An Illustrated Companion to

WORLD LITERATURE

An Illustrated Companion to

WORLD LITERATURE

Edited and adapted by Peter Quennell from the original by Tore Zetterholm

ORBIS · LONDON

Note Titles of literary works are printed in *italics* in the original language, followed by the original publication date and a translation of the title. This translated title is in *italics* only if an English-language edition has been published. The titles of less familiar languages – Russian and Scandinavian – are given only in English and the use of *italics* here does not denote that an English-language edition has necessarily been published.

Frontispiece Detail of George Bickham's frontispiece to his notable English writing book, *The Universal Penman* (1741), which included the work of some 25 contemporary penmen, mostly engraved by the master calligrapher himself.

First published under the title *Levande Litteratur – Från Gilgamesj till Bob Dylan* by Bokförlaget Bra Böcker AB, Sweden in 1981

Illustration editor: Gil Dahlström

First published in Great Britain by Orbis Book Publishing Corporation Limited, London, 1986
A BPCC plc company
Greater London House, Hampstead Road, London NW1

British Library Cataloguing in Publication Data

Zetterholm, Tore
Illustrated companion to world literature
1. Literature—History and criticism
I. Title II. Quennell, Peter
III. Levande litteratur. *English*
809 PN523

ISBN 0–85613–566–6

Printed in Portugal by Resopal

PREFACE

The author of this survey of world literature is very properly a world-traveller, whose journeys have had a strong influence upon his historical and cultural points of view. Besides visiting the United States, where he has lectured at an American university, he has made no less than seven expeditions to China, and four to Tibet after the Dalai Lama's fall. Towards the latter country, many of whose leaders, past and present, he has interviewed, he has always felt particularly drawn; and, though he has set foot in nearly every other region of the globe, it is the Far East that, apart, of course from his Scandinavian native land, he knows best and has most sympathetically observed.

Tore Zetterholm was born in 1915. His birthplace was Stockholm; but he today inhabits Sweden's earlier capital, the ancient city of Sigtuna. His literary career began in 1940 with a novel entitled *Stora Hoparegränd Himmelriket* (Great Hooper's Lane and Heaven); and since then he has devoted much of his time to imaginative fiction and dramatic writing. His journeys, however, have prompted a series of books, *China – the Dream of Man, Tibet Between Buddha and Marx* and *Voyage to Our Past,* which describes his impressions of Iraq.

In its original Swedish form, the present survey proved especially successful; and Tore Zetterholm has now revised and amplified his whole text. The role that I myself have played, while helping to prepare his translated narrative for an English-speaking reader, has been very largely editorial. The length of some sections I have ventured to reduce; others I have amplified and, here and there, a little changed. But, whenever our opinions of a subject differed, as occasionally, I must admit, they did, with remarkable generosity he has allowed me all the latitude I needed.

PETER QUENNELL

CONTENTS

GILGAMESH WHO SOUGHT LIFE

Although the word 'literature' is derived from *littera*, the Latin word for letter, it would be mistaken to assume that, until the invention of script, mankind had no songs or poems. Ever since *homo sapiens* first employed language, story-tellers and poets have told tales and recited poems describing adventures of their people, the dramas of war and love, the creation of the world and the mystery of death. We can gain some idea of these vanished works from the study of modern primitive peoples. The aboriginal inhabitants of Australia have still no written language; but they cherish sagas and myths that are handed down from family to family. In the earliest literary works, too, we find traces of an oral tradition and references to the singers and story-tellers of a far-off past.

Cuneiform script was created by the Sumerians at the end of the 4th millennium BC but not deciphered until the first half of the 19th century by, among others, the German expert G.R. Grotefend and the English Assyriologist Sir Henry Rawlinson. (British Museum, London)

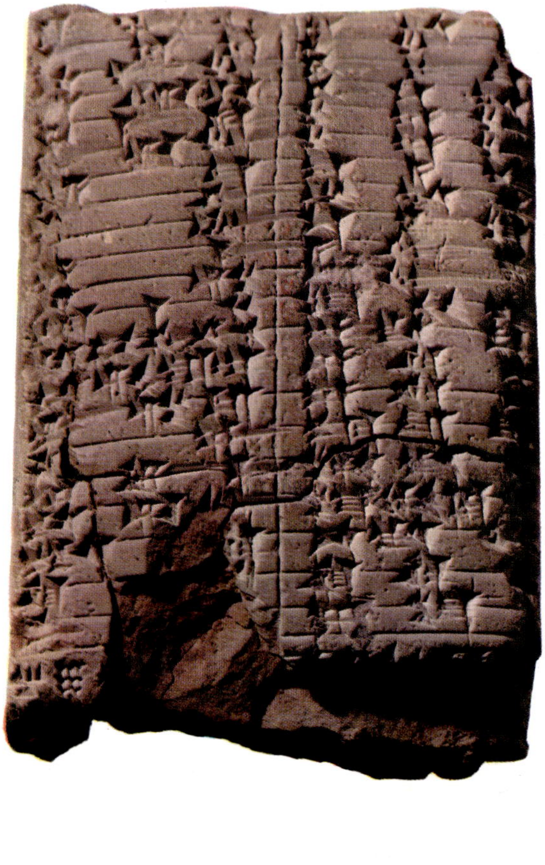

The earliest human cultures almost all developed on the banks of rivers, where riparian silt made farming easy. This happened some five thousand years ago along the Euphrates and the Tigris, the Nile, the Indus, the Yangtze Kiang (now known as Ch'ang Chiang) and the Yellow River. Script was discovered at about the same time, and literature began to take shape.

The most ancient of known scripts, called *cuneiform* owing to its wedge-like strokes (*cuneus* being Latin for wedge), was produced by the Sumerians, a people who settled some 3500 years BC on the territory around the Euphrates in the Persian Gulf, where they continued to rule for another fifteen hundred years. They were then conquered by a Semitic people, who founded the Babylonian and Assyrian Empires, and whose language is usually called Akkadian. Cuneiform script was written with reeds on damp clay tablets, which, once dried, became extremely durable. Archaeologists have unearthed at least half a million such tablets, either undamaged or in fragments; and students of language have succeeded in deciphering the Sumerian and the Akkadian inscriptions that they bear.

The great majority of these inscriptions concern calculations and financial records; but they also preserve the remains of an ancient Middle Eastern literature – hymns, prayers and myths, as well as songs and epics that describe the creation of the world, and gods and heroes of Sumerian and Babylonian legend. Only two whole epic poems have been found or reconstructed. One of them, *Enuma elish*, tells of the Creation. Another is the *Gilgamesh Epic*, now usually accepted as the oldest surviving work of human literature, which still possesses a strong imaginative appeal.

Gilgamesh was a hero who came from Uruk in Babylonia:

> ... When the gods created Gilgamesh they gave him a perfect body. Shamash the glorious sun endowed him with beauty, Adad the god of the storm endowed him with courage, the great gods made his beauty perfect, surpassing all others. Two thirds they made him god and one third man.
>
> In Uruk he built walls, a great rampart, and the temple of blessed Eanna for the god of the firmament Anu, and for Ishtar the goddess of love...

Gilgamesh probably represents an historical king, who lived in the Land of Two Rivers about 2600 BC. Of the first song devoted to the exploits of this splendid hero, composed by the Sumerians as early as 2000 BC, only a few fragments are all that remain. The present *Gilgamesh Epic*, written in Akkadian, is inscribed on twelve clay tablets that come from the library of King Assurbanipal, established in Nineveh in the seventh century BC.

The theme of the *Gilgamesh Epic* concerns Man's vain attempts to understand his mortal destiny. A great warrior, the hero defeats giants and monsters. Enkidu alone, a hairy child-of-nature, who becomes his faithful companion, can equal Gilgamesh in strength; and, when Enkidu sickens and dies, his master is overcome with anguish at the prospect of his own extinction. He then sets out to seek life, and crosses the wide Sea of Death, seeking the ancient Utnapishtim, a

predecessor of the biblical Noah, who has escaped the Great Flood and knows every secret. From him, Gilgamesh learns that, except for Utnapishtim, no one can escape death:

> ... Utnapishtim said, 'There is no permanence. Do we build a house to stand for ever, do we seal a contract to hold for all time? Do brothers divide an inheritance to keep for ever, does the flood-time of rivers endure? It is only the nymph of the dragon-fly who sheds her larva and sees the sun in his glory. From the days of old there is no permanence. The sleeping and the dead, how alike they are, they are like a painted death ...

Nevertheless, Utnapishtim is persuaded by Gilgamesh to tell him of a life-giving plant that the hero carries up from the sea-bed. But, before he has had time to eat the magic herb, it is stolen by a serpent. Frustrated, Gilgamesh turns back; and the last scene of the poem describes his melancholy meeting with Enkidu's spirit, which rises from the ground and begs him to become resigned to the 'order of the earth'.

Above *Assyrian warriors of the 7th-century* BC *King Assurbanipal. Tens of thousands of cuneiform script tablets were discovered in the ruins of his library at Nineveh by the English archaeologist and diplomat, Sir Henry Layard, in 1849. Among these was the* Gilgamesh Epic, *thought to be the oldest preserved work of literature. Alabaster bas-relief, 600* BC. *(British Museum, London)*

Left *Cultural man has always dreamed of the unspoiled child-of-nature and in the* Gilgamesh Epic *the hero's rival who became his brother-in-arms, Enkidu (depicted here), is the first in world literature's long line of 'noble savages'. Alabaster statue, c. 2500* BC. *(Iraq Museum, Baghdad)*

THE CULT OF THE DEAD

The hieroglyphics – picture writing – and figures inscribed on this stone relief, dating from 1200 BC, tell the story in truly graphic form of a lame man on his way to visit the goddess Ashtaroth or Ishtar (the Eastern equivalent of the Greek Astarte) in search of a cure. (Glyptothek, Copenhagen)

Since almost all ancient literature is both anonymous and largely impersonal, we are fascinated, in one of the oldest extant literary works, to meet an author who strikes a strong individual note. In the *Dispute Between a Man and his Ba*, a poem written about 1800 BC during the era of the Egyptian Middle Kingdom, we read of a man who longs to be able to die, though his *ba* (soul) opposes him and urges him to enjoy existence, but is finally persuaded to follow him into the Kingdom of the Dead. The man's plea for death is expressed with moving eloquence in the following extract:

Death is before me today
Like a well-trodden way,
Like a man's coming home from
warfare.

Death is before me today
Like the clearing of the sky,
As when a man discovers what he
ignored.

Death is before me today
Like a man's longing to see his home
When he has spent many years in
captivity.

Ideas of death and of the after-life dominated many aspects of Egyptian civilization, which arose, at about the same time as Sumerian culture, during the third millennium BC, but soon acquired the distinctive characteristics that it retained until the beginning of the Christian era. Bound by tradition, the Egyptian system of life and ways of thought tended to grow more and more static, and its state-religion increasingly conservative. The cult of the dead became more and more important; and tombs and temples were the most grandiose Egyptian buildings, the largest, of course, being the Pyramids, built to ensure a pharaoh's immortality.

Literature, which was almost exclusively religious, has been preserved on the sarcophagi of the dead, on papyrus scrolls or pyramid inscriptions. The famous *Book of the Dead*, a guidebook placed in burial chambers, advises the dead how they should conduct their last journey, and describes places and divine figures they will meet in the Underworld.

Not that literary and artistic expression was completely fettered. During the Middle Kingdom (1991–1786 BC, Dynasty XII) sculptors produced some almost alarmingly life-like portrait–statues; while in the New Kingdom or New Empire (1552–1069 BC, Dynasties XVIII–XX) writers were encouraged to employ a simpler, more popular language. An important literary form was now the saga. Collections of sagas – or folk-tales – that, during the Middle Ages, would spread all over the West included Egyptian motifs many thousand years old.

The Cult of the Sun

Of writers, whose names we know, in the New Kingdom, the most remarkable is Amenophis IV, called **Akhenaten** (*c.*1375–1358 BC), the heretical Pharaoh who sought to introduce a new religion, the monotheistic cult of the Sun, and who, in his verses, even in his edicts, used colloquial language. But his religious revolution failed; the existing priesthood was too powerful. Akhenaten's feeling for Nature – a sentiment that also appears in contemporary love lyrics – may have been the product of literary sophistication rather than the sign of a renewed vitality. His *Hymn to the Sun*, however, has triumphantly survived him:

When thou settest in the western horizon, the earth is in darkness after the manner of death. The night is passed in the bedchamber, heads covered, no eye can see its fellow. Their belongings are stolen, even though they be under their heads, and they perceive it not. Every lion is come forth from its lair and all snakes bite. Darkness is (the sole) illumination while the earth is in silence, their maker resting in his horizon.

The earth grows bright, when thou hast arisen in the horizon, shining as Aten in the daytime. Thou banishest darkness and bestowest thy rays. The Two Lands are in festival . . .

Below *In Dynastic Egypt during the New Kingdom (Dynasty XVIII–XX, c. 1552–1069 BC) both art and literature grew increasingly realistic, as in this wall painting of reapers on a 16th-century BC tomb at Deir el-Medina, Thebes, Egypt.*

Above *From the reeds along the Nile came some of Mankind's oldest writing materials to inscribe cuneiform script and hieroglyphics. The latter were first deciphered in 1822 by the French Egyptologist J.P. Champollion, based on a clue from the Rosetta Stone inscription, the tablet discovered by Napoleon's soldiers near the Rosetta mouth of the Nile.*

Above *Pharaoh Akhenaten ('he who pleases Aten'), wife Nefertiti and daughter, hold up offerings to the sun-god, Aten, to whom Pharaoh wrote his famous* Hymn. *The sun-disc symbolizes the god, and rays ending in hands holding ankh-signs are bestowing life on Akhenaten and his family. Relief from Tell el-Amarna, c. 1350 BC. (Egyptian Museum, Cairo)*

'HEARKEN, O ISRAEL!'

Neither Babylon nor Egypt provided many literary examples for the West to follow. That was the achievement of a minor nomadic people, who had settled along the River Jordan about the middle of the fourteenth century BC in the ancient fatherland of the Canaanites, and who founded the Kingdoms of Israel and Judaea.

The spiritual faith of the Jewish people was their chief strength. *'Schma Israel!'* – 'Hearken, O Israel!' said the Lord to His people, the Fifth Book of Moses (Deuteronomy 4) tells us; and those words have been included in the Jewish profession of faith, and repeated by Jewish believers every day since that remote period. The walls of Babylon fell, and the armies of Pharaoh were dispersed; but Israel's holy scripts upheld the spirit of Judaism despite persecution and a long exile.

Incorporated in the Old Testament are the remains of myths and sagas, hymns and proverbs gathered from many Near Eastern countries, a literature much of it so ancient that the Hebrews may have brought it with them, no doubt largely as an oral tradition, when they reached the Promised Land. Such, for instance, is the story of the Flood, which Abraham himself may have heard before he left Ur in Chaldaea. Out of this multifarious material poets and prophets, historians and legislators, evolved the existing Old Testament. The oldest books – the Books of Moses – were probably written about 900 BC; and the most recent, the Book of Daniel, about 165 BC. The Old Testament did not acquire its present shape until a century after Christ. For many hundreds of years, we possessed no manuscripts earlier than those of the tenth century; but then, in 1947 some Bedouins discovered what are today known as 'the Dead Sea Scrolls', some of which are at least a thousand years older.

Even if the First Book of Moses (Genesis) were not the record of a world religion, it would be a magnificent literary work. Its narrative skill, the realism, part lofty, part burlesque, with which the Patriarchs are described, and its shrewd psychology, all distinguish its construction; and that Book and its four successors, which the Jews call the Torah (Teachings), together with the Book of Joshua, the Book of Samuel and some other narrative books, constitute a prose epic that unfolds the history of Jehovah's Chosen People; while the Books of Ruth, Esther, Daniel and Jonah, also written in prose, contain legends and stories, often based on some historical event. The Book of Job stands between prose and poetry. Derived from an old folk-tale, in its present form it is usually assigned to the fifth century BC. Its central character, the sorely-tried Job, who appeals to God as he seeks to solve the problem of human suffering, is a Jewish Prometheus or Faust. With its use of dialogue, its dramatic vigour and limited array of characters, the Book of Job is reminiscent of Greek tragedy, although, when it was composed, it is unlikely to have been regarded as a drama. Yet few passages in the Bible are more eloquent than Job's final plea:

Construction work in progress for Noah's Ark. Geologists today consider that a real catastrophe was the basis of the ancient myth of the Flood recorded in the Bible – Genesis, 6:17. Detail from a 14th-century mosaic. (St Mark's Basilica, Venice)

> When I looked for good, then evil
> came unto me: and when I waited
> for light, there came darkness.
> My bowels boiled, and rested not: the
> days of affliction prevented me.
> I went mourning without the sun; I
> stood up, and I cried in the
> congregation.
> I am a brother to dragons, and a
> companion to owls.
> My skin is black upon me, and my
> bones are burned with heat.
> My harp also is turned to mourning,
> and my organ into the voice of
> them that weep.

Job, 30:26–31

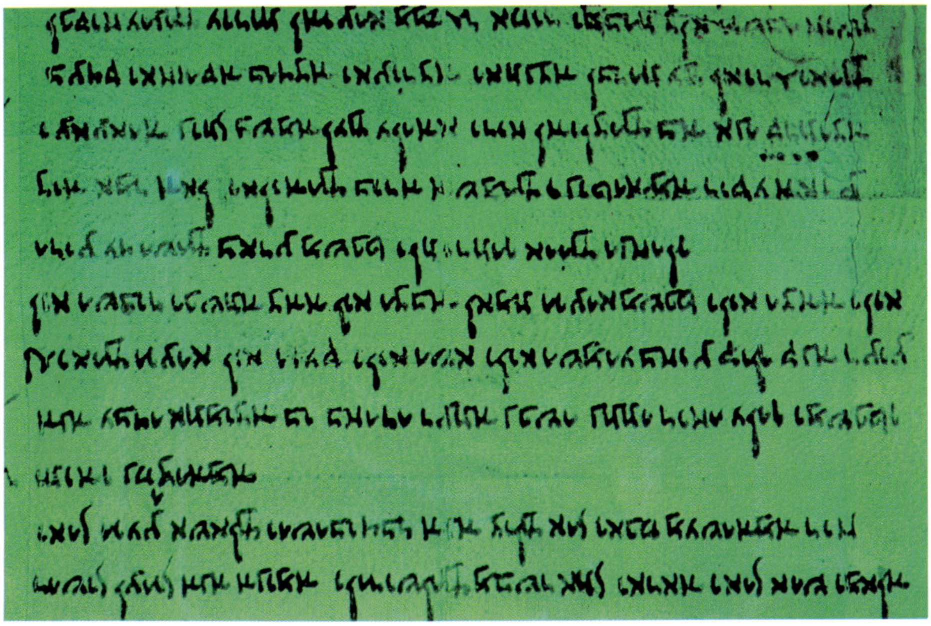

Above *Jonah about to be swallowed by the Whale, from one of the early biblical legends – Jonah, 1:15. Detail of late 15th-century fresco by the Swedish artist Albertus Pictor, known as 'Albert the Painter'. (Härkeberga Church, Uppland, Sweden)*

Left *Fragment from the complete Book of Isaiah on one of the scrolls of leather found in 1947 by a Bedouin boy near Khirbet Qumran by the Dead Sea. The scrolls (now known as the Dead Sea Scrolls) had been hidden by a Jewish sect, the Essenes, when their community was destroyed by the Romans in the 1st century AD. (Israel Museum, Jerusalem)*

THE BOOK OF PSALMS AND THE SONG OF SOLOMON

Of all the poetic books in the Old Testament, The Book of Psalms has had most effect on Western literature and the rites of Christian worship. It was evidently the work of many unknown authors; and King David is unlikely to have written the various songs attributed to him. The book, as a whole, appeared after the Exodus; but many of the psalms are certainly very ancient. Prayers and invocations here, that must have been part of the Jews' most ancient traditions, are easily distinguishable, as is the influence of Sumerian, Babylonian and Egyptian poetry; while the great hundred-and-fourth psalm has certain likenesses to Akhenaten's invocation to the Sun. Otherwise, the contents of the Book are uneven. Some Psalms tell only of the Pharisees' racial hatreds; but others, especially the pilgrims' songs, have a true poetic grace.

The Song of Solomon may at first have been a series of lyrics chanted in a dance—drama, which then merged into an ancient fertility rite and found a place in organized religion. Both in Jewish and in Christian society, however, the faithful have preferred to give it a wholly religious and allegorical meaning. That such was its original significance is just as improbable as that King Solomon himself was really its author. Above all else, it is a love-poem, a descant on the theme of sensuous beauty:

My beloved is white and ruddy, the
chiefest among ten thousand.
His head is as the most fine gold; his
locks are bushy and black as a raven.
His eyes are the eyes of doves by the
rivers of waters, washed with milk,
and fitly set.
His cheeks as a bed of spices, as sweet
flowers: his lips like lilies dripping
sweet smelling myrrh.
His hands are as gold rings set with
the beryl; his belly is as bright ivory
overlaid with sapphires.
His legs are as pillars of marble, set
upon sockets of fine gold; his
countenance is as Lebanon, excellent
as the cedars.
His mouth is most sweet: yea, he is
altogether lovely. This is my
beloved, and this is my friend, O,
daughters of Jerusalem.

Song of Solomon, 5:10–16

The sensuous beauty of the Song of Solomon has inspired many artists. Here, tribute is paid to the prince's daughter whose 'two breasts are like two young roes that are twins' (7:1–13). Illustration by Arnošt Paderlík, for a Swedish edition of Song of Songs *(1967).*

THE ROARING OF THE LORD

When Uzzia ruled over the Kingdom of Judaea, and Jeroboam over Israel, the Lord uttered a roar of anger, writes the Prophet Amos:

> ... because they have ripped up the women with child of Gilead, that they might enlarge their border ... because they sold the righteous for silver, and the poor for a pair of shoes ... so shall the children of Israel be taken out that dwell in Samaria in the corner of a bed, and in Damascus in a couch ... they afflict the just, they take a bribe and they turn aside the poor in the gate from their right ... thy wife shall be an harlot in the city, and thy sons and thy daughters shall fall by the sword, and thy land shall be divided by line, and thou shall die in a polluted land ...
>
> Amos, 1:13; 2:6; 3:12; 5:12; 7:17

Amos lived in the eighth century BC and is considered the first of the so-called 'script prophets'; and his prophesies show for the first time how Jehovah, a savage tribal god, began to be transformed into a spiritual and moral deity. Amos was not only a seer and diviner of oracles, but also a truth-teller, a guardian of his people's conscience, a harsh critic of mankind and its rulers, preaching the gospel of universal righteousness.

It has been said that, whereas the older, pre-Babylonian Conquest prophets warned of national doom and ruination, and limited the scope of their prophesies to the future of their own people, those who survived exile, and witnessed the fall of Jerusalem, increasingly abandoned their vision of a peaceful, united Israel. Even before the Dispersal, the idea of the Messiah existed; but it was often a hope confined to the Jews alone rather than a promise that the whole world shared.

The prophet Jeremiah, whose suffering shows through the lyrical style of his Book in the Old Testament. A particularly doleful lamentation – a jeremiad – is named after him. Facsimile of 15th-century German woodcut from Schedel's Weltchronik *(1493). (Royal Library, Stockholm)*

This hope found its most sublime expression in the First Isaiah's prophecy on the coming of the Prince of Peace:

> The people that walked in darkness have seen a great light: they that dwell in the land of the shadow of death, upon them hath the light shined.
>
> Isaiah, 9:2

The prophet Jeremiah himself suffered a heavy blow in his old age when, having impetuously plunged into politics, he found himself in bitter opposition to the leaders of the state. As a stern recluse, standing alone before his Maker, his relationship with the God he served grew peculiarly individual. Jeremiah has been styled 'the first suppliant in the history of religion'; and his violent lyrical style reflects the intensity of his private anguish:

> Cursed be the day wherein I was born; let not the day wherein my mother bare me be blessed.
>
> Cursed be the man who brought tidings to my father, saying, a man child is born unto thee; making him very glad.
>
> And let the man be as the cities which the Lord overthrew, and repented not and let him hear the cry in the morning, and the shouting at noontide ...
>
> Jeremiah, 20:14–16

The Books of the Prophets seldom contain narrative passages, and usually lack artistic unity; they resemble a collection of political tracts, written in verse by a divinely gifted poet, and interspersed with autobiographical asides. It is doubtful whether any other part of the Old Testament has had so strong an influence. Echoes of Amos' 'Roaring of the Lord' have rolled on through European history. The language of the prophets has been echoed not only by holders of other faiths, but also, and perhaps with even greater energy, by secular controversialists and critics, even by the active opponents of religion. A host of social reformers and revolutionaries have found inspiration in the Jewish Prophets.

A NEW HEAVEN AND A NEW EARTH

The New Testament, unlike the old, has a single, self-explanatory theme – the redemption of mankind through the death of Jesus Christ. The Epistles of St Paul were the first parts to be written, probably as early as AD 50 or 60; and, by the beginning of the third century, the New Testament as a whole had taken shape. The oldest manuscript fragments were written on papyrus from about AD 120. It is almost impossible today to regard it solely as literature; but among the masterpieces of the Western World it unquestionably deserves a high place. The story of the life and sufferings of Jesus, if we compare the Gospel's narrative with other religious documents, has a strongly realistic and dramatic quality; while the account of Paul's shipwreck in the Acts of the Apostles is one of the most detailed records of ancient seafaring that we now possess.

Not long after there arose against it a tempestuous wind, called Euroclydon.

And when the ship was caught, and could not bear up into the wind, we let her drive.

And running under a certain island which is called Clauda, we had much work to come by the boat:

Which when they had taken up, they used helps, undergirding the ship; and fearing lest they should fall into the quicksands, strake sail, and so were driven.

And we being exceedingly tossed with a tempest, the next day they lightened the ship;

And the third day we cast out with our own hands the tackling of the ship.

And when neither sun nor stars in many days appeared, and no small tempest lay on us, all hope that we should be saved was then taken away.

The Acts, 27:14–20

The Book of Revelation has had a lasting effect on Western religious literature. It belongs to a visionary tradition, common in the Near East during the pre-Christian centuries, at a time when seers and prophets were increasingly preoccupied with the approaching end of the world, as, in the Old Testament the Book of Daniel shows. Thanks to the Book of Revelation, visionary writing spread to the West, and has flared up again at certain periods – for example, during the Middle Ages. Since the explosion of an Atom Bomb, the apocalyptic words of the Epistle of Peter, have a hideous contemporary significance:

... the heavens shall pass away with great noise, and the elements shall melt with fervent heat, the earth also and the works that are therein shall be burned up.

II Peter, 3:10

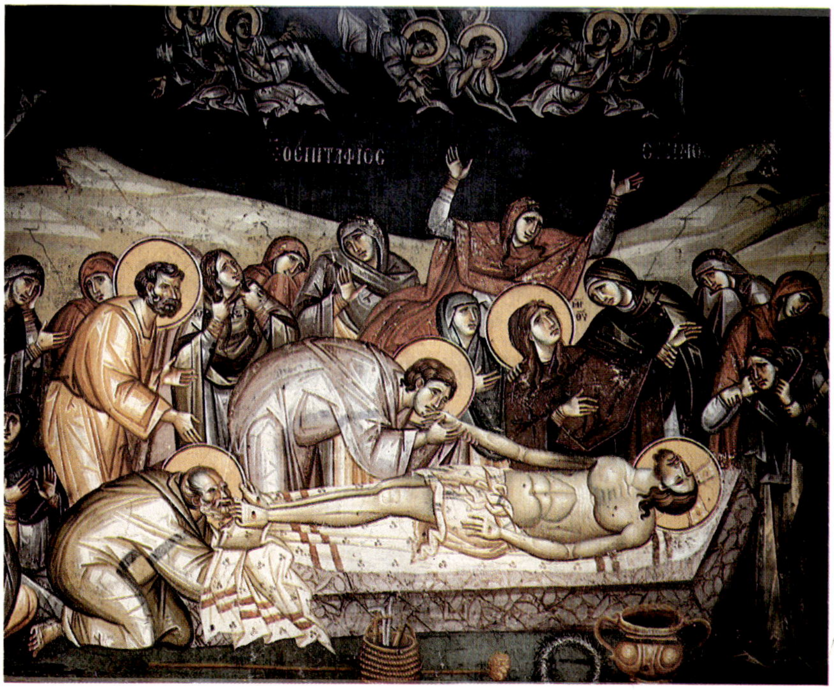

The New Testament Gospels provided an endless source of inspiration for artists from the 1st millennium AD onwards. Detail of 14th-century fresco of The Deposition in the Church of St Clement in Ohrid, Macedonia, Yugoslavia.

GODS AND HEROES

The Avesta, the most important religious document of Ancient Persia, is thought to have been partly written about 600 BC by the prophet **Zarathustra** (**Zoroaster**). This strange and difficult work was not known in Europe until the eighteenth century, when it was translated by the French orientalist Abraham-Hyacinthe Anquetil-Duperron. A rewritten and extremely imaginative version, *Thus Spoke Zarathustra*, produced by the German philosopher Friedrich Nietzsche, has played an important part in Western thought.

Until recent times little was known in the West of ancient Indian Literature. Indian religious writings, called the Veda, were first composed and assembled during the second and first millennium before Christ, the most important being *Rigveda* and *Upanishad*, both collections of prayers and hymns.

The greatest of Indian heroic epics, the *Mahabharata*, which runs to more than a hundred-thousand couplets, was compiled, as it exists today, between AD 300 and 500, but includes much earlier material; and its most important section is a didactic poem, the *Bhagavad Gita*, a philosophical dialogue between the hero and the god Krishna. India's other great Sanskrit epic, *Ramayana*, was probably written by a single author, **Valmiki**, who lived during the third and second centuries BC.

Kalidasa, the finest poet of India's classic period, who lived in the fifth century AD, wrote not only epics, but lyrics and dramas. His play *Sakuntala*, translated in the eighteenth century, is said to have had an influence on Goethe when he was producing his two-part verse–drama *Faust* (published in 1808 and 1832).

Ramayana, *the great Sanskrit epic, centres on the battle between Good and Evil. Ravana, the evil many-headed King of the Demons, has abducted Sita, wife of the exiled Prince Rama. Here the 'good' King of the Monkeys, Hanuman (standing right of Ravana), is caught while trying to rescue Sita. Detail from an Indian water-colour,* c. *AD 1800. (National Museum of India, New Delhi)*

The Indian god Krishna with Prince Arjuna (at right), one of the Pandava brothers who were disinherited by the rival Kaurava brothers but regained their kingdom with the help of Krishna. Scene taken from the 4th to 5th-century AD heroic Indian epic, Mahabharata. *According to tradition, this was written by the Hindu anchorite, Vyasa, who is himself one of the main characters in the work. Detail from a 17th-century edition. (Bibliothèque Nationale, Paris)*

CONFUCIUS AND TAOISM

The Han Dynasty spanned the years 206 BC to AD 221 and was one of the golden ages of Chinese culture. This bronze horse and chariot, excavated in 1969 in Wu-wei in the province of Kansu, dates from the later, Eastern Han period (AD 25–220). It is an example of the narrative art depicting everyday life that was characteristic of the time. (National Museum, Peking/Beijing)

The sixth century BC was a noteworthy epoch in the history of mankind. It was then that Buddha appeared in India, the first Greek philosophers in Europe, and in the Far East the Great Chinese philosopher and religious sage, K'ung Fu-tzu (Kong Fuzi in pinyin – the modern script), whose name means Master K'ung or master, generally known as **Confucius**.

Like Jesus and Socrates, Confucius himself wrote nothing down; but his sayings were recorded by his disciples in a book entitled *Lun Yu*, or *Analects*. Confucianism, which is concerned primarily with wisdom, morality and social ethics, had a tremendous effect on Chinese civilization. Under the old Empire, every educated Chinese citizen studied it, and all aspirants to official status were obliged to take examinations in Confucian lore. The moral standards that the *Lun Yu* preaches are high; and some of Confucius' 'Rules of Life' recall the teachings of the New Testament:

Master K'ung said: What I do not wish people to do to me, neither do I wish to do to people.

The main defect of Confucius, from a modern Chinese point of view, is his intense conservatism and deep respect for authority, which were used by the ruling class to impede any form of political or social progress.

China's other great native religion was Taoism (Daoism), founded on the *Tao te ching* (*Jing*), or *The Classic of the Way and Its Power*, said to have been written by **Lao Tzu** (**Lao Zi**), Master Lao, in the sixth century BC. Nothing is known of the Master himself; but legend has it that he was born with white hair and spoke to a plum tree as he left the womb. Later scholars have doubted his real existence, and suggested that the *Tao te ching*, an extremely obscure work, may have had several different authors. Tao is usually translated as 'the Way'; but it also signifies the strength that supports everything, controls the universe, and is the origin and end of all things, like water, the lowly element from which everything comes, and to which everything returns. The secret strength of weakness and pliancy is a favourite Taoist theme. Tao, to true believers, represents all that is elevated in life, but is itself formless and beyond the reach of words. A very interesting early Chinese poet was **Chuang Tzu** (**Zhuang Zhou**), a Taoist and mystic, who wrote about 300 BC, and conveyed his anarchistic philosophy in prose–poems that reveal both humour and imagination.

From **The Dream of the Butterfly**
by Chuang Tzu

Once upon a time, I, Chuang Tzu, dreamt I was a butterfly, fluttering hither and thither, to all intents and purposes, a butterfly. I was conscious only of following my fancies as a butterfly, and was unconscious of my individuality as a man. Suddenly I awaked, and there I lay, myself again. Now I do not know whether I was then a man dreaming I was a butterfly or whether I am now a butterfly dreaming I am a man.

From **The Canon of Reason and Virtue** in *Tao te ching* by Lao Tzu

Man during life is tender and delicate. When he dies he is stiff and stark. The ten thousand things, the grass as well as the trees, while they live they are tender and supple. When they die they are rigid and dry. Thus the hard and strong are the companions of death. The tender and delicate are the companions of life. Therefore he who in arms is strong will not conquer. When a tree has grown strong it is doomed. The strong and great stay below, the tender and delicate stay above.

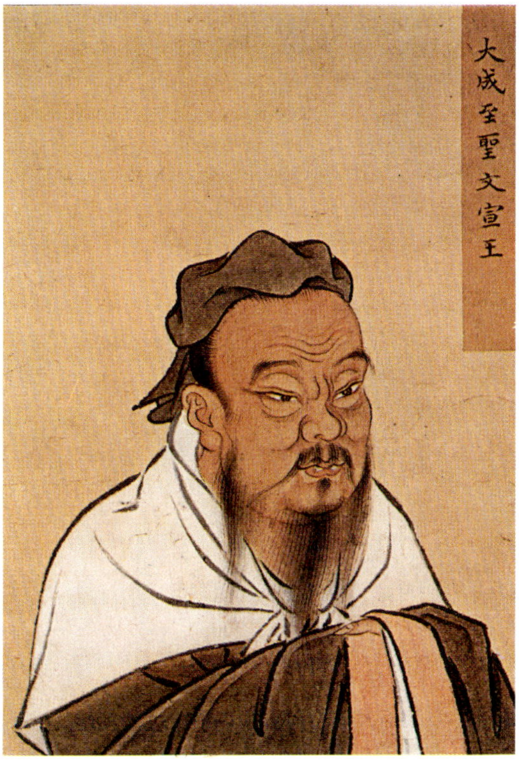

Above *China's teacher and wise man, K'ung Fu-tzu (Confucius), gave rise to the philosophy of Confucianism but was himself sceptical of all metaphysical speculation. To a pupil pondering on death, he said: 'As long as you do not know life, how can you know death?' (National Museum, Peking/Beijing)*

Right *Lao-Tzu riding on a buffalo, a popular motif with Chinese artists as it was on his journey on a buffalo away from civilization that the legendary 'Master Lao' was supposed to have written the sacred script of Taoism,* Tao te ching. *Painting by Chang Lu of the Ming Dynasty (1368–1644). (National Museum, Peking/Beijing)*

THE RISE OF THE GREEK EPIC

The oldest works of Western literature are two Greek epic poems, *The Iliad* and *The Odyssey*, traditionally attributed to a blind poet named **Homer**. Although seven cities competed for the honour of being his birthplace, nothing is known of Homer's life; and scholars have been unable to decide just what is the link between these two great poems – whether we can still assume that they were the work of a single man, or must conclude that they were produced by several hands during the course of centuries. According to one theory, that certainly deserves attention, they were indeed written by a single poet, who used older material; and much has since been added to his text. But, whatever their origin, their sudden appearance was an almost miraculous event.

Both *The Iliad* and *The Odyssey* are written in hexameters, unrhymed verse in six metrical feet (a 'foot' being the unit of rhythm in a verse); and each begins with an invocation to the Muse. 'Sing, O goddess, of the wrath that burned in Achilles, Peleus' son' is the first line of *The Iliad*, which tells how the Greeks besieged the city of Ilium (Troy) in Asia Minor. They had attacked Troy, it was said, because Paris, a young Trojan prince, had stolen from her homeland the beautiful Helen, daughter of Zeus and Leda, and wife to King Menelaus of Sparta (Lacedaemon), younger brother of Agamemnon, King of Argos; whereupon the Greek chieftains, under Agamemnon's leadership, set sail to bring her home again. The central theme in *The Iliad* is the bitter dispute between Agamemnon and the great bulwark of the Greek forces, 'swift-footed Achilles', over the possession of two female captives. Achilles retires in anger from the field; and Trojans prevail against Greeks until he can be persuaded to return.

Archaeological excavations have shown that the story of the siege of Troy has some historical basis; and that, around 1200 BC, a city on the site of ancient Troy was burnt to the ground. This happened at the end of the Greek Bronze Age, when iron had begun to come into general use. At the same time, the last of the Greek tribes, the Dorians, swept down from the north, and, during the struggle that followed, the Kingdom of Mycenae collapsed. The fall of Troy was long celebrated by poets and bards, both in Greece and in the Greek colonies on the coast of Asia Minor. Among these colonists, about 700 BC, a great poet is thought to have arisen, who extracted the best of the songs and heroic poems that had already gained currency, and, with the help of his own vigorous imagination, forged a magnificent poetic structure.

The Odyssey, which may have been produced in much the same way as *The Iliad*, but, according to some scholars, about a century earlier, tells of the wanderings at sea of an intrepid Greek chieftain. The enterprising and lively tribes who made up the Greek people did not always settle down upon the mainland; even before the Dorian migration, they had reached the coast of Asia Minor. Then, about 750 BC, a new wave of emigrants colonized southern Italy and spread as far afield as the site of modern Marseille. The story of *The Odyssey* was undoubtedly derived from tales of the sea that had been in circulation among sea-faring Greeks since far-off Mycenaean times.

The theme of *The Odyssey* is linked with that of *The Iliad*. It depicts the homeward journey, after Troy had fallen, of the Greek hero Odysseus (whom the Romans renamed Ulysses). Having offended the sea-god Poseidon, before he can reach Ithaca, his beloved island-home, he is obliged to wander around the shores of the Mediterranean, where he meets with strange and terrifying adventures among savage men – who include a race of one-eyed giants – and ferocious sea-monsters. Only after nine long years of suffering does he again set foot on Ithaca, where his wife Penelope awaits him, and make short work of a gang of greedy neighbours, who have been wooing Penelope and eating up his goods.

Each of these poems is a living picture of a vanished age; but what characterizes them above all else is

Above left *The Greek poet Homer, believed to be the author of the oldest works of Western literature,* The Iliad *and* The Odyssey, *probably written from 800 to 700 BC. (National Archaeological Museum, Naples)*

Opposite *Head of Odysseus, King of Ithaca, whose journey home after the Trojan War forms the basis of* The Odyssey. *1st-century BC fragment excavated at the 'Cave of Tiberius' near Sperlonga in the late 1950s. (National Archaeological Museum, Sperlonga, Latina, Italy)*

The death of Achilles during the Siege of Troy where, according to The Iliad, *he was fatally wounded in one heel by the Trojan prince, Paris. To make him invulnerable, Achilles' mother, the sea-goddess Thetis, had immersed her baby son – except for the heel by which she held him – in the 'infernal' river Styx which surrounded the Underworld. From a Roman sarcophagus, 2nd century* BC. *(Louvre, Paris)*

The return of Odysseus to Ithaca from his nine-year odyssey. After slaying Penelope's treacherous suitors, with the help of his son Telemachus, Odysseus finally reveals himself to his faithful wife. From a tomb relief, c. *300* BC, *found at Gölbasi, near Ankara, Turkey. (Kunsthistorisches Museum, Vienna)*

their poetic realism. Some details, however, may already have seemed archaic during the poets' own period. A scholar, for example, has pointed out, that, although the poet introduces chariots, he would appear to have forgotten the strategy of chariot-warfare – the warriors who drive in chariots to the battlefield then dismount to fight. There as elsewhere, he is evidently thinking of a remote heroic past.

In his descriptions of human nature, on the other hand, of men's passions and impetuous actions, of their hopes and fears, and loves and hatreds, Homer shows unequalled genius. He excels, too, in his evocations of the sea and, now and then, of splendid landscapes, such as his glimpse of the Trojan plain at night, scattered with watch-fires beneath the ancient city's walls. Nor does the pathos of the human existence escape him. It was a barbaric age. Having slain the noble Hector, Achilles drags the corpse behind his chariot wheels. Yet his meeting with Hector's aged father, Priam, who has come to reclaim the brutalized body, is a deeply moving narrative. And so is the account in *The Iliad* of Hector's last conversation with his wife, and of his parting from his little son Astyanax:

> '... All that, my dear,' said the great Hector of the glittering helmet, 'is surely my concern. But if I hide myself like a coward and refused to fight, I could never face the Trojans and the Trojan ladies in their trailing gowns. Besides, it would go against the grain, for I have trained myself always, like a good soldier, to take my place in the front line and win glory for my father and myself. Deep in my heart I know the day is coming when Holy Ilium will be destroyed, with Priam and the people of Priam of the good ashen spear. Yet I am not so much distressed by the thought of what the Trojans will suffer, or Hecabe herself, or King Priam, or all my gallant brothers whom the enemy will fling down in the dust, as by the thought of you, dragged off in tears by some Achaean man-at-arms to slavery. I see you there in Argos, toiling for some other woman at the loom, or carrying water from an alien well, a helpless drudge with no will of your own. "There goes the wife of Hector", they will say when they see your tears. "He was the champion of the horse-taming Trojans when Ilium was besieged." And every time they say it, you will feel another pang at the loss of the one man who might have kept you free. Ah, may the earth lie deep on my dead body before I hear the screams you utter as they drag you off!'

As he finished, glorious Hector held out his arms to take his boy. But the child shrank back with a cry to the bosom of his girdled nurse, alarmed at his father's appearance. He was frightened by the bronze of the helmet and the horsehair plumes that he saw nodding grimly down at him. His father and his lady mother had to laugh. But noble Hector quickly took his helmet off and put the dazzling thing on the ground. Then he kissed his son, dandled him in his arms, and prayed to Zeus and the other gods: 'Zeus, and you other gods, grant that this boy of mine may be, like me, pre-eminent in Troy; as strong and brave as I; a mighty king of Ilium. May people say, when he comes back from battle, "Here is a better man than his father." Let him bring home the blood-stained armour of the enemy he has killed, and make his mother happy.'

Odysseus was held captive for a year and his men turned into swine by the evil enchantress, Circe, on the island of Aeaea. He escaped with the help of a magic herb called Moly, given to him by the god Hermes, which forced Circe to reverse the spell on his companions. From a 1st-century BC *Etruscan sarcophagus. (Museo dell' Opera del Duomo, Orvieto, Umbria, Italy)*

THE BIRTH OF DEMOCRACY

Hesiod, 'The Father of Greek Didactic Poetry', traced the genealogy of the gods and the beginnings of the world, leading to Olympian Zeus as 'Father of Gods and Men', in his Theogony. *From a French edition of 1584.*

Mountainous, arid Greece was not united until the year 338 BC when, at the decisive Battle of Chaeronea, the Greek city-states, at length defeated by Philip of Macedon, had lost their independence. Meanwhile, Athens, Sparta, Thebes, Corinth were constantly at war. Yet they preserved a certain spiritual unity, thanks to their common religion and language; and to this unity Homer's poems contributed. *The Odyssey* and *The Iliad* were always their common property.

In Homer, the ruling caste is still predominant. But in the works of **Hesiod**, who lived in about 700 BC, we meet peasants and other ordinary people, even the hard-working author himself. His great didactic work, *Works and Days*, has little dramatic action. Hesiod offers advice and observations on country life, which may perhaps best be compared with the old advisory manuals of northern Europe; and here the poet begins to speak in person. He complains about the peasant's hard lot, and about his own good-for-nothing brother, but also lauds pleasures of the country and benefits of daily labour.

In the eighth century BC there were great changes in the Greek social system, caused by the development of a money-based economy. Crafts, industry and trade flourished and created new classes, which provoked sharper class antagonisms, not only between the upper and lower classes, but also between the old land-owning class and the new monied aristocracy. This ferment continued through succeeding centuries. The lower classes became conscious of their power; and, during what is called 'the Period of Tyrants', the road towards the democracy was paved, most of all in the largest Greek city, Athens, where during the sixth century, two great statesmen, Solon and Cleisthenes, framed a democratic constitution. We should not assume, however, that democracy, as we know it today, was the immediate result of their efforts. The Greek slave was almost without rights. But, though it may shock us to reflect that slavery was one of the most important prerequisites of ancient civilization, according to some historians it opened wide the door for Greece's days of intellectual and spiritual glory.

A NEW POETIC MODE

The lyric stage of Greek poetry (700–500 BC) coincided with the progress of a social revolution, in which poets often passionately took sides. New conditions demanded an art-form better able to express the spirit of the times than the calm swell of Homeric hexameters. Greek lyric verse was a far more adaptable medium, which might express either the poet's political opinions or his voluptuous sense of beauty. Unfortunately only fragments of Greek verse, once so rich and important a literary field, have survived; and it is as difficult to recreate its glories, or evoke the characters of individual poets, as to form an impression of some splendid Greek vessel from a heap of ancient shards. We know, however, that it was closely linked with music, and probably sung to the accompaniment of the flute or of the Greek lyre, made of tortoise-shell, goat's-horn and strings of gut.

The Greek lyric had two main forms – the personal lyric, which expressed individual emotions and opinions, and the choral lyric, which pleaded the cause of a larger group. In poems of the first kind three different types of metre – iambic, elegiac and that of the Aeolian ballad – were usually employed, each for a separate purpose. The iambic (of which the swift cadences resembled the rhythm of speech) was the measure judged appropriate for satirical and political verse, its greatest exponent being **Archilocus**, a citizen of the island of Paros, born in the seventh century BC, who lived and died a soldier. His poems tell of the hardships and joys of military life. They have about them an acrid whiff of the smoke of camp-fires.

The elegy was also used by Archilocus – at first, in lamentations for the dead, but, later, in erotic verse, political verse and battle-songs:

My spear wins bread, my spear wins
 Thracian wine:
To drink it, on my spear's head I
 recline.

Archilocus was an often savage and hot-tempered poet, famous for the hatreds he expressed. Although only remnants of his work remain, he is one of the few authors of that time to survive as a recognizable personality.

Polymnia. Muse of lyric poetry. The other Muses – goddesses of poetry, music and song – were: Calliope (heroic epics), Clio (history), Erato (elegy), Euterpe (music), Melpomene (tragedy), Terpsichore (dance), Thalia (comedy), and Urania (astronomy). Detail of vase painting, c. 400 BC, from Apulia (Puglia), Italy. (Staatliche Antikensammlung, München)

*Orpheus, poet and singer, was founder of the mystic cult of Orphism which taught that Hades – the Underworld – was a place of punishment for the soul before it could be purified. When his wife, Eurydice, died and descended into the Underworld it was his magical playing (**above**) on the kithara (the professional Greek lyre with a large soundbox) that gained Orpheus her release – provided he did not look at her when she followed him back to life. He could not resist turning round, and so death claimed her once more. Orpheus spent the rest of his life wandering in Thrace, singing of his love, until the Thracian women, jealous of his constancy to Eurydice, tore him to pieces. According to legend, his head, still singing, and lyre floated out to sea to Lesbos, home of lyric music. Detail from a vase painting of scenes from the Underworld, c. 320 BC, found in Canosa, Apulia (Puglia), Italy. (Staatliche Antikensammlung, München)*

The greatest collection of elegies in existence today has been attributed to **Theognis**, who flourished during the civil wars fought about 500 BC. A member of the aristocratic party, he was driven into exile when the democratic faction triumphed. Memories of past feuds and of his own unhappy fate often give his verses a powerful intensity:

Ah, could I drink their dark-red blood!
Could some just power
Govern it so, and grant me at last, to
have my hour.

Aeolian verse, on the other hand, was always associated with music; and, as its home was the island of Lesbos, famous for its beautiful women and good wines, naturally enough its finest works were either love-poems or drinking-songs. The greatest name in the history of Aeolian song is that of the poet **Sappho**, who wrote from about 600 BC onwards. Her life and personality have given rise to a great deal of unreliable and ambiguous guesswork. We know, however, that she kept a school of elocution for young women, and that some of her poems are addressed to them. But, although homosexual love was seldom disapproved of by the Greeks, Sappho's tendencies may perhaps have been misjudged, or, at least, somewhat over-emphasized, since the most distinguished families of Lesbos seem to have entrusted their daughters to her care.

The few remaining fragments of her work show that Sappho was one of Europe's finest lyrical poets. Her brief tributes to an idolized woman-friend have been called the first significant love-poems in Western literature. Like so much lyrical poetry, they are almost impossible to translate; but their passion and pure tone still reach us across the centuries.

It is to be a God, methinks, to sit before you and listen close by to the sweet accents and winning laughter which have made the heart in my breast beat so fast and high. When I look on you – my speech comes short or fails me quite – In a moment a delicate fire has overrun my flesh, my eyes grow dim and my ears sing, the sweat runs down me and a trembling takes me altogether; till I am green and pale as the grass, and death itself seems not very far away...

In Sappho, too, we find a new feeling for Nature. It has been said that she was the first European poet to discover flowers. In one poem, for example, she writes of the hyacinth, 'which the mountain shepherd tramples underfoot, and it still blooms purple on the ground'. In another, of the beauty of an orchard: 'By the cool waterside the breeze rustles amid the apple-branches, and the quivering leaves shed sleep'.

Sappho's contemporary, **Alcaeus**, one of the earliest literary exiles, like Theognis driven out by the popular faction, is usually regarded as the originator of drinking-songs, but was also known for his political and erotic verses. Though comparatively little of his work has survived, in the opinion of Greek critics he ranked next to Sappho – 'pure Sappho of the violet tresses and the gentle smile', as he calls her in a fragment.

Choral Verse

Greek choral poetry is less accessible to the twentieth-century reader. From the outset it was in the service of religion, and later used to celebrate victories at the great Olympic Games, and to speak on behalf of the city or the people. Thus, it had originated in Sparta, where patriotic feeling always ran high, but afterwards developed in other cities with the rapid evolution of the Greek drama.

During the first half of the fifth century, relations between the Greek states were put to the test by the struggle against the Persians, during which, although Greece at length prevailed, Athens itself was burned down by Xerxes. The choral poet **Pindar**, who lived at this time, now came to be looked on as a national poet. His poems are difficult to understand, since they are filled with obscure images and legendary allusions. He was essentially a religious poet, a conservative and strict conformist at a time when freethought was beginning to emerge, a writer who defended the sacred truth embodied in the Oracle of Delphi.

Simonides, Pindar's contemporary rival as a choral poet, is best known for his epigrams, short poems in elegiac metre, often used for sepulchral inscriptions. With their brevity and concentrated feeling, they sometimes achieve incomparable expressiveness. This, for example, is Simònides' epitaph on the Spartan warriors who had died defending Greece against the Persians:

Go tell the Spartans, stranger passing-by,
That here, thus faithful to their laws, we lie.

Sappho, by Renaissance artist Raphael who was to redecorate a series of rooms in the Vatican in 1508/14. Detail of the wall representing Poetry; the other three walls symbolized Philosophy (see page 37 for Raphael's famous painting of 'The School of Athens' – Plato's Academy for this subject), Theology and Jurisprudence. (Stanza della Segnatura, Vatican, Rome)

HARMONY AND SLAVERY

The development of Greek civilization between 500 and 300 BC produced one of the noblest periods in Western history. Its focal point was the city of Athens; and what was achieved during those two centuries remains the ultimate basis of all Western culture.

Those centuries, however, had a stormy social background. Not long after the devastating Persian War, the rivalry between the Greek city states provoked a long, embittered struggle, in which many of the great writers and thinkers, among them Socrates and the tragedian Aeschylus, were obliged to play a military part.

Yet, despite these clashes, the cities grew prosperous, especially Athens, which became a centre of industry and commerce, thanks to the strength of the Athenian fleet, to the exploitation of rich mineral resources, and to the wise statesmanship of public leaders, among whom Pericles was the best-known and the most enlightened.

The political atmosphere of the various Greek states had undoubtedly a marked effect on the contribution they made to literature and art. Sparta, for example, ruled by an aristocratic minority, could not measure up to democratic Athens. But even in Athens, class-antagonisms were, and would remain acute. Physical labour, whether within a household or a commercial enterprise, was still largely carried out by slaves.

The cultural age with which we are dealing is usually called the 'Attic Period' (after Attica, the tongue of land on which the Athenians had settled); and the keyword of its prevailing style was harmony. Balance, symmetrical proportions and harmonic limitation were its governing ideals – the ideals that shaped the glorious Parthenon; but we have gradually come to perceive that, beneath this harmonious surface, sometimes threatening to break through, there lay an element of conflict. Poets projected their own fears and sufferings into the classic forms of poetry and drama. The old religion and ways of thought were challenged; and frequently the theatre became the battlefield on which the conflict was enacted.

The Acropolis in Athens, with its temples and statues, was a centre of Greek religion in the 5th century BC. During the many religious festivals, there would be competitions for song, music and dance as well as symbolic processions and gymnastic contests.

THE THREE TRAGEDIANS

Going to the theatre for an ancient Athenian was no mere relaxing social pastime. For him the play was a religious festival, celebrated in grandiose literary style. Performances lasted three days in a great marble amphitheatre open to the sky. The State itself and rich citizens sponsored the performances; and several dramatists took part, each competing for the winner's laurel-wreath.

The Tragedies had their origin in feasts and songs, honouring the wine-god Dionysus. Their composition and performance followed strict rules; and the number of actors was limited. Greek plays also introduced choruses, whose task was to evoke the atmosphere as the story unfolded, and to comment on the action, either expressing 'the voice of the people', or sometimes putting forward the dramatist's own views. Greek tragedies were written as trilogies – three plays by the same author that formed a single unit and were performed on the same day. As a finale, a so-called Satyric Drama was performed, its theme being linked, more definitely than that of the others, with the cult of Dionysus. The subject matter of plays was, almost without exception, derived from Greek mythology.

The history of Greek tragedy may itself be divided into three sections, and its pillars were three great poets, Aeschylus, Sophocles and Euripides.

It was **Aeschylus** (*c.* 525–456 BC), once a soldier in the Persian War, who introduced the use of two actors. Before his day, tragedy had consisted largely of narrative and choric poems. Not only did he create the tragic drama, but he is still regarded as one of its noblest exponents. Critics speak of 'the thunder of Aeschylus'. His genius had a

Above *Scene from a Satyric Drama showing two musicians, and a member of the chorus dressed as a satyr in goatskin and carrying a grinning mask. Detail from a 500 BC vase painting celebrating the marriage of Dionysus and Ariadne. (National Museum of Villa Giulia, Rome)*

Left *The 5th-century BC amphitheatre – with perfect acoustics – at Epidaurus in the Peloponnese, where performances at festivals often lasted several days.*

tempestuous strength and violence, and is seen at its most powerful in the use to which he put the chorus. Although the action of the play is described by a series of messengers, who relate what is happening 'off-stage', the effects that he creates are extraordinarily vigorous – as in *The Persians,* his only play he produced with a contemporary theme – and a work that is particularly memorable because Greece's former opponents are here magnanimously treated.

Aeschylus is said to have written ninety tragedies, of which seven have been preserved. Again and again in his work he dwells on the mystery of human life; and, although he expresses his reverence for the gods, his faith seems to have been painfully achieved. In *Prometheus Bound,* his main character is the defiant Titan who had dared to steal the heavenly gift of fire. Aeschylus portrays this heroic rebel with sympathy; but in the other plays of the trilogy, now lost, he probably intended to justify his hero's terrible punishment by Zeus, the all-powerful Father of the Gods.

In *The Oresteia,* the only trilogy by Aeschylus that has been preserved intact, he depicts the hideous crimes committed by the family of Agamemnon. The King, having sacrificed his daughter to secure his own success in war, on his victorious arrival home is himself murdered by his wife Clytemnestra, and her paramour Aegisthus. His son Orestes then kills his mother on the orders of Apollo; and the god later saves him from the Furies, the Spirits of Revenge, who are hunting down the matricide. Orestes, Aeschylus maintains, has been merely the tool of divine justice; for he is reluctant to accuse the gods of injustice, however harsh their rule may seem.

One of the magnificent repoussé gold masks (c. 1500 BC) found in the shaft graves at Mycenae by the German amateur archaeologist Heinrich Schliemann. 'I have gazed upon the face of Agamemnon', he telegraphed to King George of the Hellenes; but the masks are now thought to be at least 300 years older than that Homeric king. Schliemann had discovered the site of Troy in 1873, beneath modern Hissarlik, in north-west Turkey. (National Archaeological Museum, Athens)

Nothing is more dangerous to weak Man, Aeschylus repeatedly suggests, than, in his moment of mortal glory, to fall into the sin of hubris, or presumptuous arrogance, and to suppose himself the equal of the gods. Thus, when Clytemnestra spreads out the purple carpet of victory for her returning husband, Agamemnon at first declines to tread it:

> Stop this crawling on the ground, and howling like wolves at me! I won't be softened. I am the king of a small Greek city, not an Asiatic despot or Ethiopian headman. My people would laugh at me if they saw me swaggering on these embroideries and spoiling them. This is ritual for the Gods. I am a man. I insist on being honoured as a man. As long as I follow the law of my kingdom, the Gods will preserve me.

Although **Sophocles** (*c.*496–406 BC) by introducing a third actor took a decisive step towards the modern conception of dramatic poetry, his great contribution was on a psychological level. The conflicts he portrayed were not only a struggle against external forces, but a state of warfare within Man himself. In *Antigone* King Creon decrees that the body of the rebellious Polynices should be thrown to the dogs; but the dead man's sister defies

Top *Aeschylus, the Greek dramatist famous for his tragedies, wrote his own epitaph before he died, where he spoke proudly of his part in the Battle of Marathon but failed to mention his contribution as dramatic poet. Engraving from antique bust. (Royal Library, Stockholm)*

Above *Sophocles, a generation younger, defeated Aeschylus for the Prize of Tragedy in 468 BC. (Capitoline Museums, Rome)*

the tyrant and gives the corpse a decent burial. Here the conflict is no dispute for power – Antigone recognizes that she is powerless – but a clash between opposing wills, one of which represents the authority of the state, the other the emotions of humanity. Both Creon and Antigone are right, but each from a different point of view.

Spiritual conflict was what most concerned Sophocles. Unlike Aeschylus, he does not attempt to clarify the operations of divine justice. In *Oedipus Tyrannus,* the main character is crushed by his inexorable fate. Oedipus' offences have been committed inadvertently. In the past, through no fault of his own, he has killed his father and been the incestuous consort of his mother. What he has done he himself reveals by his actions. He owes his fall to the inscrutable irony of the gods.

Sophocles was famous for the beauty of his choric passages; and it was said that, when his undutiful son took the old poet to court, accusing him of feeble-mindedness, he won his case by reciting a chorus from his latest drama, *Oedipus at Colonus,* where he writes of his beloved country home near Athens:

Stranger, where thy feet now rest
In this land of horse and rider,
Here is earth all earth excelling,
White Colônus here doth shine!
Oftenest here and homing best
Where the close green coverts hide
her,
Warbling her sweet mournful tale
Sings the melodious nightingale,
Myriad-berried woods her dwelling,
And the wine-hued ivy, where
Through the sacred leafage lonely
No sun pierces or rude air
Stirs from outer storm, and only

Those divine feet walk the region –
Thine, O Reveller, thine,
Bacchus, following still that legion
Dear, thy nursing Nymphs divine.

Euripides (*c.*484–*c.*406 BC) continued the religious debate. He was influenced by the scientific and philosophical thinking of his period – a subversive dramatist who did not hesitate to question the wisdom and moral standards of the Olympian divinities. This he could not do openly, as his plays were performed at religious festivals; but his touches of criticism are easily discerned. Nor did he refrain from altering the old myths to suit his own purposes. At the same time, besides adding a narrative prologue, he reduced the part played by the chorus and presented a more involved plot. The religious element of his plays is minimized; and, although now and then he allows a god to appear, it is as a dramatic device rather than as a manifestation of the dramatist's religious faith.

Gods and demi-gods, moreover, are given realistic, even comic features – like the drunken Heracles in *Alcestis,* the earliest of Euripides' extant dramas. He was also one of the first dramatists to portray women in detail and analyse erotic passion. *The Medea,* for example, depicts a scorned woman, who becomes the murderess of her children; while in *Hippolytus,* it is Phaedra's illicit love for her stepson that precipitates her downfall. But in *Hippolytus,* too, the gods are accused of bearing the responsibility for human suffering; and Euripides repeats this accusation in the *Ion,* where, in still harsher terms, he seems to turn against the Oracle of Apollo at Delphi. 'If gods do ill, gods they are not!' a character declares.

Towards the end of his life, Euripides wrote dramas that had direct links with the political situation of the day. In *The Trojan Women,* he speaks bitterly of war, and of warriors, 'the fools who ravage cities', and depicts the misery of a conquered people.

Euripides' last drama, *The Bacchae,* is the only complete Dionysiac play that has survived – an extraordinary evocation of the wine-god's frenzied women worshippers running wild upon the mountains. King Pentheus, who attempts to repress their orgies, provokes the anger of the god they serve, falls into their hands and is eventually torn to pieces.

Here, as so often in the work of Euripides, his attitude towards his subject is obviously ambivalent. Is Pentheus, a sane man slaughtered by maddened women, an innocently suffering hero, whose only real offence is that he has disobeyed the gods? Did he deserve his fate? Yet the irrational ecstasy, to which he falls a victim, is conveyed in a wonderfully expressive chorus.

Chorus from **The Bacchae** by Euripides

A MAIDEN

O glad, glad on the mountains
To swoon in the race outworn,
When the holy fawn-skin clings,
And all else sweeps away,
To the joy of the quick red fountains,
The blood of the hill-goat torn,
The glory of wild-beast ravenings,
Where the hill-tops catch the day;
To the Phrygian, Lydian, mountains!
'Tis Bromios leads the way.

ANOTHER MAIDEN

Then streams the earth with milk, yea, streams
With wine and nectar of the bee,
And through the air dim perfume steams
Of Syrian frankincense; and He,
Our leader, from his thyrsus spray
A torchlight tosses high and higher,
A torchlight like a beacon-fire,
To waken all that faint and stray;
And sets them leaping as he sings,
His tresses rippling to the sky,
And deep beneath the Maenad cry
His proud voice rings:
'Come, O ye Bacchae, come!'

ALL THE MAIDENS

Hither, O fragrant of Tmolus the Golden,
Come with the voice of Timbrel and drum;
Let us the cry of your joyance uplift and embolden
The God of the joy-cry; O Bacchanals, come!
With pealing of pipes and with Phrygian clamour,
On, where the vision of holiness thrills,
And the music climbs and the maddening glamour,
With the wild White Maids, to the hills, to the hills!
Oh, then like a colt as he runs by a river,
A colt by his dam, when the heart of him sings,
With the keen limbs drawn and the fleet foot a-quiver,
Away the Bacchanal springs!

Left *Dancing maenad (or Bacchante), a priestess of the cult of Dionysus, god of wine and the theatre. Roman copy of a relief by Callimachus (c. 400 BC), the first Greek sculptor to achieve such faithful effects of drapery in marble. (Palazzo dei Conservatori, Capitoline Museums, Rome)*

Opposite *Euripides (shown here) and his seniors Aeschylus and Sophocles are acknowledged to be the three greatest Greek playwrights. Euripides was the first dramatist to portray women in detail, and his* The Bacchae *is the only complete Dionysiac play to have survived. (Glyptothek, Copenhagen)*

COMEDY

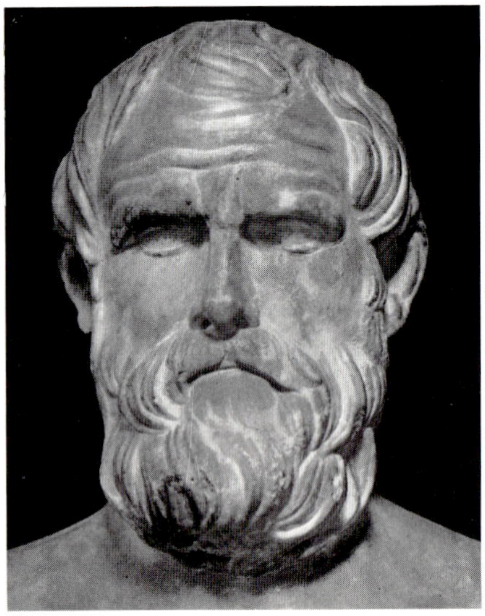

Above *Aristophanes, the master of comedy. Although his political satires have dated, he can still amuse audiences and his highly inventive* The Birds *is successfully performed to this day. Stephen Sondheim even adapted* The Frogs *as a musical project in the mid-1970s. Bust from the Villa Hadrian (Adriana) at Tivoli, near Rome. (Louvre, Paris)*

Greek comedy, like tragedy, has its roots in religious festivals, though in celebrations of a much more cheerful kind, held to mark the yearly vintage. In comedy the choice of subject matter was far freer than in tragedy; and plays were full of satirical references to public figures and political conditions.

The most famous comic dramatist was **Aristophanes** (*c.*445–385 BC), whose first plays were performed during the war between Athens and Sparta. A supporter of the aristocratic party, he was strongly opposed to the war itself and to war-mongering politicians, especially to the bellicose demagogue Cleon, whom he ridicules in the comedy called *The Knights*. Among his other targets were Socrates, the speculative philosopher whose educational influence he deplored, shown in *The Clouds* floating high above the earth, and Euripides, the revolutionary modern playwright, fancifully derided in *The Frogs*.

A born conservative, Aristophanes attacked all supposedly 'progressive' movements. But his finest and most poetic play, *The Birds*, has a much wider and more interesting scope. Here he draws a poetic picture of the Kingdom of the Birds, in which he finds a parallel to the human society he knew. 'Cloud Cuckooland' is as splendid a piece of literary invention as Swift's Brobdingnag and Lilliput.

Lysistrata, in which he again voices his opposition to the self-destructive war with Sparta, is a very different type of comedy, and emphasizes the sexual side of the Dionysiac cult; for here the peace-loving Athenian women are shown refusing their husbands' embraces so long as the struggle is permitted to continue. *Plutus*, on the other hand, is a non-political comedy, which deals with basic human failings. Aristophanes' last play, it foreshadows the New Attic Comedy that dominated the stage during the next hundred years, and of which **Menander** (342–290 BC) was the chief dramatist.

Left *Menander, famed for his 'New Attic Comedy', featured many typical characters of comedy in his plays – the miserly father, clever servant, boastful soldier. Few of his works have survived but the Roman playwrights of a century and more later, such as Plautus and Terence, adapted his original themes for their comedies. Fresco, c. 1st century BC, from the House of Menander at Pompeii, near Naples. He did not live here. It was thus named because the famous fresco of Menander was found on a wall facing the peristyle garden.*

One of a series of erotic illustrations by Picasso inspired by Aristophanes' satyric anti-war play Lysistrata *(411* BC*), for the Limited Edition Club of New York (1934). In the 1930s Picasso set up an etching workshop and illustrated many classic works, including Ovid's* Metamorphoses *in 1931.*

THE DAWN OF SCIENCE

Greek drama lost its imaginative force at about the same time as the Athenian city-states vanished. But Athens still made valuable contributions to the civilization of the West.

Towards the end of the fifth century, when a knowledge of political science and the art of public speaking were particularly valued, a new school of teachers arose – the so-called **Sophists**, or professors of wisdom, who, although they had a salutary effect on prose-literature, were said, at least by their opponents, often to indulge in sterile quibbling. A far more liberating voice was that of the Athenian **Socrates** (*c.*469–399 BC). No Sophist himself – unlike them, he never founded a school or delivered lectures, but took his message to the market-place – he aroused the same criticisms, and was eventually put to death.

We have no extant works from Socrates' own hand. His teachings were wholly oral; and nothing remains of them except for his pupils' records, which reveal his passion for truth and his acuteness of perception. When he was condemned to death by his countrymen on the charge that he 'corrupted youth', he made a speech in his own defence that will never be forgotten.

Socrates' Speech of Defence, as we read it today, is the work of his disciple, **Plato** (427–347 BC), who undoubtedly caught his master's spirit; but elsewhere it is sometimes hard to distinguish between the two sages. Plato, it has been said, built up a philosophical system, whereas Socrates wished only to give practical advice on the moral conduct of existence. One might add that Socrates prompted men to think, whereas Plato did their thinking for them. Thus a scholar has suggested that Plato's most Socratic works are those which do not put forward a solution to the problems raised.

The basis of Plato's philosophy is his idealism – his belief that what we call 'reality' is nothing but an incomplete reflection of a higher reality, the world of ideas. He expressed his views by means of Dialogues, conversational encounters in which well-known Athenian citizens take part. The main character is usually Socrates himself. Plato's dialogues are memorable not only for their philosophic content, but as vivid pictures of Athenian social life.

Plato is one of the thinkers who have left a decisive mark on the intellectual history of the West. Platonism helped to shape the doctrines of the early Christian Church and, much later, at the beginning of the nineteenth century, coloured the Romantic Movement.

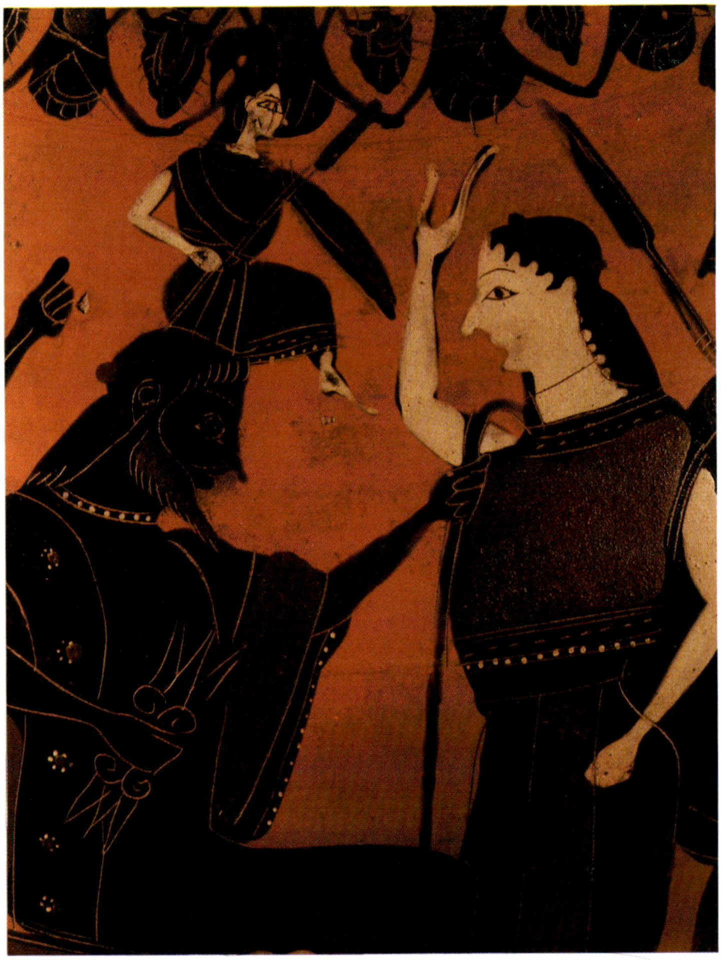

Athene being born from the head of Zeus after he had swallowed his first wife, Metis (the representative of wisdom) when she was about to give birth. The chief festivals of the cult of Athene, goddess of war and peace, wisdom and the crafts, took place in the city of Athens, centre of art and culture. From a vase painting, c. *400* BC. *(Louvre, Paris)*

'The School of Athens' – Plato's Academy (c. 1509), by Raphael, represents Philosophy, one of the four main topics of literature commissioned for the walls of the Vatican Stanza (see Sappho from the Poetry wall on page 27). In the centre, Plato – his head modelled on Leonardo da Vinci – talks to his pupil, Aristotle, surrounded by other great figures of the time such as Homer, Socrates and Euclid. (Stanza della Segnatura, Vatican, Rome)

SCIENCE AND HISTORY

Aristotle (384–322 BC), a pupil of Plato and the tutor of the future Alexander the Great, spent his middle years in Athens, where he lectured on philosophy. With his theories on ethics, metaphysics and the art of poetry, he made a lasting contribution to the Western world. Medieval thought was largely derived from his teachings, until, nearly two thousand years after his death, Francis Bacon and other philosophers began to question his authority and recommend alternative sources of knowledge – scientific experiment, for example. But our present system of defining literary types still goes back to Aristotle and his treatise on the *Art of Poetry*.

During the fifth century BC the historian first emerged as a literary artist. **Herodotus** (*c*.484–*c*.420 BC) has been called 'The Father of History', a title he certainly deserves; for, although a keen collector of legends and travellers' tales, he was also a pioneer in the field of historical research; and, when he was preparing his history of the struggle between Greeks and Persians, he familiarized himself, so far as he could, with all the countries he described, visiting Egypt, the great Mesopotamian cities, the tribes on the Black Sea and the coasts of Asia Minor. To the best of his ability he assembled facts, but he was never averse from telling romantic stories; and the result was an extraordinarily lively and interesting narrative.

His successor **Thucydides** (*c*.460–*c*.399 BC) is said to have shed tears as a young man on hearing Herodotus read his work aloud at the Olympic Games; but the method he employed in his *History of the Peloponnesian War* was far more scientific, and had a literary shape he had borrowed from the drama, as when he shows the Athenians committing the fatal act of hubris that would ultimately bring about their miserable defeat at Syracuse. **Xenophon**, too (*c*.430–*c*.354 BC) also dealt with contemporary history, as in his *Anabasis*, his graphic account of how ten thousand Greek mercenaries made their famous escape from Persia back to the Black Sea in 400 BC.

Two great Greek historians, Herodotus and Thucydides. They both thought Greece was the centre of the universe just as their contemporaries believed that the earth was the centre of the solar system. But by 200 BC it was known that the earth was round and its circumference could be calculated almost exactly. Herodotus, although acknowledged as 'The Father of History', was sometimes called 'The Father of Lies' for his indulgence in colourful anthropological or geographical digressions. (National Archaeological Museum, Naples)

HELLENISM

The warring Greek states never achieved unity. This was first established by the prince of a small country on the outskirts of Greece proper, Alexander the Great (356–323 BC) of Macedon. The period that followed his foundation of a Macedonian empire, and that lasted until the Romans conquered Greece, is called the Hellenistic Period. Greek literature now became the property of the civilized Western world. But Hellenistic literature itself often displayed refinement, taste and learning rather than originality.

Apollonius Rhodius, who flourished at Alexandria during the third century BC, in his poem the *Argonautica*, on Jason's voyage to the Black Sea in search of the Golden Fleece, made a bold attempt to revive the ancient Homeric tradition; and, although it never reaches Homeric heights, it contains some fine imaginative passages.

Theocritus, however, a Sicilian (born between 300 and 310 BC) who received his education at Alexandria, became the first of the Greek Pastoral Poets, and cast his memories of his youth near Syracuse into nostalgic and romantic form. In his *Idylls*, shepherds and country girls are seen through the affectionate eyes of a cultured city-dweller, looking back, like A.E. Housman in our own age, to a 'land of lost content'.

Another genuine innovator was the Sophist **Longus** (his dates of birth and death are uncertain; but he probably lived in the second or third century AD) whose exquisite pastoral–erotic tale *Daphnis and Chloe* was one of the earliest precursors of the modern novel.

Above left *The story of Jason and the Argonauts, with their good ship Argo, has inspired poets of all times. It was taken up by Homer and Hesiod, by the great tragedians, by the Greek lyric poets Pindar and Theocritus, by Apollonius Rhodius in his epic* Argonautica *(3rd century BC) and by more recent literary figures such as William Morris (in 1867) and Robert Graves (in 1944). Detail of a painting by Lorenzo Costa the Elder (c. 1460–1535). (Museo Civico, Padua, Italy)*

Above *'Daphnis and Chloe', the 'children-of-nature' in the pastoral–erotic story of the early centuries AD by the Greek writer, Longus. A translation by George Moore,* The Pastoral Loves of Daphnis and Chloe, *was published in a limited edition in 1924. These lovers also inspired Saint-Pierre's romance,* Paul et Virginie *(1787) and Ravel's music for his ballet of that name (1912). Sensuous woodcut (1937) by the French artist Aristide Maillol.*

THE GREEK HERITAGE

The She-Wolf suckling the twins Romulus and Remus. Thrown into the Tiber by their uncle who deposed their father as King of Alba Longa, saved by a she-wolf and reared by a shepherd, they returned to found the city of Rome on the Palatine Hill about 753 BC and Romulus became first King of Rome. The Golden Age of Roman literature was not to come for over 600 years. This Etruscan bronze sculpture dates from the 6th century BC, but the figures of the twins were added in the 15th century AD by the Florentine artist and goldsmith, Antonio Pollaiuolo. (Capitoline Museums, Rome)

There is a certain grim truth in the legend that the founders of Rome, the twins Romulus and Remus, were the foster-children of a she-wolf; for it was thanks to the courage and fierceness of the Roman nature that, during the course of a few hundred years, Rome grew from a small pastoral village in Latium into an Empire that dominated Asia Minor, the whole extent of the Mediterranean world and much of Northern Europe. Meanwhile, the Roman conquerors absorbed the civilizations of the peoples whom they swallowed up.

Seldom has a victorious power been more tolerant of foreign cultures and alien religions. Only the traditional institutions of the Roman state were always held sacred.

Up to the middle of the first century BC, Roman literature was overshadowed by imported Greek models. The most vigorous native works were the **Atellan Farces** *(fabula atellana),* from Atella in the ancient Campania region – popular comedies, of which the main characters, renamed Harlequin, Columbine, Pierrot, still figured on the stage in eighteenth- and nineteenth-century pantomimes.

The earliest interesting Roman writers are two comic playwrights, Plautus and Terentius. Of the two, **Plautus**, who died in 184 BC, was the better humoured. He aimed solely to amuse, and appears to have been completely untroubled by ethical or social problems. His gallery of characters was, in fact, largely taken from the New Attic Comedy: the dissolute young man, his miserly and unsympathetic old father, the kept-lover, the courtesan, and the witty, insolent, outspoken slave who constantly extricates his master from unpleasant situations.

Scene from one of the Comedies, possibly by Menander, chief dramatist of the New Attic style (in the 4th century BC) which was carried on by the Roman playwrights Plautus and Terence. The large-mouthed mask at left is often seen on terracotta statues, the lady's mask (centre) is typical of the older Comedy style, and the figure on the right is recognizably a servant from her plainer and shorter dress. 1st-century AD fresco from a house in Region I,6,II at Pompeii, near Naples.

Left *Terence's* Comedies *were still popular in the Middle Ages, as shown by this title-page to a 16th-century edition. (Royal Library, Stockholm)*

Above *The Roman Forum was a chief centre of political and economic life in the ancient world for over 500 years.*

Many of his plays, such as *Mostellaria* (*The Ghost*) and *Miles gloriosus* (*The Boastful Soldier*), are still sometimes revived; and his character-types and plots were adapted by later masters such as Molière, Holberg and other playwrights.

Terence or **Terentius** (*c.*195–159 BC), born a slave, was a more refined dramatist and portrayed his personages with greater subtlety. He had assimilated Greek culture, and studied the comedies of Menander. One of his most important plays, the *Adelphoe* (*The Brothers*), describes the advantage of an upbringing that is based on trust, and on love rather than on violence. Terence was long considered superior to Plautus; but today the somewhat rougher Plautus is more generally admired.

Left *Ruins of the Appian Way, the great route south from Ancient Rome to Brindisi on the Adriatic, begun in 312 BC by Appius Claudius, the Roman dictator – and founder of Latin prose and oratory.*

THE GOLDEN AGE OF ROMAN LITERATURE

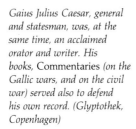

Gaius Julius Caesar, general and statesman, was, at the same time, an acclaimed orator and writer. His books, Commentaries *(on the Gallic wars, and on the civil war) served also to defend his own record. (Glyptothek, Copenhagen)*

In Roman history, the last century BC was a period of rapid expansion and fierce internal crises. New social groups clamoured for a place in the sun; while frequent wars increased the strength of the army, and encouraged the rise of power-seeking adventurers. Yet, despite military and political conflicts, cultural activity did not diminish; and during the century that preceded the death of the first Roman Emperor, Augustus (63 BC–AD 14), Roman literature enjoyed its Golden Age.

The first great poet to emerge was Titus Lucretius Carus, known as **Lucretius**, who lived about 95–55 BC. Greek ideas and Greek standards form the basis of his long philosophic poem *De Rerum natura* (*On the Universe*). But his pessimism and often dry, didactic tone – enlivened, it is true, by passages of wonderful poetic beauty – seem to reflect the spirit of his own age. His basic subject is the Human Condition. Lucretius was a materialist, who regarded everything, the soul included, as built of atoms; and he gives a grandiose, but gloomy picture of life, in which the gods have lost their position and the only directing force is blind Fate. Christian thinkers have always resented him, and reminded us of the story, probably apocryphal, that he was driven mad by a love-potion and committed suicide. Less prejudiced critics, however, have hailed him as Rome's greatest poet, and maintained that his pessimistic resignation may help to liberate his readers from the weakening fear of death.

In **Catullus** (*c.*84–*c.*54 BC) Rome produced an outstanding lyric poet. Many of his exquisite love-poems are addressed to the fashionable mistress he called Lesbia, whose real name was Clodia, the promiscuous wife of a senior Roman official, and the sister of the dissolute revolutionary politician Clodius. They depict a desperate sensual passion, doomed to bitter disillusionment, in melodious, deeply moving lines:

My Lesbia, let us live and love
And not care tuppence for old men
Who sermonize and disapprove.
Suns, when they sink, can rise again,
But we, when our brief light has shone,
Must sleep the long night on and on.

Here, the sonorous dignity of Catullus' last line – *'nox est perpetua, una, dormienda'* – could have been achieved only in Latin.

Other Roman poets of the same stamp as Catullus were the Elegiac Poets, **Tibullus** (48?–19 BC) and **Propertius** (*b.*54/48–*c.*16 BC), both cultivated young men, who, at a time when Augustus and his rivals were battling for command of the Roman world, occupied themselves chiefly with the pleasures and sorrows of the individual life, and with their devotion to the 'learned girls' they loved.

Latin Prose Writers

Latin prose, too, now found an individual style. With his public orations and philosophic writings – for instance, *De Senectute* (*On Old Age*) – the lawyer and philosopher **Marcus Tullius Cicero** (106–43 BC) created the type of 'classical Latin'; while his letters to his friends, of which eight hundred still survive, have an easier personal tone. In them we meet Cicero himself, with all his strength, all his limitations, continuing to think and write until the year when he was at length assassinated on the orders of his political opponent, Antonius, whom Shakespeare introduces as Mark Antony.

The great general and statesman **Julius Caesar** (100–44 BC) was also a master of Latin prose; and his accounts of his own martial exploits, such as his subjugation of tribal Gaul, are masterpieces of concise dramatic narrative.

Left *Title-page of a French edition of* The Works of Lucretius *(1692). As Plato was the favourite philosopher of the Romantics, so Lucretius appealed to the materialists and atheists of the 17th and 18th centuries.*

Below *Cicero, whose prose style was to become the model for 'classical Latin'. His name has given rise to the term 'cicerone', meaning a guide. (Uffizi, Florence)*

PAX ROMANA

The Emperor Augustus, who brought about a moral and literary rebirth known as the age of the pax romana. This statue was found at the 'Villa of Livia' (his wife) in Prima Porta, near Rome. The breastplate reliefs celebrate the return of the Roman Standards in 20 BC, captured at the Battle of Carrhae in Parthia (53 BC). (Vatican Museums, Rome)

Once the Civil War had ended, Octavianus (who was later to become Emperor Augustus) successfully re-established peace and order; and the period of internal calm that then began, and would last almost two hundred years, has been named the age of the *pax romana*, of the Roman Peace which, after the extinction of the Republic, encompassed the whole Western world. Few rulers have intervened in cultural life as effectively as did Augustus. Although his own previous career had been cruel and destructive, he determined that he would raise his country's civilization to the same high level as its military prowess, and bring about a patriotic and moral rebirth. In this campaign, literature, he saw, had an important part to play, by glorifying memories of the Roman past and celebrating solid traditional virtues.

The poet who best exemplified Augustus' design was **Virgil** or **Vergilius Maro** (70–19 BC). In his first important works, the *Eclogues* and the *Georgics*, Virgil writes of the charms of country life and of his own idyllic existence on his farm in northern Italy. Sometimes his poems remind us of Isaiah's prophecies; for, in one of his *Eclogues*, he speaks of a mysterious male child, born to rule over the Kingdom of Peace, where the ox and the lion shall lie down together. In the four books of the *Georgics*, he describes the life of the Italian peasant and, now the horrors of the Civil War have gone, preaches a peace-giving return to Nature – advice that, during the eighteenth century, Jean-Jacques Rousseau and his followers would insistently repeat.

Virgil's greatest production, however, was the *Aeneid*, begun at the suggestion of the Emperor who, while temporarily absent from Rome, had

written to him, asking for some memorial of his poetic genius. Virgil worked on the manuscript for eleven years. 'I lick my verses as a bear licks her cubs', he himself remarked. His plan was to emulate the Homeric poems by chronicling the ancient origins of Rome. In his poem, the Trojan hero Aeneas is described wandering, like Odysseus, hither and thither, and at last reaching Italy to lay the foundations of the Roman Empire, on his way having met, loved and eventually deserted Dido, Queen of Carthage, a country the Roman Republic had attacked and destroyed, and, again like Odysseus, he ventured down into the Kingdom of the Dead.

During the Middle Ages, Virgil was the most esteemed of ancient poets, and also reputed to have been a magician and a seer, who had foretold the advent of the Christian faith. In the *Divina commedia*, he acts as Dante's guide through the Inferno and the realms of Purgatory.

Above *Pan (god of woods and pastures), a forest-god, Silvanus, and Apollo as a shepherd-god are three of the deities who appear in the Tenth Song of Virgil's* Eclogues *(or* Bucolics*). Woodcut by Aristide Maillol for a 1928 edition with Latin and English texts, handmade paper by Gaspard Maillol, decorative type cut by Eric Gill. (Royal Library, Stockholm)*

Above *Virgil, the Roman poet whose* Aeneid *was written at the suggestion of the Emperor Augustus, with the Homeric epics as model. From a 3rd-century AD mosaic found at Hadrumetum (now Sousse) in Tunisia. (Bardo Museum, Tunis)*

Left *Stone mask of Tragedy, from late 1st century AD, at the ancient Roman port, Ostia.*

DREAMS OF PEACE

Horace, with his philosophy of enjoyment and stoic morality combined with satire, became a favourite poet of the Age of Enlightenment, and has been constantly translated and quoted by writers of every age. Relief, c. 1st century BC. (Museum of Fine Arts, Boston)

Though he, too, played his part in the Emperor's master-plan, Quintus Horatius Flaccus, better known as **Horace** (65–8 BC) was personally very unlike Virgil. He was a member of the literary circle that gathered around Augustus' friend and minister Maecenas, who gave him generous support and had granted him the farm in the mountains that forms the background of so many of his poems. There he did his best to shun the storms of life, cultivate his art in quietude, meditate peacefully and drink good wine. Above all else it was tranquillity he valued:

Peace and calm seas the voyager begs the gods for
When storms blow up in mid-Aegean, and black clouds
Muffle the moon, and sailors miss the usual
Stars in the sky;

And peace is what the battle-maddened Thracians
And the fierce Parthians with their painted quivers
Pray for – the peace no gold or gems or purple
Grosphus, can buy.

A pasha's bribes, a consul's rodded lictors
Can soon disperse a riot of the people,
But not the grey mob of the mind, the worries
Circling the beams

Of fretted ceilings. He lives well on little
Whose family salt-dish glitters on a plain-laid
Table; no fears or ugly longings steal his
Innocent dreams.

Despite his love of the country, Horace also enjoyed Rome with its 'smoke and wealth and noise', and addressed many of his Epodes to the city and its characters, among whom we read of the arrogant upstart 'parading along the Sacred Way in a toga three yards wide'. But, as a rule, his satires are good-humoured. He was essentially an artist, whose pursuit of the appropriate image and the right word was undoubtedly his strongest passion.

His younger colleague, the poet **Ovid** (43 BC–AD18), having been unwise enough to defy the Emperor, had to pay a heavy penalty. A brilliant young man, he entered the fashionable Roman world, whose sophisticated views of life and love he expressed in his *Ars amandi*, or *The Art of Love*, a poetic manual written on the technique of courtship and seduction; while *Remedia amoris*, or *Cures of Love*, offers instruction as to how the satisfied amorist may regain his previous liberty.

Though Augustus was no puritan himself, the poet's cynicism seems to have offended the Emperor; and Ovid, warned to improve his moral tone, in his next poem, *Metamorphoses* or *Transformations*, adopted a far less provocative subject – the fabulous changes of shape undergone by gods and mortals, described in a series of richly imaginative tales.

Ovid's own transformation came too late. Involved in a court scandal that concerned one of Augustus' kin, he was exiled to Tomi, a wretched settlement on the shores of the Black Sea, where he remained until his death, and wrote the lamentations that he entitled *Tristia*, or Sorrows.

ROMAN HISTORIANS

Romans were always mindful of their own victorious past; and **Livius**, or **Livy** (59 BC–AD 17), another writer patronized by the Emperor Augustus, set out to gratify their historical sense with a *History of Rome* in a hundred-and-forty-two books, extending from the foundation of the city until the year 9 BC. He produced a lively and graphic narrative – he is said to have 'canonized Rome' as the Ideal Commonwealth – which was much applauded by his readers; though modern historians have sometimes criticized his unscholarly methods of research.

Both **Tacitus** (*c.*AD 55–?) and **Suetonius** (*c.*69–*c.*14) lived at a time when the *pax romana* had been established on a firm foundation, and looked back on the reigns of such dissolute earlier emperors as Tiberius and Nero, of whose conduct they repeat many appalling stories, from a sternly hostile point of view. Suetonius, the private secretary of the upright Emperor Hadrian, produced in his *Lives of the Caesars* a particularly scandalous account of former Imperial misdeeds; but Tacitus' *Histories*, a history of his own times, of which only four complete books have survived, and his *Annals*, which begin with the death of Augustus and end with the suicide of Nero, are far more considerable works of literary art. Tacitus had a peculiarly original prose-style; he was a master of the succinct, expressive phrase, as when, in four damning words, he describes an unsuccessful ruler (Galba) – *'capax imperii nisi imperasset'*: 'he might have seemed capable of governing had he never governed'.

'Believe me, love's desire shall not be hastened too quickly. No, tempt it out gradually, carefully and gently ...' wrote Ovid in his Ars amandi *or* The Art of Love, *an early manual on the technique of courtship and seduction, which inspired this woodcut (1935) by Aristide Maillol. (Royal Library, Stockholm)*

THE LATTER DAYS OF THE EMPIRE

Rome was long to retain its imperial supremacy; and when, in AD 410, the sacred city was sacked by a Barbarian chief, Alaric, King of the Visigoths, a cry of horror resounded throughout the Latin-speaking world. The causes of Rome's fall were numerous, and included the breakdown of the fiscal system, barbarian incursions across her eastern frontiers and the engagement of barbarian armies, as well as the growth at home of a huge unemployed urban proletariat, who demanded a constant supply of 'bread and circuses' – free meals and endless gladiatorial games in the Circus Maximus, which could hold some 320,000 people.

During the reign of Nero (54–68), a picaresque novel appeared – the *Satyricon* – possibly the work of one of his favourite companions, **Petronius** (*d.* AD 66), called the Emperor's *'arbiter elegantiae'*, or Arbiter of Elegance. The *Satyricon* gives us a vivid, sometimes horrific picture of contemporary low-life, the most famous episode being an account of an immense and tasteless banquet held by the vulgar parvenu Trimalchio. The author was a satirist, but never a moralist. He merely observed and depicted, with amusement, and often relish, the vices and aberrations of his fellow men.

During this period, the art of poetry declined. The satirist **Martial** (*c.*40–*c.*104) is no match for Horace, but provides some lively glimpses of the social background; while **Juvenal** (*c.*55–*c.*135) who is usually regarded as the last important Roman poet, has left us sixteen ferocious satires, aimed at the follies of women – particularly women who engaged in the Gladiatorial Games – urban dirt and overcrowding, and the arrival of pestilent foreigners. They pour into the Tiber, he says, all the filth of the Orontes and the Tigris.

The only Latin tragic dramatist of note was **Seneca**, (4 BC–AD 65), the tutor and private counsellor of the Emperor Nero, who eventually ordered him to kill himself; which he did with Stoic courage. Seneca's ten tragedies

Above *Seneca the Younger although at one time adviser to Emperor Nero was later accused of conspiracy and ordered to take his own life, which in his bath he duly did. He had a talent for moralistic maxims such as: 'He who has little is not poor, but he who wants to have more is'. Facsimile of woodcut from Schedel's* Weltchronik, *printed in Nürnberg in 1493. (Royal Library, Stockholm)*

Opposite *Scene of the freed slave Trimalchio's banquet from 'Fellini Satyricon' (1969), the Italian director's film based on the notorious novel of 1st-century AD Roman low-life,* Satyricon, *attributed to Petronius. Trimalchio (at right) was played by Mario Romagnoli.*

Left *Messalina, lecherous third wife of Emperor Claudius I, appears in Juvenal's* Sixth Satire. *Her sinister character is here portrayed by Aubrey Beardsley in* The Yellow Book *(1897), of which he was the first art editor. (British Museum, London)*

include some fine rhetorical flights, but are as full of horrors as Shakespeare's early *Titus Andronicus*. He was much admired and imitated, often to their detriment, by lesser Elizabethan playwrights.

Other literary Stoics were the freed slave **Epictetus** (*c.*50–130) whose collection of improving discourses, *Enchiridion*, was recorded by a pupil, and the philosophic **Emperor Marcus Aurelius** (121–180), who, sometimes even on active service against barbarian invaders, wrote in Greek a series of *Meditations* that reveal the Stoic creed at its most dispassionate and morally exalted.

The fact that, like Marcus Aurelius, many poets and scientists now preferred to use the Greek language shows the gradual decline of Latin literature. Thus Lucianus, usually called **Lucian** (*c.*115–*c.*180), a native of Syria, composed his *Dialogues* in Greek. The form is taken from Plato; but the lively humour they display is much nearer to that of Aristophanes. Best known are his *Conversations in the Kingdom of the Dead*, where he frequently makes broad fun of the religious and philosophic beliefs he saw flourishing around him.

During the last centuries of the Roman Empire, many alien faiths began to replace the ancient State religion; and chief among them, of course, was Christianity, which the Emperor Constantine (272–337) officially authorized in the year 312 after the Battle of the Milvian Bridge. Meanwhile, as early as the second century AD, the New Testament had been translated into Latin. The Latin version of both Testaments, the Vulgate, did not appear, however, until the opening years of the fourth century.

Above *'The Unexpected Homecoming' from Lucian's humorous* Dialogues, *written in Greek. In these* Dialogues *(or* Conversations*) he satirizes society, philosophers and the gods of mythology. Illustration by Bele Bachem for a West German edition of* Heterae Dialogues *(1957).*

Right *The 2nd-century* AD *philosopher Apuleius is best-known for his satire on Man's vices and follies,* The Metamorphoses *or* The Golden Ass, *which with its mixture of adventure and frivolity could be called the earliest modern novel. It was first translated into English in the 16th century. The sorcerer's apprentice, Lucius, who was accidentally transformed into the likeness of an ass, is brought back to human form by the Egyptian goddess, Isis. This interpretation of an erotic episode is by Hans Erni for a Swiss edition (1960).*

THE TRIUMPH OF CHRISTIANITY

A new and significant literary form, the Christian hymn, was first created some hundred years earlier; and, by depending on rhyme and accent instead of syllabic length, it produced a poetic revolution. Here the greatest names are those of **Ambrose** (339–397), son of the Governor of Galilee, and **Prudentius** (384–410), who has been described as the earliest Christian poet to exhibit true imaginative genius.

The scion of a rich North-African family, **St Augustine** (354–430) had enjoyed, as a young man, all the pleasures of the pagan world and delighted in the Gladiatorial Games; until, having heard a mysterious voice that bade him 'take and read' the Epistles of St Paul, he was converted to the Christian faith. Later, having become Bishop of Hippo on the African coast, he learned with horror in the year 410 of the tragic fall of Rome, entered and pillaged by the Visigoths – an event that inspired the book he entitled *The City of God*. Augustine's masterpiece, however, was his *Confessions*, an extraordinarily vivid account of his youthful sins, and of his escape from sin through Christianity. Here, for example, is the Bishop's candid description of his licentious early days:

> To Carthage I came, where a whole frying-pan full of abominable loves crackled round about me – I was not in love as yet, yet I loved to be in love, and with a more secret kind of want, I hated myself for having little want. I sought about for something to love: security I hated – and all because I had a famine within me – It was very pleasurable to me, both to love, and to be loved; but much more, when I obtained to enjoy the person whom I loved.
>
> I defiled, therefore, the spring of friendship with the filth of uncleanliness – My God, my Mercy, with how much sourness didst thou of thy goodness to me besour that sweetness! – even that I might be scourged with the iron burning rods of jealousy and suspicions, and of fears, and angers, and brawls.

Apart from his Confessions, *St Augustine's most important work is* De Civitate Dei *(*The City of God*). It has greatly influenced the understanding between the Christian Church and State. Woodcut from a French edition (1486). (Pierpont Morgan Library, New York)*

4 *The Middle Ages/Europe*

DANCE OF DEATH AND JOY OF LIFE

Devils tormenting the lost in Hell, an image the Church often urged the faithful to contemplate. 16th-century woodcut.

In AD 476, Romulus Augustulus, the last Roman emperor of the West, was deposed by Odoacer, a barbarian war lord, who then declared himself King of Italy, and reigned until he himself was overthrown, in the year 493, by Theodoric, King of the Goths. The Dark Ages, which lasted throughout the seventh and eighth centuries, now descended upon Europe; for its new rulers, though they sometimes aped Roman modes, had comparatively little understanding of the civilization that they had brought down.

Yet some remains of learning were still kept alive in Christian monasteries and churches; and from them a fresh civilization gradually emerged. It was the Church that, during the Middle Ages, shaped European ways of life and thought, and mankind's general conception of the world. Latin became an international language; pilgrims flocked to the Christian holy places; and, in 1096, Pope Urban II was able to gather knights of all the continent under the banners of the First Crusade.

But divisive forces were also at work, and grew steadily more powerful, as emperors and princes resisted the political pretensions of the Church. Charlemagne's Holy Roman Empire, which had been blessed by the Pope in 800, collapsed on his death in 814; and his imperial structure broke up. The Feudal System gave almost unrestricted power to the war-like ruling class; the peasantry was reduced to servitude; only the urban middle class retained some degree of independence.

Education, reserved for the few, was largely conducted in cathedral- and monastery-schools, and later in the universities that had started to appear during the twelfth century. Students from all over Europe came to the University of Paris, whence they took home with them both new ideas and relics of the old learning. Knowledge was also disseminated by itinerant monks and priests, and by strolling singers and jesters, frequently united in the same person; and these were the men who contributed much to the formation of medieval literature.

The Church preached a gospel of purity and self-denial (which churchmen themselves did not always follow) and urged the faithful to contemplate images of death and, after death, either of heavenly bliss or of eternal punishment. The Dance of Death, in which a horrific skeleton intrudes on Man's everyday existence, was a favourite medieval theme. But the natural *joie de vivre* of a hearty, lusty race proved stronger than the sense of sin; and the European scene, as it is illustrated in books and pictures, appears to be full of life and gaiety and colour. The Middle Ages was a period of contrasts – of greed and asceticism, of mysticism and rationalism, of ferocious pugnacity and romantic feeling.

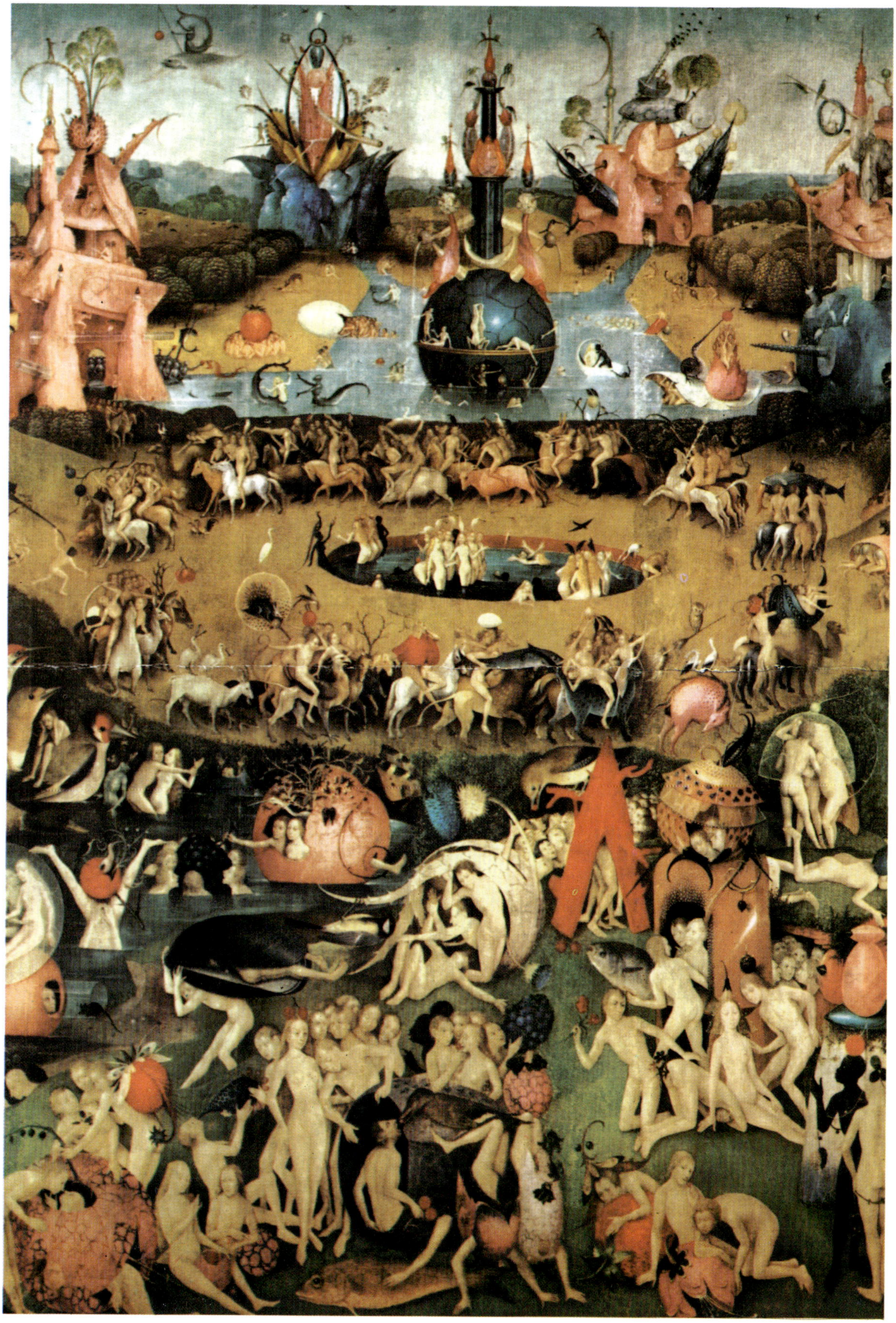

During the Middle Ages there was much fantasizing both in art and literature on the delights and terrors of temptation and torment. Scene from the central panel of the triptych 'The Garden of Earthly Delights' by the Dutch painter, Hieronymus Bosch (c. 1450–1516). (Prado, Madrid)

SAINTS AND HEROES

St Francis of Assisi devoted his life to preaching and poverty and founded the Franciscan Order. Section of a triptych by Italian artist Benozzo Gozzoli (c. 1421–1497. (National Gallery of Umbria, Perugia, Italy) **Above** *13th-century Church of S. Francesco at Assisi – in fact, one chu ch built on another one. The saint's tomb and a series of frescoes by Giotto can be seen here.*

Now that Latin had been adopted as the language of the educated classes, little remained of the literature of the ancient German tribes. While it was engaged in its missionary work, the Church endeavoured to extirpate all the relics of paganism, among which were the traditional folk-tales and songs. The little that has been preserved was often tamed and expurgated, though the original wildness sometimes breaks through.

This ancient literature largely consisted of heroic tales in verse and prose. Outside Scandinavia, one of the oldest earliest surviving texts is the eighth-century Anglo-Saxon epic *Beowulf*, the story of an Old Norse hero who slays trolls and dragons. The existing version shows a Christian influence, and it is thought that the author may have been a cleric who used Virgil as his pattern, although the subject he adopted was based on heathen legends.

During the greatest period of the Middle Ages (*c.*1050–1300), ecclesiastical culture was richest and most various. **Peter Abelard** (1079–1142) and **St Thomas Aquinas** (*c.*1225–1274) shaped a Catholic philosophy that is still accepted today; while **Francis of Assisi** (1182–1226) did his best to live in the spirit of the Gospel, and preached not only to men and women, but to beasts and birds, and wrote his famous hymn to 'Brother Sun and Sister Moon'.

This period of the Middle Ages also achieved literary expression, through the heroic poems that, in France, then the centre of Western culture, were called *chansons de geste* – songs of deeds, as in achievements of war, from the Latin *gesta*. Like the Homeric epics, they had probably been preceded by shorter songs and tales that had sprung up around historical events and celebrated places of pilgrimage, but were given their final form some hundreds of years after the happenings they describe.

The most famous *chanson de geste* is *The Song of Roland*, which appeared about 1100, its historical core being an episode taken from the war that Charlemagne, during the eighth century, had waged against the Basques. In the poem, however, the enemy have become the heathen Saracens, and Charlemagne is the defender of the Christian faith.

The Song of Roland was inspired by a burning enthusiasm for the Christian religion and the military virtues; and it is around them that the action turns. There is no hint of human love; nor is there much psychological characterization. But, within this limited framework, *The Song of Roland* possesses a bleak beauty and a lofty but simple style.

Here Roland prepares for death, having been cut off from the main body of Charlemagne's forces:

Now Roland feels that he is at death's door;
Out of his ears the brain is running forth.
Now for his peers he prays God call them all,
And for himself St Gabriel's aid implores;
Then in each hand he takes, lest shame befal,
His Olifant and Durendal his sword.
Far as a quarrel flies from a cross-bow drawn,
Toward land of Spain he goes, to a wide lawn,
And climbs a mound where grows a fair tree tall,
And marble stones beneath it stand by four.
Face downward there on the green grass he falls,
And swoons away, for he is at death's door.

Heroic figures defeating dragons or demons appear in many legends at different periods and from different cultures, such as St George and the Dragon, Perseus and Andromeda in Greek mythology, and Rama and the Demon King in the early Sanskrit epic, Ramayana. *St George was said to be a Christian soldier who died a martyr's death at Lydda, in Palestine, at the turn of the 3rd century. In medieval times St George represented the good Christian overpowering the evil dragon who had captured a princess. Painting by German artist, Lucas Cranach the Elder (1472–1553). (Hamburger Kunsthalle, Hamburg)*

CHIVALRIC LOVE

Contemporary miniature of 'master-singers' – poets and musicians who developed from the minnesingers, lyric poets dating from the 12th century. They were organized into Guilds, and the German poet Heinrich von Meissen *(c. 1250–1318) is said to have founded the first school of* meistersingers *in Mainz in 1311. He was known as* Frauenlob *for his poems in praise of ladies and of the Virgin Mary.*

Even during the warlike Middle Ages, the rattle of swords and the braying of trumpets did not wholly satisfy an audience; and many delightful lyrics were composed, often written by poor wandering students. Fresh and popular, they celebrated the pleasures of a vagrant life, and the joys of love and the spring. As the twelfth century approached, love-poems grew popular with the rich, and developed under the influence of Latin prototypes. This fashion came from Provence, and then spread all over Western Europe. The singers, who performed at courts, singing in their national tongues, were called troubadours; and among the most famous were **Bernart de Ventadorn** (*c.*1145–1180) in Provence, and **Walther von der Vogelweide** (*c.*1170–*c.*1230) in Germany where they were called minnesingers. The love they described was romantic and exalted; and their verses were usually addressed to a married noblewoman whom the troubadour worshipped from afar. He did not necessarily expect a physical reward; and, if he were given the slightest sign of favour, he was apt to faint with ecstasy. Large singing-competitions were often held. Although, in itself, this type of verse was not always very distinguished, it brought a new element into contemporary literature, and helped to refine the martial manners of the day.

Another literary form that arose during the twelfth century in France were the so-called *romans bretons*, or chivalrous epics. As in the *chansons de geste*, the poet tells of war and adventure, and his main characters are valiant knights; but what inspires these knights to do tremendous deeds is romantic love rather than hatred of the heathen or devotion to the art of war. Several *romans bretons* take their subjects from legends and songs spun round a Celtic sovereign called King Arthur and 'The Knights of the Round Table.'

Best-known of such subjects is the story of Tristan and Isolde, a theme that has inspired many poets, of whom one of the earliest is **Chrétien de Troyes** (*c.*1135–*c.*1183). It tells how the young knight Tristan is sent by his liege lord, King Mark, to escort Isolde, the monarch's future wife; and how, by a mischance, Tristan and Isolde drink a love potion that causes them to betray the King. They are obliged to part; Tristan marries another woman; but he cannot forget Isolde, and, as he lies wounded, he sends her a farewell message. She hastens to join him; but Tristan is already dead, his wife having persuaded him that Isolde has played him false; at which she dies beside his body. Another subject that Chrétien de Troyes also treated was the legend of Perceval (or Parsifal), the pure youth, guardian of the legendary Holy Grail, the sacred chalice believed once to have held the Blood of Christ.

Romans bretons were admired all over Western Europe. German poets elaborated on the Tristan and Parsifal stories; and in Italy and Spain chivalrous verse–novels, that revived the same legends, were still read far into the seventeenth century. Even in rough, distant Sweden, attempts were made to rewrite earlier chivalric tales.

Meanwhile, in Germany, an unknown writer, perhaps an Austrian, from the material of the ancient Teutonic tales evolved the *Nibelungenlied*, which has become the German national epic, now well-known thanks to Wagner's operas. The *Nibelungenlied* may be placed between the *chansons de geste* and the *romans bretons* since it is more chivalrous and courtly than the former, but harsher and more primitive than the latter. Its atmosphere bears some resemblance to that of the Greek tragedies; but here it is not blind Fate, but the dramatis personae's own characters that precipitate the tragedy. The hero, Siegfrid, is married to the Burgundian princess, Kriemhild; and, with the help of his cloak of invisibility, he assists his brother-in-law Gunther to conquer the Valkyrie Brunhild. When Brunhild learns of his action, she has Siegfrid slain; but, after his death, Kriemhild, now remarried to Etzel (or Attila), the King of the Huns, with her new consort's assistance herself takes a bloodthirsty revenge.

Page from an unfinished German manuscript (1200–1216) of the earliest-surviving story of the Holy Grail, Perceval or Le Conte du Graal, *by Chrétien de Troyes, the 12th-century French poet renowned for his Arthurian romances. Although based on Celtic legends, these tales stemmed from France, being inspired by the medieval Breton minstrels. (Stadtmuseum, München)*

'THE REYNARD' & 'THE ROMANCE OF THE ROSE'

Although, during the Middle Ages, the more sophisticated type of literary productions did not reach the peasant or the town-labourer, the people had always had their own poetry – hymns of invocation, or songs to mark the rhythm of the weaving-loom and rowing bench, as well as love-songs that were not invariably chivalrous. These ditties were seldom written down, but carried on by word of mouth from generation to generation.

A no-less anonymous, and again a purely oral form, were the folk-tales that seem to have been told in every country, and were often transmitted from race to race. In medieval days, there was a considerable exchange of tales and sagas between the West and East; and the greatest favourites were the animal-tales, which can be traced as far back as Ancient Egypt. Both hero and villain are frequently the cunning fox; and the tales told about him were worked up by medieval narrators into a long mock-heroic poem entitled *Le Roman de renart* (*The Reynard*) in French, and *Reinke Vos* in Low-German dialect.

Another kind of verse that was popular at the time, and clearly intended for an audience neither aristocratic nor unduly pious, was the *fabliau* – a form of short story in verse, probably written by itinerant jesters or unfrocked priests. The hero is usually one or the other; and it is always the poor student who tempts the middle-class housewife to leave the path of virtue, and who makes fun of greedy clerics. The tone of the *fabliau* is cheerful and coarse, realistic and malicious; and no one escapes ridicule, from the stupid peasant to St Peter. Here the rough treatment of women is in sharp contrast to the worshipful attitude expressed by the Provencal poets. But beneath ribald satire we occasionally notice genuine sympathy for the poor and the oppressed. Class differences begin to be underlined; and sometimes we catch a murmur of revolutionary discontent.

The Romance of the Rose, *an allegory of a young man courting his loved one, symbolized by the rose, was written by two different people. The French poet Guillaume de Lorris wrote the first 4000 lines (c. 1230) for a fastidious court audience, and some 40 years later French writer Jean de Meung wrote the remaining 18,000 lines for bourgeois readers with more robust tastes. This subject was frequently illustrated in contemporary and later miniatures, such as this 15th-century French example. (Bibliothèque Nationale, Paris)*

In short, beside literature aimed at an educated and aristocratic audience, another arose that appealed to the more robust taste of the rising middle class. A third type of poetry, the allegorical, which was probably popular with both classes, is reflected in the preachings of the Church. The author of allegories personifies virtues and vices as men and women he names Hope, Timidity or Evil Tongue.

Le Roman de la rose (The Romance of the Rose), a widely popular medieval poem, is a long allegorical narrative that describes a young man's pursuit of his beloved, symbolized by the Rose, which itself symbolizes the idea of Love. The authors were two thirteenth-century poets, one of whom exemplified the Provençal style of chivalrous poetry with long theological digressions, while the other completed it in the racy satirical manner of the *fabliau* – a collaboration that made their portrayal of Woman and Love somewhat contradictory, but, perhaps for that reason, all the more interesting and realistic.

Title-page woodcut by Ignatio Meurer of a Swedish edition (1621) of the mock-heroic epic, Reynard the Fox. *In the disguise of animal stories, poems could serve not only as moral tales but also criticize those in power. Early examples were the fables of Aesop (c. 6th century* BC*) and Phaedrus (1st century* AD*).*

Reyncke Foss.

Thet är:

En skön och nyttigh Dicht/ full medh Wijßheet/godh Låro/och lustige Exempel: Vthi hwilken alle Menniskiors wäsende/ Handel/ Otroo/ List och Snillheet affmålat warder/ sampt medh thet sedliga Förståndet och thenne Books brukk.

Allom Menniskiom i thenna sällsamma tijden ganska tienligh och nödigh at weta/ etc. Medh sköne Figurer beprydd.

Tryckt och vplagdt i Stockholm/ aff Ignatio Meurer/ 1621.

DANTE

Death-mask of Dante Alighieri, the great Italian poet. (Private Collection, Florence)

In the most productive period of the Middle Ages, France was the cultural centre of Europe; but, during the fourteenth century and the convulsions of the Hundred Years' War, its imaginative activities were much curtailed; and at that time, another flowering took place south of the Alps, where Italian began to be recognized as a fruitful literary medium. This development showed itself first in poetry, profiting from Provençal influence.

The Italian language came of age with **Dante Alighieri**, who was born in Florence in 1265 and died in Ravenna as a political refugee in 1321. In *La Vita nuova* (The New Life), a series of poems, linked together by short passages of prose, he tells of his love for the young Beatrice, and of his sorrow when she dies. Dante's passion for the dead maiden, to whom in life he had never dared to speak, is both ethereal and romantic. She is not so much a creature of flesh and blood as the marvellous personification of beauty and goodness.

Having played a vehement part in the political conflicts of his day, when the 'black' Papal faction overcame the 'white' and the group that supported the Holy Roman Emperor, Dante was forced to leave his birthplace for ever; and, as an exile, he wrote a succession of learned works, in which he triumphantly demonstrated how much the Italian language could achieve. But today his reputation largely rests on the work that he completed not long before his death – the greatest poetic masterpiece of the Middle Ages, perhaps, indeed, of our Western civilization, *La Divina commedia* (*The Divine Comedy*). The title 'comedy' is now somewhat misleading. Dante's poem is an epic account of a poet's journey through the diverse, often terrifying regions that, after death, await the human soul. It includes a hundred cantos, divided between the *Inferno*, *Purgatorio* and *Paradiso*. To guide him through the *Inferno* and *Purgatorio* Dante has the first-century Roman poet Virgil, and, through *Paradiso* his lost Beatrice. Although Dante declares that the poem came to him in a vision, it is the product of an acutely intellectual waking mind, which, with brilliant clarity, reflects the current view of the universe that he had derived from the teachings of the Catholic Church.

The allegorical message of the *Divina commedia* is timeless; but, as a realistic narrative, it also fascinates the modern reader; for it has something of the matter-of-factness of a detailed guide-book. Dante describes every place in the three realms, and every stretch of the long path that he and Virgil are obliged to tread. Many of his contemporaries must have read his poem as a detailed description of the experiences they themselves would one day suffer. The souls punished in the *Inferno* are almost painfully lifelike; and among them he depicts his own political enemies, painted with an intensity of hatred that spares neither cardinals nor popes. On the frozen bottom layer of hell lurks Satan, with Judas, Brutus and Cassius in his jaws – the men who had betrayed Christ and the Empire.

It has often been said that the *Inferno* is the most absorbing section of the work; and it is certainly the most dramatic. But today the lyrical and architectural beauty of the later parts has begun to arouse more interest. In the *Inferno*, Dante's evocation of Paolo Malatesta's and Francesca de Rimini's forbidden love, and of their plight as they are swept along together on an eternal storm-wind, is exquisitely moving and pathetic:

> Love, that to no loved heart remits
>   love's score,
> Took me with such great joy of him,
>   that see!
> It holds me yet and never shall leave
>   me more.
>
> Love to a single death brought him
>   and me; . . .

Then, in the *Purgatorio*, we meet a different kind of love – that of Beatrice, as she approaches him to lead him forward into Paradise:

And instantly, for all the years between
Since her mere presence with a kind of fright
Could awe me and make my spirit faint within,

There came on me, needing no further sight,
Just by that strange, outflowing power of hers,
The old, old love in all its mastering might.

And, smitten through the eyesight unawares
By that high power which pierced me, heart and reins,
Long since, when I was but a child in years,

I turned to leftward – full of confidence
As any little boy who ever came
Running to mother with his fears and pains –

'Dante and Virgil crossing the Styx', one of the most notable paintings by Eugène Delacroix (1798–1863), a leader of the French Romantic school. Dante regarded the 1st-century Roman poet, Virgil, as 'our greatest poet', and it is Virgil who guides Dante through Hell and Purgatory in his Divine Comedy. *(Louvre, Paris)*

THE CLOSE OF THE MIDDLE AGES

Right *Woodcut of François Villon, from the first edition of his* Grand Testament *(c. 1460), which consisted of 173 stanzas, including ballads and rondeaux. (Bibliothèque Nationale, Paris)*

Cy comence le grant codicille qte ftamét maiftre françois Billon

The Cité of Carcassonne in France was often the setting for Mystery and Morality Plays, and some of the best remains of medieval fortifications in Europe are to be found there. The town was greatly restored by the 18th-century architect, Viollet-le-Duc.

No sharp boundary can be drawn between the Middle Ages and the Renaissance, which merge during the fourteenth and fifteenth centuries. But typical medieval literature began to decline as the Catholic Church weakened, and the world of chivalry was gradually thrust aside by royal power and the emergent middle class. Poetry, however, still developed; and the vogue of the ballad spread from France all over Europe, the most famous ballads being those which glorified Robin Hood and other rustic champions.

Simultaneously, the reputation of the great universities dwindled; learning was replaced by sterile academic pedantry; and students were considered rascals. Such a rascal, halfway through the fifteenth century, was the extraordinary poet **François Villon** (*b.* 1431), an arch-bohemian, who extracted poetic inspiration from the squalor and misery amid which he lived, and who wrote both of outcasts, drunkards and street-girls, and of his own corroding sense of sin. He was haunted by the idea of death. Thus, in his *Ballade des dames du temps jadis* (*The Ladies of Bygone Days*) with the melancholy refrain, '*Mais où sont les neiges d'antan?*' (*But where are the snows of yesteryear?*) he reminds us how mortal beauty vanishes; and in *L'Epitaphe*, written at a moment when he and his cronies were expecting to be hanged, he may perhaps have prophesied his own fate. Most of his poems are collected in his *Great Testament*. He himself completely vanished from record about 1463, when he was thirty-two years old.

The Medieval Stage

Having no classical foundation to build on, the playwrights of the Middle Ages had perforce to make a fresh start; but, like the Ancient Greek dramatists, they found it in contemporary religious faith. At Christmas and Easter, the Church dramatized biblical texts to explain them to the more ignorant believers. Thus plays became 'the Bible of the poor'; and the result was liturgical drama, first written in Latin, later in ordinary speech. Soon church-buildings became too small to house the performers and their audience; and, as early as the twelfth century, plays were moved to secular surroundings. They were called Mystery Plays so long as they adhered to strictly biblical themes; but their subjects moved further and further away from the stories told in Holy Writ. Whereas Mystery Plays related the lives of the Saints, Morality Plays often took the form of allegories, in which characters appeared who represented an array of moral attributes. An example, the English play *Everyman*, is still frequently revived.

Epitaph by François Villon

Oh brothers, you live after us,
because we shared your revenue.
God may have mercy upon you,
if you have mercy upon us.
Five, six – you see us tied up here,
the flesh we overfed hangs here,
our carrion rots through skin and shirt,
and we, the bones, have changed to
dirt.
Do not laugh at our misery:
pray God to save your souls and ours!

We hang in chains to satisfy
your justice and your violence,
brother humans – surely, you see
that all men cannot have good sense!
Here no man may look down on us –
Oh Child of Mary, pity us,
forgive our crimes – if dying well
saved even the poor thief from hell,
the blood of Christ will not run dry:
pray God to save your souls and ours!

The rain has soaked and washed us
bare,
the sun has burned us black. Magpies
and crows have chiselled out our eyes,
have jerked away our beards and hair.
Our bodies have no time to rest:
our chains clank north, south, east and
west,
now here, now there, to the winds'
dance –
more beaks of birds than knives in
France!
Do not join our fraternity:
pray God to save your souls and ours!

Prince Jesus, king of earth and air,
preserve our bodies from hell's
powers –
we have no debts or business there.
We were not hanged to make you
laugh.
Villon, who wrote our epitaph,
prays God to save your souls and ours!

This fresco in the Church of S. Anastasia in Verona by Italian artist Antonio (Pisano) Pisanelli (1395–1455), which antedates Villon's poem Epitaph *by some 25 years, evokes the gruesome prospect before the artist when facing the gallows, accused of theft.*

Comic Drama had a more complex origin. The jester had flourished since ancient times; and a part of the traditional comic repertoire can be traced back to the comedies of the Roman Empire. Popular games and frolics were woven into the action; and the best-known medieval comedy is the cheerful French farce about the ridiculous misadventures of the *Lawyer Pathelin*, in *La Force de Maistre Pierre Pathelin*. The literature of the Middle Ages, like other aspects of medieval life, spans a huge register of contrasted ideas and feelings, from the earthy coarseness of a *fabliau* to the subtle sweetness of a Provençal lyric and the ethereal beauty of Dante's picture of Paradise. Again and again the imaginative genius of an unknown artist shines through, just as it does in the sculptured ornament of a thirteenth-century cathedral.

Medieval stages were often circular with the audience seated all round them. This miniature (c. 1400) celebrates the theatre of comedy with Calliope, the Muse of heroic epics, inscribed on the curtained booth, and Terence, the 3rd-century Roman master of Comedy drama, portrayed below. (Bibliothèque Nationale, Paris)

MAGIC RUNES

Sigurd's runic inscription on Ramsund mountain in Sweden. This hero of Germanic legend appears in numerous song–poems, in the Icelandic Poetic Edda *and the German* Nibelungenlied *cycle among others.*

> You will be able to find runes and the legible letters, letters of great power, which might have been painted by the great sage; made by the mighty gods and cut by Odin, chief among the gods.

These runes, which come from the god Odin himself, were thought to possess magical powers and help to decipher the riddle of experience. Introduced to Scandinavia in the second century AD, inscribed on stones and staves of wood, on spear-shafts and household goods, were used until the twelfth century. The clumsiness of writing materials limited their scope; but the same sturdy substances preserved them. At first, the main purpose of runes appears to have been magical. From obscure invocations carved on the Norwegian Eggjum rune stone, we learn that they were designed to protect the dead against evil spirits and call forth vengeance on a killer.

For all their brevity, runes illuminate the life of the Nordic peoples throughout a whole millennium. No pyramids were ever built in honour of Scandinavian rulers; instead, thousands of rune stones were raised to commemorate the free peasants, who sailed their own Viking ships. An obituary was the only form of immortality on which the Viking race depended.

EDDAIC AND VIKING POETRY

Iceland was colonized by the Norwegians about AD 900. Like all migratory people, the Icelanders cherished old traditions, which, in a hazardous life, represented permanence. During the centuries after they had established themselves, ancient Icelandic literature arose almost as miraculously as that of the Judaean people a thousand years earlier.

Again, poetry came first. Eddaic poems are anonymous, their authors all unknown, their subjects ancient gods and heroes, the metres employed few and simple. Most of the songs, written down from about 1270 onwards, are called *Elder Edda, Edda of Saemund* or, more correctly, *Poetic Edda.*

The rune stone inscription in Olafur Brynjulfsson's Edda *manuscript of 1760 reads: 'Here rides Oden on the horse, Sleipner.' Runes originated with the Teutonic god Woden or Wotan (known as Oden or Odin in the North), god of nocturnal storms, who was gradually transformed into the god of war and of spiritual life as the Latins equated him with Mercury. (Arnamagnean Institute, Copenhagen)*

The first of the songs of the Edda, *Voluspá* (*Sibyl's Prophecy*) is a vision of the creation of the universe and its destruction, and relates how the gods lifted the earth out of the sea, how the first Golden Age began; how the Days of the Axe and the Days of the Knife dawned, and tells of the Twilight of the Gods, when gods and giants perished, and of the new Golden Age. The *Voluspá* is an inspiring prophecy rather than a didactic work. The poet was a kind of Scandinavian Isaiah; and his final passages depict the earth once more rising from the ocean and the unsown fields turning green.

The proverbial poem *Hávamál,* (*Sayings of the High One* – Odin), on the other hand, which urges that evil should be met with evil, and that only a man's fame survives his death, reflects a wholly pagan spirit. Like the Greek gods, those of the Edda are always close to human kind.

The human heroes in the Edda, too, like Homeric heroes, are closely related to the gods. Sigurd and Volund have the same superhuman dimensions as Hector and Achilles. The historical origins of the stories can often be traced, but time has blended them with myth and saga. Despite this process, however, the soldiers and rulers of the great period of migration can be detected in the Edda poems and about half the Edda songs are usually classed as heroic poems. But their historical background is always somewhat vague. They deal for the most part with individual tragedies and family feuds.

The greatest collection of sagas concern Sigurd Fafnesbane and his royal relations, and they use much the same material as the German *Nibelungenlied.*

Whereas the Edda poets remain mysterious, the authors of Viking (scaldic or skaldic) poetry seem intensely living, and are not only named, but have been vividly portrayed.

One of these was **Egil Skallagrimsson**, who died about the year 900. He appears in the family saga that describes him. A terrible Viking, cruel and ruthless and cunning, he was also Iceland's greatest poet. Skallagrimsson's verse was different from the Edda songs. Scaldic poetry was topical, and unconcerned with the gods and heroes of the past. It had a practical purpose, either to wound or destroy, or else to applaud a chieftain or some other powerful man. When Egil was shipwrecked on the English coast, and fell straight into the jaws of his old enemy, he saved his head by means of a laudatory poem, *Hofudlausn* (The Head Ransom) that he hastened to recite.

In literary form, the scaldic poem far outdid the Edda. The more complex its metre, and the more elaborate and allusive its imagery, the finer it was thought to be. The first scalds originated at the Scandinavian peasant courts and chieftains' gatherings; but, after colonization had begun, the island people became specialists in this type of verse, until foreigners believed that every visiting Icelander was a scald, which, indeed, was very nearly true. During the classical period of the tenth and eleventh centuries, the scaldic poem was an exquisite instrument that expressed the poet's strongest feelings. Later, it grew more artificial and lost a good deal of its spontaneity.

The masterpieces of both eddaic and scaldic literature were produced in pagan times; and it is significant that Christianity was brought to Iceland only some ten years after the death of Egil Skallagrimsson.

Egil Skallagrimsson, Iceland's cruel killer and greatest poet of scaldic verse. This pagan Viking used poetry both as invocation and to insult his enemies. Late 17th century manuscript. (Arnamagnean Institute, Copenhagen)

FAMILY SAGAS AND ROYAL SAGAS

The great Icelandic hero, Snorri Sturlason, wise man, poet and chronicler of Royal Sagas. Drawing by Christian Krohg. (Royal Library, Copenhagen)

Iceland became Christian by public decree in AD 1000; and, since the Church was a centre of literacy, secular works were now written down. But the heathen view of life persisted, as the core, not only of poetry, but also of much later prose-works, more especially in the Family Sagas, Iceland's greatest literary contribution to the world. An Icelandic 'saga' does not tell stories of trolls and gnomes, but gives an historical episode imaginative shape. It unfolds the history of this island people as it was handed on from family to family.

The basic tone of the sagas is heathen; the community is built on the family; and a man's honour is valued more than anything else that he possesses. The Christian God does not yet rule; dark Destiny controls existence. Yet here and there, we can detect a different view of life. In the best of the Family Sagas, the mighty *Njall's Saga*, which dates from the end of the thirteenth century, Gunnar of Lidarande exclaims, 'I do not know if I have less courage than others, because I am reluctant to kill my fellow men'. This remark may also have served what scholars have called the highest artistic aim of a saga – to suggest an aspiration towards the world of the spirit.

The isolated life that the Icelandic islanders led may partly account for their keen interest in history, which extended to Norway, their old motherland. It was they who, in the Royal Sagas, told of the remote historic past; and these sagas, again, are based on an oral tradition, later written down by learned men. One of them, **Snorri Sturlason** (1179–1241), has given its name to the tragic Sturlunga period that came to an end when Iceland lost her independence and submitted to Norwegian rule. Snorri himself took part in the struggle, a great Icelandic hero who bore some resemblance to an early Renaissance prince, both in his learning and broadminded attitude and in his ambition and talent for intrigue. His diplomacy was great, but his lust for power even greater; and a rival eventually destroyed him. Snorri's two main works are *Edda* and *Heimskringla*, the former being a religious and didactic poem, not to be confused with *The Poetic Edda*. Most of our knowledge of the Icelandic scaldic poetry has come from Snorri.

The word 'saga' therefore has for Icelanders a special meaning. A group of poems more recent than those discussed above are called Fornaldersagor (Sagas of Ancient Times) and tell of the old days, but are closer to folk-sagas, and based on material derived from periods far earlier than the Family and Royal Sagas. They are not regarded today as strictly historical, but as Lögnsagor (Lying Sagas), and are much looser in composition, and have a larger cast of trolls and dragons and straightforward saga-themes. Eroticism, which makes them ancestors of the novel, is also an element they introduce. Many are related to heroic eddaic poems like the *Volsunga Saga*; others like *Frithiof's Saga*, tell of early Viking days. They incorporate, moreover, some Oriental and other alien themes in strange Nordic disguise.

CHRIST IS VICTORIOUS

The struggle between heathendom and Christianity was far more savage in Sweden than in neighbouring Scandinavian countries. In Sweden, Uppsala, with its sacrificial groves, was the strongest fortress of paganism; and the old idols were not destroyed there until about AD 1100.

Unlike Iceland and, to some extent, Norway, Sweden and Denmark have preserved almost nothing of their ancient literature. One exception is the Danish **Saxo Grammaticus**'s chronicle *Gesta Danorum* (*c.*1200), which expresses the national mood of the time of Valdemar the Great.

The literature later produced in Scandinavia after its move towards Christianity is somewhat less remarkable, partly because it was usually written in Latin, which diminished its originality, and partly, too, because it served a religious purpose. The freshest examples of secular literature were the folk songs, which, as in France and Germany, whence the custom came, were sung to dancing. Danish songs have a place among the finest poems of the Middle Ages, although they are little known outside their native land.

Birgitta

The only Swedish writer whose reputation, during the Middle Ages, spread all over Europe was **Birgitta** (**Bridget**) (1303–1373), who was eventually canonized. Both as woman and as a poet, she is an imposing figure, and would appear to have lived two separate lives. After a worldly career as the wife of an important man and the mother of eight children, when her husband died she was at last free to follow her religious calling; and in 1349, she moved to Rome, where she eventually breathed her last. Meanwhile, she wrote more than six hundred 'Heavenly Revelations', which she maintained she had received straight either from Christ or from the Virgin Mary. For many years, most of them could be studied only in the Latin of her father confessors; but now, they have been translated into English, *The Revelations and Prayers of St Bridget*, as well as Swedish, the language in which she herself received them.

The coffin of St Birgitta (Bridget), the visionary and poet. Her remains were taken from Rome, where she died, back to her homeland on her canonization in 1391. Fresco by Johannes Rosenrod (1437), in the Tensta Church in Uppland.

ISLAM

Top *First Sura of the Koran, the sacred collection of the prophet Muhammad's revelations, from an Egyptian edition.* **Above** *Celebrating the end of Ramadan, the ninth month of the Arab year when the Muslim must fast from sunrise to sunset. Arab miniature. (Bibliothèque Nationale, Paris)*

Opposite *After Muhammad's legendary journey from Mecca to Jerusalem he travelled through the seven heavens with the archangel Gabriel, where he was touched by the hand of God and eventually carried back to Mecca. Turkish miniature. (Bibliothèque Nationale, Paris)*

When the poor camel-drover, **Muhammad** (570–632) was forty years old, he was commanded by the Angel Gabriel to become a prophet and his people's guide. The religion he founded is called Islam; its leaders were styled Caliphs, or followers.

The third Caliph, Othman, had the oral and written testimonies of Muhammad's revelations collected, and then appointed a commission to draw up Islam's holy scriptures. They were given collectively the name *Qur'an* (the Koran), which means reading or recitation, and contain 114 chapters, or Suras. The early Suras are written in rhymed prose and the later portions in a more straightforward prose style. The language of the Koran became the literary language of the Arab countries. It thus describes the Day of Judgment:

When the sun shall be darkened,
When the stars shall be thrown down,
When the mountains shall be set
moving,
When the pregnant camels shall be
neglected,
When the savage beasts shall be
mustered,
When the seas shall be set boiling,
When the souls shall be coupled,
When the buried infant shall be asked
for what sin she was slain,
When the scrolls shall be unrolled,
When heaven shall be stripped off,
When Hell shall be set blazing,
When Paradise shall be brought nigh,
Then shall a soul know what it has
produced.

In less than a hundred years, the Caliphs of Islam had conquered the whole of the Near East, in 711–712 taken Spain and pushed beyond the Indus to the borders of China. The religious teachings of Islam cannot alone explain its militant impetus, which is largely attributable to the fact that the rise of the new faith coincided with the development of an aggressive warrior society; where, as would happen during the Christian Crusades, the faith that the warriors held added lustre to their conquests.

Of the wealth of Arab poetry that arose in Cairo and Cordoba, in Damascus and Baghdad, only fragments ever reached the West, since Islam was now the chief enemy of Christian Europe. A translation of the Koran, however, was first printed in the sixteenth century, with the approval of the religious reformer Luther, who regarded it as a cautionary document.

Then, at the beginning of the eighteenth century, a glimpse of Islamic secular literature was provided by Galland's French translation of the *Thousand and One Nights.* These stories, which the beautiful Schéhérazade is said to have told night after night, came from all over the Orient; and their origins can often be traced back to Ancient Egypt.

It was during the nineteenth century, that the West next became aware of Arab, usually Persian, poetry and recognized its literary merits. The poet **Hafiz** (1320–1389), whose works were translated at the beginning of the century, inspired Goethe; and in 1859, the English writer Edward Fitzgerald published a free rendering of *The Rubáiyát of Omar Khayyám*, a large collection of quatrains attributed to the late eleventh-century Persian poet, philosopher and mathematician, which delighted the Pre-Raphaelite Brotherhood, and has now made Fitzgerald's adaptation one of the most often quoted of minor English poems.

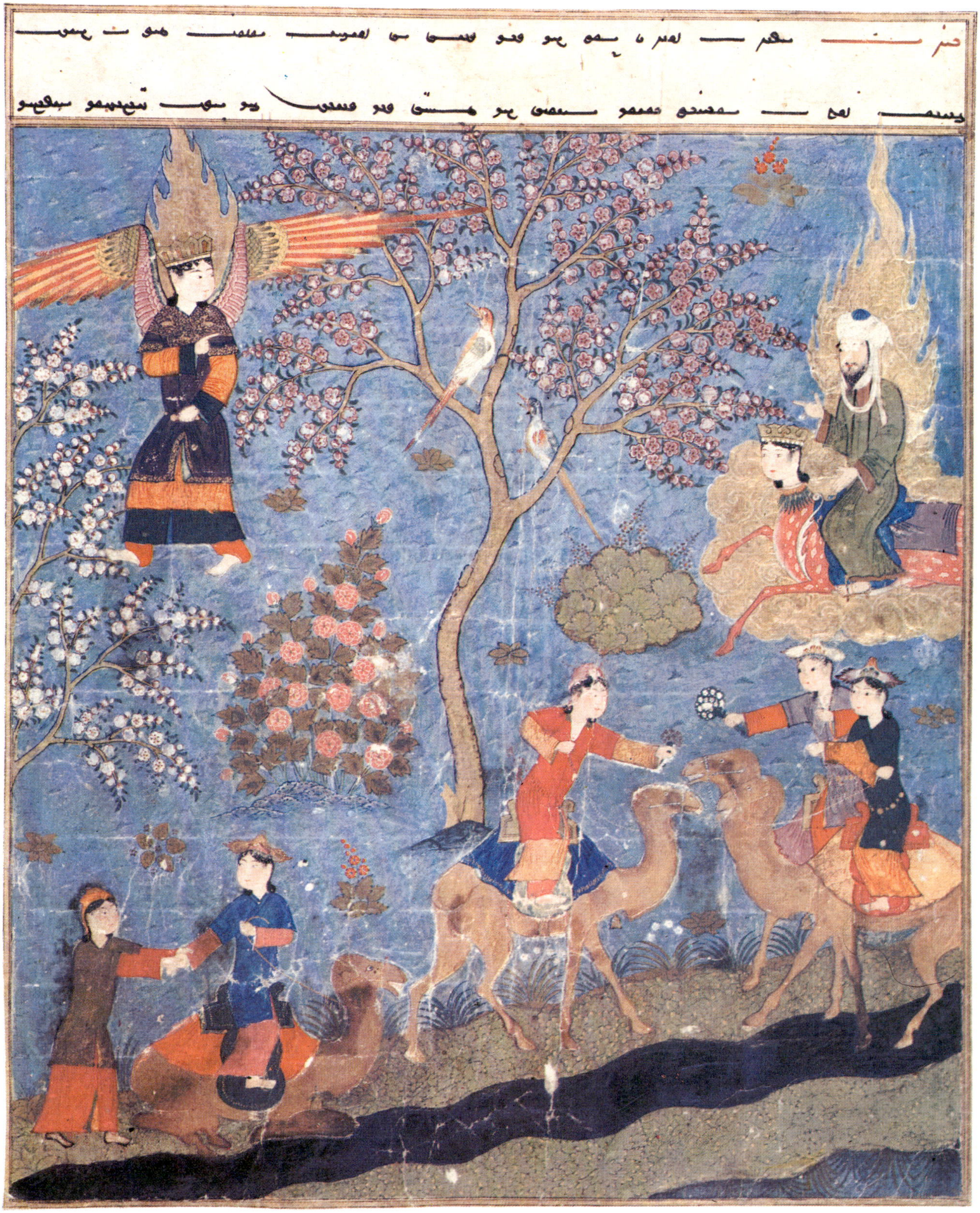

THE GOLDEN AGE OF CHINESE LITERATURE

靜夜思 李白

牀前明月光 疑是地上霜

舉頭望明月 低頭思故鄉

Above *One of Li Po's quatrains in its Chinese script. The difficulties of conveying the style of an original Chinese or Japanese poem are apparent when the characters have first to be transliterated into the Western alphabet – from which a literal translation is made – and then turned into a free version by a poet. After transliteration the title of this four-line poem would read:*

Tsing ye si

Ch'uang ts'ien, ming yüe
kuang
i shï, ti shang shuang
kü t'ou, wang ming yüe
ti t'ou, sï ku hiang

After literal translation by a sinologist comes the free version:

A Still Night's Thought

The clear moon lights my
bed,
There is frost on the
ground.
I raise my eyes to the
clear moon,
I bow my head and think
of my homeland.

With a few exceptions, the early Chinese poets were little known in the West until the present century. The T'ang Dynasty (618–906) has been called the Golden Age of Chinese literature; and the three best-known poets of the time are **Li Po** (**Li Bo**, AD 701–762), **Tu Fu** (712–770) and **Po Chü-i** (772–846). Both Li Po and Po Chü-i were philosophic wine-bibbers, concerned above all else to catch the beauty of the passing moment. Among the forms that T'ang poets perfected was the *chüch-chu*, or 'stop-short' poem, which, in only four lines, set out to record the impression made on them by an emotion or a scene.

Japanese verse was profoundly affected by the importation of Chinese culture during the Yamato and Nara periods, which lasted until 794, when the Heian age, a peak of Japanese civilization, opened. Early Japanese poets, too, were greatly concerned with the transience of human life.

Here, for example, is a poem by the eighth-century lyricist, **Lady Kasa**:

Like the pearl of dew
On the grass in my garden
In the evening shadows,
I shall be no more.

Drinking Alone by Moonlight
by Li Po

A cup of wine under the flowering
trees;
I drink alone, for no friend is near.
Raising my cup I beckon the bright
moon.
For he, with my shadow, will make
three men.
The moon, alas! is no drinker of wine;
Listless, my shadow creeps about at
my side.
Yet with the moon as friend and the
shadow as slave
I must make merry before the spring is
spent . . .

The Cranes by Po Chü-i

The western wind has blown but a few
days;
Yet the first leaf already flies from the
bough.
On the drying paths I walk in my thin
shoes;
In the first cold I have donned my
quilted coat.
Through shallow ditches the floods are
clearing away;
Through sparse bamboos trickles a
slanting light.
In the early dusk, down an alley of
green moss,
The garden-boy is leading the cranes
home.

Left *There were many scholars who were also poets and artists in China. They considered landscape painting to be important for its religious, philosophical and symbolic overtones and for the chance it gave to express Man's involvement with the universe. This example of an early 16th-century scroll painting on silk is by Chu Tuan. (Museum of Far Eastern Antiquities, Stockholm)*

Opposite *Stig Södersten's evocative illustration to a brief poem by the 8th-century Japanese lyricist, Shami Mansei, in which the transience of Man's life is compared with the fragility of a rowing-boat on the open sea. From a Swedish edition of Japanese poetry (1956).*

5 *Renaissance – Reformation – Baroque*

REBIRTH AND REFORMATION

Right *With three small ships and 120 men, Christopher Columbus* (**below**) *first sailed across the Atlantic in 1492, hoping to reach Asia by sailing due West. He mistook the West Indies for India and the first land he sighted (actually Watling, one of the Bahamas), he named San Salvador; he then sailed along the north coasts of Cuba and Haiti (Hispaniola). On his second voyage a year later he founded the first European town in the New World, Isabela on Haiti. Other Bahamian islands are named on this contemporary woodcut – Conceptión, Cape Sta Maria. Despite further expeditions, he died alone and forgotten in 1506, but his discoveries opened a new world to scholars as well as adventurers.*

Below right *From ancient times there have been astronomers who thought the earth moved round the sun and not vice versa. The Polish astronomer Nicolaus Copernicus's (1473–1543) views of the universe, then considered heretical by Church and State, were those of today. Artist unknown (1575). (Collegium Maius/Old University, Cracow, Poland)*

The Renaissance, a great 'Rebirth' of interest in the civilization of the classic past, began during the fourteenth century to sweep across Europe, and travelled gradually northwards until, two hundred years later, it had reached the Scandinavian countries.

Artists and scholars did not merely rediscover the culture of Antiquity – which, indeed, had never been entirely forgotten – but were inspired to build a new world and abandon the medieval image of the universe. It was a time of momentous geographical discoveries, and also a period of revolt against the dominion of the Catholic Church and the philosophical concepts of the Middle Ages, an era that produced, besides Vasco da Gama and Columbus, Copernicus and Galileo. The joy of discovery can still be felt today in every aspect of Renaissance life and art.

Man, at the same time, became the Measure of Existence, and was no longer regarded as part of a larger unity to which it was his duty to conform. The rights of the individual were emphasized. He was entitled to develop his own abilities and realize his private aims. Renaissance Man sought for omniscience. Typical of the age was **Leonardo da Vinci** (1452–1519), painter, mathematician, poet, scientist, who took all knowledge as his province. Another, and less attractive side of Renaissance individualism appears in the character of **Niccolò Machiavelli** (1469–1527), whose masterpiece *Il Principe* (*The Prince*) is a treatise on clever statecraft and on the art of successful ruling, which even some modern dictators and political opportunists have at times taken as their guide.

Left *Machiavelli, the statesman and author. Artist unknown.*

Below *Title-page of the first edition of Machiavelli's* The Prince, *published in 1532. This work, with its theories of government and shrewd statesmanship, influenced many Renaissance sovereigns, among them King Henry VIII.*

Below left *Original manuscript of Copernicus's revolutionary work* (c. 1530) De Revolutionibus orbium coelestium. *He delayed publication until 1543 for fear of the Church's disapproval, and is said to have received the first proofs on his deathbed. (University of Cracow, Poland)*

IL PRINCIPE DI NICCOLO MACHIAVELLI AL MAGNIFICO LORENZO DI PIERO DE' MEDICI.

LA VITA DI CASTRVCCIO CAstracani da Lucca a Zanobi Buondelmonti, & à Luigi Alamanni, composta per il medesimo.

IL MODO CHE TENNE IL DVCA Valentino per ammazare Vitellozo, Oliverotto da Fermo, il S. Pagolo, & il Duca di Gravina discritta per il medesimo.

I RITRATTI DELLE COSE DELla Francia, & della Alamagna per il medesimo, nuovamente aggiunti.

M. D. XXXII.

In the literary field the most important event of the Renaissance was the discovery of modern printing methods. In Europe during the fourteenth and fifteenth centuries, single pages had been printed with the help of wooden plates; and these pages could then be stapled together, as in the famous *Biblia pauperum* (The Bible of the Poor). About 1438, however, the German Johann Gutenberg (1395–1468), a native of Mainz, learned the art of printing text with loose-cast typeface; and, in the years 1455–56, the first Bible was produced by this method. The importance of Gutenberg's discovery cannot be over-emphasized. Both for good and for ill, our employment of the printed word has shaped the history of modern mankind.

Above left *Gutenberg's press, which produced the first printed book in the mid 15th century, has been reconstructed in his native Mainz and public demonstrations in the Gutenberg Museum there show how the original press worked. (Gutenberg Museum, Mainz, West Germany)*

Left *Great strides were made in anatomical knowledge during the Renaissance period. This lecture hall for anatomical studies and dissections, the oldest-preserved, is at the University of Padua in Italy. It was built in the 16th century in the form of an amphitheatre.*

Opposite *Dissection of the principal organs and the arterial system of a female figure from Leonardo da Vinci's (1452–1519) unfinished work on human anatomy that reveals his advanced views on the construction of the human body. He is said to have discovered the theory of circulation of the blood. The annotations are in his left-handed 'mirror' writing. (Royal Library, Windsor Castle, Berkshire, by gracious permission of H.M. Queen Elizabeth II)*

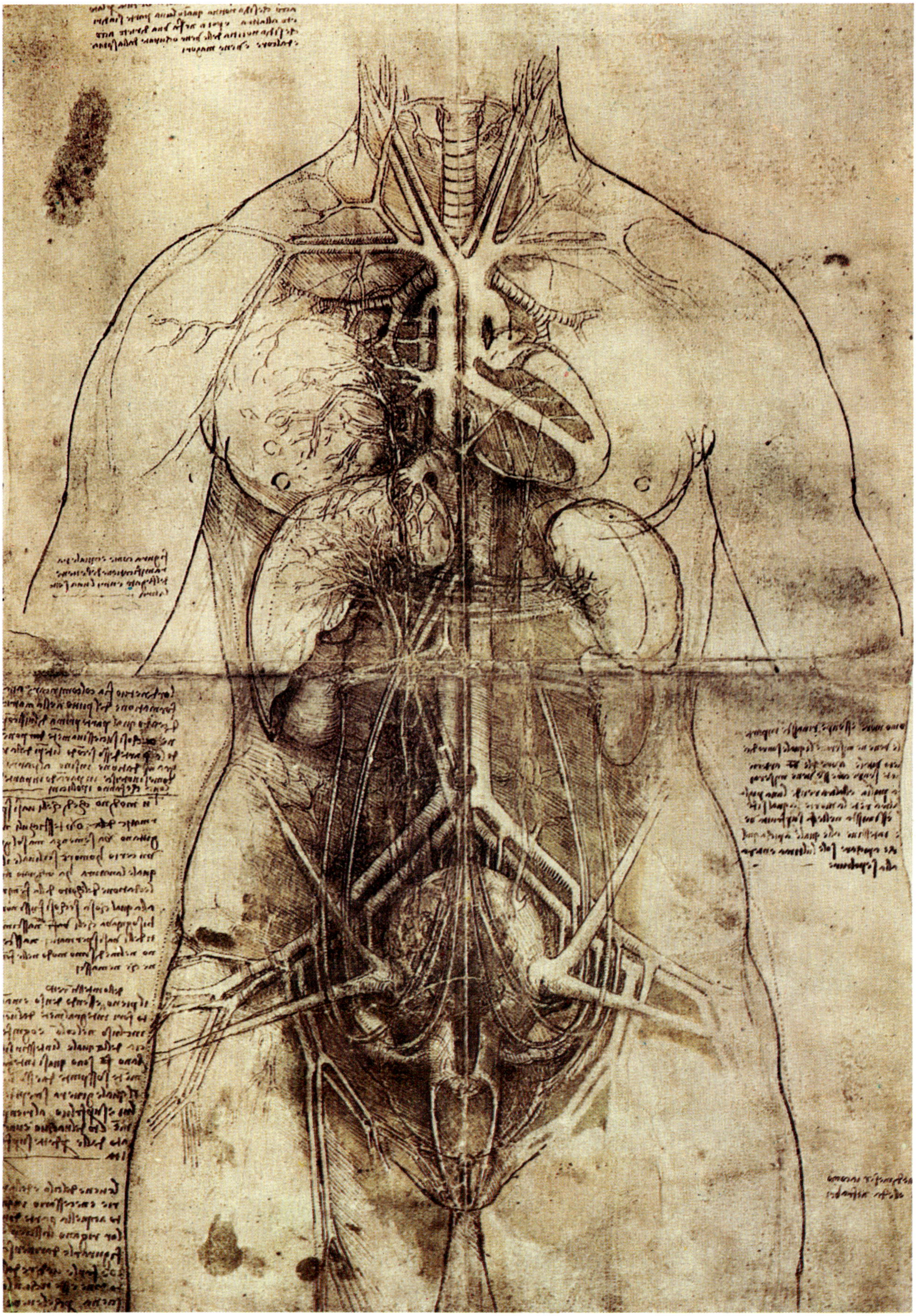

THE RISE OF THE INDIVIDUAL

The Renaissance originated in Italy for a variety of reasons – among them being the emergence of small princely states and independent cities, where a new social group, the middle class, was acquiring power and influence, a development that favoured the rise of distinctive human characters.

At first, Renaissance poets sought to create a new literature in the ancient Latin forms. But the plan did not entirely succeed; and the greatest poets of the Renaissance used the living language of the day.

Petrarch (Francesco Petrarca, 1304–1374) the earliest Renaissance poet of genius, though a keen collector of classical manuscripts (including Greek texts he could not read himself), and the author of various Latin theses and poems, is now remembered for his Italian sonnets and *canzoni*, in which he celebrated his love of his native landscape and his attachment to the idealized mistress he called Laura. Petrarch's famous poem *Italia mia* (My Italy) is one of the first signs of a romantic patriotism largely unknown in the Middle Ages.

Another aspect of the Renaissance spirit is revealed by **Giovanni Boccaccio** (1313–1375), whose lyrics and narrative verse, such as *Il Ninfale fiesolano* (The Nymph of Fiesole) and *Elegia di Madonna Fiammetta*, have a classic grace, but whose most famous work is the collection of stories, *Il Decamerone* (The Ten Days), which has a contemporary framework. In 1348, the year of the Great Plague, a company of distinguished Florentine ladies and gentlemen sought a rustic refuge, where, to while away the time, each of them agreed to tell a story. Some of these stories are derived from medieval legends, others from social gossip of the day. The latter give us a vivid impression of the life and customs of late fourteenth-century Florence. *The Decameron* has often been called improper; and it is true that Boccaccio was no prude. His great virtue is that, besides being an excellent story-teller, he emphasizes the individual quality of the men and women he describes. During his last years, however, he was troubled by what he then believed to have been the sinfulness of his early work, and passed the remainder of his life in erudite studies and devotional meditations.

Petrarch, 'the first modern man' and father of Italian humanism. From an early miniature. (Biblioteca Civica, Trieste, Italy)

As the first wave of the Italian Renaissance receded, it was followed, about 1470, by the so-called High Renaissance. Petrarch and his contemporaries had associated themselves with the culture of Antiquity. The poets who succeeded them hoped to found a new literary tradition that would equal the literature of Greece and Rome. So the spirit of the ancient epics was revived, and employed on the subject-matter of native folk-songs and tales; and poets remembered the medieval legend of the hero Roland (Orlando in Italian) and adapted the style of the chivalric *chansons de geste*. Thus **Luigi Pulci** (1432–1484) wrote a mock-heroic poem about Roland and

the giant Morganto, his faithful man-at-arms; while in *Orlando innamorato* (Roland in Love) **Matteo Boiardo** (1441–1494) abandoned burlesque, and adopted a genuinely heroic theme.

Their example was followed by the most important poet of the High Renaissance – **Ludovico Ariosto** (1474–1533). In his *Orlando furioso* (Roland Run Mad), of 1516, the story no longer concerns the Crusades and the struggle against the infidel, but Orlando's love for Angelica, which ultimately drives him mad. The gentle irony with which Ariosto introduces his characters is itself characteristic of the Renaissance – for instance, when Astolfo travels to the moon on a

Left *Petrarch's 'Laura' – possibly Laure de Noves who died in 1348. 15th-century miniature from a MS of his* Il Canzoniere. *(Biblioteca Laurenziana, Florence)*

Below *Boccaccio's friendship with Petrarch strengthened his classical studies, and his stories in* Decameron *provided a source of inspiration for many artists, among them Sandro Botticelli. His painting here (c. 1486) illustrates the tale of the husband avenging himself on his unfaithful wife, to the consternation of the guests at an alfresco celebration. (Prado, Madrid)*

Above *In 1791 Jean-Georges Noverre, one-time ballet-master to the Count of Württemberg, executed a series of sketches for a 'modern dress' stage version of Tasso's epic poem* Jerusalem Delivered. *This costume is that of the sorceress Armide who delayed Rinaldo from joining the First Crusade by holding him captive in her enchanted gardens. This poem has been the source of several ballet scenarios. (Royal Library, Stockholm)*

Above right *In his* Orlando furioso, *the High Renaissance poet Ariosto continued the story of Orlando and Angelica begun by an earlier Chivalric poet, Boiardo, in his* Orlando innamorato *(1487). Contemporary view of Orlando by Italian artist Niccolò dell' Abbate (*c. *1512–1570). (Pinacoteca Nazionale, Bologna, Italy)*

winged horse to recover Orlando's wits, which he brings home in a bottle. Here is no trace of medieval credulity. Ariosto has often been compared to Raphael; both for the poet and for the painter, stylistic grace was more admirable than violent feeling.

Then, towards the middle of the sixteenth century, the High Renaissance was followed by Late Renaissance, as the Catholic Counter-Reformation resisted both Protestant reforms and aesthetic paganism. **Torquato Tasso** (1544–1595) was a poet who championed orthodoxy, and whose Catholic piety, which under the influence of mental illness, sometimes assumed fantastic guises, inspired him to produce an epic on the First Crusade, *Gerusalemme liberata* (*Jerusalem Delivered*) in 1580.

His narrative has also a worldlier side. Even more destructive than the other perils that his valiant Crusaders face is the lure of sensual love, personified in the sorceress Armida, on whose island the hero Rinaldo is for a while imprisoned. Tancred, the melancholy knight who kills his own mistress, the Saracen amazon Clorinda, is said to bear some resemblance to the poet. Once he had completed his work,

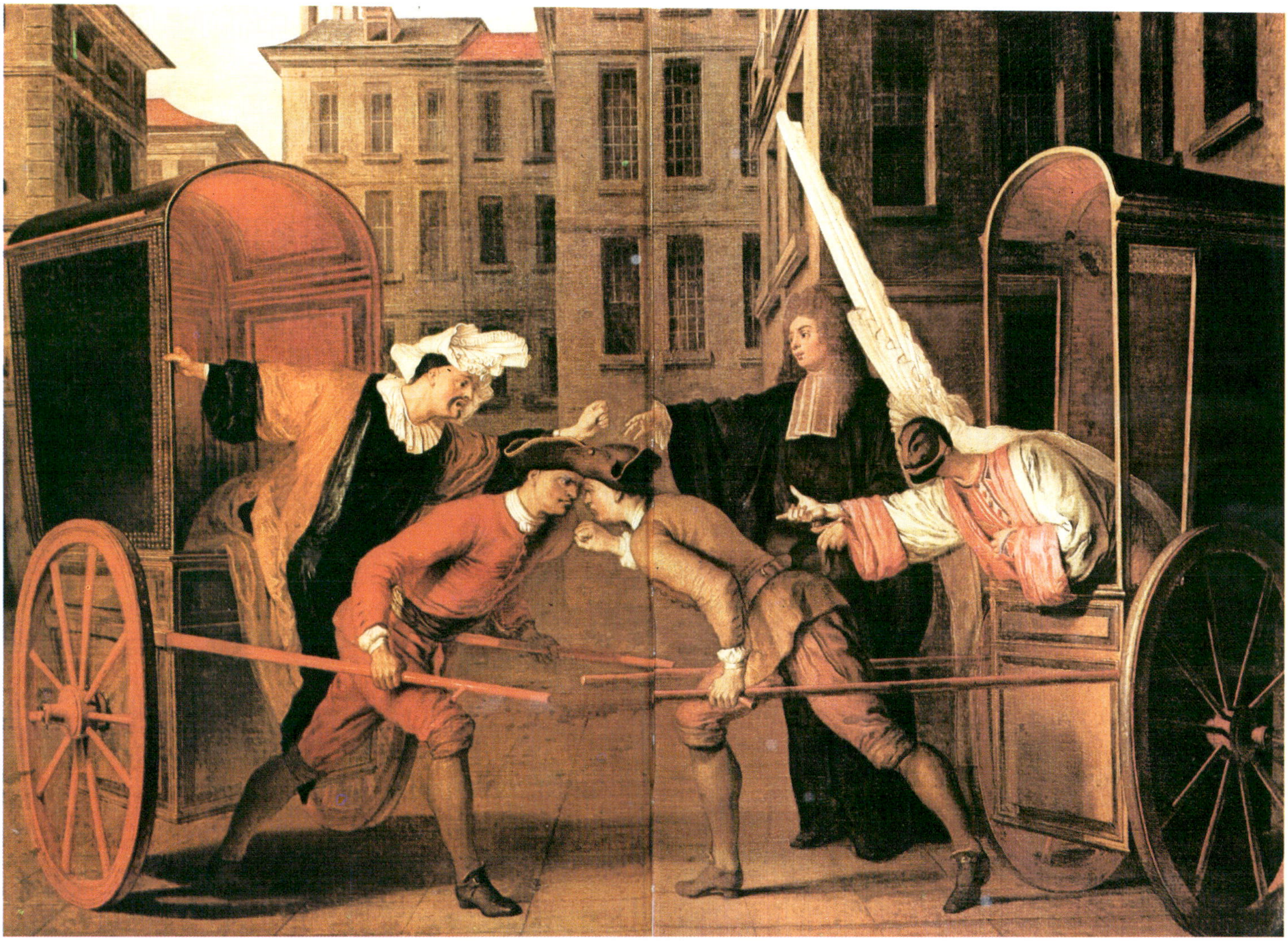

Tasso sought the advice of theologians, and, on their advice, began to bowdlerize his text; but luckily the original has survived. His pastoral play, *Aminta*, a rather over-sweet production, is only important today because it has provided material for future operas.

Most Italian Renaissance plays are more or less unreadable, except for the popular comedies called the *commedia dell'arte*, where the dialogue was largely improvised by the comedians themselves, who enacted a variety of stock roles – Harlequin, Columbine, Pierrot, pedantic Doctor, braggart Soldier – which have never quite left the stage.

Above *Typical* commedia dell'arte *scene with the traditional setting of houses grouped round a town square. From the middle of the 16th century this type of farce was performed by professional actors who specialized in particular parts, which were often handed down from father to son. The style of improvised comments in* commedia dell'arte *performances inspired the 17th-century French actor–playwright, Molière. Painting by Claude Gillot (1673–1722), designer at the Paris Opera. (Louvre, Paris)*

Left *Torquato Tasso, the Late Renaissance poet, was also an astronomer and a mathematician of note. Portrait by Italian Mannerist artist Federico Zuccaro (c. 1542–1609), whose drawings of Queen Elizabeth I of England are preserved in the British Museum.*

'DO NOT BIND THE SPIRIT'

'I want to be a citizen of the world,' declared **Erasmus of Rotterdam** (1466?–1536), when offered the honorary citizenship of Zürich. Born in Holland, he studied and worked in France and Germany, but refused to submit to any kind of national allegiance. Erasmus wrote his own books in Latin, among them being *Moriae encomium* (The Praise of Folly), an attack on the shortcomings of monastic life, and *Colloquia familiaria* (Intimate Conversations). Although he never definitely broke with the Church, as a Humanist and the spokesman of intellectual liberty he was a great precursor of the Reformation; and his critical edition of the New Testament, written in Latin in 1516, was one of the most dangerous weapons that the partisans of Protestantism employed.

Martin Luther (1483–1546), with his translation of the Bible, his collection of sermons and his reported table-talk, had almost as strong effect on the German language as Dante had had on the Italian tongue. He was no fastidious stylist; but, like a huge blacksmith, he hammered German into a sturdy instrument. Even today, the tone of his hymns echoes through the religious verse of many European countries.

Above left *Portrait sketch (1520) by the master-draughtsman, Albrecht Dürer, of the Dutchman, Gerhard Gerhards, who became the world citizen Desiderius Erasmus. Although a precursor of the Reformation, he dissociated himself from the more aggressive reformers such as Martin Luther. (Louvre, Paris)*

Left *Hans Holbein the Elder's illustration for Erasmus's satire on theologians,* The Praise of Folly *(1509), written at the suggestion of Sir Thomas More. The artist's son, Hans Holbein the Younger, established his international reputation after completing several portraits of Erasmus.*

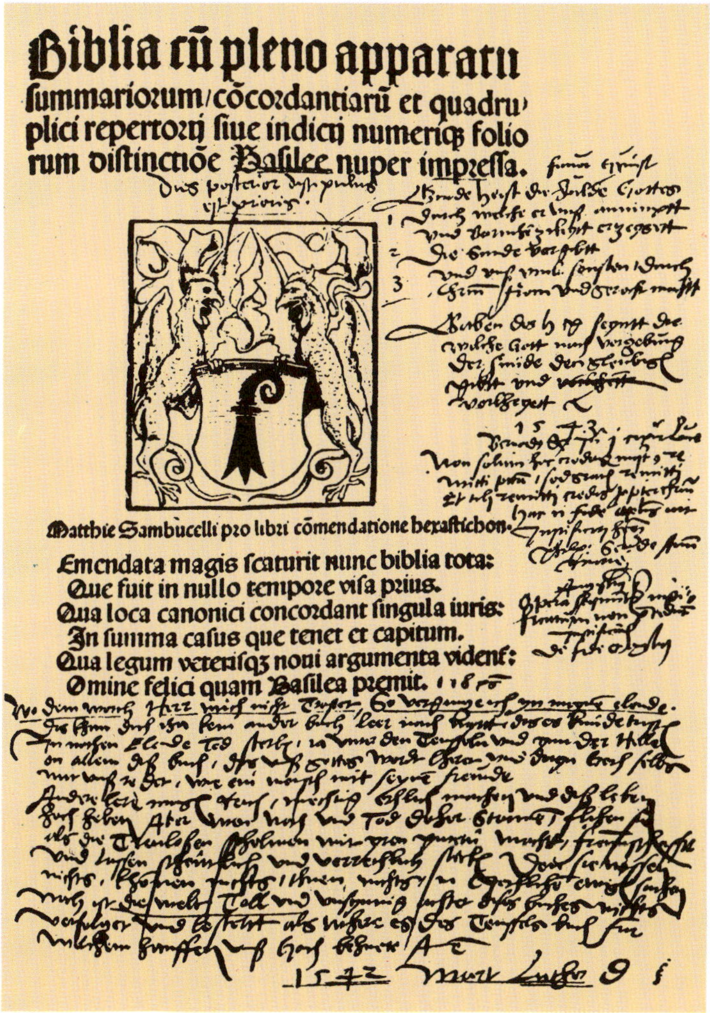

Biblia cũ pleno apparatu summariorum/cõcordantiarũ et quadruplici repertorij siue indicij numeriq3 foliorum distinctiõe Basilee nuper impressa.

Matthie Sambucelli pro libri cõmendatione hexastichon.

Emendata magis scaturit nunc biblia tota:
Que fuit in nullo tempore visa prius.
Qua loca canonici concordant singula iuris:
In summa casus que tenet et capitum.
Qua legum veterisq3 noui argumenta videns:
Omine felici quam Basilea premit.

Above *Title-page of a Latin Bible with annotations in the hand of Martin Luther, whose translation of the Bible from Greek into German in 1534 – known as the Lutheran Bible – involved researching the correct terms for all the plants, animals, precious stones and household goods occurring in the text.*

Above right *Martin Luther, father of the Reformation in Germany, who became an Augustinian friar. He later attacked the Church's sale of indulgences, posting his notices to that effect on the church doors at Wittenberg in 1517, after which he was excommunicated for a time. Portrait by his friend, the German artist Lucas Cranach the Elder (1472–1533). (National Museum, Nürnberg)*

Wider das Bapstum zu Rom vom Teuffel gestifft/
Mart. Luther D.

Wittemberg/1545.
durch Hans Lufft.

Right *Controversial to the end, Luther chose as title for his last pamphlet,* Papacy at Rome, Founded by the Devil *(1545). Title-page of a first edition, printed in Wittenberg.*

'DO AS YOU WISH'

France accepted the Renaissance all the more readily because Gaul had once been a populous Roman province, and had still many links with Southern Europe. In France, too, as in Italy, the doctrines of Humanism, which emphasized the needs and rights of the individual, were already flourishing; and, in the religious conflicts of the sixteenth-century, French Protestants, or Huguenots, adopted a strongly Humanist position.

The French Renaissance, however, did not definitely gain impetus until the reign of François I (1494–1547), when the short story developed both from the country's nativé traditions and from Italian prototypes. The authors of *Cent nouvelles nouvelles* (A Hundred New Short Stories) learnt their technique from Boccaccio; and the King's sister **Marguerite de Navarre** (1492–1549) modelled her *Heptaméron* (Seven Days) on the same pattern. But the narrators of these tales, instead of fleeing the Plague, are said to have been driven by floods to seek shelter in a monastery.

François Rabelais (1494?–1553?), the great literary master of the French High Renaissance, was first a monk, but later studied medicine and classical languages. Parodying ancient chronicles, he wrote fantastic and often lubricious romances, about the giant Pantagruel in 1532, and about Pantagruel's father Gargantua in 1534. Although his books were banned by the theologians of the Sorbonne, with the help of powerful patrons he was able to distribute them. Rabelais's narrative style is distinguished by the vein of grotesque exaggeration he borrowed from ancient folk-tales and by its sensual out-spokenness. The storyteller is evidently in revolt against all inhibiting conventions; but, at the same time, he impresses the reader as a learned and deeply thoughtful man. Despite his early monastic and medical training, Rabelais makes broad fun of priests and doctors alike, and shows equally little respect for lawyers and philosophers. On the other hand, he champions the new science, and advocates the Renaissance ideal of individual freedom. At his imaginary monastery of Thélème, there is only one rule: 'Do as you wish!'; which, at first, may sound a no less dangerous piece of advice than the command that 'The Oracle of the Divine Flask' delivers in the single word: 'Drink!' Yet Rabelais does not recommend inordinate licence and intemperance. Free people, he believed, have an instinct that will always preserve them from self-destructive vices.

Michel de Montaigne (1533–1592) had a less robust character than Rabelais. A discreet egoist, he lived a withdrawn life in his pleasant country house, observing life and studying the classics. With his *Essais*, of which the first collection came out in 1580, he became the originator of this literary form. *Essai* means 'attempt'; and Montaigne attempted always to reveal his true self, and to distinguish the

Above *Marguerite of Navarre, whose* Contes de la reine de Navarre *was later re-titled* Heptaméron *(Seven Days) after the style of Boccaccio's* Decameron *(Ten Days). She shared the same tolerant view of love as Rabelais, but had a greater respect for faithfulness. Detail of drawing by François Clouet* (d. 1572). *(Musée Condé, Chantilly, France)*

Left *His sympathy for Humanism always underlay the parodies of François Rabelais, the Franciscan friar-turned-Benedictine monk who later became an eminent physician. From an early 16th-century illustration. (Bibliothèque Nationale, Paris)*

literal truth of events and feelings amid the vast accumulation of prejudices and prepossessions. A sanguine sceptic, he had the phrase *Que sçay-je?* (What do I know?) painted on the rafters of his library. His tolerance and distrust of any kind of fanaticism made him a typically Renaissance man. 'Our minds stray blindly in the dark,' he wrote. Yet he never lost his appreciation of human pleasures or his splendid capacity for friendship.

During the 1540s, a group of seven young poets arose in France who resembled Ariosto's school, like them determined to create a national literature that should be worthy of the classic past. They called themselves the *Pléiade*, after the sevenfold constellation of stars; and the brightest of the cluster were **Pierre de Ronsard** (1524–1585) and **Joachim du Bellay** (1522–1560). Ronsard, wrote André Gide, 'dominates French poetry; and until we reach Victor Hugo we do not find again such a noble lyric flow.' His love-poems are especially admirable:

> When you are very old, at evening, by candlelight, sitting near the fire spooling and spinning the wool, you will say, in wonder, as you sing my verses: 'Ronsard praised me in the days when I was beautiful.'
>
> Then not one of your servants who hears that news, though already half asleep over her work, but will start awake at the sound of my name, and bless your name of immortal renown.
>
> I shall be under the ground, a boneless ghost, taking my rest in the myrtles' shade; you will be an old woman crouching by the hearth, regretting my love and your own proud scorn. Heed me and live now; do not wait till tomorrow. Gather today the roses of life.

Left *Michel de Montaigne, French essayist and sceptic, who had a lasting influence on both French and English literature. Portrait by an unknown artist. (Musée Condé, Chantilly, France)*

Below left *The giant Pantagruel from Rabelais's lubricious romance of that name. Hand-painted design for a French edition (1943) by André Derain, the noted modern French artist.*

THE SPANISH GENIUS

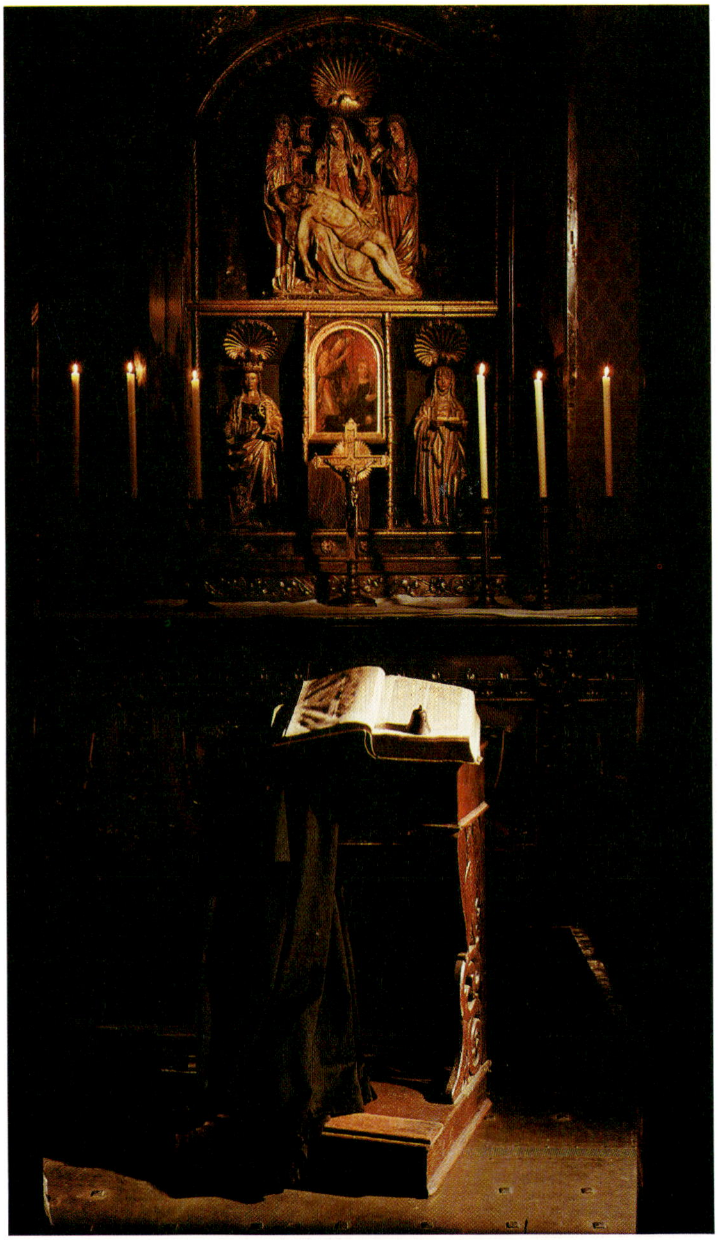

St Ignatius of Loyola's (1491–1556) prayer-book and cloak in the Silver Chapel, Santuario de San Ignacio Loyola, Azpeitia, Guipúzcoa, Spain. This Spanish soldier (born Inigo de Oñez y Loyola) gave up his military career to become an ecclesiastic, and founded the Jesuit Order – in 1534.

In the sixteenth century, Spain was the strongest of the great European powers. The Moors had been driven out of the peninsula; across the ocean, Spanish conquerors had seized vast tracts of land and untold riches; and gifted and unscrupulous rulers, such as Ferdinand and Isabella, had united the country in the name of the Catholic faith. Spain continued her triumphal progress until Philip II's 'Invincible Armada' was shattered by the English fleet in 1588.

As has happened so often elsewhere, in Spain national power and prosperity provided breeding grounds for literature and art. This period the Spaniards themselves have entitled their 'Golden Century', when, strangely enough, Spain stood at the centre of Renaissance, yet a little outside the general European movement. The Spaniards, too, had their Romantics and their Humanists, and also developed a magnificent national language, as Castilian gained supremacy over every other dialect. In Spain, nevertheless, the Catholic Church kept its grip on the souls and bodies of men more effectively than in any other country. The Inquisition was a Spanish device; the Counter-Reformation originated in Spain; and the founder of the Jesuit order, Ignatius of Loyola, was a Spaniard. **Teresa de Jesús** (1515–1582) and **San Juan de la Cruz** (1542–1591) were religious mystics of a typically Spanish kind; but their allegories and poems were allowed to appear only after they had been scrutinized by Inquisitorial censors.

Although fanaticism and ecstasy appealed to the national temperament, Spaniards had a strain of realism and a vigorous sense of humour. These attributes certainly distinguish the Span-

ish novel, which appeared during the sixteenth century, and, besides chivalrous and pastoral stories, of a kind then popular throughout most of Europe, included picaresque tales. In this field *Lazarillo de Tormes*, by an unknown author, was particularly popular. Such narratives were named after the Spanish word *picaro*, or rogue; and the hero, who often tells his own story, is usually a poor youth thrown into the world to make his way as best he can, who is there bullied and deceived, but whose native cunning invariably prevails. Such books were meant primarily to entertain. Some specimens, nevertheless, for example *Guzmán de Alfarache* by **Mateo Aleman** (1547–1614), give a satirical picture of the Spanish social world, with its rigid class divisions, in the so-called Golden Century.

Above *Victims of the Spanish Inquisition, established in 1478 during the reign of Ferdinand and Isabella and only finally abolished in Spain in 1820, depicted here in a 17th-century engraving.*

Left *Pinje Madonna of the Spanish Gran Canaria. At religious festivals, especially in Holy Week, such elaborately dressed images would be carried round the streets in procession to commemorate the 'Sorrows of Our Lady' while a few impromptu lines, known as* Saetas, *were chanted in a Flamenco-style dirge.*

CERVANTES

Apart from his masterpiece Don Quixote de la Mancha *(produced when he was 58), Cervantes is known for his short stories* Novelas ejemplares *(1613, Twelve Tales), on which the 17th-century playwright John Fletcher drew for inspiration. Before becoming a writer, Cervantes had served his country at war, and been captured by pirates who held him hostage as a slave in Algeria. Portrait by Juan de Jáurequi (1600). (Real Academia Española, Madrid)*

The master of Spanish prose, **Miguel de Cervantes Saavedra** (1547–1616), was equally at home in the chivalric and the picaresque style. He himself had known adventure and hardship, as a soldier had taken part in the sea-fight against the Turks at Lepanto, and had been gravely wounded. Later, captured by pirates, he had languished as a slave in Algeria for five years. Then, back at home again, he became a professional writer and worked for a quarter of a century, making very little progress, until, at the age of fifty-eight, he produced the masterpiece that secured him immortality, *Don Quixote de la Mancha*, of which the first part came out in 1605, and the second in 1615.

Cervantes' original purpose was to write a hilarious parody of contemporary best-sellers, the exceedingly successful chivalric romances of the day. The hero, a poor country gentleman, has lost his wits through reading too many stories of the kind, and decides that he himself will play the part of knight errant. Having set forth to combat the powers of evil, he finds it difficult to distinguish between reality and fantasy. Mounted on the elderly charger he re-christens Rocinante, and accompanied by Sancho Panza, the amiable dullard he has appointed his squire, he hopes to accomplish tremendous deeds in honour of the noble Dulcinea, a simple peasant-girl from Toboso. Alas, demons and giants he attacks are windmills and a flock of sheep; and all his heroic sorties end in ignominious disaster.

Cervantes' parody, however, as the novel develops, takes on a very different colouring. Almost against his will, his hero's character changes, and develops into a symbolic representation of frustrated idealism, lost in an unfriendly world; and the reader asks himself whether we can afford to neglect innocent enthusiasts of Don Quixote's breed. As a French critic writes: 'The world would perhaps collapse if everyone were like Don Quixote, but it would undoubtedly collapse if there were no Don Quixotes in our midst.'

Beside 'The Knight of the Sorrowful Countenance', as Don Quixote was sometimes called, rides Sancho, his personal antithesis, the Castilian peasant whose jovial gossip and crude commonsense constantly interrupt his master's declamations and help to bring him down to earth. The pair of them, the sublime enthusiast and the earthy realist, even today still hold their place among the great legendary figures of the Western World.

From **Don Quixote** by Cervantes

At that moment they caught sight of some thirty or forty windmills, which stand on that plain, and as soon as Don Quixote saw them he said to his squire: 'Fortune is guiding our affairs better than we could have wished. Look over there, friend Sancho Panza, where more than thirty monstrous giants appear. I intend to do battle with them and take all their lives. With their spoils we will begin to get rich, for this is a fair war, and it is a great service to God to wipe such a wicked brood from the face of the earth.'

'What giants?' asked Sancho Panza.

'Those you see there,' replied his master, 'with their long arms. Some giants have them about six miles long.'

'Take care, your worship,' said Sancho Panza; 'those things over there are not giants but windmills, and what seem to be their arms are the sails, which are whirled round in the wind and make the millstone turn.'

'It is quite clear,' replied Don Quixote, 'that you are not experienced in this matter of adventures. They are giants, and if you are afraid, go away and say your prayers, whilst I advance and engage them in fierce and unequal battle.'

As he spoke, he dug his spurs into his steed Rocinante, paying no attention to his squire's shouted warning that beyond all doubt they were windmills, and no giants, he was advancing to attack. But he went on, so positive that they were giants that he neither listened to Sancho's cries nor noticed what they were, even when he got near them. Instead he went on shouting in a loud voice: 'Do not fly, cowards, vile creatures, for it is one knight alone who assails you.'

At that moment a slight wind arose, and the great sails began to move. At the sight of which Don Quixote shouted: 'Though you wield more arms than the giant Briareus, you shall pay for it!' Saying this, he commended himself with all his soul to his lady Dulcinea, beseeching her aid in his great peril. Then, covering himself with his shield and putting his lance in the rest, he urged Rocinante forward at a full gallop and attacked the nearest windmill, thrusting his lance into the sail. But the wind turned it with such violence that it shivered his weapon in pieces, dragging the horse and his rider with it, and sent the knight rolling badly injured across the plain. Sancho Panza rushed to his assistance as fast as his ass could trot, but when he came up he found the knight could not stir. Such a shock had Rocinante given him in their fall.

'O, my goodness!' crid Sancho. 'Didn't I tell your worship to look what you were doing, for they were only windmills? Nobody could mistake them, unless he had windmills on the brain.'

'Silence, friend Sancho,' replied Don Quixote. 'Matters of war are more subject than most to continual change. What is more, I think – and that is the truth – that the same sage Friston who robbed me of my room and my books has turned those giants into windmills, to cheat me of the glory of conquering them. Such is the enmity he bears me; but in the very end his black arts shall avail him little against the goodness of my sword.'

'God send it as he will,' replied Sancho Panza, helping the knight to get up and remount Rocinante, whose shoulders were half dislocated.

Left *Sancho Panza looks on with horror as Don Quixote: '... covering himself with his shield and putting his lance in the rest, urged Rocinante forward at a full gallop and attacked the nearest windmill, thrusting his lance into the sail ...' Illustration by Teodoro Delgado for a Spanish study of 'Don Quixote' (1970).*

Below *Don Quixote on his deathbed, a memorable portrayal (1863) by the famous wood-engraver, Gustave Doré, who also illustrated the works of Dante, Rabelais and Balzac.*

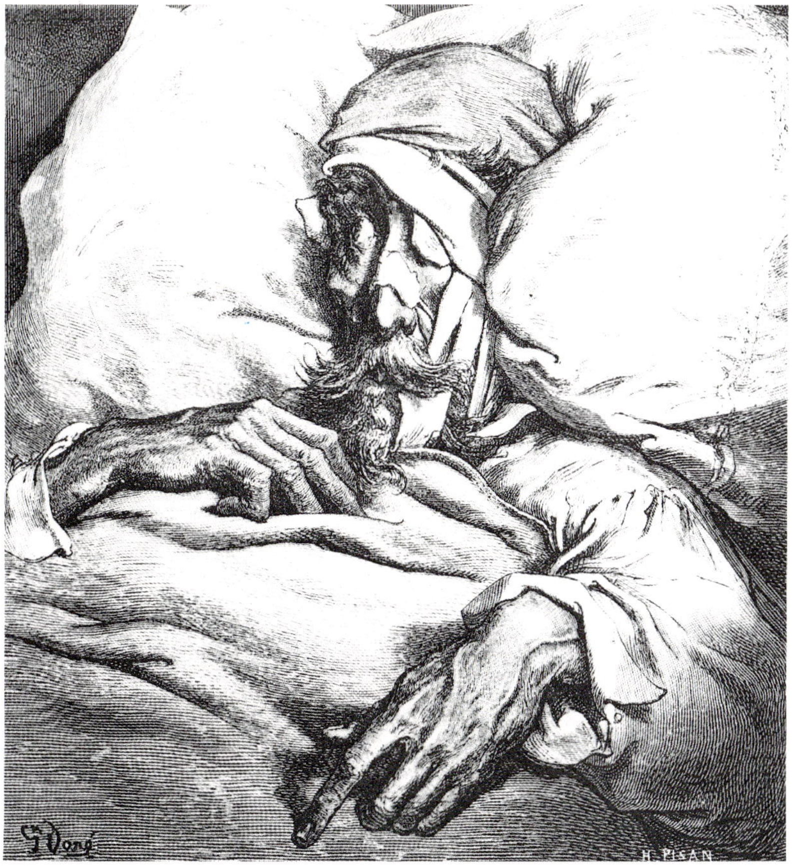

CULT OF HONOUR

Lope de Vega considered his plays to be without much value, although posterity has judged otherwise. Title-page of an Italian edition of The Best of Lope de Vega.

Spanish drama, based on a creed of which the corner-stones were the Catholic Church and the power and grandeur of the monarchy, was the Golden Century's second great achievement. The central value of the system was Honour, for which humanity, love and reason were all sacrificed.

In the works of **Lope de Vega** (1562–1635) this outlook on life jarred with a light-hearted nature. A man of the world and a soldier, who accompanied the Invincible Armada when it set sail against England, he was also a writer and, eventually, a priest; but, both before and after his ordination, he was involved in endless love affairs and scandals, and, as a result of one of these incidents, was banished from Madrid for several years. Meanwhile, he found time to produce an immense variety of works, and is said to have written 3000 sonnets and nearly 1600 plays. Of the latter, more than 600 have survived, for the most part of remarkably high quality. All have well-constructed plots, and show a grasp of human psychology that is often convincing, provided we can accept the fact that his characters will commit any kind of cruelty and idiocy to uphold their outraged honour. Lope de Vega took his subjects from the Bible, the myths of Antiquity, Spanish history and the scandalous records of aristocratic life. *Peribáñez* (1614) and *El Castigo sin venganza* (1634/35, Punishment without Revenge) are examples of his tragic style; *El Acero de Madrid* (1614, The Steel of Madrid), of his comic vein, a play about the intrigues undertaken by a young man and his mistress to enable them to meet. Sometimes Lope does his best to show that peasants, too, have human feelings – a revolutionary idea in sixteenth- and seventeenth-century Spain. Thus *Fuente Ovejuna* (1619), which depicts a group of villagers rebelling against their oppressive overlords, reveals a genuinely democratic spirit. At the same time, he wrote religious plays called *autos*; and these and his poetry, such as the *Canción de cuna para la Virgen* (*Cradle Song for the Madonna*), suggested that piety and a light-hearted approach to life may be reconciled through art:

Holy angels and blest,
  Through the palms as ye sweep
Hold their branches at rest
  For my babe is asleep.

And ye Bethlehem palm-trees,
  As stormy winds rush
In tempest and fury
  Your angry noise hush; –
Move gently, move gently,
  Restrain your wild sweep;
Hold your branches at rest
  My babe is asleep.

My babe all divine,
  With earth's sorrows oppressed,
Seeks in slumber an instant
  His grievings to rest;
He slumbers, – he slumbers, –
  O, hush then and keep
Your branches all still, –
  My babe is asleep.

Cold blasts wheel about him, –
  A rigorous storm, –
And ye see how, in vain,
  I would shelter his form; –
Holy angels and blest
  As above me ye sweep,
Hold these branches at rest, –
  My babe is asleep.

The effects of Spanish mysticism are even more apparent in the plays of **Pedro Calderón de la Barca** (1600–1681). Although in *El Médico de su honra* (*The Surgeon of his Honour*) the dramatis personae's cult of honour would strike a modern audience as inhuman, it is still dramatically effective. Among some hundred plays, a large number, called *autos sacramentales*, are designed to celebrate the glories of the Mass; while his religious 'comedies', *commedias divinas*, mix lyrical and romantic with pietistic themes. *El Príncipe constante* (The Steadfast Prince) concerns the martyrdom of a patient Portuguese prince in a dreadful Turkish gaol. But the most fascinating of Calderón's dramas, *La Vida es sueño* (*Life's a Dream*), is a philosophical comedy about the imprisoned hero Sigismund, who is chastened and ennobled by the degradation he endures. The tone of the play is set, and its title explained, in a central monologue:

SIGISMUND

That's true. Then let us curb this fierce vexation,
This fury, this ambition, lest by chance
We dream again. For we shall dream again.
We are in a world so singular, that living
Is only dreaming; and experience
Teaches, that men who live, dream what they are
Until they wake.

The King dreams he is King, –
And lives in this illusion, – ordering, –
Disposing, – governing; – while even the praise
He wins – is borrowed, written in the wind,
And changed by death to ashes. – Tragedy
Bitterest of all! Who then would be a King,
Knowing that he must wake in the sleep of death?

The rich man dreams his riches, dreams his cares;
The poor man dreams his poverty, his want.
He dreams who prospers, dreams who toils, and dreams
Who's piqued and sulks. Throughout the world, all men
Dream what they are, although they know it not.

I dream that I am here, loaded with chains;
I dreamt another state, more flattering.
What is life? A frenzy. What is life? Illusion.
A shadow, a fiction; – and the greatest good's
A little thing. For all life is a dream,
And dreams themselves are – dreamstuff.

SEGVNDA
PARTE DE
COMEDIAS,
DE DON PEDRO CALDERON DE LA
Barca, Cauallero del Abito de Santiago.
RECOGIDAS
POR DON IOSEPH CALDERON DE LA
Barca su hermano.
DIRIGIDAS,
AL EXCELENTISSIMO SEÑOR DON RODRIGO de Mendoza Roxas y Sandoual de la Vega y Luna Señor de las Casas de Mendoza y Vega, Duque del Infantado y Marques de Cenete, &c.
CON PRIVILEGIO.
En Madrid: Por *Maria de Quiñones* Año de M.DC.XXXVII

Left *Title-page of the first edition of Part II of Calderón's* Comedies *(1637), collected by his brother Joseph and dedicated to the many-titled Don Rodrigo de Mendoza Roxas.*

Below *Calderón, the dramatic successor to Lope de Vega in Spain. After a career as a soldier he became a priest in 1651, and honorary chaplain to Philip IV. In 1853 Edward Fitzgerald (better-known for his version of the* Rubáiyát of Omar Khayyám*) made blank verse and prose translations of his plays, published under the title* Six Dramas of Calderón. *(Museo Lazaro Galdiano, Madrid)*

SEA ROUTE TO INDIA

During the fifteenth and sixteenth centuries, Portugal established a colonial empire with settlements in Africa, Asia and South America. Silver and gold, spices and silk, were transported to Lisbon, which became the centre of the European import trade; and commerce provided the climate for a cultural flowering.

Humanism and Renaissance literature presently reached Portugal despite the strenuous resistance of the Catholic Church; and, for many years, Portuguese poets adopted Italian and Provençal models. But there was one great exception – **Luis de Camões** (or **Camoëns**, 1524–1580), who wrote his country's national epic, *Os Lusíadas* (The Lusiads) in the Virgilian spirit. This immense poem, which consists of ten sections, deals with Vasco da Gama and the Lusiads – the journey of the Portuguese to India. Like the classical poets, Camões allows the gods to intervene in the story – the beautiful Venus on the side of the Portuguese, Bacchus and Neptune, on behalf of their foes.

A picturesque impression of Portugal's national poet, Camões, made a year after his death. He led an adventurous life, banished from the court at Lisbon for an amorous misdemeanour, campaigning against Morocco (where he lost an eye – evident in this painting) and soldiering in India and Goa – before he returned to favour under King Sebastian, when his epic Lusiads *was finally published (1572). Painting by Riyo Tomoto (1581). (Private Collection, Lisbon)*

'ROBBERS, VAGRANTS AND PUBLIC ACTORS'

In Westminster Abbey, the tombs and memorials of great English poets are assembled around Poets' Corner; and the first man of genius to be buried there was **Geoffrey Chaucer** (1340?–1400), who had come under the influence of the Italian fourteenth-century Renaissance. But his masterpiece, *The Canterbury Tales*, has a wholly English tone and setting – a collection of versified stories, said to have been exchanged by a company of pilgrims who plan to visit the shrine of St Thomas à Becket at Canterbury, and at their London inn, before they set out, agree to relieve the tedium of the journey by each one of them contributing a separate tale. They include a knight, his son and squire, a monk, a nun, the innkeeper of the Tabard, a prosperous widow, a merchant and a miller; and the stories they relate are suited to their characters and callings, some poetic and romantic, some realistic and some gross and bawdy. In combination, they produce an extraordinarily vivid picture of medieval England, its gaiety and free speech, its love of pageantry and colour, and its devotion to terrestrial joys. The poet was both a brilliant narrator and a consummate master of the changing English language.

The English Renaissance, however, was short-lived; and the fierce civil conflict, known as the 'Wars of the Roses', caused a setback that lasted until the instalment of the Tudor Dynasty. Under the second of that line, Henry VIII, literature returned to England with two accomplished court-poets, **Sir Thomas Wyatt** (1503–1542) and **Henry Howard, Earl of Surrey** (1517–1547). The Renaissance had at last arrived; the arts of Italy were now well-known; and, during the second half of the next century, in the glorious reign of Queen Elizabeth I who, after the deaths of her brother and her pious Catholic sister, succeeded to the throne in 1558, a new era of creative activity opened. The Queen, a formidably gifted woman, who had once thanked God that 'I am endued with such qualities that if I were turned out of the realm in my petticoat, I were able to live in any place in Christendom', was both a good modern linguist and a fluent Latinist. Her Court was the most magnificent in Europe; and, although she did not patronize the visual arts – Nicholas Hilliard was the only distinguished English artist of the day – luckily for the Elizabethan dramatists, she was extremely fond of the theatre. During her reign, she was surrounded by adoration; no Christian sovereign has been more nearly deified; and a succession of poets, describing her as 'Gloriana' or as 'Cynthia', added distinction to her cult. **Edmund Spenser**, for example, (1552?–1599) produced his long allegorical poem *The Faerie Queene*, with the Queen as his semi-divine heroine and her arch enemy, Mary Queen of Scots, as Duessa, the malevolent enchantress.

Although actors still ranked among 'robbers and vagrants', the performances they gave soon became immensely popular; and the *Spanish Tragedy* (1587) by **Thomas Kyd** (1558–1594) and **Christopher Marlowe**'s *Tamburlaine the Great* (staged in the same year), both poetic melodramas on a tremendous scale, proved extraordinarily successful.

Christopher Marlowe (1564–1593), a true Renaissance desperado alleged by the authorities to have been a homosexual and an atheist, was eventually stabbed to death in a tavern brawl, possibly provoked by a dispute about the bill, though the fact that he is thought to have belonged to the Elizabethan Secret Service may have had something to do with his assassination. His three best-known plays, *Tamburlaine*, *Edward II* and *Doctor Faustus*, contain long passages of ebullient rhetoric and sudden flashes of astounding poetry. Thus Marlowe expresses his idea of Beauty through the mouth of the Mongolian world-conqueror.

The Wife of Bath, one of the main characters in Chaucer's Canterbury Tales *(c. 1387). First she describes her life with five successive husbands, then relates the story of an aged hag who persuades an Arthurian knight to marry her if she saves him from death with the right answer to the question: What do women love most? This is 'sovereignty'; whereupon she is transformed into a beautiful young woman. Woodcut by Rockwell Kent for an American edition of the* Tales *(1934).*

TAMBURLAINE

What is beauty, saith my sufferings,
then?
If all the pens that ever poets held
Had fed the feelings of their masters'
thoughts ...
If all the heavenly quintessence they
still
From their immortal flowers of poesy,
Wherein, as in a mirror, we perceive
The highest reaches of a human wit;
If these had made one poem's period,
And all combined in beauty's
worthiness,
Yet should there hover in their restless
heads
One thought, one grace, one wonder,
at the least
Which into words no virtue can digest.

Above *Elizabeth I. Queen of England, during whose long reign (1558–1603) the British Court became the most splendid in Europe, literature flourished, and the Queen, a learned woman who spoke fluent Latin, as 'Gloriana' was the centre of a romantic royal cult. Portrait by Anglo-Flemish painter Marcus Gheeraerts the Younger (1561–1635), with pictures celebrating the defeat of the Spanish Armada. (National Maritime Museum, London)*

Left *Christopher Marlowe, the ill-fated young dramatist apostrophized by Shakespeare in* As You Like It. *An eloquent extract from Marlowe's famous play,* Tamburlaine, *is quoted at left. Detail from portrait by an unknown artist (1585). Marlowe is said to have requested the artist to include the words:* Quod nutrit me destruit *(What feeds me, destroys me) around this painting. (Corpus Christi College, Cambridge)*

SHAKESPEARE

William Shakespeare (1564–1616), the greatest name in Elizabethan or, indeed, in English literature, was born at Stratford-upon-Avon, a riverside Warwickshire town, the son of John Shakespeare, an important middle-class citizen, who followed a variety of trades as glover, butcher, dealer in corn and malt, leather, hides and raw wool, and who, when William his eldest son was four years old, became Stratford's mayor or 'bailiff'. Though we know nothing of the poet's childhood, he almost certainly received a sound education at the local grammar school; and afterwards, John Shakespeare having lost money, he is said to have worked for a time in his father's slaughterhouse. Then, in November 1582, he was abruptly plunged into wedlock, married off, presumably by their anxious relations, to a young woman eight years older than himself. Anne Shakespeare bore him their first child, Susanna, in May 1583, and twins, a boy and a girl, Hamnet and Judith, in 1585.

Otherwise we have no record of the poet's married life, and no descriptions of his wife's character; but two plays, the first written at the beginning, the second at the end of his career, contain references to the unhappiness that often results from 'wedlock forced'; and fairly soon afterwards, probably about 1587 according to his earliest biographer, 'an extravagance he was guilty of' – he had been caught poaching in a local justice's park – obliged him to leave Stratford and make his way to London, perhaps with a company of itinerant players passing through the town. We hear no more of him until 1592, when he suddenly emerges as a successful London playwright, satirized by Robert Greene, one of the so-called 'University Wits', a disappointed literary man who, in a scurrilous pamphlet, wrote of 'an upstart crow, beautified with our feathers, that ... supposes he is as well able to bombast out a blank verse as the best of you, and ... is in his own conceit the only Shake-scene in a country.' The fact that Greene's publisher then hastened to issue a profuse apology, declaring that the victim of the satire was known to be both an upright and a civil person and an accomplished man of letters, suggests that Shakespeare had already a growing reputation and that he was much liked by his friends.

The poet, so far as we can judge today, had an unusually harmonious disposition – 'a handsome, well-shaped man', reported the seventeenth-century memorialist John Aubrey, 'and of a very ready and pleasant smooth wit'; and it is clear that, in the hazardous profession he had adopted, he showed considerable business-sense. Not only did he manage his affairs shrewdly, so that, by the time he reached middle age he had accumulated a modest fortune, but, as a dramatist, he was a sound judge of what the contemporary public needed.

Shakespeare's life as a creative writer is usually broken up into four main creative periods – the period that lasted until 1594, during which he produced his earliest historical plays and a series of comedies, among them

The 'Chandos' portrait, said to be of Shakespeare, is sometimes attributed to Richard Burbage, his fellow–actor. (National Portrait Gallery, London)

The Globe Theatre in Southwark, in south-east London, which was built in 1599 from some of the original materials of the old Globe (of which Shakespeare owned a tenth share). This new Globe was burned down during a performance of Shakespeare's Henry VIII *in 1613.*

The Taming of the Shrew, as well as two narrative poems, *Venus and Adonis* and *The Rape of Lucrece*; the period between 1594 and 1599, that saw the production of *Julius Caesar, Romeo and Juliet, A Midsummer Night's Dream, The Merchant of Venice* and his later historical dramas, *Richard II, Henry IV, Parts I and II* and *Henry V*; the epoch of the great tragedies, *Hamlet, Othello, King Lear* and *Macbeth*, of his majestic Roman plays, *Antony and Cleopatra* and *Coriolanus*, yet, at the same time, of his most delightful comedies, *Much Ado About Nothing, Twelfth Night, As You Like It*, and of three 'bitter-sweet' plays, *Troilus and Cressida, Measure for Measure* and *All's Well That Ends Well*, that lasted from 1599 to 1608; and his last phase, from 1608 to 1616, when both his technique and his point of view seem to have been slowly changing; and he wrote his magnificent farewell to the stage, in his finest romantic comedy *The Tempest*, performed before the King in 1611.

There can be no doubt that this tremendous imaginative achievement was the product of a single mind; and that the author's name was William Shakespeare. In the past, many wild attempts have been made to attribute his works to Lord Oxford, Sir Francis Bacon, even to Christopher Marlowe after his supposed death; but they create many more problems than they solve. There is no reason why a middle-class actor–manager should not have described the doings of great statesmen, or the lives of courts and aristocratic houses. Shakespeare dedicated his two juvenile poems, *Venus and Adonis* (1593), which he called 'the first heir of my invention', and *The Rape of Lucrece* (1594) to Henry Wriothesley, Earl of Southampton, a handsome young courtier with whom he was evidently on good terms.

Meanwhile, about 1592, he had joined a company of players, afterwards named 'The Chamberlain's Men', and, in 1599, acquired a tenth share of a new playhouse named the Globe on the south bank of the Thames. By that time he had grown so prosperous that he had already purchased New Place, an imposing house in Stratford; and his financial position showed a steady improvement until he eventually left the stage. As we study Shakespeare's life and works, we must soon face the fact that his was a divided character – a poet of astonishing genius, yet a professional opportunist, who never hesitated to satisfy his audience's taste. He worked for two sovereigns – Elizabeth I and her successor James I – both of whom he did his best to please. The Queen, he knew, delighted in the theatre and wished to see more of Sir John Falstaff – hence *The Merry Wives of Windsor*. The King was fascinated by the supernatural and had written a learned treatise upon witchcraft – hence the Scottish tragedy *Macbeth*.

That the great imaginative dramatist and the successful businessman should somehow have coexisted continues to puzzle the modern literary historian. But so it was; and Shakespeare's commercial instincts seem not to have in any way hindered the evolution of his genius.

One of the distinctive features of Shakespeare's genius was its many-sidedness. Coleridge would call him 'myriad-minded'. No other poet or dramatist has had so wide an imaginative scope, and created such a multitude of extremely different characters, from the genial, life-loving Sir John Falstaff to Hamlet, gloomy, embittered Prince of Denmark. 'Shakespeare', wrote that excellent critic William Hazlitt, 'does not stand reasoning on what his characters would do or say, but at once *becomes* them, and speaks and acts for them.' Sometimes a character seems to escape his control, and develops unexpected qualities. Thus, Shylock in *The Merchant of Venice*, originally intended, no doubt, as the portrait of a wicked Jew, at a time when Queen Elizabeth's Jewish physician Dr Lopez was accused of trying to poison her, took on – perhaps almost against the dramatist's will – an air of tragic dignity, which (as Heine, the nineteenth-century German writer, noted when he visited a London theatre) moved members of the audience to tears.

Equally many-sided was Shakespeare's use of language. Having admired 'Marlowe's mighty line', he made blank verse as a method of dramatic expression even nobler and more effective; while the songs with which he harmonizes his comedies – the Elizabethan Age was intensely musical – are among the most beautiful English lyrics ever written. He mastered the sonnet too; and in 1609, evidently without the author's permission, a certain Thomas Thorpe published 'a book called Shakespeare's sonnets', adding a mysterious dedication to their 'onlie begetter ... Mr W.H.'.

The identity of Thorpe's dedicatee, despite whole volumes of most learned discussion, has never been satisfactorily established; nor is the story these poems tell always completely understandable. But their hero, the golden youth whom the poet adores, was probably his friend and patron Lord Southampton; and some critics have described the series as 'a monument to homosexual love raised by an otherwise heterosexual poet'. Often Shakespeare contrasts his own age and mercenary profession with his hero's

Left *Titania, Queen of the Fairies, in* A Midsummer Night's Dream. *She loves the changeling boy 'stol'n from an Indian' and refuses to give him up to her Master, Oberon, but the magic herb induces her to fall in love with Bottom and forget all else. Oberon then: 'did ask of her her changeling child; which straight she gave me, and her fairy sent to bear him to my bower in fairy land.' Illustration by the British artist Arthur Rackham for a special children's edition of the play (1908).*

Below *Mark Antony is beguiled by Cleopatra at the feast for which he was 'barber'd ten times o'er' in* Antony and Cleopatra. *Detail from a painting by the 17th-century Dutch artist and writer, Gérard de Lairesse. (Rijksmuseum, Amsterdam)*

Above *Hamlet (Amblet) from a Danish verse-chronicle written in 1597, at least five years before Shakespeare's* Hamlet. *This Danish work portrays Hamlet as a powerful Renaissance prince, following the tradition of Saxo Grammaticus's 'Amleth' in his* Danish History *(c. 1200). Royal Library, Stockholm.*

Above right *The great French tragedians, François Talma (1763–1826) and Mlle Duchesnois (1777–1835) in their roles of Hamlet and Gertrude. Talma, so admired by Napoleon, played many Shakespearian leads, including Othello, Macbeth and Henry VIII. (Bibliothèque de l'Arsenal, Paris)*

Opposite *The Swan Theatre in London in Shakespeare's time, from a pen-and-ink sketch by a Dutchman, Johannes de Witte, in 1596.*

youth and glorious energy. Here, for example, is Sonnet LXXIII:

That time of year thou mayst in me
behold
When yellow leaves, or none, or few,
do hang
Upon those boughs which shake
against the cold,
Bare ruin'd choirs, where late the sweet
birds sang.
In me thou see'st the twilight of such
day
As after sunset fadeth in the west;
Which by and by black night doth
take away,
Death's second self, that seals up all in
rest.
In me thou see'st the glowing of such
fire,
That on the ashes of his youth doth lie,
As the death-bed whereon it must
expire
Consum'd with that which it was
nourish'd by.
This thou perceiv'st, which makes
thy love more strong,
To love that well which thou must
leave ere long.

To illustrate Shakespeare's gifts as a master of blank verse would require many pages of quotations; but four famous passages, from *The Merchant of Venice*, *Hamlet*, *Measure for Measure*, and *The Tempest* show them at their most magical. In *The Merchant of Venice* (*c.*1595), Lorenzo and his love Jessica, Shylock's faithless daughter, gaze up at the starry heavens:

How sweet the moonlight sleeps upon
this bank! ...

Sit, Jessica: look, how the floor of heaven
Is thick inlaid with patens of bright gold:
There's not the smallest orb which thou behold'st
But in his motion like an angel sings,
Still quiring to the young-eyed cherubins;
Such harmony is in immortal souls!
But, whilst this muddy vesture of decay
Doth grossly close it in, we cannot hear it.

Like other Elizabethan poets, Shakespeare, as T.S. Eliot said of a slightly later dramatist, was 'much possessed' by the idea of death. But it did not distort his imagination, and in *Hamlet* (*c.*1601/02) the story of Ophelia's suicide has a wonderfully lyrical background:

There is a willow grows aslant a brook,
That shows his hoar leaves in the glassy stream;
There with fantastic garlands did she come
Of crow-flowers, nettles, daisies, and long purples
That liberal shepherds give a grosser name,
But our cold maids do dead men's fingers call them:
There, on the pendent boughs her coronet weeds
Clambering to hang, an envious sliver broke;
When down her weedy trophies and herself
Fell in the weeping brook. Her clothes spread wide;
And, mermaid-like, awhile they bore her up:
Which time she chanted snatches of old tunes;
As one incapable of her own distress,
Or like a creature native and indued
Unto that element: but long it could not be
Till that her garments, heavy with their drink,
Pull'd the poor wretch from her melodious lay
To muddy death.

In *Measure for Measure* (1603), a somewhat uneven play, the human fear of death is terribly expressed:

Ay, but to die, and go we know not where;
To lie in cold obstruction and to rot;
This sensible warm motion to become
A kneaded clod; and the delighted spirit
To bathe in fiery floods, or to reside
In thrilling region of thick-ribbed ice;
To be imprison'd in the viewless winds,
And blown with restless violence round about
The pendent world; or to be worse than worst
Of those that lawless and incertain thought
Imagine howling; 'tis too horrible!
The weariest and most loathèd worldly life
That age, ache, penury and imprisonment
Can lay on nature is a paradise
To what we fear of death.

In *The Tempest* (1610/11) on the other hand, Prospero's farewell, both to the real world and to the visionary universe he has conjured up, is at once sad and philosophic:

Our revels now are ended. These our actors,
As I foretold you, were all spirits and

Are melted into air, into thin air:
And, like the baseless fabric of this vision,
The cloud-capp'd towers, the gorgeous palaces,
The solemn temples, the great globe itself,
Yea, all which it inherit, shall dissolve
And, like this insubstantial pageant faded,
Leave not a rack behind. We are such stuff
As dreams are made on; and our little life
Is rounded with a sleep ...

As Prospero retired from his island, Shakespeare himself retired to Stratford, and left behind him all his magic books – no library is mentioned in his will. He died, after a 'merry meeting' with a pair of fellow poets at which, we are told, they 'drank too hard' – on 23 April 1616.

THE BAROQUE STYLE

Meanwhile, throughout Western Europe, during the sixteenth and seventeenth centuries, a new style was developing – the 'Baroque', which affected both art and literature, and was characterized by its exuberance, its wealth of fantastic detail, and, as in pictures of Rubens (1577–1640), by its sensuous vitality. In Italy, it was called *marinismo* after the poet **Giambattista Marino** (1569–1625); in Spain *gongorismo* after another poet, **Luis de Góngora** (1561–1627).

Baroque was a product of the Counter-Reformation, a movement to revive and enrich the Roman Catholic Church. But, although English writers often appreciated sumptuous elaboration, they escaped its full force. Shakespeare's work cannot be styled Baroque; nor can the plays and poems of **Ben Jonson** (1572–1637). A friend and sometimes a critic of Shakespeare, Jonson was a learned writer and erudite classicist, yet, as his many comedies and tragedies show, possessed a vein of genuine originality and a delightful lyric gift. His best-known comedy is *Volpone* – presented at Shakespeare's Globe theatre – the study of a miser, who feels an almost religious passion for his accumulated wealth.

The English seventeenth century saw the emergence of the Scientific Spirit; for **Francis Bacon** (1561–1626) then became one of the originators of modern scientific methodology with *Novum organum*, the book he published in 1620. It was also a particularly fruitful period in the history of English verse; and, during its earlier decades, a new school of writers appeared upon the literary scene. Called the 'Metaphysical Poets', they employed 'wit' as a favourite poetic weapon – a trait that, during the next age, gravely offended Samuel Johnson, who declared that 'their only wish was to say what they hoped had never been said before', and that in their poems 'the most heterogeneous images . . . were linked by violence together.' Of this school the earliest and finest member was **John Donne** (1572–1631), an adventurous young man, who, after a rakish youth, when he wrote a series of memorable love-poems, in 1619, at the instigation of King James I, took Holy Orders and proved the most puissant preacher of his day. His sermons are famous. Here, for example, is a celebrated extract, from which Ernest Hemingway would take the title of a novel:

> No man is an Island intire of it selfe; every man is a peece of the Continent, a part of the maine; if a Clod bee washed away by the Sea, Europe is the lesse, as well as if a Promontorie were; any man's death diminishes me, because I am involved in Mankinde; & therefore never send to know for whom the bell tolls; it tolls for thee.

The term 'Baroque' does not refer only to the exaggerated 17th-century style of painting, sculpture and architecture that revelled in using classical forms in an unclassical way; it may also denote a literary style such as we sometimes find in Shakespeare, Ben Jonson and John Donne. Peter Paul Rubens (1577–1640) was sometimes called the greatest Baroque artist of the North, and his celebration of 'The Feast of Venus' (**opposite**) *is typically Baroque. (Kunsthistoriches Museum, Vienna)*

LYRICS AND SERMONS

John Milton, now blind, dictates to his daughters, Deborah and Mary. He was for a time helped in his official duties by the young poet, Andrew Marvell. By George Romney (1734–1802), well-known portrait-painter and contemporary of Gainsborough and Reynolds. (Whitbread Collection, Biggleswade, Bedfordshire)

The struggle between the British Monarchy and Parliament, which grew more bitter after the accession of King Charles I in 1625, led to the hard-fought Civil Wars, and finally, in 1649, to the execution of the King. Great Britain then became a republican Commonwealth under the Protectorate of Oliver Cromwell, whose followers, called the Puritans, established a political and religious tyranny, which invaded every sphere of life. Literature and art were tolerated; but the playhouses were closed.

The greatest poet of the age was **John Milton** (1608–1674), at one time Cromwell's Latin secretary. Before he framed his masterpiece *Paradise Lost*, he had been stricken by blindness; but, as a magnificent sonnet shows, he bore this affliction with exemplary patience:

When I consider how my light is spent,
Ere half my days, in this dark world and wide,
And that one talent, which is death to hide
Lodged with me useless, though my soul more bent
To serve therewith my Maker, and present
My true account, lest he returning chide,
'Doth God exact day-labour, light denied?'
I fondly ask. But Patience, to prevent
That murmur, soon replies, 'God doth not need
Either man's works or his own gifts; who best
Bear his mild yoke, they serve him best, His State
Is Kingly: thousands at his bidding speed
And post o'er land and ocean without rest;
They also serve who only stand and wait.'

In *Paradise Lost* (1667), Milton produced what so many Renaissance poets failed to achieve – a Christian epic that deserved comparison with the great epics of Antiquity. Here he recreates the Biblical story of the Creation and the Fall, and justifies 'the ways of God to Man'; but his portrait of Satan, God's defeated yet still rebellious adversary, conveys now and then something of the majesty of evil. Milton, said William Blake, was 'of the Devil's party without knowing it.'

What though the field be lost?
All is not lost; the unconquerable will,
And study of revenge, immortal hate,
And courage never to submit or yield:
And what is else not to be overcome?

In *Paradise Regained* Milton celebrates the victory of Good and Christ's eventual triumph. His tragic drama, *Samson Agonistes*, follows the pattern of an ancient Greek play, where the blinded Samson represents both his own plight and the hardships experienced by his fellow Puritans. For 1660 had seen the Restoration of a Stuart ruler, Charles II; and it was now the Puritans' turn to suffer persecution.

John Bunyan (1628–1688), a pious Puritan believer, was one of those cast into gaol; but his imprisonment was not excessively rigorous. He was able to continue writing; and *The Pilgrim's Progress*, his allegorical story of a man's journey in search of salvation, appeared in 1678. It gained a popularity that it has never since lost. Few religious works have been more widely read.

Restoration Comedy, of which we owe the liveliest, boldest and most elegant specimens to **William Congreve** (1670–1729), **William Wycherley** (1640–1716) and the architect **Sir John Vanbrugh** (1664–1726), reflects the carefree spirit of the Stuart Court, its cult of pleasure and relentless pursuit of love. No other English comedies quite so polished and amusing were seen on the English stage until the advent of Richard Brinsley Sheridan's plays in the 1770s.

Two distinguished diarists record the everyday social life of the period. **John Evelyn** (1620–1706), polymath and founding father of the Royal Society, a centre of contemporary scientific learning, was the more serious-minded and less entertaining of the two. **Samuel Pepys** (1633–1703), a distinguished civil-servant and himself a member of the Royal Society, between 1660 and 1669, kept in cypher an unsparing record not only of such important public events as the Plague and the Great Fire, but of his squabbles with his wife and his own disreputable amours. What especially delights us in Pepys's diary are his passion for music and tremendous enjoyment of life. 'Mighty pleased with this day's pleasure', he wrote, after an alfresco concert, on 8 April 1667.

Above *Bunyan and John Gifford, Nonconformist Minister at Elstow, near Bedford, as Christian and Evangelist in* Pilgrim's Progress. *This stained-glass window in Elstow Church commemorates the tercentenary in 1950 of their meeting. Bunyan became Minister there for the last 17 years of his life – after he had been imprisoned in Bedford for 12 years for preaching without a licence.*

Below *Samuel Pepys, whose inimitable diary, written in cipher during the 1660s, was not published until 1825 – and then in heavily expurgated form. The first unexpurgated edition did not start to appear until 1970. Portrait by John Hayls (1666). (National Portrait Gallery, London)*

EPOCH OF THE SUN KING

Above *During the years 1661/84 the Sun King, Louis XIV, transformed the original small Palace at Versailles, near Paris, into the symbol of French Classicism and the* de facto *artistic capital of France. Shown here is the Western façade with the South Wing (at right). The Hall of Mirrors spans the first floor of the centre and faces two 'water-parterres' bordered by bronze statues.*

Top *The Music Room of Madame Adélaïde at Versailles. Marie-Adélaïde of Savoie was the grand-daughter of Louis XIV and mother of Louis XV. The French writer and prelate, Fénelon, had been tutor to her husband Louis, duc de Bourgogne, and wrote* Télémaque *(1699) for him. Thought to contain satirical references to Louis XIV and his policies, it brought disgrace on the author.*

During the reign of Louis XIV (1661–1715), a treatise was published that, in perfect seriousness, likened the French Sovereign to God the Father. Louis was also styled the Sun King, *le Roi Soleil*, around whom society revolved. The nobility, so turbulent in his father's reign, had now been reduced to a kind of courtly servitude, and were expected to live at Versailles and pay daily homage to the King.

Naturally, the writers of the day showed little rebellious spirit, since they, too, depended on royal patronage; and Louis' approval or disapproval determined the fate of any work of art. The Académie Française, founded by Cardinal Richelieu in 1635, remained the arbiter of taste.

French Classicism originated as a protest against Baroque literature, which had survived in the salons of the *Précieuses* – a group of cultured ladies who assembled in one another's drawing-rooms, and favoured sentimental love stories with pastoral backgrounds. *L'Astrée* by **Honoré d'Urfé** (1567–1625) was a novel they especially admired.

François de Malherbe (1555–1628) has been called the founder of French Classicism; he was a fine poet, whose work set a high standard of correctitude and clarity. But the same ideals were carried even further by **Nicholas Boileau** (1636–1711), whose satires demolished *précieuse* fiction, and whose *L'Art poétique* (1674) made him the literary legislator of Europe. His leading principle was Reason; his aim, to seek the Truth through the observation of Nature. 'Nothing is beautiful except the truth' was his famous dictum; and, as his models, he looked back to the great poets of Antiquity.

DUTY OR LOVE

In 1637, **Pierre Corneille** (1606–1684) opened the period of French classical drama by his production of *Le Cid,* a work distinguished by its obedience to certain rules that the ancient dramatists had followed, among them being the rule of the 'Three Unities' – those of Action, Time and Space – which were to be carefully maintained, and meant that an action must occur on a single day, and in the same place.

Le Cid is based on a psychological conflict that was to be repeated again and again throughout the history of literature under many different guises – the conflict between love and duty; and the plot presents a Spanish nobleman, obliged for his honour's sake to kill his mistress' father in a duel.

Most of Corneille's plays describe a similar conflict and exalt the victory of heroic Will. In *Horace* (1640), love gives way to patriotism; in *Cinna* (1641) and *Polyeucte* (1641/42), Corneille's subject is the sacrificial fate of Christian martyrs. Will is, above all else, the controller of unruly passions.

'The Father of Tragedy', Pierre Corneille, who introduced the period of French classical drama in the 1630s. In later years he was deserted by audiences and actors in favour of the younger dramatist, Jean Racine, who preferred the drama of 'passion' to that of honour and 'duty'. Portrait from the first edition of his collected works (1644). (Bibliothèque Nationale, Paris)

RACINE

Above *As a young man, the tragic dramatist Racine studied at Port-Royal, the headquarters of the Jansenists, the puritanical sect who opposed the Jesuits, and their stern morality influenced his early life and work. He abandoned them for a period of success at Louis XIV's court but for his last two tragedies returned to religious themes. (Bibliothèque Nationale, Paris)*

Above right *Madame de Maintenon, spiritual confidante and unacknowledged second wife of Louis XIV, is said to have had a strong effect on Racine's later choice of themes. Portrait by French painter and engraver Augustin de Saint Aubin (1737–1807). (Bibliothèque Nationale, Paris)*

French classical drama was perfected by **Jean Racine** (1639–1699), the composition of whose plays is strictly logical. All unneccessary minor characters are eliminated; and, unlike Corneille, Racine did not find it in the least difficult to preserve the Unities. That, however, is not the only difference between them. For Corneille, Will–Power was the most powerful human force. He created the drama of duty, whereas, in Racine's view of existence, Passion took its place. Critics have said that Corneille demonstrated the strength, and Racine the weakness, of humanity; and that Corneille's heroes arouse admiration, but Racine's, compassion.

French classical poetry is almost exclusively concerned with moral values, and pays little attention to their social background. Racine's first great tragedy, *Andromaque* (1667), for example, is founded on a terrible Greek legend of violence and madness. Yet it was performed at the court-theatre, in the presence of the King; and both the actors and the audience wore the fashionable costumes of the day. No armed conflicts took place on the stage; and there were, of course, no comic episodes. An air of patrician dignity prevailed.

How, one may ask, can such a presentation be reconciled with a realistic pursuit of Nature? Well, Nature, according to Boileau, was unalterable and universal. It did not depend on outward appearances or on picturesque detail. What counted was the verisimilitude with which the dramatist displayed his theme.

In Racine's other works, the interest of the drama is primarily psychological. The hero of *Bérénice* (1670) is the Emperor Titus, who, for the benefit of

the state, gives up the woman whom he loves; while the subject of *Phèdre* (1677) is derived from Euripides' *Hippolytus*, a Queen's guilty passion for her youthful stepson. As almost always in Racine's plays, a woman is the main character; and he develops the original plot with a high degree of subtlety. *Phèdre*, however, had an unfriendly reception; and its failure, complicated perhaps by some spiritual or moral crisis, caused him to retire from the stage, until Madame de Maintenon, the King's spiritual guardian and unacknowledged wife, persuaded him to produce two dramas with biblical themes, *Esther* in 1689 and *Athalie* in 1691.

Opposite *One of Racine's last tragedies,* Esther, *portrays King Ahasuerus's new Queen, the Jewish heroine whose people were ill-treated by the King's chief minister, Haman. Esther intercedes with the King on behalf of the Jews and of her cousin Mordecai who is to be hanged. Revealed as a tyrant, Haman makes an unsuccessful plea for his life with the Queen, as shown in this drawing by English artist Henry Anelay (fl. 1850–1870).*

Right *Françoise Dumesnil and Brizard performing in histrionic style (1750) in Racine's* Athalie. *The play was inspired by the story in 2 Kings, 11 of how the High Priest Jehoida had restored Joash to the throne his grandmother Athaliah had usurped. Racine's plays have been performed by some of the most brilliant actresses, among them the incomparable Rachel. (Bibliothèque d'Arsenal, Paris)*

Below *The great French actor, François Talma, in a late 17th-century production of Racine's* Andromaque, *portrayed here by de Rasculon y Grabado de Coqueret. Talma, who insisted that costumes and settings should be historically accurate, would not have approved of the original staging of this play in contemporary dress at the court of Louis XIV. (Bibliothèque Nationale, Paris)*

MOLIÈRE

Right *Molière, the actor–manager and author who had also inherited the post of furnisher to the royal household. Detail from a painting by Pierre Mignard (1612–1695), portrait-painter to the court of Louis XIV.*

Below right *Molière as Arnolphe in his own* L'École des Femmes (School for Wives). *A few days after performing in his last play,* Le Malade imaginaire *(1673), he died without formally renouncing his profession of actor, and so, according to the law of the Church, was not allowed a Christian burial.*

The third important playwright of the age was the comic dramatist **Molière** (1622–1673), the pseudonym adopted by the actor–manager Jean-Baptiste Poquelin. He took a more liberal view of histrionic rules and conventions than did Racine and Corneille, and constantly infringed the Three Unities. Mindful of the audience he had to entertain, he accepted the traditions of popular farce, and used comic personages who date back to Greek and Roman times – the miserly father, the cunning servant, the two impatient young lovers – but gave them the dignity, and sometimes the complexity, of living men and women.

Molière made his name with *Les Précieuses ridicules* (1659), an exuberant attack on fashionable literary salons, which soon afterwards he followed with *L'École des femmes* (1662), this time aimed at social snobbery. Now recognized as a powerful satirist, he did not hesitate to challenge rank and privilege. But he had one great ally – Louis XIV himself. A professional actor and the son of a paper-hanger, Molière belonged to the rising middle class, whom the King was glad to favour; and once he enjoyed the supreme distinction of being invited to dine at the royal table.

In *Don Juan* (1665), where his plot was taken from a Spanish play about the celebrated seducer, Molière depicts the ruthless amorists of his own age; and in *Tartufe* (1664), he draws an alarming picture of religious hypocrisy and cant, that aroused the antagonism of the Church. To round off his play, he used the device also employed by Euripides with his *deus ex machina*; though here it is not a divinity, but the King, whom Molière brings on to the stage in the last act to resolve the situation and establish order.

The characters Molière created have a universal application. Tartufe, lusting after Orgon's wife and money, remains the type of pious hypocrite. Although Molière has sometimes been blamed for falling back on the simplified characters of farce, his genius usually enabled him to present his personages as individuals. Harpagon in *L'Avare* (1668, The Miser) is at once a type and a separate human being; while Alceste in *Le Misanthrope* (1666) is both a typically stubborn, dogmatic man, and a dignified, even a tragic figure.

Molière had pleased the monarchy; but, as he died on stage, the Church refused him Christian burial.

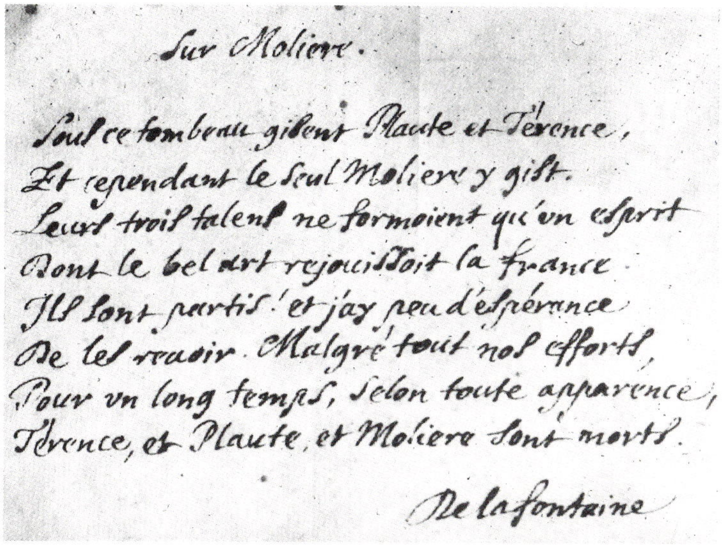
Sur Moliere.

Sous ce tombeau gisent Plaute et Térence,
Et cependant le seul Moliere y gist.
Leurs trois talens ne formoient qu'un esprit
Dont le bel art rejouissoit la france.
Ils sont partis! et jay peu d'espérance
De les revoir. Malgré tous nos efforts,
Pour un long temps, selon toute apparence,
Térence, et Plaute, et Moliere sont morts.

De la fontaine

Left *La Fontaine, although best remembered as the great French fabulist, also wrote poems, plays and opera librettos. He penned this graceful epitaph for his friend Molière, whose talents he links with the two earlier dramatic masters, Plautus and Terence, whose deaths he also mourns. (Bibliothèque Nationale, Paris)*

Below *Molière and the actors of the Comédie Française, at a reception given by Louis XIV (seated and wearing his hat as was the royal custom). This French national theatre, devoted to classical repertory – and at one time known as 'La Maison de Molière' – was founded in Paris in 1680 by royal decree. It is still organized along lines originally established by Molière in the 1650s. Painting by Ingres (1857), upholder of the Classic style as opposed to his Romantic contemporary, Delacroix, who once said of him 'His art is the complete expression of an incomplete intelligence.' (Théâtre Comédie Française, Paris)*

THE NATURAL STYLE

Above *La Fontaine's* Le Loup et la cigogne (Fables I, The Wolf and the Stork) – *spelt Latin-style as 'cicogne' here, and* (**above right**) Le Meunier, son fils et l'âne (Fables III, The Miller, His Son and the Ass) – *'The greatest ass of the three is not the one you would think.' This great fabulist was inspired by Greek, Roman and Eastern sources as well as drawing from parallels of his own time. Engravings from a French edition of his* Fables *(1755). (Royal Library, Stockholm)*

Opposite, top *Charles Perrault, who diverted French literature from its preoccupation with Antiquity, was also noted for his fairy-tales. His* Little Red Riding Hood *was probably first translated into English as early as 1729, and is here illustrated in characteristic 19th-century style.*

Wit and style and worldly good sense are the characteristics of **Jean de la Fontaine** (1621–1695), whose *Fables* (of which the first collection was made in 1668) have become an imperishable part of European literature. As a moralist, he is scarcely suited to the schoolroom; the conclusion he draws is often cynical, and he is not always on the side of innocence and virtue. But, as a storyteller and master of light poetic narrative, he possessed a dazzling gift. His animals – the Ant, the Heron, the Fox, and many others – remain animals, yet become astonishingly human. Thus, in his *The Grasshopper and the Ant*, the Ant is a crafty capitalist; the Grasshopper, an improvident dilettante:

A Grasshopper the summer long
Sang her song,
And found herself when winter came
Without a morsel to her name.
Not one scrap of worm or fly
Had the careless thing put by!
So she took her tale of want
To her neighbour, Mistress Ant,
Begging for a small advance
Of the needful sustenance
Till the spring came round next year.
'I'll repay you, never fear,
Interest and principal,
Sure as I'm an animal.'
The Ant has many faults, I own,
But being too ready with a loan
Is not among them. 'Well, my dear,
Tell me how you spent the summer?'
'Night and day, to every comer,
Please you, ma'am, I sang my ditty.'
'Singing, were you? Very pretty!
Now's your chance,
Mistress Grasshopper, to dance.'

The great French classical writers as a rule were poets; but now three prose writers enlarged the outlook of their age. One was **Blaise Pascal** (1623–1662), a precocious scientist and mathematician, whose treatise on conic sections, written at the age of sixteen, astonished Descartes. He had also a profoundly religious strain, and became a member of the puritanical Jansenist movement (which disputed the doctrine of Free Will); and from its headquarters, the Monastery of Port-Royal, published his *Lettres provinciales*, a brilliant anonymous attack on the Jansenists' adversaries the Jesuits. But his most memorable work was his collection of scattered thoughts, his *Pensées*, which appeared after his death in 1670. Here he emerges as a great aphorist and a superbly succinct, at times poetic writer. 'Man is no more than a reed, the feeblest part of nature; but a *thinking reed*', is among his most often-quoted observations.

Pascal was preoccupied with the spiritual life; **La Rochefoucauld** (1613–1680), once a courtier and adventurous soldier, with his Man's social psychology; and, during his later years he settled down to produce a volume entitled *Réflexions ou sentences et maximes morales,* which appeared in 1665. He had a polished style, an acute wit and a mordant insight into human failings. Characteristic of La Rochefoucauld's observations is his remark that 'in the mishaps of even our best friends we often find something that does not altogether displease us'.

La Bruyère (1645–1696) drew in his *Caractères* (1688/96) a series of typical contemporary portraits; and, among seventeenth-century writers, he was one of the few who described the wretched condition of the peasantry:

> One sees certain wild animals, male and female, scattered over the country, black, livid, and burned by the sun, who are chained, as it were, to the land they are always digging and turning over with an unquenchable stubbornness; they have a sort of articulate voice, and when they stand up, they exhibit human features: they are men.

Nature, Reason and a respect for Antiquity were the three corner-stones of the French classical tradition. So long as a belief in these persisted, classicism lived on. But, towards the end of the century, the last was removed, when the authority of ancient literature was questioned. Its main defender at the time was Boileau, and its antagonist **Charles Perrault** (1628–1703), author of critical works, burlesque verses and celebrated fairy-tales, among which were 'Little Red Riding Hood' and 'Puss in Boots'. He based his criticism on the idea of Human Progress. If Progress were advancing in other fields, why not in the realm of modern literature?

Above *Blaise Pascal's cell at Port-Royal, near Paris, where he came under the influence of Jansenism, and a posthumous portrait (***above right***), perhaps from his death mask. He was a mathematician and physicist as well as a moralist. (Musée de Port-Royal des Champs, Paris)*

LET THERE BE LIGHT!

Above *The room at Woolsthorpe Manor, near Grantham in Lincolnshire, where Isaac Newton was born. Lying open at the frontispiece is the third edition of his* Principia *(1687), written, it is said, after seeing an apple fall in his garden – which inspired him to develop the idea of universal gravitation.*

Right *Isaac Newton. He was knighted in 1705 and his statue at Trinity College, Cambridge, was commemorated by Wordsworth in his* Prelude: *'. . . The marble index of a mind for ever voyaging through strange seas of thought alone.' Both Newton and the German philosopher, Leibniz, claimed priority for their discoveries in the field of calculus. Portrait by Vincenzo Milone.*

After the 'Glorious Revolution' of 1688, an event dear to liberal nineteenth-century historians, James II, the last of the Stuart line, an avowed Catholic, was replaced by William of Orange, a determinedly Protestant ruler; and, during the next hundred years, Great Britain came to represent in Europe the idea of freedom and enlightenment. British scientists and philosophers gained Continental renown. In 1687, the physicist **Isaac Newton** (1642–1727) published his revolutionary discoveries on the laws of gravitation, *Philosophiae Naturalis Principia Mathematica*; and the philosopher **John Locke** (1632–1704), in *An Essay Concerning Human Understanding* (1690) and *Some Thoughts Concerning Education* (1693) examined the processes of thought and defined the limitations of human knowledge by carefully studying the mechanism of his own intelligence.

Meanwhile, British society was growing increasingly commercial; and when, early in the next century, in 1726, Voltaire paid his momentous visit to England, he was impressed not only by the wealth but by the culture and dignity of London merchants, who seemed to hold almost as exalted a position as any European prince. Learning and literature flourished; the individual enjoyed far greater freedom than he had ever done in France; and from that moment, we are told, Voltaire resolved to 'destroy all the prejudices of which his country was the slave'.

An Age of Reason appeared to have begun; but, as we shall soon observe, the eighteenth-century Cult of Feeling had also a strong influence on many contemporary novelists and poets.

PROSE COMES OF AGE

During the second half of the seventeenth century, two great writers, **Daniel Defoe** (1660–1731) and **Jonathan Swift** (1667–1745) helped to revolutionize English prose-style by their equally bold and direct, though very different, use of language. Each was a many-sided character. Defoe, for example, preparatory to becoming a novelist, followed many different trades; the son of a London butcher, he was first an unsuccessful businessman, then a government spy, an industrious journalist and a prolific political pamphleteer. His earliest novel, *The Life and Strange Surprising Adventures of Robinson Crusoe*, did not come out until 1719, when he had almost reached his sixtieth year, but soon earned him European fame. Crusoe, his shipwrecked hero, is essentially a modern personage, the product of a mercantile era, who, once he has overcome the shock of being cast away and grown accustomed to his solitude, transforms his well-stocked desert island into a prosperous colony, with Friday, the 'Noble Savage' he has rescued, as his loyal native adjutant, and himself as a benevolent proprietor and governor. The charm of Defoe's narrative is its air of sober realism, and the effect of verisimilitude he manages to produce by the keen attention that he pays to detail, though the story has also an imaginative aspect, and here and there a single vivid touch suddenly lights up the scene.

Moll Flanders, however, published in 1722, is unquestionably his masterpiece. The first true English 'novel', as we understand the word today, it follows the progress of a poor but adventurous young woman against the background of contemporary English life. A foundling, deprived of any proper education but put to work in early childhood, she already longs to be a 'gentlewoman'; and, though her adult career is often disreputable – she is a sneak-thief, a whore and a receiver of stolen goods and on one occasion, nearly a murderess – respectability and economic security are the aims that she has set herself. Defoe's prose-style is splendidly straightforward, and echoes the language spoken by ordinary people in the London that he knew; but, should the subject demand it, as when Moll is tempted to strangle a little girl she has just robbed, he is capable of reaching tragic heights. Defoe was neither an analyst of character nor was he a moralist; he was less concerned with feelings than with facts; but his resolute adventuress and his resourceful castaway are still among the most memorable figures in the history of English fiction.

Whereas Defoe was a Londoner born and bred, Jonathan Swift, born in

Below left *Crusoe and Friday from a 19th-century illustration of Defoe's* Robinson Crusoe, *based on the true story of Alexander Selkirk, who survived several years alone on the uninhabited island of Juan Fernández, off the South Pacific coast of Chile.*

Below *Contemporary engraving of Defoe, who created some of the more memorable characters in English fiction. (British Museum, London)*

Above *Jonathan Swift, a man of many parts, pamphleteer, humanist, satirist, novelist, whose* Gulliver's Travels *expressed, among much else, his 'savage indignation' with the contemporary European world. Portrait (c. 1718) by Charles Jervas. (National Portrait Gallery, London)*

Right *'Gulliver bestrides the army of Lilliput'. Swift's account of this miniature race is a diverting caricature of modern society. Illustration by Thomas Morten for an 1870 edition.*

Dublin of English parents, was a man who lacked a settled home, a champion of the hard-pressed Irish people, yet always happiest with his English friends. Two bold satires, *The Tale of a Tub* and *The Battle of the Books*, which both appeared in 1704, established his position as a London wit; and, through the services that, as a vigorous pamphleteer, he did the political leaders of the day, having taken Holy Orders in 1695 he hoped that he might one day become a bishop. He was always disappointed; and disappointment, sharpened by life-long ill-health and some unhappy personal relationships, gave Swift's attitude towards mankind at large a peculiarly aggressive turn. *The Tale of a Tub* was an attack on the divisions of the Christian Church; *The Battle of the Books*, on the pedantry of modern critics. But his finest and most popular work, *Gulliver's Travels*, which appeared in 1726 – a masterpiece, he admitted himself, designed to 'vex the world rather than divert it' – had an immensely wider scope. Like *Robinson Crusoe* presented as a genuine traveller's tale, it contains a fantastic exposition of human weaknesses and vices. Wherever he goes – first, to Lilliput, whose tiny inhabitants reproduce the worst aspects of contemporary life; next, to Brobdingnag, the land of the giants, where he is regarded by its huge sovereign as an amusing but ignorant and wrong-headed dwarf; then to Laputa, the domain of mad, conceited scientists; finally, to the country of the Houyhnhnms, a race of enlightened horses who have reduced their human subjects, the 'abominable Yahoos', to the status of ferocious slaves – Gulliver finds little consolation or relief. For example, having delivered a solemn lecture to the King of Brobdingnag about the virtues of European government and the beauties and advantages of modern warfare, he is dismissed with a majestic smile:

> ... Taking me into his hands, and stroking me gently, [the King] delivered himself in these words ... 'By what I have gathered from your own relation, and the answers I have ... extorted from you, I cannot but conclude the bulk of your natives, to be the most pernicious race of little odious vermin that Nature ever suffered to crawl upon the surface of the earth.'

Yet, despite the plan he had formed of 'vexing the world', Swift, when he published *Gulliver's Travels*, succeeded in giving it enormous pleasure. As sound a stylist and fine a story-teller as Daniel Defoe, this savage critic, an angry, unhappy man himself, made an extraordinarily generous contribution to the happiness of mankind.

ESSAYISTS AND NOVELISTS

Both Swift and Defoe, besides their success as story-tellers, had also won fame in the role of pamphleteers and controversialists; and, during the early eighteenth century, journalism of various kinds became increasingly popular with the educated Englishman. The vogue of the magazine began in 1711, when **Joseph Addison** (1672– 1719) joined **Sir Richard Steele** (1672–1729), who had launched the *Tatler* two years earlier; and they then founded the *Spectator*, a daily periodical that published 555 essays during the course of 21 months. The aim of this daily journal, its editors declared was 'to enliven morality with wit, and to temper wit with moral sentiment'. The *Tatler*, an off-spring of the seventeenth-century news-sheet, was a blend of gossip, news and literary essays; but the *Spectator* discussed moral and social questions, and sought to bring 'philosophy' out of schools and colleges to dwell in clubs, at tea-tables and at coffee-houses. Addison was a graceful stylist and an able popularizer of serious topics.

Among the *Spectator*'s successors, in the middle years of the century, were the *Rambler* and the *Idler*, in which **Samuel Johnson** (1709–1784), sometimes called 'the English Socrates' – the greatest literary law-giver of his age, and the hero of the immortal biography written by his friend and disciple, **James Boswell** (1740–1795) – first showed his talents as an imaginative essayist.

In 1740, when a romance named *Pamela; or, Virtue Rewarded* appeared on English bookshelves, the modern novel came into its own. The author, **Samuel Richardson** (1689–1761), a printer by trade, did not reveal his gifts and achieve fame until he had reached the age of fifty-one; but *Pamela* was immediately successful, and quickly ran through four editions. Casting his narrative in letter-form, he told the story of an innocent servant-girl whom her master's son endeavours to seduce, but who, thanks to a rare mixture of virtue and commonsense, contrives to thwart him, with the result that he eventually offers her marriage. In *Clarissa Harlowe* (1747/49), one of the longest English novels ever issued, the heroine, though equally virtuous, is at length betrayed and ravished, her seducer being Lovelace, a fascinating rake, who believes that it is his task in life to strip the last vestiges of prudish self-deception from the women he beguiles. On the one hand, Richardson is a conventional moralist; on the other, a wonderfully shrewd psychologist. His analysis of character is often extremely subtle. His portrait of Lovelace struck the contemporary imagination, and was long discussed and imitated by foreign writers. Richardson's work had a considerable effect on the development of the European novel.

Henry Fielding (1707–1754), who twice wrote cruel parodies of *Pamela* in *An Apology for the Life of Mrs Shamela Andrews* (1741) and in *The Adventures of Joseph Andrews and his friend Mr Abraham Adams* (1742), had a quality that Richardson could never have claimed, an uproarious sense of humour, coupled with a warm affection for mankind at large. His greatest novel, *Tom Jones* (1749), which has some affinity with the Spanish picaresque novels, though it contains many discursive asides, where the novelist buttonholes his reader, gives us a boldly realistic account of a young man's headlong progress through the world. Tom himself is by no means

Below *Dr Johnson, 'the Great Cham of Literature', whose* Dictionary *(1747/55) was 'for the use of such as aspire to exactness of criticism or elegance of style'. From an unfinished portrait (c. 1777) by James Barry. (National Portrait Gallery, London)*

Bottom *Samuel Richardson, who influenced the development of the European novel. Detail from a portrait by Mason Chamberlain the Elder.*

Henry Fielding, self-styled 'Founder of a new Province in Writing', and literary guiding-light to Thackeray and Dickens. He mercilessly parodied Samuel Richardson's romance Pamela. *Caricature by William Hogarth (1697–1764). Fielding described Hogarth's highly original style of subject painting (illustrated here) as 'comic history'. (British Museum, London)*

strictly upright; he is both unscrupulous and keenly amorous. But he declares that, 'to procure pleasure to myself', he would not 'be knowingly the cause of misery to any human being'. Fielding, who claimed that he was 'the Founder of a new Province in Writing', and had set out to produce 'a comic-epic in prose', was the forerunner and literary guiding-light of such Victorian novelists as Thackeray and Dickens.

Of all the eighteenth-century English novelists, **Laurence Sterne** (1713–1768) was the most peculiarly unorthodox, and popularized a new word, 'sentimental', used as a term of high praise, in the vocabulary of contemporary readers and writers. It signified, above all else, the ability to feel and sympathize and look beneath the surface of existence. 'What a large volume of adventures', Sterne wrote, 'may be grasped ... by him who interests his heart in everything ...'. Like the philosopher **David Hume** (1711–1776), he believed that the human personality consisted of a 'bundle ... of different perceptions' in a state of 'perpetual flux and movement'; and, when he described a character, instead of giving it a definite outline, he set out to describe that flux. An eccentric country clergyman, Sterne published his long novel *Tristram Shandy* in 1759/67 – a strange medley of reflections, personal anecdotes, romantic musings and comic portraiture hung on a single thread of story, that begins with a ludicrous account of his own conception, which nearly fails to take place because at a critical moment his mother suddenly asks his father if he has forgotten to wind up the clock!

Sterne's method of narration is deliberately discontinuous; and he employs a similar technique in his entertaining travel-book, *A Sentimental Journey through France and Italy*, published in 1768. Here the subjects with which he sympathizes range from a pretty shop-girl to a dead donkey and an unhappy caged bird. At a French inn, he hears a pathetic voice 'which I took to be of a child . . . I heard the same words repeated twice over; and looking up, I saw it was a starling hung in a little cage; – "I can't get out, – I can't get out", said the starling'.

Compared with Sterne, whose treatment of his material bears a strong resemblance to that of James Joyce, **Tobias Smollett** (1721–1771) was a prosaic story-teller, whose novels *Roderick Random* (1748), *Peregrine Pickle* (1751) and *Humphrey Clinker* (1771), in the well-established picaresque tradition, send his heroes travelling across land and sea, through a long series of adventurous exploits and serio-comic misadventures. The great caricaturist Rowlandson illustrated *Peregrine Pickle*; and Smollett's stories, at their best, have a caricatural vitality and gusto. It is not surprising that Smollett detested Sterne, who lampooned him as the abominable 'Smelfungus'.

Oliver Goldsmith (1730–1774), an Irish man of letters, with many of the qualities said to be typically Hibernian – he was loquacious, good-hearted, imaginative, but also thoughtless and extravagant – after wandering around Europe 'with no more than a few halfpence', settled down to London literary life, and in 1766, encouraged by Samuel Johnson, produced *The Vicar of Wakefield*, a simple but cleverly turned story, with a charming domestic background, about the trials and subsequent rewards of virtue, which proved immediately successful. Later, he wrote a brilliant play, *She Stoops to Conquer* (1773), one of the few eighteenth-century dramatic works that, besides *The Beggar's Opera* (1728), by **John Gay** (1685–1732) and *The School for Scandal* (1777) by **Richard Brinsley Sheridan** (1751–1816) are still revived upon the London stage.

THE ENGLISH AUGUSTAN AGE

Left *John Dryden, whose mastery of the English language was shown in works that ranged from dramatic and lyric poetry to ferocious satire. Engraving from a drawing by Thomas Uwins (1782–1857) in the collection of the 19th-century romantic author, Sir Walter Scott.*

Above *Alexander Pope. Detail of portrait by J. Richardson. (National Portrait Gallery, London)*

Although prose-literature had made striking advances, the Poetic Spirit had never declined in England. Few periods have produced more delightful minor poets, both religious and profane, than the strife-torn seventeenth century; and after the death of Milton in 1674, his place was taken by **John Dryden** (1631–1700) as an acknowledged master of the language. He was at once a splendid poet, a fine poetic dramatist and a distinguished literary critic, who, during his later years, held court at his favourite coffee-house, where younger poets and playwrights gathered round him. His scathing political satire *Absolom and Achitophel* (1681) is a masterpiece of vituperative eloquence; while, besides comedies and baroque historical dramas written in heroic couplets, he produced a blank-verse tragedy, *All for Love* (1678), based to some extent on Shakespeare's *Antony and Cleopatra*, that rises here and there to an almost Shakespearian level. It was his finest play, and the only drama, he said, that he had written solely 'for himself'. In 1700, Dryden bade good-bye to his century in his famous *Secular Masque*, of which the last two lines strike a deeply poignant note:

'Tis well an old age is out,
And time to begin a new . . .

Alexander Pope (1688–1744) presently succeeded to the master's throne, whence he dominated contemporary literature. Crippled since his boyhood and very nearly a dwarf, a mere four feet and six inches high, he was a man of powerful genius, who towered far above his fellow poets. In 1717, having reached his twenty-ninth birthday, he decided to publish his collected *Works*, which already included his ambitious *Essay on Criticism* and his exquisite mock-heroic poem, *The Rape of the Lock*. Between 1715 and 1726, Pope translated both the *Iliad* and the *Odyssey*, and between 1713 and 1738, completed his *Moral Essays* and his *Imitations of Horace*; while his *Essay on Man*, intended as a philosophic preface to the *Moral Essays*, was writ-

The name of Ossian, alleged to have been a 3rd-century Celtic bard, occupies an important place in the history of Romantic literature. Though Goethe, Blake and the Emperor Napoleon were all devoted to his works, they were almost certainly fabricated during the 1760s by a Scottish man of letters named James Macpherson, who claimed that they were translations of ancient poems he had luckily discovered. Here, the French artist A.L. Girodet-Trioson depicts the 'Apotheosis of the French Heroes' (1801), who had fallen under Napoleon's command, and whom Ossian welcomes into a Celtic Elysium. (Napoleonic Museum, Malmaison, Rueil)

ten in 1733 and 1734. Like Dryden, he became a ferocious satirist; and the original version of *The Dunciad*, a savage attack on contemporary poetasters, came out in 1728.

Pope was a classical writer, the chief luminary of the so-called Augustan Age. Yet, many of his poems, for example, his *Eloisa to Abelard* and *Elegy to the Memory of an Unfortunate Lady*, have a strong Romantic colouring. Himself he was devoted to the 'Gothick' past, to medieval ruins, desolate landscapes and ideas of mystery and 'horror'. The early eighteenth century witnessed the first glimmerings of what has been called the 'Romantic false-dawn', which also appear in the poems of **Thomas Gray** (1716–1771). He, too, had a 'Gothick' turn of fancy, an aspect of his work that Samuel Johnson sternly criticized. But, although Johnson declared that Gray's attempts to recreate the medieval past, as in *The Curse Upon Edward* (supposed to be pronounced by an indignant Welsh patriot, whose people the English monarch had subjugated) where examples of the 'false sublime' abound, he agreed that Gray's famous *Elegy Written in a Country Churchyard* (1750) contained 'images which find a mirror in every mind, and ... sentiments to which every bosom returns an echo'. Solitude and death were both themes that evidently haunted the poet's imagination:

> For who to dumb forgetfulness a prey,
> This pleasing anxious being e'er
> resigned,
> Left the warm precincts of the cheerful
> day,
> Nor cast one longing lingering look
> behind.

During his later life, Gray conducted scholarly researches into Celtic and Icelandic verse. Primitive literatures had begun to fascinate students; and when, in 1760, a certain imaginative Scotsman, **James Macpherson**, (1736–1796) published his *Fragments of Ancient Poetry* and other verses, alleged to have been the work of a mysterious third-century Celtic bard named **Ossian**, although they were almost certainly fraudulent, they enthralled a multitude of readers, among whom, at a much later period, was Napoleon Bonaparte. By this time, the Romantic Movement was well under way; and not only mountains and waterfalls, but the architecture of the Industrial Revolution, mines, factories and blast-furnaces, were regarded as 'horrid', 'terrible' and 'sublime'.

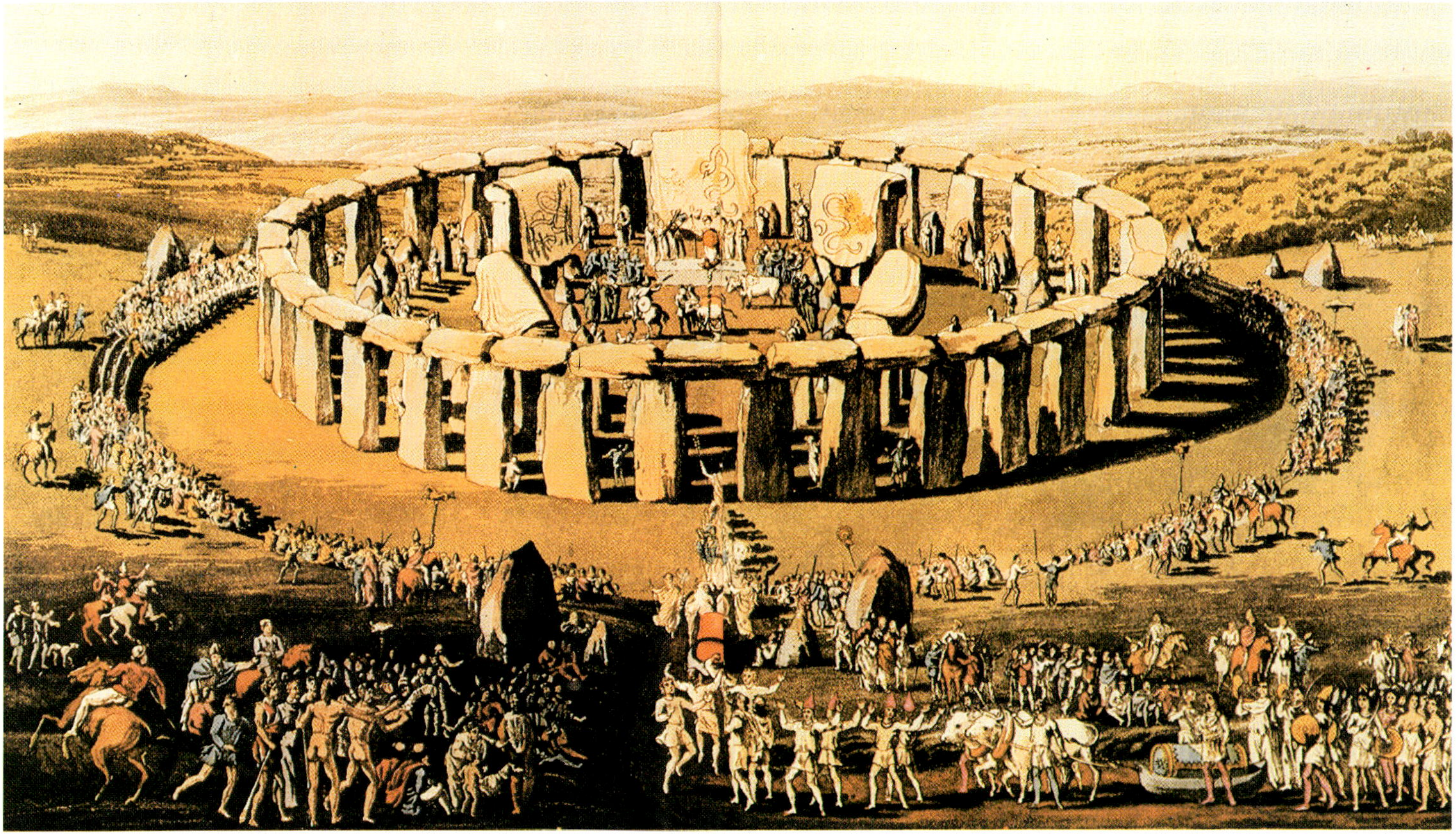

More important than the legendary Ossian, who caught the imagination of early Romantics, was Thomas Percy's Reliques of Ancient English Poetry *(1765). An anthology of genuine, mostly medieval ballads, it quickened the study of national ballad literatures throughout Europe. An ancestor of all modern 'folk' movements, it restored a vital part of the European tradition. The 17th-century British antiquary John Aubrey had first associated the Druids with Stonehenge, the prehistoric stone circle on Salisbury Plain* (**above**)*, where they were thought to have held their secret rites. In fact, it belongs to a much earlier period of history.*

Right *Blake's 'The Flight of Moloch' (1809) illustrates Milton's* On the Morning of Christ's Nativity. *(Whitworth Art Gallery, Manchester)*

Below *Robert Burns in 1787 by Alexander Nasmyth. (National Portrait Gallery, London)*

Scotland's national poet, **Robert Burns** (1759–1796), came far closer than Ossian to the spirit of the ancient folk-songs. A self-educated poet, at his best he used his native dialect to describe his many love-affairs and the jollifications of his friends. The poems he wrote in the Augustan English of his day are a great deal less effective.

William Blake (1757–1827) has been described as 'one of the strangest and most variously gifted figures in the history of English art and writing', the son of a London shopkeeper, who, even in childhood, had had ecstatic visions, seen the face of God looking through the window, and a flight of angels roosting amid suburban trees. Yet his visionary turn was combined with great practical abilities; and, from 1789, when he produced *Songs of Innocence* (to be followed by a complementary group of lyrics, *Songs of Experience* in 1794), having learned the engraver's trade, he not only illustrated his own books, but engraved, coloured and distributed them. A religious prophet, he also invented his own mythology, which included a host of spirits, demons, demiurges, and preached a highly individual creed, asserting that behind the 'delusive World of Nature', lay the spiritual reality of human life. The first of his mysterious 'Prophetic Books', appeared in the same year as *Songs of Experience*; and this vast series was completed by *Jerusalem* and *Milton* in 1804. The most memorable, certainly the easiest to read, is *The Marriage of Heaven and Hell*, published in 1790, a masterpiece of revolutionary writing, where, besides attacking the framework of orthodox Christianity, he announced that 'Man has no Body distinct from his Soul ... that Energy is Eternal Delight' and, elsewhere, that 'the road of excess leads to the palace of wisdom'. Blake's symbolism has frequently a sexual colouring; and the new Jerusalem he sought to build on earth was to be the home of individual freedom, whence Christian puritanism had long ago been banished.

Although the 'Prophetic Books' are often densely obscure, they contain passages of splendid clarity. Blake was an exquisite lyric poet; and his most famous lines, taken from *Milton*:

And did those feet in ancient time
Walk upon England's mountains green?

still inspire a modern audience, despite the fact that those who respond to its rapturous music may not always fully grasp its meaning.

THE LAWS OF REASON AND THE GOSPEL OF FEELING

During the great days of pre-Revolutionary rule, the sovereign was the apex of society. But in 1793, the French sent Louis XVI to the scaffold, and instituted the Cult of Reason. Meanwhile, the monarchical system was being slowly undermined, not only by the underprivileged but by the upper and middle orders, for whom the endless discussion of human rights had become an intellectual pastime. Before the system finally collapsed in 1789, it was already slowly breaking down.

When, in 1685, by the Revocation of Nantes, religious freedom was abolished, nearly a quarter of a million French Protestants were summarily driven into exile. Most of them fled to England, where they came into contact with many new ideas on political and social issues; and these ideas filtered back to France, at a time when an increasingly powerful middle class was providing literature with a host of new readers.

Montesquieu (Charles de Secondat, Baron de la Brède et de Montesquieu, 1689–1755) was among the first writers to publish a reasoned criticism of the existing social scheme. This he did in *Lettres persanes* (1721), a series of imaginary letters supposed to have been written by a young Persian tourist who gives a vividly critical account of European institutions. With his other main work, *L'Esprit des lois* (1748, On the Spirit of the Laws), Montesquieu is said to have been 'one of the most broad-minded precursors' of the Revolution that he did not live to see.

Montesquieu, man of letters and political philosopher, whose work On the Spirit of the Laws *influenced the provisions of the US Constitution and of the French constitution after the Revolution of 1789. Engraving from a portrait by Garnerey. (Royal Library, Stockholm)*

VOLTAIRE

The best known and most powerful leader of the Enlightenment was **François Marie Arouet** whose pseudonym was **Voltaire** (1694–1778). Although a man of middle-class origin, he quickly made a place for himself in the aristocratic framework of eighteenth-century French society – despite some early setbacks, as when he was thrashed by the servants of an angry nobleman and cast by the authorities into the Bastille.

His visit to England early in 1726, where he was much impressed by the comparative liberality of the British social system, met Alexander Pope and other distinguished literary characters, and almost everything he saw delighted him, left a deep impression on his mind; and from that moment, we are told, he determined to destroy all the prejudices 'of which his own country was the slave'. His fame as an established writer very soon spread throughout Europe, and he conducted long correspondences with the two most enlightened monarchs of the day, allegedly Frederick the Great of Prussia and the Russian Empress Catherine. At the Château of Ferney, near Geneva, he at length himself became a kind of intellectual sovereign and received his guests in princely state.

Voltaire's tragedies, such as *Zaïre* (1732), and his epic poem *La Henriade* (1723), seldom appeal to modern readers. It was through his controversial works and some of his brilliant short stories that he exhibited his true genius. 'Tolerance' was always Voltaire's watchword. His *Lettres philosophiques* (1734), the product of his visit to England, and a collection of essays, *Dictionnaire philosophique* (1764), were both decisive volumes in the history of French thought.

From a literary point of view, Voltaire's *contes*, short novels or long short-stories, are his most memorable work. They combine an element of fantasy with a strong colouring of social and political satire. Thus, *Zadig* (1747) gives us a young Babylonian's first impressions of contemporary

Above *Voltaire, one of the principal figures of the Enlightenment in France. Having attacked the injustices of the French social system, he fled to London, as an exile, where from 1726 to 1729 he became a devotee of all things English from Newtonian physics to the comparative freedom of English politics and society. Detail from a portrait by Garnerey.*

Right *Voltaire welcomed to the Elysian fields by Henri IV, whom he had eulogized in* La Henriade. *From a drawing by L. Fauvel.*

'The Philosophers' Supper' – leaders of the French enlightenment involved in producing the great Encyclopedia, *which embodied their rationalistic, democratic and scientific outlook. Voltaire, arm raised, (and on his left and right) Diderot, general editor (1751/72), and author–critic La Harpe. (Left and centre foreground) mathematician d'Alembert who wrote the introduction, and the revolutionary Marquis de Condorcet. (Bibliothèque Nationale, Paris)*

Paris; while *Micromégas* (1752), a story in the spirit of Swift, tells us of an imaginary monster's visit to Earth from one of the planets of Sirius.

As a young man, Voltaire had shared the optimism of his period and its conception of human progress. Then, in 1755, the terrible earthquake that destroyed Lisbon darkened his vision of the universe and inspired not only his poem on the tragedy, but his finest short story *Candide* (1759), in which he tore to pieces the specious theory, expressed by the German philosopher Leibniz, that 'everything is for the best in the best of all possible worlds.'

THE ENCYCLOPEDISTS

The War of Ideas sharpened midway through the eighteenth century; and in 1751 two great pioneers of the Enlightenment, the writer **Denis Diderot** (1713–1784) and the mathematician **Jean Le Rond d'Alembert** (1717–1783) launched the publication of the great French encyclopedia *L'Encyclopédie ou dictionnaire raissoné des sciences, des arts at des métiers*. As French was the cultural language of the day, it was distributed all over the educated Western world, and became the Enlightenment's most active force. Among its contributors were Voltaire, Jean-Jacques Rousseau and Montesquieu; while d'Alembert explained the project in his opening introduction.

The *Encyclopedia* was not merely a reference book, as we understand the word today; nor was it a survey of the latest scientific trends. It also adopted a combative attitude and produced radical opinions on politics, religion and philosophy, indeed, on almost every type of controversial subject. Now and then, its publication was banned. It was

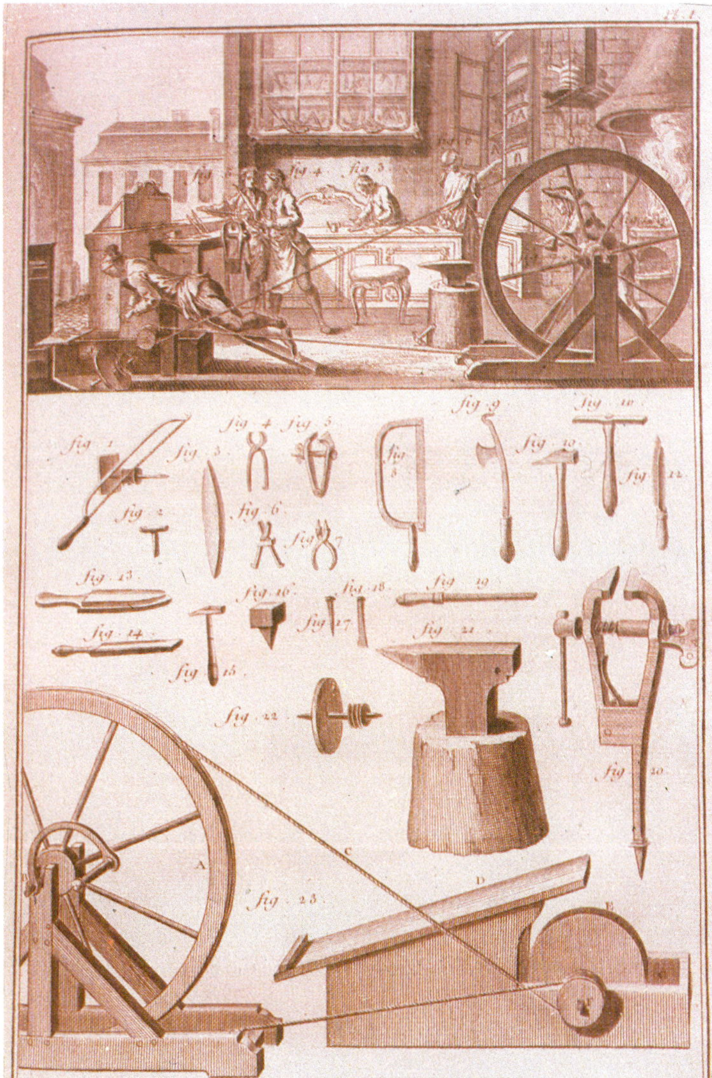

Above *Denis Diderot. As general editor of the* Encyclopedia *he wrote a diversity of articles, which included many on professional and technical subjects. A* Supplement *was added in 1776/80 to the original 28-volume set. Portrait by Franco-Flemish artist Louis-Michel van Loo (1707–1771), and* (**right**) *A Lathe Workshop, one of the superb copper engravings that appear in the section devoted to trade. (Bibliothèque Nationale, Paris)*

consigned to the papal Index of forbidden books; and not until 1772 were all twenty-eight volumes printed as a whole. Diderot was a skilful journalist and an adventurous novelist, whose *La Réligieuse* (The Nun, written in 1760, published in 1796) attacked the Church and the abuses of conventual life. At the same time, he wrote contemporary dramas, *Le Fils naturel* (1757, The Illegitimate Son) and *Le Père de famille* (1758, The Head of the Family).

'Business in the pamphlet shops in Paris is incredible. One can scarcely squeeze from the door to the counter. Nineteen-twentieths of the productions are in favour of liberty', wrote Arthur Young in his popular first-hand account of the Revolution. French engraving (1797). (Bibliothèque Nationale, Paris)

ROUSSEAU

Jean-Jacques Rousseau (1712–1778), though he, like Voltaire, must be accounted one of the revolutionary liberators of the European mind, and himself contributed to the *Encyclopedia*, was also strongly opposed to some of the principles of the Enlightenment. Rather than preach the benefits of civilization, he advocated a return to Nature; while for Reason, as a guide to human conduct, he substituted Feeling. Thus, in his first thesis, *Discours sur les sciences et les arts* (1750, On Science and Art) he denied that art and science had contributed to the purification of morality; and, in the next, he declared that social education and the right to property had destroyed Natural Man and engendered misery and strife.

In Rousseau's controversial vocabulary 'Virtue' was a favourite word; but, as the *Confessions* (written 1765/70) he produced during his later years show, he had frequently betrayed his own moral code – for example, by relegating the bastard children of his common-law wife to the Parisian Foundling Hospital where it was unlikely that they would survive.

Meanwhile, he had had a strangely bohemian career, wandering from place to place, and from employment to employment. Besides his literary genius, he had uncommon musical gifts, and in 1752 dashed off a rustic operetta, *Le Devin du village* (The Village Soothsayer), that was enthusiastically acclaimed at the Court of Louis XV. His most important books – those which secured him world-wide fame – belong to the second half of his existence. His novel, *Julie ou la nouvelle Héloïse*, was published in 1761, and almost immediately became a sort of Lovers' Bible – a paean in praise not only of amorous passion but of matrimonial fidelity. The action takes place among the foothills of the Alps; and Rousseau was one of the first of his day to describe the romantic magnificence of Alpine landscapes.

With *Du contrat social* (1762, *The Social Contract*) a theoretical essay on the origins of the modern social system, he emerged as a leader of contemporary political thought, and helped to prepare the ground for the Revolution that broke out in 1789.

Émile, ou traité de l'éducation (1762, *Émile, or On Education*) is a treatise on the education of children, and how it should be employed to protect and encourage what is best in man. Though Rousseau's programme is scarcely scientific, his underlying theories have found wide acceptance; and the book also contains Rousseau's ideas of a religious faith that is both morally elevating and entirely undogmatic.

During Rousseau's lifetime, his *Confessions* were never published as a whole. Here, in what is one of the western world's most fascinating self-portraits, he attempts valiantly, if not always quite successfully, to lay bare the deepest and darkest secrets of his mind and heart. The following extracts are from Rousseau's messages to the world in his *Discours sur l'inégalité parmi les hommes* (*Discourse on the Origin of Inequality*, second part) and *Émile*.

Top *Rousseau, philosopher, author and educationalist, contributed to the sections of the* Encyclopedia *that discussed music and political economy. He quarrelled with many of his associates – Diderot, Voltaire, and the Scottish philosopher and historian, David Hume, with whom he stayed in England during the 1760s.*

Above *'The Execution of Robespierre and his Fellow-Conspirators Against Liberty and Equality' (1794), victims of their own 'Terror'. (Bibliothèque Nationale, Paris)*

From **Discourse on Inequality**

... The first man who, having enclosed a piece of ground, bethought himself of saying 'This is mine,' and found people simple enough to believe him, was the real founder of civil society. From how many crimes, wars, and murders, from how many horrors and misfortunes might not any one have saved mankind, by pulling up the stakes, or filling up the ditch, and crying to his fellows: 'Beware of listening to this impostor; you are undone if you once forget that the fruits of the earth belong to us all, and the earth itself to nobody.'

So long as men remained content with their rustic huts, so long as they were satisified with clothes made of the skins of animals and sewn together with thorns and fish-bones, adorned themselves only with feathers and shells, and continued to paint their bodies different colours, to improve and beautify their bows and arrows, and to make with sharp-edged stones fishing boats or clumsy musical instruments; in a word, so long as they undertook only what a single person could accomplish, and confined themselves to such arts as did not require the joint labour of several hands, they lived free, healthy, honest, and happy lives, so long as their nature allowed, and as they continued to enjoy the pleasures of mutual and independent intercourse. But from the moment one man began to stand in need of the help of another; from the moment it appeared advantageous to any one man to have enough provisions for two, equality disappeared, property was introduced, work became indispensable, and vast forests became smiling fields, which man had to water with the sweat of his brow, and where slavery and misery were soon seen to germinate and grow up with the crops ...

From **Émile, or On Education**

... With the age of reason the child becomes the slave of the community; then why forestall this by slavery in the home? Let this brief hour of life be free from a yoke which nature has not laid upon it; leave the child the use of his natural liberty, which, for a time at least, secures him from the vices of the slave. Bring me those harsh masters, and those fathers who are the slaves of their children, bring them both with their frivolous objections, and before they boast of their own methods let them for once learn the method of nature.

I return to practical matters. I have already said your child must not get what he asks, but what he needs; he must never act from obedience, but from necessity.

The very words *obey* and *command* will be excluded from his vocabulary, still more those of *duty* and *obligation*; but the words strength, necessity, weakness, and constraint must have a large place in it. Before the age of reason it is impossible to form any idea of moral beings or social relations; so avoid, as far as may be, the use of words which express these ideas, lest the child at an early age should attach wrong ideas to them, ideas which you cannot or will not destroy when he is older. The first mistaken idea he gets into his head is the germ of error and vice; it is the first step that needs watching ...

Top *Illustration for Rousseau's* Julie ou la nouvelle Héloïse, *the 'lovers' Bible', after a drawing by Jean-Michel Moreau le Jeune (1788).*

Right *Illustration for* Émile, *his treatise on education, by Louis Petit (1791). Rousseau considered practical subjects such as gardening to be an essential part of a full modern education.*

FROM REALISM INTO REVOLUTION

Rousseau was not the only French writer to preach the Cult of Feeling in the Age of Reason; and, among novelists and dramatists, he had both forerunners and successors. During the seventeenth century, French fiction had grown increasingly realistic; and, later, the **Abbé Prevost** (1697–1763) produced a single masterpiece, *Manon Lescaut* (1731), his pathetic story of a courtesan's rise and fall, and of the undying passion she inspires in an impressionable young man's heart.

Meanwhile, as a dramatist, **Marivaux** (1688–1763) continued the tradition of Molière, adding light-hearted contemporary touches. **Beaumarchais** (Pierre Augustin 1732–1799), however, whose comedies, *Le Barbier de Seville* (1775), and *Le Mariage de Figaro* (1778), are today best known through Mozart's and Rossini's operas, took a bolder and more dangerous line, showing the poor as outspoken critics of the rich; and *Figaro*, at first banned by the French government, was not permitted to appear until 1784, when the Revolution was already fast approaching. During those bloody years, literature was almost silenced; and the only considerable young poet of the age, **André Chénier** (1762–1794), was sent to the guillotine in 1794. On his way to the scaffold, he struck his forehead, exclaiming *'J'avais pourtant quelque chose là!'* – 'Yet I did have something there!'

Top *Marivaux's comedies were written with a graceful subtlety –* 'marivaudage' *– which was to inspire the later dramatists Giraudoux and Anouilh. He also produced a French imitation of Addison's* Spectator *in 1722/23. Portrait by L-M. van Loo.*
Above left *Scene from an 18th-century production of Mozart's opera from Beaumarchais's* The Marriage of Figaro. *(Musée de la Comédie Française, Paris)*

'STURM UND DRANG' AND THE CLASSIC SPIRIT

While Frenchmen had begun to lament the coarseness of Molière, German audiences had scarcely outgrown their taste for clowns and tight-rope dancers. In Germany, the influence of the Middle Ages was not quickly overcome; and, during the sixteenth century, the religious verse of the Reformation alone had any real poetic value. The terrible wars that swept Germany in the seventeenth century next impeded literary progress. But *Der abenteuerliche Simplicissimus Teutsch* (1669, *Simplicissimus*) by **H.J.C. von Grimmelshausen** (1625?–1676) is a realistic picaresque novel, a story of the Thirty Years' War that gives us a vivid picture of contemporary brutality and confusion. Otherwise, the only noteworthy German writer of the period was the philosopher **G.W. von Leibniz** (1646–1716), whose optimistic conviction that 'everything was for the best in the best of all possible worlds' would be memorably ridiculed by Voltaire; and who wrote not in German but in French, just as the great Dutch–Jewish philosopher **Baruch Spinoza** (1632–1677) had decided to write his treatise *Ethica ordine geometrica demonstrata* (1677) in Latin.

Anxious to realize the contemporary ideal of the Enlightened Sovereign, Frederick II of Prussia (1712–1786) summoned to his Court a succession of poets and philosophers, among them, Voltaire. But it was not part of his plan to create a German culture, for he himself wrote in French and regarded French civilization as his great example. A major task thus awaited his compatriots – to give the Enlightenment a truly German shape; and a school arose that sought to reject the influence of modern France and turn back to the Ancient World and the German heritage itself. The main leader of this movement was **F.G. Klopstock** (1724–1803), who wrote *Messias* (1748, *The Messiah*), Germany's first important epic modelled on Antiquity. He was also indebted to the Scottish

Top *From Jacques Callot's series of etchings (1633) on the miseries of the Thirty Years' War which Grimmelshausen also vividly depicted in his* Simplicissimus. *(Army Museum, Stockholm)*
Above *Spinoza, the philosopher whose* Ethics *proclaimed that goodness and piety brought their own reward. (Bibliothèque Nationale, Paris)*

'Laocoön and his Sons' by El Greco (c. 1680) reinterprets a famous 1st-century BC group of statuary, now at the Vatican Museum. Rediscovered (in Rome) in 1506, the anonymous work depicted the fate of Laocoön, Apollo's priest in Troy who, with his sons, was attacked and killed by serpents, on the god's orders. The sculpture was hailed as a masterpiece of classical art and became a focus of debate among German aestheticians of the mid-18th century, such as Winckelmann and Lessing, both of whom saw the ancient work as a model of heroic grandeur. El Greco's passionate painting would seem to anticipate the 'storm and stress' of German literature in the 1770s, which Lessing influenced but did not approve. (National Gallery of Art, Washington DC)

Ossianic poems and borrowed some visions of the Romantic False-Dawn.

Gotthold Ephraim Lessing (1729–1781) was another writer who successfully devoted himself to adopting what was best in the Enlightenment, but remained a patriot who sought to develop an independent German literature. In the field of aesthetics, he produced a valuable thesis *Laokoön* (1766) defining the limits of poetry and art. But it was the drama he loved best; and the publication of his *Hamburgische Dramaturgie* (1767/68), was an epoch-making event in the history of dramatic criticism.

To the new German drama, Lessing himself contributed *Miss Sara Sampson* (1755), a middle-class tragedy, and *Minna von Barnhelm* (1767), a comedy in the French style, but with German overtones, its hero, Major von Tellheim representing the noblest aspect of the Prussian officer-class; while *Nathan der Weise* (1779, Nathan the Wise), set in Jerusalem at the time of the Crusades is an enlightened plea for spiritual and racial tolerance.

Among exemplars of the so-called New Classicism the most representative name is that of the art-historian **Johann Winckelmann** (1717–1768); and, simultaneously, the new Romantic trends found expression through the literary school called *Sturm und Drang* (Storm and Stress) after a play by **Maximilian von Klinger** (1752–1831), whose followers reacted against French literary rules and preached the independence of creative genius. The German Romantic Movement also received a decisive impetus from the works of **J.G. Herder** (1744– 1803). A poet and philosopher, he collected folk-songs and advocated the foundation of a national school of poetry.

Yet, despite the growth of the Romantic spirit, the eighteenth century's belief in Reason was never wholly superseded. Its basis was *Kritik der reinen Vernunft* (1781, *The Critique of Pure Reason*) that we owe to **Immanuel Kant** (1724–1804). It has been said that human thought has probably never reached further than when Kant set out to determine its basis.

Lessing started his Laokoön: on the Boundaries of Painting and Poetry *(1766) from a comment by Winckelmann on Virgil's treatment of the story and its interpretation by an anonymous classical sculptor. Whereas the sculptor showed the victims suffering their torment with nobility, the poet described their agonized screams, which, Lessing argued, showed the different attitudes that the poet and the sculptor adopted. Portrait (c. 1760) by J.H. Tischbein the Elder.*

Johann Winckelmann, the German writer on archaeology and aesthetics whose works such as The History of Ancient Art among the Greeks *(1764) formulated a long-unchallenged view of Greek art that stressed its 'noble simplicity' and 'tranquil grandeur'. Portrait by Anton Maron. (Schlossmuseum, Weimar, E. Germany)*

GOETHE

Above *Goethe, the universal genius of his age, was not only the greatest figure in German literature but a scientist who published revolutionary theories on the optics of colour perception and on plant morphology. His career as a writer covered nearly a century of German literature, from his rococo and romantic periods to his anticipations of symbolic realism in the* Novellen *(1827). A silhouette of 1816. (Goethe Museum, Frankfurt-am-Main)*

Right *The young Goethe takes farewell of Friederike Brion, who inspired his youthful lyrics but whom he was to betray. Illustration by Eugen Klimsch (1886).*

Below *Design for* Erlkönig *by Lotte Reiniger (1899–1981).*

As a young author, **Johann Wolfgang von Goethe** (1749–1832) had shared the feelings of the *Sturm und Drang* school, but, later, worked towards an artistic harmony that he distinguished in the Greek classics. By doing so, critics have suggested, he may have impaired his youthful talents, with the result that the young Goethe is superior to the old. This, however, is a largely misleading conclusion. The blood of the young genius still coursed through the older man's veins.

Goethe's early novel, *Die Leiden des jungen Werthers* (1774, The Sufferings of Young Werther) voices the emotions of *Sturm und Drang* at their most vehement. A short novel about a young man who rebels against the conventions of society and finally kills himself for love, it expresses the poignant sufferings of youth. There is a period in every young man's life, said Goethe, when he imagines that the story must have been written for his especial benefit.

The same rebellious and impulsive mood pervades Goethe's youthful drama *Götz von Berlichingen* (1771/73, *Iron Hand*), a play set in the Middle Ages, that depicts its knightly hero's struggle against authority.

In his poems, Goethe unreservedly gave the world almost all he had to give. Despite his scholarly, even pedantic disposition, he was a typical Man of Feeling, constantly involved in passionate love affairs; and his betrayal as a young man of the priest's daughter, Friederike Brion, left behind it a haunting sense of guilt that afterwards, when he composed *Faust*, inspired the tragic Gretchen episode.

In 1775, Goethe entered the service of the Duke of Weimar and rose to ministerial rank. His poetic works were now more disciplined; and, during the next few years at Weimar, he published a prose drama *Iphigenie auf Tauris* (1787), as well as a play about the Netherlandish hero *Egmont* (1787) and some of his most vigorous poems, including ballads such as *Der Fischer* (The Fisherman), *Erlkönig* (The Fairy King) and, on a larger scale his famous *Über allen Gipfeln* (Above the Treetops) from *Wanderers Nachtlied II* (1815, Traveller's Night Song).

To escape from his passion for Charlotte von Stein, he spent the years 1786–88 in Italy, and then, having returned to Weimar, settled down as an industrious official, married Christiane Vulpis, and, encouraged to some extent by his friend Schiller, began a period of

rich creative activity, during which, as his verse drama *Torquato Tasso* (1790) and his Homeric epic *Hermann und Dorothea* (1796/97) show, he moved more and more deliberately towards a classic style. To this period also belong his sensuous *Römische Elegien* (Roman Elegies) and *Venezianische Epigramme*.

Goethe's autobiography, *Aus meinem Leben. Dichtung und Wahrheit* (From My Life: Poetry and Truth) appeared after his sixtieth birthday; while the poems he published in *West-östlicher Diwan* (1819, *The West-Eastern Divan*) when he was already seventy show that he was still prepared to plunge into new amorous experiences. *Selige Sehnsucht* (*Blessed Yearning*) from *Buch des Sängers* (*The Book of the Singer*) follows:

In coolness of those nights of love
Which thee begat, bade thee beget,
Strange promptings wake in thee and
move,
While the calm taper glimmers yet . . .

Distance can hinder not thy flight;
Exiled, thou seekest a point illumed
And, last, enamoured of the light,
A moth, art in the flame consumed.

Throughout the years, Goethe worked on his verse drama *Faust*, which

Goethe admiring the Colosseum in Rome. His visit to Italy in 1786 was of fundamental importance in his life and has become one of the classic events in the history of German literature. The art, archaeology and architecture, the very idea of Italy experienced at first hand, made an immense impression on his mind, and is recorded in such works as his Römische Elegien *(1788/90) and his later* Italienische Reise *(1816/17,* Italian Journey*). Painting by J.P. Hackert (1787). Goethe Museum, Frankfurt)*

Below left *Scene from Part I of Goethe's* Faust, *with the ill-fated Gretchen, Faust and Mephistopheles, evoked by the painter and illustrator Julius Schnorr von Carolsfeld (1794–1872). (Austrian National Gallery, Vienna)*

Below right *Alternative interpretation of the main characters of* Faust. *His deserted love Friederike Brion is said to have inspired some 'Gretchen' episodes. From a set of lithographs (1828) by Eugène Delacroix.*

he had begun in 1772 and did not complete until 1831, the year before his death. It is based on the old story of the scientist who, to acquire knowledge, forms a secret bargain with the Devil. But Goethe takes it a great deal further. The agreement that Doctor Faustus signs with his blood puts at his service Mephistopheles, the Prince of the Underworld, who offers him, not only knowledge, but all that he desires of worldly sensations and delights; while Mephistopheles is entitled to claim his soul the moment he is satisfied with what he has achieved and wishes time

to stand still – that is to say, when he has reached a point where the human soul has ceased to struggle and aspire.

The second part of Faust is less dramatic than the first; it has a haunted, brooding atmosphere, that reflects the ageing poet's struggles to solve the riddle of existence. Here Faust is transported through time and space, and demands no less a consort than the beautiful Helen, who gives birth to a son, Euphorion – a symbol of Goethe's yearning for the Ancient World. But the moment Mephistopheles has long expected, when he will hear his predestined victim cry 'Wait!', does not occur until Faust watches the inhabitants of a rugged northern coastline fighting to protect their fields. Faust's course, however, is not yet fully run. He is acquitted by a heavenly court, and wafted up to blessedness by Gretchen, the love of his youth, now the representative of 'Eternal Woman', destined to redeem the human race.

Goethe's main theme in *Faust* is Man's salvation through activity. It has been called 'the drama of Western Man', since it insists that 'freedom and life' can only be achieved by a man's own unceasing efforts.

What is most fascinating in Goethe is his huge range. Besides being a great poet and strikingly original thinker, he was an outstanding scientist and a practical politician. Right into old age, moreover, his senses remained alert, and his heart always retained its capacity to love.

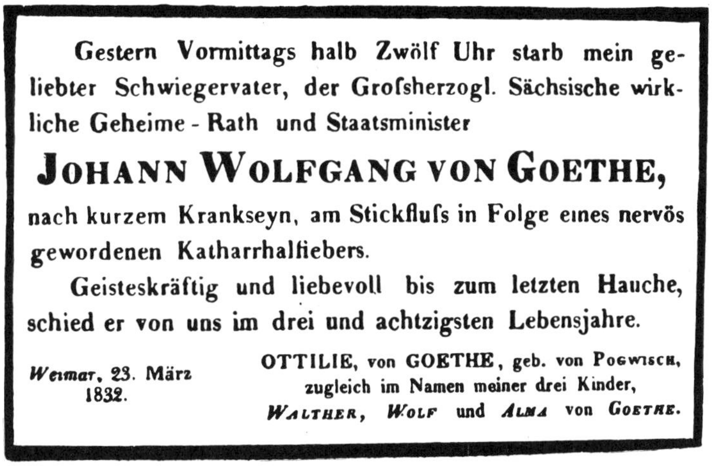

Gestern Vormittags halb Zwölf Uhr starb mein geliebter Schwiegervater, der Groſsherzogl. Sächsische wirkliche Geheime-Rath und Staatsminister

JOHANN WOLFGANG VON GOETHE,

nach kurzem Krankseyn, am Stickfluſs in Folge eines nervös gewordenen Katharrhalfiebers.

Geisteskräftig und liebevoll bis zum letzten Hauche, schied er von uns im drei und achtzigsten Lebensjahre.

Weimar, 23. März 1832.

OTTILIE, von GOETHE, geb. von POGWISCH, zugleich im Namen meiner drei Kinder, *WALTHER*, *WOLF* und *ALMA* von *GOETHE*.

Above *The ageing Goethe, of whom Napoleon said after meeting him at Erfurt. 'Voila un homme!' – 'There is a man!'. Drawing by Gebbers.*

Right *Goethe died at Weimar, announced his daughter-in-law Ottilie, after a short illness, 'alert of mind and loving to his last breath.'*

SCHILLER

Top right *Friedrich von Schiller in 1793, shortly before he began a fruitful and creative friendship with Goethe and in 1799 moved to Weimar. The youthful poet began his career in the Stuttgart Military Academy but was not cut out for a soldier. Portrait by Ludowika Simonowitz (Schiller Nationalmuseum, Marbach, W. Germany)*
Above *In 1789 Schiller became professor of history at Jena and married the following year. The poet-professor-husband in pensive mood here, on one of his country rides.*

The talent of **Friedrich von Schiller** (1759–1805), though equally original, was not so far-reaching. But, whereas Goethe's hatred of tyranny had faded with time, it remained a distinguishing feature of Schiller's outlook – perhaps because for seven long years in his youth he had been a pupil at a German military school.

Schiller's greatest contribution was to the drama; and the title-page of his first play, *Die Räuber* (1781, The Robbers), bears the Latin dedication *'in tyrannos'* – against tyrants. With many variations on *Sturm und Drang* themes, the work combines an ardent plea for freedom; and, a hundred years later in *Son of a Servant* (1886/87), Strindberg would describe how he had first felt its influence. The hero, a kind of Teutonic Robin Hood, steals from the rich to relieve the sufferings of the poor. After its opening night, Schiller was exiled from the petty dukedom where he then lived; and although, later, out of sheer necessity he was forced to seek princely patronage, he would never cease to express his strongly libertarian views – in such plays as *Fiesco* (1781/82), *Kabale und Liebe* (1784, Intrigues and Love) and particularly in *Don Carlos* (1787). The last-mentioned play, which shows the Spanish Crown Prince and his friend, Marquis Posa, carrying on a struggle for civic rights and religious tolerance, also does justice to the opposition. The arch-despot, King Philip II, is one of Schiller's most impressive and convincing characters.

As a working dramatist, Schiller broke many of the rules of French theatrical composition – for example, the 'Unities' of time and place. Meanwhile, his mood grew less Romantic, and he did his best to write in what he himself considered to have been the harmonious and objective spirit of Antiquity. His critical essays, among them *Über naive und sentimentalische Dichtung* (1795/96, On Naive and Sentimental Poetry) achieved European fame; and his historical dramas – the *Wallenstein* trilogy (1798/99), *Maria Stuart* (1800), *Wilhelm Tell* (1804) and others show him putting his theories into practice. They illustrate both his youthful passion for freedom and his considered adult vision of the world, and have a truly classic grace.

In his poems, *Die Künstler* (1788/89, The Artists), *Das Lied von der Glocke* (1799, Song of the Clock), *An die Freude* (Ode to Joy), Schiller was equally concerned with ideas – on the task of art and the brotherhood of mankind; and the last inspired the final chorus of Beethoven's 'Ninth Symphony'.

In Germany, the period of Lessing, Goethe and Schiller was the equivalent of the Classic Age in France – an epoch when some of a nation's noblest qualities assumed distinctive literary form.

As Goethe observed, Schiller's constant theme was freedom. His famous 'Ode to Joy' (1786), used by Beethoven in his 'Choral (Ninth) Symphony', is a triumphant hymn to the free human spirit, and it was his passion for liberty that forced him into exile.
Above right *Contemporary Hamburg production of* William Tell *(1804), his drama that proclaimed the theme of romantic revolution. (Goethe Museum, Düsseldorf)*
Above *William Tell and his son, from a fresco in the church of Burglen, where the Swiss hero is said to have been born.*

Die
Räuber.
Ein Schauspiel
von fünf Akten,
herausgegeben
von
Friderich Schiller.
in Tirannos
Zwote verbesserte Auflage.
Frankfurt und Leipzig.
bei Tobias Löffler.
1782.

Title-page for the 'second revised edition' of Schiller's play Die Räuber (The Robbers) *published in Frankfurt and Leipzig in 1782. The division of Germany into scores of independent principalities, though it offended the growing sense of German national identity, had its obvious advantages. Whereas the ducal authorities of Mannheim, where* Die Räuber *had its* première *in January 1782, had found its libertarian principles subversive, the work was welcomed in the free self-governing city of Frankfurt and elsewhere. (Schiller Nationalmuseum, Marbach, W. Germany)*

From **The Life of Schiller** by Thomas Carlyle (1823/24)

He had a mind of the highest order, grand by nature, and cultivated by the assiduous study of a lifetime. It is not the predominating force of any one faculty that impresses us in Schiller, but the general force of all. Every page of his writings bears the stamp of internal vigour, new truths, new aspects of known truth, bold thought, happy imagery, lofty emotions. Schiller would have been no common man though he had altogether wanted the qualities peculiar to poets. His intellect is clear, deep, and comprehensive, its deductions, frequently elicited from numerous and distant premises, are presented under a magnificent aspect, in the shape of theorems embracing an immense multitude of minor propositions. Yet it seems powerful and vast, rather than quick or keen, for Schiller is not notable for his wit, though his fancy is ever prompt with its metaphors, illustrations, comparisons, to decorate and point the perceptions of reason ...

Perhaps his greatest faculty was half poetical, half philosophical imagination: a faculty teeming with magnificence and brilliancy, now adorning, now aiding to erect, a stately pyramid of scientific speculation; now brooding over the abysses of thought and feeling, 'til thoughts and feelings, else unutterable, were embodied in expressive forms and palaces and landscapes glowing in ethereal beauty rose like exhalations from the bosom of the deep ...

Schiller's heart was at once fiery and tender, impetuous, soft, affectionate, his enthusiasm clothed the Universe with grandeur, and sent his spirit forth to explore its secrets and mingle warmly in its interests ...

The young Schiller, still in his military uniform, reads from Die Räuber *to a group of friends. But he had left his army medical post without leave to attend the first night of his play in Mannheim, and this, combined with government objections to the play's theme, forced him to leave his regiment. Painting by* C.A. von Heideloff *(1855), from a drawing by his father who took part in the reading. (Schiller Nationalmuseum, Marbach, W. Germany)*

Below *Beethoven's dedication of his: 'Symphony with final chorus on Schiller's ode: To Joy' (the Ninth Symphony) to Friedrich Wilhelm III of Prussia.*

During his last fifteen years he wrote his noblest works; yet ... no day of that period could have passed without its load of pain. Pain could not turn him from his purpose or shake his equanimity; in death itself he was calmer and calmer ...

On the whole we may pronounce him happy. (The) kingdoms which Schiller conquered were not for one nation at the expense of suffering to another; they were soiled by no patriot's blood, no widow's, no orphan's tear; they are kingdoms conquered from the barren void of darkness ... a 'possession for ever' to all the generations of the Earth.

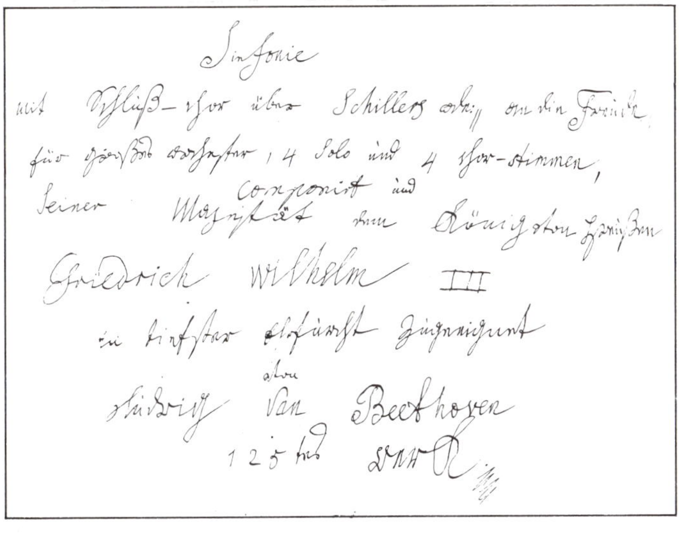

Sinfonie
mit Schluß-Chor über Schillers Ode: an die Freude
für großes Orchester, 4 Solo und 4 Chor-stimmen,
componirt und
Seiner Majestät dem Könige von Preußen
Friedrich Wilhelm III
in tiefster Ehrfurcht zugeeignet
von
Ludwig van Beethoven
125tes Werk

'BARBARITY ALONE WAS ONCE PATRIOTIC'

Georg Stiernhielm, 'The Father of Swedish Poetry', who requested the following to be inscribed on his tombstone: Vixit, dum vixit, leatus – *He lived happily, as long as he lived. Portrait by D.K. Ehrenstrahl (1663). (Gripsholm Castle, near Stockholm)*

During the sixteenth and seventeenth centuries, Swedish writers – and the situation was much the same in Denmark and Norway – had still to forge their literary weapons; and in Sweden the master-smiths were **Olaus Petri** (1493–1552), the translator of the Bible, and **Georg Stiernhielm** (1598–1672), whose epic *Hercules* (1648) has been called the first work of art in Swedish literature. Scandinavian languages were not adapted to a literary purpose until the eighteenth century; nor, apart from a small cultivated élite at Court, was the reading-public numerous.

Even the great dramatist of Norway and Denmark, **Ludvig Holberg** (1684–1759), is not widely known in other parts of Europe, though he was greatly admired both in his two native countries and in Sweden. Born in Bergen, he began his adult life as an official and pedagogue, then took his first steps as a writer with the comic epic *Peder Paars* (1719/20). While he lived in Copenhagen, he wrote no fewer than fifteen comedies in eighteen months, including *The Political Theorizer* (1723), his masterpiece *Jeppe on the Mountain* (1722) – about the peasant who woke up in the Baron's bed and became a gentleman for a day – *The Fidget* and *Erasmus Montanus* (both *c.*1724/27), the latter deriding the pomposity of learned men.

Holberg's master was Molière; and, according to the custom of his day, much of his work is unselfconsciously derivative. But, as often as he creates characters and describes their backgrounds, he shows true originality. It has been said that, if all other evidence had been destroyed, it would be possible to find in his work almost every detail of life in contemporary Copenhagen. His dialogue, too, reveals his understanding of life, shown, for example, in the remark made by one of his dramatis personae: 'People around here say that Jeppe drinks; but they never say *why* Jeppe drinks ...'

A product of the European Enlightenment, the Swede **Carl von Linné** (1707–1778) – **Linnaeus** – became famous all over the Western world as a scientist and botanist; and, in Sweden, his works, particularly his accounts of his scientific travels, became a cornerstone of prose literature.

Emanuel Swedenborg (1688–1772), on the other hand, illustrates the struggle between scientific rationalism and visionary mysticism. In *Arcana coelestia* (1749, *Arcana or Heavenly Mysteries*), *De coelo et eius mirabilibus et de inferno* (1758, *Heaven and Hell*), *De cultu et amore Dei* (1745, *On the Worship and Love of God*) he combines metaphysical speculation with an almost comically detailed description of the after-life. Thus, in Paradise, according to Swedenborg, the blessed enjoy a heavenly replica of earthly meals and social pastimes; even wines are offered to the faithful. Swedenborg wrote in Latin, which enabled him to extend his religious message throughout the whole of Europe.

At home, Sweden's national poet, **Carl Michael Bellman** (1740–1795) is celebrated for, among much else, his drinking-songs; but the fact that his verse is difficult to translate into other languages has so far dimmed his reputation.

Right *Linnaeus, the Swedish botanist founder of the modern system of nomenclature. The Linnean Society of London (1788) purchased his collections. Statue by A. Almqvist, at Lund in Sweden.*

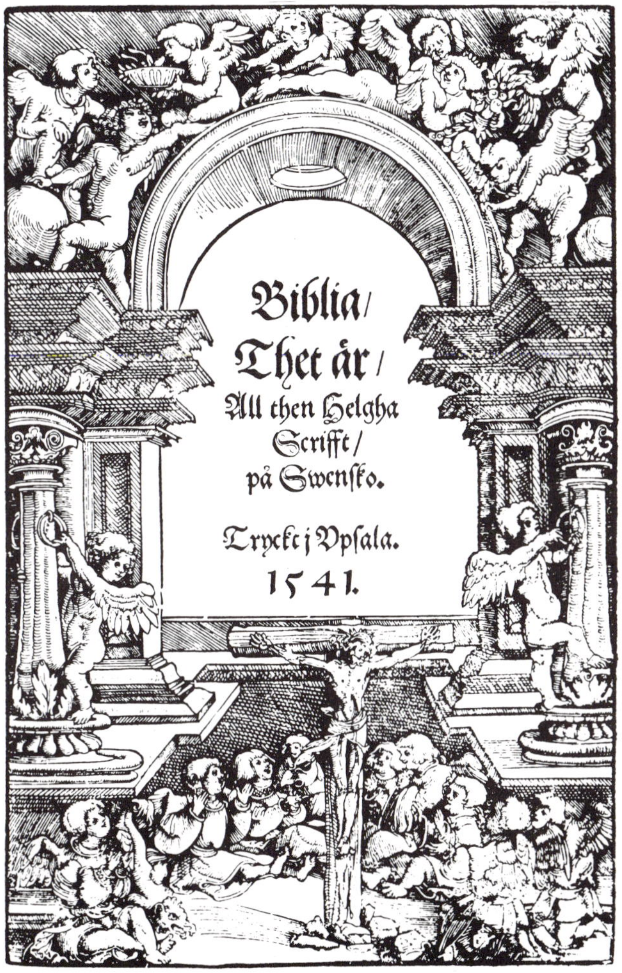

Title-page of the 'Gustav Vasa' Bible of 1541, the first complete translation of the Bible into Swedish. It was printed in Uppsala. (Royal Library, Stockholm)

Right *Emanuel Swedenborg, mystic and visionary, was in the view of the poet Kellgren 'an absolute fool', while to Goethe, Emerson and Strindberg, he was one of the great human spirits. Portrait by Per Krafft. (Nationalmuseum, Stockholm)*

Far right *C.M. Bellman, poet-musician and literary adviser to King Gustav III, wrote drinking songs and biblical parodies. Portrait (1781) by Pehr Hilleström the Elder. (Nationalmuseum, Stockholm)*

Below *'Death' is often a guest in Bellman's drinking parties; see the coffin in his illustration (1793) of his own song* The Temple of Bacchus. *(Royal Library, Stockholm)*

DRAMA AND NOVEL

During the Mongolian Yuan Dynasty (1280–1368), traditional Chinese drama developed into the kind of operatic performance that, despite the Social Revolution, is still staged today.

Another literary form that reached its peak during the Mongolian period, and the Ming, and Ching (Qing) Dynasties (1368–1911), was the novel, which was usually circulated by itinerant story-tellers.

The Chinese themselves often speak of 'the four great novels': *San kuo* (*San Guo Zhi Yanyi*) – (The Romance of the Three Kingdoms), a fourteenth-century picaresque romance by an unknown author, and the three sixteenth-century novels *Shui hu chuan* (*Shui Hu Zhuan*) – (The Water Margin), by **Kin Seng-tan**, (**Jin Shengtan**), *Si yu ki* (*Xi You Ji*) – (*The Journey to the West*, or *Monkey*) by **Wu Cheng-en**, (**Wu Chengen**), and the anonymous and somewhat pornographic picture of contemporary life, *Chin Ping Mei* (*Jin Ping Mei*) – (The Golden Lotus). Later, in the eighteenth century, a fifth famous prose work appeared: *Hung Lou Meng* (*Hong Lou Meng*) – (The Dream of the Red Chamber) by **Tsao chan** (**Cao Zhan**), an extensive family chronicle, based on an older novel entitled *The Tale of a Rock*.

From the Western reader's point of view, these gigantic books do not make easy reading; for they combine touches of bold realism with fragments of Chinese history, ghost stories and traditional folk-tale; and not until the present century were most of them translated for the first time.

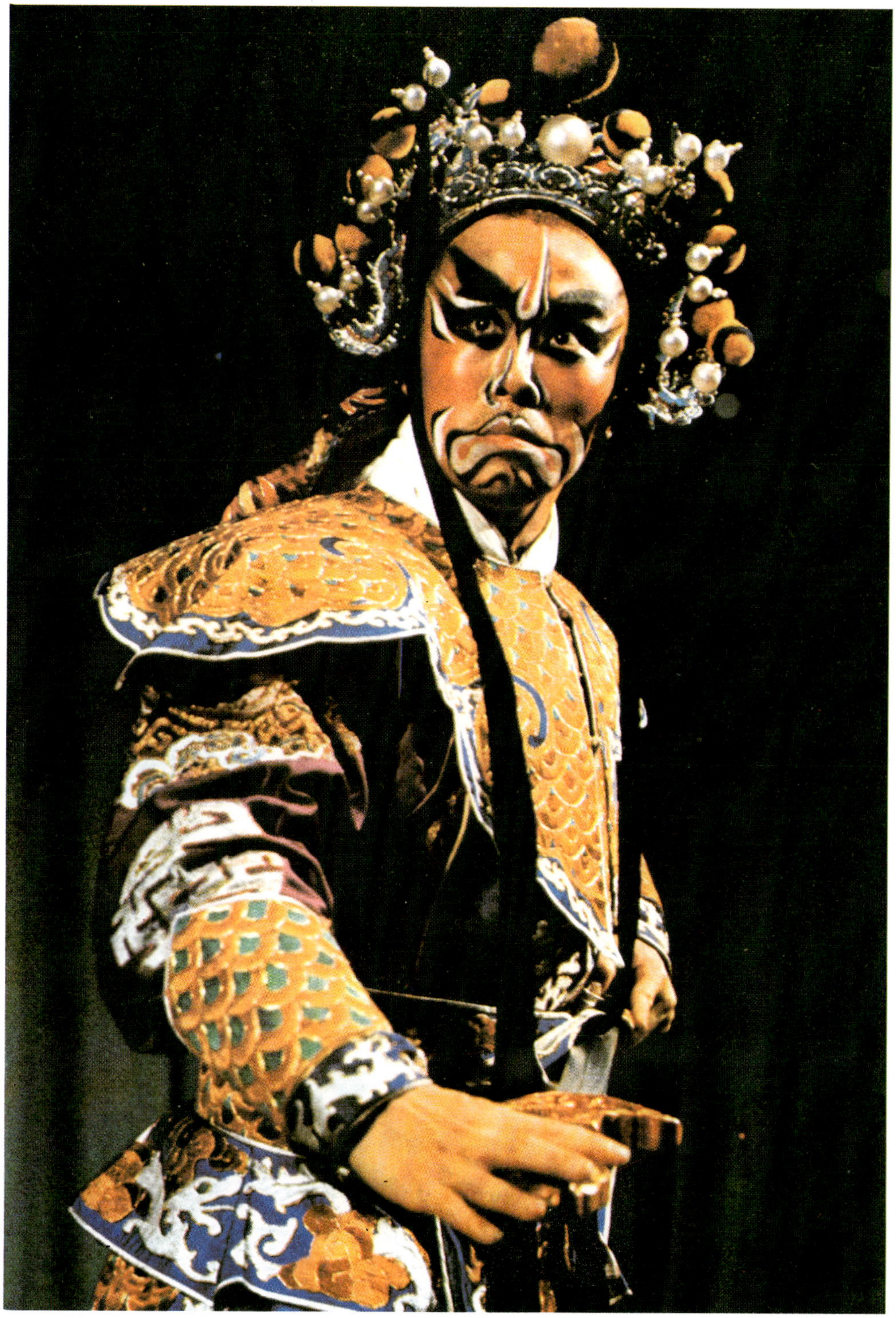

The traditions of Peking Opera reach back to the 14th century. The make-up, masks and costumes are strongly stylized, so that the character is immediately recognizable. Female roles are traditionally played by men.

'ANYWHERE OUT OF THE WORLD!'

Freedom, Equality and Fraternity had been the dreams of the French Revolution; but they were never fully realized. After a brief period of splendid hope and promise, when, an English Romantic poet declared, it was joy to be alive, high-minded visionaries such as Robespierre and Saint-Just organized a bloody Reign of Terror, which continued until they themselves were beheaded, and a young Corsican officer, Napoleon Bonaparte, began the ruthless and triumphant career that took him at last to the Imperial Throne. He made France a powerful military state. But then, in 1815, on the field of Waterloo, his 'eagles were felled', and the conqueror vanished into exile.

After the fall of Napoleon and the restoration of what Byron called 'the dull, stupid old system' of monarchical government, the hopes both of adventurous young men and of liberal idealists faded; with the result that they sought in literature a relief and stimulus they could no longer find in life.

The nature of Romanticism is difficult to define; for the early-nineteenth century Romantic Movement assumed a host of different forms. Romantic feelings had always existed; but only at this moment in history did they acquire so strong a colouring and cover so wide a field.

One of the chief characteristics of Romantic literature was its preoccupation with a legendary past, which seemed to offer a refuge from the vulgar present day. Poets, novelists and painters alike were fascinated by the Middle Ages. But, at the same time, they were obsessed by the idea of freedom; and the artist became a rebel, perpetually in revolt against conservative society, yearning after a spiritual independence that the current age denied him. He was a passionate individualist, determined to satisfy the demands of his own genius, and carry every emotion he felt to the furthest possible extent. The prosaic reasonableness of his eighteenth-century predecessors he habitually despised. Imagination was a gift that he valued above all else.

'The Shipwreck' (c. 1805) by J.M.W. Turner, who brought a power and passion to the European tradition of marine painting that was typically Romantic. His huge output included numerous paintings based on literary sources. In the early 1800s he admired Poussin's work which he saw at the Louvre's exhibition of Napoleon's looted pictures, unlike Ruskin who praised the new style, singling out Turner for admiration. (Tate Gallery, London)

German Romanticism acquired its special character from the philosophical bias of the men who helped to launch it; the last bastions of the Enlightenment were over-thrown by professional philosophers. Among them was Kant's favoured pupil, **J. G. Fichte** (1762–1814), whose work encouraged the national liberation movement, and whose *Reden an die deutsche Nation* (1808, Speech to the German Nation), delivered at Berlin University during the French occupation, became the manifesto of resistance. His views on the creative ego also played an important part in the development of German Romantic writing. Simultaneously **Friedrich von Schelling** (1775–1854) appeared, his main theme being that Nature itself is inspired, contrary to the mechanistic opinions held during the Age of Enlightenment. Both for him and for the Romantic writers, the universe was not a machine, but a sentient organism.

On the borderline between philosophy and literature are **Friedrich von Schlegel** (1772–1829) and his brother, **Wilhelm von Schlegel** (1767–1845) who together may be said to have founded the Romantic school in Germany. Its centre was Jena, where they gathered their sympathizers round them, and lectured and published their works. Wilhelm's translation of Shakespeare was probably the Schlegels' greatest feat.

Ludwig Tieck (1773–1853) showed more imaginative talent than the Schlegels, though many of his productions show the Romantic Movement at its worst – its unrestrained

For Schelling (**above**), *art was the most important of all human activities. He had a deep influence on the Romantics, for this reason and because of his insistence that Nature itself was inspired, in contrast to the mechanistic views of the Enlightenment. Portrait by J.K. Stieler. (Bayerische Staatsgemäldesammlungen, München)*

Left *The German countryside in Autumn. The modern love of landscape with its concern for Nature owes much to the Romantics.*

'The Pied Piper of Hamelin' is based on a legend dating back to the 13th century. It has been suggested that it may have connections with the Children's Crusade of 1212, when some 20,000 children followed their young leader from Cologne . . . mostly to their death. Illustration by B. Löffler for a 1902 edition of the song-book Des Knaben Wunderhorn. *(Royal Library, Stockholm)*

verbosity, tendency to sentimental over-statement and infatuation with the Middle Ages. Of his comedies, the most living are *Der gestiefelte Kater* (1797, Master Cat in Boots) and *Prinz Zerbino* (1799), plays distinguished by what was then called 'romantic irony', which meant that the poet did not always pretend to be entirely serious, and often lightened the atmosphere with a slight sardonic smile.

Friedrich von Hardenberg (1772–1801), better-known under his pseudonym **Novalis**, also belonged to the earlier Romantic school. Like so many writers of the time, he died young; and his achievement was fragmentary; but his works contain a rare distillation of the true Romantic spirit; while, in his unfinished novel, *Heinrich von Ofterdingen* (1802), he created a famous symbol, 'the Blue Flower', which conveyed the Romantic poet's longing for some subliminal state of being that awaited us far beyond our everyday existence.

The city of Heidelberg was the starting-point of a somewhat younger literary group, that had fewer philosophical interests but more poetic leanings. It produced no single great poet; and its chief monument is a collection of folk-songs, called *Des Knaben Wunderhorn* (1806/08, The Boy's Magic Horn), made by **Ludwig Joachim von Arnim** (1781–1831) and **Clemens Brentano** (1778–1842), whose own works include numerous echoes of traditional folk-songs and the ancient folk-tales.

Echoes of the folk-tale are also to be heard in *Peter Schlemihls wundersame Geschichte* (1814, The Amazing Story of Peter Schlemihl) by **Adelbert von Chamisso** (1781–1838), the story of the man who lost his shadow, which, though disguised as a simple fairy-tale, has a profound psychological significance that has kept it alive as a 'minor classic' until the present day.

Among the Heidelberg Romantics, the most genuinely creative poet was **Joseph von Eichendorff** (1788–1857). He, too, was inspired by the charm of folk-songs, particularly by their sensitive approach to Nature. At his best, he describes the pleasures and adventures of a wandering life; and much of his freshest verse is scattered through his delightful story, *Aus dem Leben eines Taugenichts* (1826, *Memoirs of a Good-for-Nothing*):

God when on Man great love
bestowing
Over the wide world bids him rove.
Unto him all marvels showing
In stream and field and hill and grove.

The lazy who at home are lying
Are cheered not, by morn's early red,
Know naught save nursling children
crying
And care and fear and thoughts of
bread.

Eichendorff had a happy harmonious nature; and even his strain of melancholy is untinged with bitterness, and merely reflects the Romantic longing for some unattainable beatitude.

A third group of writers arose in Schwaben, where the poet **Ludwig Uhland** (1787–1862) wrote ballads about his native landscape, with its memories of medieval legends.

Meanwhile, in the field of literary scholarship, an important contribution was made by the brothers **Jakob Grimm** (1785–1863) and **Wilhelm Grimm** (1786–1859), whose magnificent collection of traditional German fairy-tales, *Kinder- und Hausmärchen* (1812/14 *Grimm's Fairy Tales*), retold with great imaginative energy and a poetic feeling for the use of language, has become one of the most widely read children's books in European literature.

'Hansel and Gretel at the Gingerbread House', one of Hermann Vogel's illustrations for an 1894 German edition of the Grimm brothers' timeless Fairy Tales. *Within ten years of the original publication, the famous caricaturist George Cruickshank had illustrated an English translation. (Royal Library, Stockholm)*

VON KLEIST

The three leading German Romantics – the dramatist von Kleist, the storyteller Hoffmann and the poet Hölderlin – were not members of any literary coterie or group. In his own life, **Heinrich von Kleist** (1777–1811) was a dramatic figure constantly torn by inward conflicts that eventually drove him to commit suicide. He was passionately disturbed by his country's sufferings before its liberation, and himself fought as a soldier against Napoleon. In his plays, although he chose Romantic themes, he maintained a gravely realistic tone; and, whether his heroine is the Amazonian Queen *Penthesilia* (1808) or the medieval *Das Käthchen von Heilbronn* (1810, tr. in *Fiction and Fancy of German Romance*, 1927), she is a living personage, carefully observed. His best-known dramatic works are the popular realistic comedy *Der zerbrochene Krug* (1808, *The Broken Jug*) and the tragedy *Prinz Friedrich von Homburg* (1810), of which the main theme is a soldier's sense of duty.

Von Kleist also produced a masterpiece of narrative prose in his long short story, *Michael Kohlhaas* (1808), where an honest peasant is driven to revolt against the injustices that he has undergone – a poignant tale, told with calm realism, of the struggle between the individual and society.

Left *Von Kleist, the vigour of whose work recalls the 'storm and stress' period while its searching psychology anticipates the plays of Büchner. Portrait (1801) by Wilhelmina von Zenge. (Staatsbibliothek, West Berlin)*

Right Die Marquise von O, *von Kleist's erotic novella, was first published with his collected stories (1810/11). This scene from Erich Rohmer's film of 1976, 'The Marquise of O', shows Edith Clever as the widowed noblewomen who finds herself pregnant but cannot remember her rapist and so advertises in a local newspaper that she will marry whoever admits to the deed. She finally agrees to marry the man who responded – whom she loves and cannot, at first, believe is guilty of her rape. However, her acceptance of him turns on her eventual reaction, 'How could I love you if I had not hated you first?'*

HOFFMANN

Like Kleist, the wizard of German Romanticism, **Ernst Theodor Amadeus Hoffmann** (1776–1822), did not belong to any Romantic schools. Both as a writer and as an individual, he moved in a strange world poised between fantasy and reality; and, although he earned his livelihood as a bureaucrat, was, at the same time, a poet, a draughtsman and a fine musician. He was fond of mystifying his friends, and would sometimes vanish no one knew where.

In his novels and short stories, he mixes the prosaic with the fantastic, and thus produces a ludicrous and yet ghostly effect. Hoffmann, when he adopted a realistic tone, was as good a story-teller as Hans Andersen; but beneath the amusing surface of his tales often lurks a bitter truth. His novel *Die Elixiere des Teufels* (1813/16, *The Devil's Elixir*) is a tale of horror, where the devil's potion that the monk drinks evidently symbolizes the powers of evil. In *Der goldene Topf* (1813, *The Golden Pot*), a legendary guest, the 'Prince of Salamanders' joins a prosaic Dresden gathering of craftsmen and officials. His volume of collected stories *Die Serapionsbrüder* (1818/21, *The Serapion Brethren*), includes some of his most famous narratives, among them *Nussknacker und Mäusekönig* (The Nutcracker and King Mouse) and *Klein Zaches* (Little Zaches).

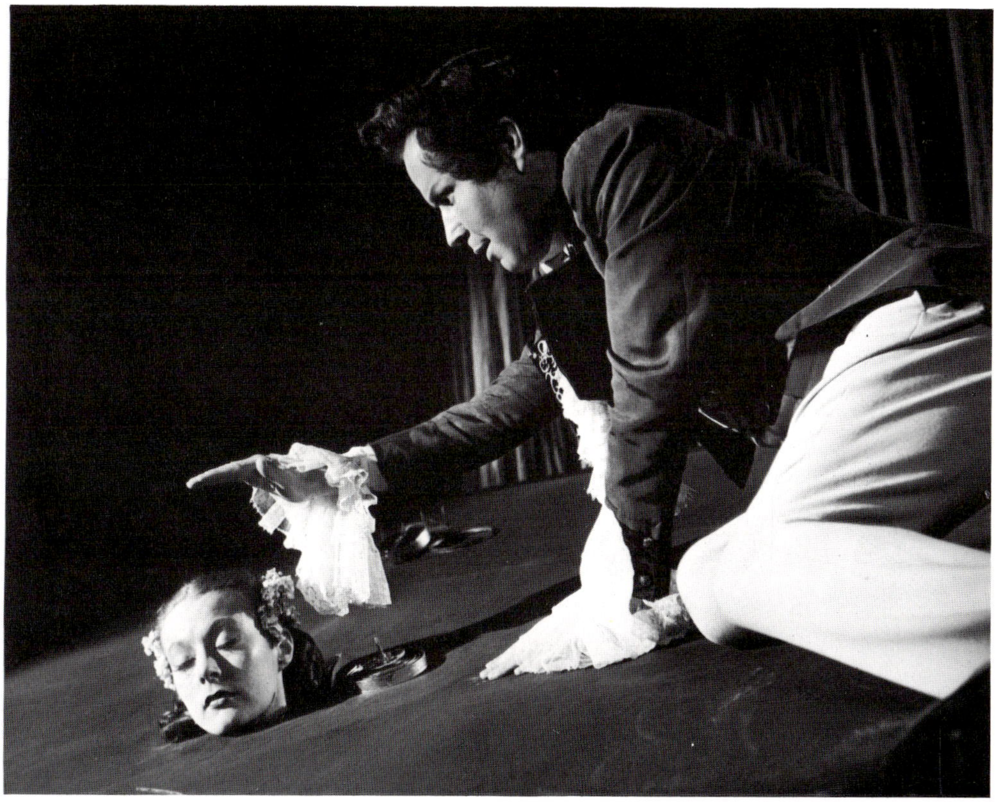

Top *E.T.A. Hoffmann, a self-portrait. His opera* Undine *(1816) was the inspiration for Delibes's ballet, 'Coppélia', of 1816 and Offenbach's later operetta 'The Tales of Hoffmann' (1881). It was adapted yet again for the film* (**right**) *'The Tales of Hoffmann' (1951) by Michael Powell and Emeric Pressburger. Here, Hoffmann (Robert Rounseville) finds the head of Olympia (Moira Shearer) after the wicked Coppelius had destroyed his puppet.*

HÖLDERLIN

Friedrich Hölderlin (1770–1843) represents another phase of the Romantic Movement. A gentle visionary, he was ill-equipped to confront the brutality of real life, and at thirty began to show signs of an incurable mental illness. Earlier, and during his brief periods of good health, he wrote the works that have given him a place among the greatest German poets.

In his nature the Romantic yearning for distant scenes took the shape of a passion for ancient Greece; and, besides his classic novel *Hyperion* (1797/99), he wrote translations of Greek tragedies. His most important achievement, however, was his adaptation of antique metrical forms – in clear and simple verses, through which he expresses his own unrest and sorrow.

Diotima, the female figure to whom some of his poems are dedicated, reflects his love for Suzette Gontard, the wife of a banker, but also embodies his Romantic cult of the unattainable ideal. In all his poems Hölderlin's dominant theme is the basic human tragedy. The quotation that follows is taken from Hyperion's *Schicksalslied (Song of Fate)*:

But we are fated
To find no foothold, no rest
And suffering mortals
Dwindle and fall
Headlong from one
Hour to the next,
Hurled like water
From ledge to ledge
Downward for years into
the vague abyss

Simultaneously, Hölderlin suggests how Man may rise above his fate – through his experience of love, his devotion to Nature and Art, and religious beliefs that have no dogmatic background. His *Sonnenuntergang* (*To the Fates*) is quoted here:

One summer grant me, you powerful
fates,
And one more autumn only for
mellow song,
So that more willingly, replete with
Music's late sweetness, my heart may
die then.

. . . . .

Then welcome silence, welcome cold
world of shades!
I'll be content, though here I must
leave my lyre
And songless travel down, for *once* I
Lived like the gods, and no more is
needed.

Top *Hölderlin, a disturbed genius whose poetry was despised and forgotten for many years. Portrait by F.K. Heimer (1792). (Schiller Nationalmuseum, Marbach)*
Above *The late-5th century* BC *Temple of Soúnion, in Attica. Greece, the subject of his* Hyperion, *was the spiritual home he was never able to visit.*

GREAT ROMANTIC POETS

The Romantic Movement began to take shape in England many years before it emerged in France, where it would reach its highest point during the productive 1830s. The first two great English Romantic poets (as distinct from eighteenth-century poets like Alexander Pope who had shown Romantic tendencies) were **William Wordsworth** (1770–1850) and **Samuel Taylor Coleridge** (1772–1834); and together in 1798 they published *Lyrical Ballads*, which exemplified an entirely new attitude towards the art of poetry. While Coleridge, whom his collaborator had immediately recognized as 'a very great man', contributed a fantastic narrative poem, his most substantial masterpiece, *The Ancient Mariner*, Wordsworth chose subjects 'from ordinary life'. Both did their best to dispense with the artificial diction of the famed Augustan poets, and to employ the 'real language' of contemporary men and women – of human beings, however, 'in a state of vivid sensation', when their natural eloquence appeared. Coleridge was the more philosophic of the two; and Wordsworth particularly valued his gift of 'throwing out ... grand central truths from which might be evolved the most comprehensive systems'.

Wordsworth's chief contribution to *Lyrical Ballads* was his wonderful landscape-poem *Tintern Abbey*, in which, for the first time, he voiced his pantheistic cult of Nature:

> The sounding cataract
> Haunted me like a passion; the tall rock,
> The mountain, and the deep and
> gloomy wood,
> Their colours and their forms, were
> then to me
> An appetite; a feeling and a love,
> That had no need of a remoter charm
> By thought supplied ...

In 1790 Wordsworth had visited France, and enjoyed the prospect of what he believed to be a glorious new society –

> France standing on the top of
> golden hours,
> And human nature seeming born
> again.

But, when middle age approached, he grew increasingly conservative, and in 1818 was denounced by his fellow Romantic Shelley as a 'beastly and pitiful wretch', who had betrayed his former revolutionary principles. In later life, his poetic productions certainly grew more and more commonplace. Meanwhile, he had written fine sonnets, evocative lyrics and his impressive *Ode on Intimations of Immortality from Recollections of Early Childhood*, published in 1807. But undoubtedly his noblest work was his lengthy autobiographical poem. *The Prelude*, which was never published in his lifetime, describes the development of a poetic genius, and both the joys, and the fears, doubts and anxieties of childhood. Thus, for example, he remembers the pleasures of skating with his friends:

> All shod with steel,
> We hissed along the polished ice in
> games
> Confederate, imitative of the chase ...
> So through the darkness and the cold
> we flew,
> And not a voice was idle; with the din,
> Meanwhile, the precipices rang aloud;
> The leafless trees and every icy crag
> Tinkled like iron, while far distant hills
> Into the tumult sent an alien sound
> Of melancholy not unnoticed, while
> the stars,
> Eastward, were sparkling clear, and in
> the west
> The orange sky of evening died away.

'William Wordsworth on Helvellyn' (1843) by the eccentric historical painter and autobiographer, Benjamin Haydon. Wordsworth liked it: 'I think myself it is the best likeness, that is the most characteristic, which has been done of me.' Not so Thomas Carlyle: 'He was a man quite other than that; a man of an immense head and great jaws like a crocodile's.' The artist painted another, full-length, version with the poet seated which he lent to Elizabeth Barrett Browning, who greatly admired it. (National Portrait Gallery, London)

Above *Coleridge aged 23, three years before his masterpiece* The Rime of the Ancient Mariner *was published. Portrait by P. Vandyke (1795). (National Portrait Gallery, London)*

Opposite *'Beyond the shadow of the ship, I watch'd the water-snakes ...' (iv.12), a scene from Coleridge's* Ancient Mariner *illustrated by Gustave Doré. This poem so obsessed the artist that in 1875 he published a remarkable series of engravings, from his own gallery in London, and at his own expense –the engraving costs alone came to some £3500. Not surprisingly, he was shocked by their commercial failure.*

Coleridge was a writer who deeply impressed all his associates, yet satisfied few of their expectations. At school, he had been a 'playless day-dreamer'; yet, even in those days, he gathered around him a host of admiring listeners once he had begun to talk. He remained a powerful talker, frequently on philosophic subjects, until the end of his existence; but his creative productions were fragmentary and, besides *The Rime of the Ancient Mariner* in 1798 (retitled in 1800 *The Ancient Mariner, A Poet's Reverie* and the archaic spelling removed) and his Gothick fantasy of a year before, *Christabel*, consisted of a few lyrics, among them being the marvellous dream-poem *Kubla Khan* (1797) – a dream from which he is said to have been woken by the inopportune appearance of a local busybody – the most often quoted of his works. Coleridge's Golden Age opened in 1797, when he formed a close friendship with William and Dorothy Wordsworth, and Wordsworth acclaimed him as 'the most *wonderful* man that he had ever known'; but in 1810 the poets quarrelled, Coleridge having become an opium addict and, according to his old friend, an intolerable domestic 'nuisance'. By that time he himself declared that 'the Poet is dead in me ... I was once a Volume of Gold Leaf rising and riding on every breath of Fancy'. Thereafter he adopted a humbler role, discoursed to his friends, delivered admirable lectures to the public and composed his major prose-work *Biographia Literaria* (1817). It was a gloomy ending. 'An archangel – a little damaged', according to his school-fellow the essayist Charles Lamb, he lived on, an invalid under medical care, for the last years of his life.

BYRON

Above *Byron in the Albanian national costume he loved to wear. From 1809 to 1811 he travelled through the Turkish Empire, which then included Albania and Greece. Detail of a portrait by J. Phillips (1823/24). (National Portrait Gallery, London)*

Right *Byron at the tomb of Bozzaris (or Botzaris), the Greek hero who had defended Missolonghi against the Turks in 1822/23, where Byron himself would die. For generations the Greeks revered the memory of the British poet with honours that equalled those they paid their national hero. Detail from a 19th-century painting. (National Historical Museum, Athens)*

George Gordon, **Lord Byron** (1788–1824) was adopted, both in England and in Europe at large, as the arch-Romantic, though he himself never quite accepted the part that it was expected he should play. He was always conscious, however, of his ancestral heritage – the grandson of an admiral nicknamed 'Foul-Weather Jack', because, wherever he sailed, he seemed to run into a storm; the great-nephew of 'the Wicked Lord', an eccentric recluse, who had killed a neighbour in a duel; and the son of a bankrupt soldier, known as 'Handsome Jack', and his second wife, the unlucky Scottish heiress Captain John Byron had married for her money and soon afterwards had ruined. The poet, moreover, had been born with a mis-shapen foot, that left him permanently somewhat lame.

Byron's 'heritage of storms', added to this slight physical deformity, distinguished him, he felt, from the majority of his fellow human beings. Yet his youth was by no means uncheerful; his private life was apparently not much more rakish than that of most of his friends; and, having published some unimportant juvenile verses and a bold satire, *English Bards and Scotch Reviewers* (1809), aimed at his unappreciative critics, like other young aristocrats he set out on the Grand Tour, which took him as far afield as Athens and Constantinople. He remained abroad until July 1811, and, during his travels (he wrote) dashed off 'a great many stanzas in Spenser's measure relative to the countries I have visited'. In March 1812, they were issued as the first two Cantos of a long poetic travelogue entitled *Childe Harold's Pilgrimage*; and Byron, to quote his own words, 'awoke and found himself famous', the hero of the literary world and the lion of fashionable society.

The next two years of his London life were extravagant and feverish. Though fame may not have transformed, it undoubtedly exaggerated his character. The melancholy Childe, who claimed to have run through 'Sin's long labyrinth' and, by his unbridled pursuit of pleasure, achieved only bitter disillusionment, had been a largely fictitious personage. But now he contrived to realize his legend, and, partly perhaps because he welcomed danger, committed a sin for which 'there was no forgiveness in this world, whatever

'The Death of Sardanapalus' (1827) by Eugène Delacroix, who was greatly inspired by Byron's work and by the Greek War of Independence. His painting is as romantically exaggerated as Byron's drama Sardanapalus *of 1821. This legendary Sardanapalus – the last king of Assyria – besieged by the Medes and the Chaldeans, died in a funeral pyre of his own making, together with his concubines and eunuchs. The real king was the 7th-century* BC *Assurbanipal, who died in the destruction of Nineveh. (Louvre, Paris)*

there might be in the next' – his illicit relationship with his half-sister Augusta Leigh, the child of Captain Byron's first alliance.

To escape from this dangerous liaison, he presently married Annabella Milbanke, a blue-stocking heiress, whose attempts to understand, and, if possible, reform her husband, soon proved desperately unsuccessful. Their parting, early in 1816, soon after the birth of their only child Ada, caused a hideous public scandal and, in April, under a dark cloud, Byron left England for the last time. There followed eight long years of exile; and, having encountered Shelley among the Swiss mountains, he moved on to Venice, where he determined to 'make life an amusement' and explored the lowest depths of dissipation, but, at the same time, wrote the Third and Fourth Cantos of *Childe Harold* (in 1816 and 1818 respectively) and his masterpiece *Don Juan* (1818/20).

Byron's works are remarkably uneven in quality. They range from such immensely popular Eastern tales as *The Giaour, The Bride of Abydos, The Corsair, Lara, The Siege of Corinth,* and *Parisina,* that delighted his readers before he left England, to his last satire, *Vision of Judgement* (1822), a gloriously comic attack on the Laureate Robert Southey (who had published a solemn panegyric on the moral virtues of King George III) and his magnificent prose-works, his letters, and his private journals. In prose, declared the Victorian prophet John Ruskin, Byron 'wrote as easily as a hawk flies, and as clearly as a lake reflects, the exact truth in the precisely narrowest terms . . .'

Although *Childe Harold* contains splendid passages, of all his poems, it is *Don Juan* that shows his genius at his most compulsive, with its blend of comedy, satire and exquisite lyrical feeling.

Byron had always hoped to become a man of action; and in 1812, the Greek War of Independence gave him the opportunity he sought, and he was able to show that his championship of freedom had not been mere poetic verbiage. He died at Missolonghi, the unhealthy seaport he made his headquarters, probably of 'uremic poisoning', exhausted and dispirited, yet still courageous, on 19 April 1824.

SHELLEY

In his defence A Defence of Poetry *(1821) Percy Bysshe Shelley argued the over-riding necessity of the imaginative arts and proclaimed poets to be 'the unacknowledged legislators of mankind.' The work was not published until after his death when he was already, for many, the personification of the revolutionary Romantic spirit. His* Prometheus Unbound *(1820), a verse–drama which develops the theme of the 5th-century* BC *dramatist Aeschylus'* Prometheus Bound, *is on one level a prediction of the ultimate triumph of revolution, at a deeper level an account of a redeeming victory of love. In Greek mythology, the Titan Prometheus, defying Zeus, the lord of the gods, brought fire to the Earth – as punishment he was bound eternally to a rock among the Caucasus mountains. In Shelley's imagination and that of other Romantic poets, he symbolized the fight for freedom. Portrait of Shelley (1819) by Amelia Curran. (National Portrait Gallery, London)*

Opposite *The body of the drowned Shelley is burned on the Italian seashore, mourned by Byron (at right) and his friend Leigh Hunt, the essayist and poet (at left). Detail of a painting by L.E. Fournier (1899). (Walker Art Gallery, Liverpool)*

The only son of a prosperous English landowner and respectable Member of Parliament, **Percy Bysshe Shelley** (1792–1822) became for the later nineteenth-century a radiant personification of the revolutionary Romantic spirit. Educated at Eton, which he detested and where he earned the nickname 'Mad Shelley', he went up to Oxford, but, having written and distributed a pamphlet entitled *The Necessity of Atheism*, was expelled by the authorities. Thanks to the meagre allowance his father granted him, he next embarked on a life of philosophic and philanthropic wanderings, accompanied by the pretty but commonplace girl, the sixteen-year-old Harriet Westbrook, whom, in 1811, he had rashly married. Their marriage broke down three years later when he became enamoured of and eloped with Mary Godwin, daughter of the celebrated feminist Mary Wollstonecraft and the radical reformer William Godwin. Shelley's moral principles were strong but sometimes conveniently elastic; and, having deserted Harriet, he suggested at one point that she should join Mary and himself in a community of kindred souls.

She refused and, after many vicissitudes and much misery, at length committed suicide. Meanwhile, he and Mary (whom he presently married) left England in 1818 never to return. In 1816, beside the Lake of Geneva, he had already met Byron; and despite many differences of feeling and opinion, the two remarkably dissimilar poets remained friends and fellow exiles, until Shelley met his death at sea, and Byron watched the burning of his body on the Italian seashore near Spezia in July 1822. As a poet, Shelley was a brilliant visionary rather than a conscientious literary artist. His earliest poem *Queen Mab* (1813) now strikes us as an ambitious piece of juvenilia; and it was during the last few years of his life that he produced his most distinguished works – his symbolic drama *Prometheus Unbound* (1820), his impressive historical drama *The Cenci* (1819), his threnody for the dead John Keats, *Adonais* (1821) – which is also a vigorous defence of the Art of Poetry – and his eloquent *Ode to the West Wind* (1820).

As a prophet, some of the ideas that inspired him had a passionately personal bias. He failed to distinguish, for example, between his detestation of political tyranny and his hatred of his father; and it was in much the same spirit that he had opened his attack on Christianity. 'Oh! how I were the Antichrist!' he exclaimed; 'that it were mine to crush the demon to hurl him to his native hell . . .'

Shelley was at his best when he temporarily forgot his prophetic message to the world, and looked into his own troubled heart – as in his melodious and deeply moving *Lines Written in Dejection near Naples, 1818*:

Yet now despair itself is mild,
Even as the winds and waters are;
I could lie down like a tired child,
And weep away this life of care
Which I have borne, and yet must bear,
Till death like sleep might steal on me,
And I might feel in the warm air
My cheek grow cold, and hear the sea
Breathe o'er my dying brain its last monotony.

Left *The legendary figure of Prometheus has long inspired artists and writers. Shown here is Prometheus as the liberator of mankind and giver of Fire, one of two versions by Piero di Cosimo (1462–1521) and part of a series of panels on 'The Early History of the World' based on Ovid. (Alte Pinakothek, München)*

KEATS

Of all the English Romantic Poets **John Keats** (1795–1821) was the most deeply committed to his art. 'A genius more purely poetic never existed', wrote his friend the ill-fated painter Benjamin Robert Haydon. He believed in nothing, he once declared, but 'the truth of great poetry' and 'the holiness of the heart's affections'; and his short life was divided between his devotion to literature (in which he believed that he had failed) and the pursuit of love, where yet again he encountered bitter disappointment.

Having first studied medicine, he soon abandoned it for poetry, and in 1817 published a volume of *Poems*, which, although it contained some of his noblest early sonnets, except among a few faithful friends attracted very little notice. It was followed in 1818 by an ambitious narrative poem *Endymion* – an evidently somewhat immature work that exposed him to savage journalistic ridicule – and in 1820 by a third collection, which included many of his masterpieces, *The Eve of St Agnes*, *Lamia*, *Isabella*, the original version of *Hyperion* and the ever-famous *Odes*. Meanwhile, early the same year, he had discovered that he was suffering from pulmonary tuberculosis – the disease that had already killed both his mother and his younger brother – and, not long before, had fallen desperately in love with Fanny Brawne, a girl he had once regarded as a frivolous modern coquette, 'beautiful and elegant, graceful, silly, fashionable and strange', but who now obsessed his thoughts.

Top *Keats in 1871, by his friend Joseph Severn. (National Portrait Gallery, London)* **Above** *'Endymion' (1903), the shepherd kept asleep for ever by the moon-goddess, the better to admire his beauty, by G.F. Watts. Keats's* Endymion *allegory shows the yearning for ideal perfection as perpetually distracted by glimpses of human beauty. (Watts Gallery, Compton, Surrey)*

As in most Romantic literature, love and death and the transience of human beauty are themes that run through Keats's works. Thus in *Ode to Melancholy* he speaks of his adored mistress as herself a passing shade:

She dwells with Beauty – Beauty
  that must die;
And Joy, whose hand is ever at his lips
Bidding adieu . . .

Byron had been one of the critics who derided Keats's early poems, which he dismissed as the mere feverish self-indulgence of a juvenile imagination; but, when he read *Hyperion* and heard of Keats's death in Rome on 23 February 1821, he decided that he must make amends and instructed his London publisher to 'omit *all* that is said *about* him in any mss of mine. His *Hyperion* is a fine monument and will keep his name'. Below are the opening lines of the first version:

Deep in the shady sadness of a vale
Far sunken from the healthy breath of
  morn,
Far from the fiery noon, and eve's one
  star,
Sat grey-haired Saturn, quiet as a stone,
Still as the silence round about his lair.
Forest on forest hung about his head
Like cloud on cloud. No stir of air was
  there,
Not so much life as on a summer's day
Robs not one light seed from the
  feather's grass,
But where the dead leaf fell, there did
  it rest
A stream went voiceless by . . .
        The Naiad 'mid her reeds
Press'd her cold finger closer to her lips.

WALTER SCOTT

Of the nineteenth-century English Romantics, **Sir Walter Scott** (1771–1832) was the only great writer to score his finest triumphs through the art of prose. True, his historical narrative-poems, such as *The Lay of the Last Minstrel* (1805) and *The Lady of the Lake* (1810), were prodigiously popular; but his development of the modern historical novel was his major contribution to the literature of the Western world.

He was well-suited to the task. A Scotsman, he came from a neighbourhood whose legends and traditions were still vigorously alive. Although he had a Romantic affection for the past, he was also an accomplished realist, with a delightful sense of humour, and applied the technique of the eighteenth-century English novel to the pictures that he drew of bygone ages. His characters are authentic men and women; and no less clearly and realistically described are their immediate surroundings.

His first novel, *Waverley; or, 'Tis Sixty Years Since*, which established his reputation in 1814, and its successors, published between 1815 and 1824, *Guy Mannering, Rob Roy, The Heart of Midlothian, The Bride of Lammermoor* and others, dealt with varying aspects of the stormy Scottish past. Then he set out to conquer new fields. *Ivanhoe* takes us back to the chivalric Middle Ages; *The Fortunes of Nigel*, to Shakespearian London; *Quentin Durward*, to the medieval Court of France.

In 1825, Walter Scott was ruined by his publisher's bankruptcy; and, being essentially a man of honour, he determined to pay off his debts, and passed the remainder of his life struggling bravely to discharge them. The effort was to kill him seven years later.

Above *Sir Walter Scott, after a sketch by Slater.* **Right** *Illustration for a Danish edition (1883) of Scott's* Ivanhoe, *published in 1819.*

In 1811 Scott purchased the estate of Abbotsford near Melrose on the River Tweed and had a neo-Gothic mansion built there for himself. Two years earlier he had supplied half the capital for a new publishing firm. Its eventual bankruptcy, caused in part by his partner's extravagance, brought about his ruin.

Napoleon's despotism alienated many literary figures, among them Mme de Staël (**above**) *who had held a progressive literary salon in her Paris home before she was exiled by the Emperor. Portrait by F. Gérard (1770–1837). (Musée de Versailles)*
Below *The disastrous 'Retreat from Moscow', climax of a campaign that fast hastened Napoleon's fall. Detail of painting by J-L-E. Meissonier (1864). (Louvre, Paris)*

Walter Scott's novels had a strong influence on the progress of the Romantic Movement in France, where both medieval modes and everything Scottish, even the wearing of tartans, almost immediately came into fashion.

Madame de Staël (1766–1817) made her chief contribution to the intellectual life of her age not as an author but as a keen critic and debater of ideas, though she published two extremely popular feminist novels, *Delphine* (1802) and *Corinne* (1807), and *De l'Allemagne* (1810), an authoritative book on Germany and its people. At first an admirer of Napoleon, once she had recognized that he was an enemy of freedom, and the arch-opponent of her libertarian views, she became one of his most forceful opponents, and was obliged to leave France. Napoleon regretted her opposition – 'A woman of great talent', he admitted; had she taken his side, he might have found her very useful!

Madame de Staël's *De la littérature* (1800, On Literature) is Europe's earliest general history of the subject. There, and in *De l'Allemagne*, she paved the way for the French Romantic Movement, defended a subjective approach to literature, and set intuition and inspiration above the claims of eighteenth-century Reason.

François René de Chateaubriand (1768–1848), an aristocrat and onetime member of the counter-revolutionary army, travelled in America, returned to France at the outbreak of the Revolution, but emigrated to Great Britain in 1792. After the fall of Napoleon and the Restoration of the Bourbons, he became Minister of Foreign Affairs and French Ambassador in London. His great work, *Le Génie du christianisme* (1809, The Genius of Christianity) is a passionate defence of the Catholic Faith. But in his novels – *Atala* (1801) which revives his American memories, and *René* (1805), with its autobiographical background and ultra-Byronic hero – he displays all the qualities, and some of the defects, of the

new Romantic school. His masterpiece, however, was the magnificent autobiography, *Mémoires d'outre-tombe* (1849/50, Memoirs from Beyond the Grave) that he wrote in his declining years, a monument of French prose and an incomparable self-portrait.

Left *Chateaubriand, exponent of the new Romantic school in 1809, by A-L. Girodet-Trioson. (Musée de Versailles)* **Right** *Girodet's 'The Burial of Atala' (1808) from Chateaubriand's tale of the Indian maiden Atala, with its rhapsodic descriptions of Nature. This is an important early example of Romantic painting. Girodet was much involved in the literary scene, and, although as a painter he had been awarded the Prix de Rome, in 1812 he gave up painting for poetry. (Louvre, Paris)*

The death in 1794 of the classical lyricist André Chénier, beheaded during Robespierre's Reign of Terror, was followed by a long poetic lull; and no major collection of poems appeared until the publication of Lamartine's *Méditations poétiques* in 1820. Thanks to **Alphonse de Lamartine** (1790–1869), French verse, it has been said, 'began to sing again'. His meditations, which often take the form of lamentations, are invariably eloquent; but, as André Gide pointed out in the preface to his admirable *Anthologie de la poésie française*, though he opens with a splendid flight, once he has reached a certain imaginative altitude he frequently ceases to rise and 'planes tirelessly' along the same level; with the result that his verse remains melodious, yet may become at length monotonous, the themes he prefers being lost love, the 'clouds that obscure his heart', and the insoluble mystery of God's existence.

HUGO

Master of the French Romantic school, Victor Hugo at the age of 78, old and tired but his spirit unbroken. His collection of poems L'Art d'être grandpère *had been published a few years earlier. Portrait by Léon Bonnat (1880). (Maison de Victor Hugo, Paris)*

Champion and master of the Romantic school in France, **Victor Hugo** (1802–1885) bore on his signet-ring the magniloquent inscription EGO HUGO. He had never the slightest doubt of his own personal or poetic value, or of the grandiose part he had to play, and believed that a poet should not only express his poignant individual feelings but become 'the voice of the century' and a leader of his fellow men. As poet, what particularly distinguished him were his amazing mastery of words and extraordinary imaginative scope. His works include passages of sonorous rhetoric, and exquisite lyrics and songs, among the most moving ever written. No other single poet has done more to extend the possibilities of French verse.

Having begun his career as a Classical poet, he soon broke away from rigid metres and created new rhythms. In *Les Orientales* (1829) and *Feuilles d'automne* (1831, Autumn leaves) he showed his gift of capturing delicately sensuous impressions; while, in *Les Chants du crépuscule* (1835, Twilight Songs) he became an acute political critic, wistfully remembering his nation's former days of glory.

As a dramatist, Hugo led a vigorous campaign against the Classical tradition. His *Préface de Cromwell* is a Romantic manifesto; and, when in 1830 his historical drama *Hernani* was produced at the Théâtre Français, he organized his followers in a militant band, who both shouted down and came to blows with their obscurantist adversaries. *Hernani* broke all the classic rules. The 'Unities' are totally disregarded; no actions take place 'off stage'; every violent episode is enacted in sight and hearing of the audience.

Hugo's novels had the same qualities and defects as his plays – they are forceful and brilliantly coloured, but often melodramatic both in subject and in style, the most popular today being *Notre-Dame de Paris* (1831), an historical novel about the great Parisian cathedral and a noble dwarf, the hideous Quasimodo, who has become its tutelary spirit.

The tragic death in 1843 of a beloved daughter overshadowed Hugo's middle age; and when, in 1851, Napoleon III seized the Imperial Throne, he was driven into exile, and retired to Guernsey, one of the Channel Isles, where he remained for the

next twenty years. During his later life, among his chief poetic productions were *Les Châtiments* (1853, *Chastisements*), a series of poetic diatribes aimed at the usurping Emperor, and *Les Contemplations* (1853/55) a tribute to the memory of his lost child. His great novel, *Les Misérables*, a study of the effects of crime and punishment, came out in 1862.

As a lyric poet, Hugo is often seen at his best in *La Légende des siècles* (1877/85, The Legend of the Centuries), a luminous review of mankind's legendary past. Here is Ruth, for example, amid 'the alien corn':

All was silent in Jezreel and Ur –
The night-fields blossomed with
  flickering stars,
And, in the deep west, among these
  flowers of the dark
The moon's thin crescent, gleaming
  above her,
Made Ruth, peering through the bars
  of heaven, ponder
What God, what reaper returning from
  the harvest of eternal summer,
Had carelessly cast down his golden
  sickle, here
In this shadow-meadow, among the
  star-flowers.

A gargoyle on the roof of Notre-Dame, Paris, the setting for Hugo's famous historical novel about the Cathedral and the dwarf, Quasimodo. Notre-Dame de Paris, *over 700 pages of it, was written in under five months and was an immediate success. Hugo had earlier written of his aim to create a novel full of drama and epic poetry 'in which Walter Scott will be set among the splendour of Homer . . .'. Hugo's one-time protégé, Théophile Gautier, referred to it as a 'true* Iliad*'.*

TO HAVE LOVED AND WEPT

Alfred de Musset (1810–1857) was the spoiled child of the French Romantic Movement, and already an accomplished versifier at the age of eighteen. Although, as a devotee of *Childe Harold*, he often struck Byronic poses, he had a distinctive music of his own and an individual view of life. *Rolla* (1833), the long poem in which he tells of a rake's suicide after a night of sensual pleasure, reflects what he called 'the sickness of our age' – an age that had lost its faith and could find no relief in dissipation. But his Romanticism was of a different kind from Hugo's; he avoided the older man's verbosity. His verse, however pathetic it may be, possesses some of the Rococo graces.

Soon afterwards, his disastrous love-affair with George Sand left him permanently disillusioned; and in *Les Nuits* (1835/37) he expressed his poignant sense of loss:

Alfred de Musset and the Paris of his time. In his novel Confession of a Child of the Century *(1836) he told of his suffering when his affair with George Sand ended. In 1859 she gave her version,* Elle et Lui *(She and Him), and Musset's brother retaliated with his,* Lui et elle. *Detail of a portrait by C. Landelle. (Musée de Versailles)*

Poet, 'tis thus with great ones of thy race,
They let the crowd that lives a day laugh on,
And feast them as a Pelican his brood,
But when they sing their song of hope betrayed,
Of grief neglected, unrequited love,
The strain is scarce a spur to merriment,
Their lofty eloquence is like the blade
That sweeps a flashing circle through the air
But ever leaves some blood-drop in its track.

In his plays, however, particularly in *On ne badine pas avec l'amour* (1834, One Doesn't Play With Love) Musset struck a fresher, lighter note. They have an almost Mozartian grace and gaiety.

Both Hugo and Musset frankly laid bare their hearts; whereas **Alfred de Vigny** (1797–1863) of all the French Romantics is the most reticent. Not until, after his death, when the whole corpus of his works appeared, together with his diary, *Journal d'un poète*, was his character – stoical, pessimistic, reticent – fully appreciated and understood. 'Only silence is great, all else is weakness', he wrote in *La Mort du loup* (1843), Death of the Wolf), an ode to a wild beast's silent, stubborn death.

In *Moïse* (1826, Moses), he describes a prophet's exalted solitude. In *Mont des oliviers* (1864, The Mount of Olives), Jesus vainly challenges the unanswering skies above Gethsemane, which appear to symbolize divine indifference. Vigny's collection of short stories, *Servitude et grandeur militaires* (1835, The Servitude and Splendour of a Soldier's Life) reveal a similar attitude towards the problems of existence.

Théophile Gautier (1811–1872) began his career as a protégé of Victor Hugo, and, wearing a bright red medieval waistcoat, commanded the Romantic troops at the 'Battle of *Hernani*'. But, unlike Hugo, he did not believe that a poet should be the spokesman and leader of the people. He originated the maxim 'art for art's sake'. A work of art, he considered, had no value apart from its aesthetic merits; 'When an object becomes useful', he declared, 'it ceases to be beautiful'. Gautier's theories had a strong influence on later nineteenth-century

literature and painting. As a poet, he was inspired by perfection of colour and form; and his chief collection of poems, *Emaux et camées* (1852, Enamels and Cameos) have a polish and brilliance that delighted a far greater artist, Charles Baudelaire, who dedicated his *Fleurs du mal* to Théophile Gautier, the 'faultless poet', he said, and 'perfect magician' of the modern literary world. The artist's achievement alone survives the passage of the centuries, as he announces *L'Art*:

... Some ancient medal found
When a ploughman turns the ground
May show
A king of long ago

The gods themselves will pass,
But sovran poesy
Will be
More durable than brass ...

The story of 'Moses and the Burning Bush' has inspired many artists as well as poets, among them Alfred de Vigny. This strange, almost Surrealist painting is by the German artist Ernst Fuchs (1956). (Österreichische Bundes-Kunstförderung, Vienna)

THE RED AND THE BLACK

George Sand, born Aurore Dupin, was brought up in her grandmother's household on Rousseauesque principles. In 1822 she married the Baron Dudevant but left him in 1831 to live in Paris as a writer. Under the name of Jules Sand she collaborated with Jules Sandeau and then became attached to a series of other distinguished figures, notably Alfred de Musset and the composer Chopin with whom she lived from 1837 to 1847. Portrait by Charpentier. (George Sand House, Nohant, France)

As we have already seen, several of the great French Romantic poets also wrote impressive prose; and Victor Hugo had launched the French historical novel. But Aurore Dupin, better known under her pseudonym of **George Sand** (1804–1876), gave contemporary fiction a very different turn. She, too, adopted the tradition of the sentimental eighteenth-century novel, which suited her impulsive and romantic nature; but the passion that she displayed, both in literature and in life, was balanced by her boundless professional industry, strong common sense and a strain of earthy realism that never quite deserted her.

The romantic aspect dominates her first novels where, as in *Indiana* (1832) and *Lélia* (1833), she preaches the Cult of Feeling and the claims of human passion. Having, at the time of the February Revolution, embraced a kind of romantic socialism, later she underwent a gradual change. But she never lost her sympathy with the poor; and *La Mare au diable* (1846, The Devil's Marsh) and *François le champi* (1850, François the Changeling), are deeply sympathetic studies of contemporary peasant-life, which she knew from close acquaintance, since she was herself a country-woman and spent the greater part of her time at her little château at Nohant, near Bourges in the heart of rural France.

George Sand was one of the forerunners of the French realistic novel. But those who followed her added the gift of psychological analysis. In that field, Henri Beyle (1783–1842), who wrote under the pseudonym **Stendhal**, was an adventurous explorer, who with the romanticism of the early nineteenth century combined the enquiring scepticism of the eighteenth-century *philosophes*. His descriptions of his chief personages show an almost clinical detachment; and, however wild the action of the story and boldly pictur-

Right *George Sand's writing-desk in her study at Nohant, where she worked and entertained her friends until she died. The portrait is of Chopin, with whom her relationship was broken off in 1847.*

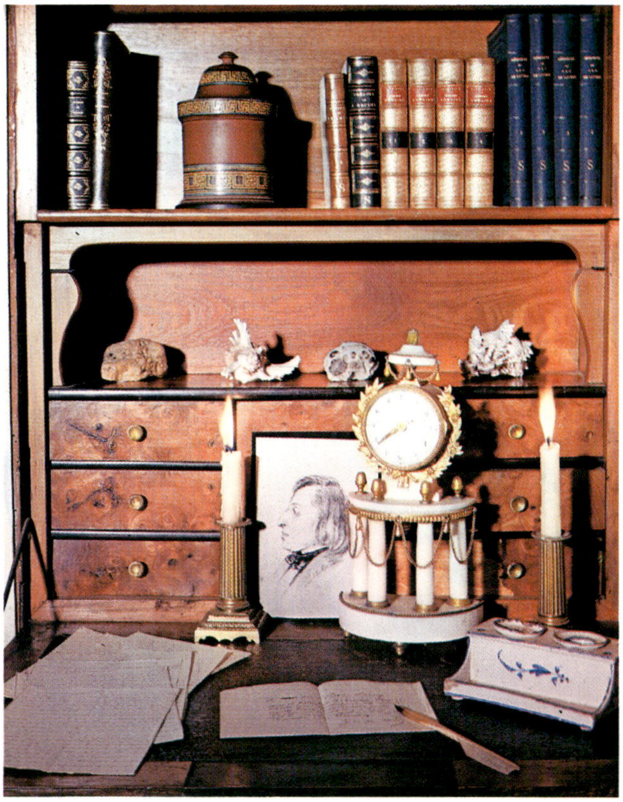

Below *The sacking of the Tuileries during the 'February Revolution' of 1848, shown in a contemporary print. During this revolution, when George Sand's sympathies were with the insurgents, she worked as a journalist.*

esque its background, he still delves into the workings of his protagonists' minds and does his best to reveal the psychological basis of any given situation. As a young man, he admired Napoleon and himself had military dreams; but, having joined the Emperor's Russian campaign, seen Moscow burning behind him and observed the horrors of the 'Great Army's' terrible retreat, he rapidly abandoned them and became a man of letters and, at length, a minor civil servant.

Stendhal's two most famous novels, *Le Rouge et le noir* (*The Red and the Black*) and *La Chartreuse de Parme* (*The Charterhouse of Parma*), were published in 1831 and 1839, when he was already middle-aged; and Balzac described the

Above *Stendhal, whose works, as he himself had prophesied, were rediscovered in the 20th century. Woodcut, one of a series of celebrity portraits by Felix Vallotton, who pioneered this graphic style in the 1890s. (Galerie Paul Vallotton, Lausanne)*

Right *Fabrizio del Dongo, the hero of Stendhal's* Charterhouse of Parma, *resigned his archbishopric and retired to a Carthusian cell at the Charterhouse after the death of his beloved illegitimate son. (National Museum, Rome)*

Left *Scene from Dumas's* The Three Musketeers *when one musketeer gains three turns of favour at De Treville's levee if he stops three others from mounting the stairs to their patron's closet. By Maurice Leloir.*

Above *Caricature of Dumas cooking* bouillabaisse – *an allusion to his mulatto grandfather (a General with the Revolutionary and Napoleonic armies) and to his extensive use of collaborators for his historical novels. Dumas père also wrote plays, memoirs, travel sketches and a cookery book.*

second as 'a masterpiece of the literature of ideas', a novel that Machiavelli might have written. Otherwise, he received little notice, but was content to prophesy that his talents would be recognized about 1880 or even 1935 – a prediction fully justified. Each of the novels listed above describes an adventurer of his own stamp, who adores women, craves for worldly success and is eventually disappointed. Stendhal was a man of tremendous energy and unbounded curiosity. His soul, he said, was 'a fire that suffers if it does not blaze. I need three or four cubic feet of new ideas a day, as a steamboat needs coal'. He wrote at breakneck speed. *La Chartreuse de Parme*, for example, was composed in less than two months.

Alexandre Dumas (1803–1870), father of the popular dramatist who shared his name, was a Romantic storyteller of a far less original type, author of such historical best-sellers as *Les Trois Mousquetaires* (1844) and *Le Comte de Monte-Cristo* (1844/45).

Meanwhile, **Prosper Mérimée** (1803–1870) helped to develop the art of the modern short story. His tales, usually set in Corsica or Spain, concern violent passions and dramatic conflicts; and his narrative style is notably clear and factual. It was Mérimée's fine Spanish novel *Carmen* (1843) that inspired Georges Bizet's opera.

BALZAC

Honoré de Balzac (1799–1850) sometimes called 'the Napoleon of the Novel', often described his imaginative operations in military terms. As the story developed, he wrote, 'Memories come charging in with flags flying ... The artillery of logic hurries along with its ammunition train ...'

Balzac was a prodigious worker, driven by his soaring literary ambitions, but, since he was seldom out of debt, constantly harassed by the need to make money; and, although he much enjoyed the pleasure of the world, he often adopted a monk's robes and lived a solitary monastic life. His aim was to depict the whole extent of modern French society, omitting not a single detail. Hence the title he chose for his tremendous series of narratives, published from 1842 – *La Comédie humaine* (The Human Comedy) in imitation of Dante's *Divina commedia*. His characters are often the victims of a fixed idea or an obsessive passion. In *Le Père Goriot* (1834, *Old Goriot*), for example, an old man's immoderate devotion to his selfish daughters provides the basis of the plot. Another of his favourite themes is the battle that an unscrupulous adventurer wages against the established social system, as in the story of a young man's upward progress that he entitled *Illusions perdues* (1837/43, *Lost Illusions*).

Balzac was a realist; yet he had also a mystic side, illustrated in such tales as *La Peau de chagrin* (1831, *The Wild Ass's Skin*), which describes a magical talisman to happiness, or *Séraphita* (1834/35), which displays a strongly Swedenborgian colouring. His prose-style has many obvious defects. But, in literature, he himself declared, 'the important thing was not to avoid mistakes but to have a quality that sweeps everything in front of it'. And that he certainly possessed.

Right *An impression of Balzac by Swiss artist Alberto Giacometti (1901–1966), better-known for his attenuated sculpture. One of the founders of the realistic novel, Balzac set out to show the effects of social environment on human personality.*

Far right *Balzac in 1846, in the monastic dressing-gown he wore when he was writing. Portrait by his friend Gavarni (otherwise Sulpice Guillaume Chevalier), the brilliant social satirist, who worked for the magazine* Charivari *and, in* La Mode, *designed and illustrated new feminine fashions.*

Above *An example of Balzac's extensive proof-correcting – in this case to* Les Employées *(1838,* Bureaucracy or A Civil Service Reformer*), his novel already serialized as* La Femme supérieure.
Right *Satirical cartoon by Honoré Daumier (1808–1879) addressed to the 'Society which has Money as its God' and headlined 'To Everyone with Capital to Lose'. He commented as strongly on the social conditions of his time as did Balzac in his writings. Any widespread business or government corruption was called 'Macairism' after the popular stage character 'Robert Macaire', archetypal charlatan made famous by actor Frédérick Lemaître and immortalized in a series of lithographs produced by Daumier and his friend Charles Philipon, publisher of* La Caricature *(1830/34) and* Le Charivari *(1832/93).*

Above *Italian patriot and guerrilla-leader Giuseppe Garibaldi. Forced to flee Italy because of his 'Freedom' activities, Garibaldi lived in the US in the early 1850s, where he became naturalized and worked as a candlemaker. Having returned to his homeland he and his Redshirts defeated the Kingdom of the Two Sicilies. He later fought with the French in the Franco-Prussian war and Victor Hugo even recommended him – without success – for election to the French Assembly in 1871. He had more success at home, becoming deputy for Rome in the Italian parliament of 1874. Detail of a romantic portrait of Garibaldi as patriotic hero, from an* Illustrated London News *supplement of 1861.*

Top *Italian Romantic poet Giacomo Leopardi, by S. Ferazzi (1830). (Palazzo Leopardi, Recanati, Italy)*
Above *Alessandro Manzoni, who became one of the originators, after Walter Scott, of the romantic historical novel with his acclaimed* The Betrothed, *set in the 17th century. Portrait by Francesco Hayez. (Brera, Milan)*

At the beginning of the nineteenth century, Italy was largely dominated by its French and Austrian overlords; but the spirit of *Il Risorgimento*, the National Awakening, had already begun to stir; and many secret societies, including the *Carbonari* (whom Byron himself aided) formed an Italian Resistance Movement.

Romanticism and Nationalism went hand in hand; and one of the earliest and greatest Italian Romantic poets was **Giacomo Leopardi** (1798–1837), the hunchbacked son of a family of conservative country gentlefolk, whose personal unhappiness and longing for spiritual freedom inspired some of the noblest poems in the language. The following is taken from his *L'Infinito* (*The Infinite*):

Here for a little while my heart is
 quiet inside me;
and when the wind lifts roughing
 through the trees,
I set about comparing my silence to
 those voices,
and I think about the eternal, the dead
 seasons,
things here at hand and alive,
and all their reasons and choices.
It's sweet to destroy my mind
and go down
and wreck in this sea where I drown.

The other great name of Italian Romanticism is **Alessandro Manzoni** (1785–1873), whose novel, *I Promessi sposi* (1821/27, *The Betrothed*) transformed the art of Italian prose-writing, and, under an historical disguise, attacked the Austrian occupiers. Its publication helped to launch the historical novel as an important literary form, on which he set forth his own view in an introductory treatise entitled *Il Romanzo storico.*

Romanticism in Denmark had never the same revolutionary ring as it did in many other countries; for there the political climate was milder.

With his lyrical skill, Denmark's leading Romantic writer, **Adam Oehlenschläger** (1779–1850), revived the poetic spirit without having to break the philosophical bonds of Romanticism as Atterbom had done in Sweden.

Henrik Wergeland (1808–1845), the first distinguished modern Norwegian poet, was a revolutionary Romantic, determined to free Norway culturally from Denmark and politically from Sweden. His love-poems and his lyrics on the beauty of Nature have a moving impetus, as in the following lines, from his *Jan van Huysums Blomsterstykke:*

Where is passion like this,
Such bliss contained by pain,
So quiet a beating heart,
So rich a blush of love,
Such harsh heartache,
As in the tulip's marvellous mouth:
That dark, self-devouring
Convulsive, strong sick flush
Of crimson night?

At the same period **Asbjørnsen** and **Moe** produced their great collection of Norwegian folk-tales.

In Finland, *Kalevala* (1835), by **Elias Lönnrot** (1802–1884), an Orpheus of the wilderness, was a stirring book.

The nineteenth century began in Sweden during the reign of the unfortunate Gustav IV Adolf, with a period of political reaction. As in other countries, Swedish Romanticism took very often an escapist turn, but was far less revolutionary and intentionally surprising than in the rest of Europe. Much influenced by German philosophy, it became an academic movement, and flourished for the most part in the university towns, where it attacked the Enlightenment, preached religious faith and Platonic idealism, championed the rights of the individual and inculcated an enthusiasm for Scandinavian antiquities.

A starting-point was provided by the magazine *Phosphoros,* launched from Uppsala in the year 1810. Its contributors were called the Phosphorists; and their leader was a precocious poet and playwright, **Per Daniel Amadeus Atterbom** (1790–1855). During his tragically short life, **Erik Johan Stagnelius** (1793–1823) wrote poems that, with their sensuous imagery and stylistic grace, are among the most vigorous productions of Swedish Romantic verse.

Thanks to *Frithiof's saga* (1823) **Esaias Tegnér** (1782–1846) became Sweden's greatest Romantic poet. **Erik Gustaf Geijer** (1783–1847) with his cult of Scandinavian antiquity, was another genuine Romantic. **Carl Jonas Love Almqvist** (1793–1866) pursued a similar course. Through his collection, *The Book of the Thorn-Rose* (1832/50), runs an exotic and demonic strain, which also appears in the conduct of his tragic personal life. Charged with the attempted murder of a money-lender, he was driven into exile. But he had already shocked his readers by the publication in 1839 of his realistic novel *Sara Videbeck* (1839), where he expressed boldly feminist ideas at least a hundred years too early.

Top *The Swedish writer Carl Jonas Love Almqvist fled Sweden for America in 1857 to avoid a murder charge. It is said that he supported his vagabond life there 'by illusionism and bigamism.'* **Right** *'The Happiness of Frithiof', illustration for a 19th-century edition of Tegnér's Romantic saga.*

Pushkin, the national poet of Russia, created a Byronic hero for his masterpiece Evgeni Onegin. *Here he is depicted in Byronic pose in 1932 by V.E. Popkov. With the advent of Romanticism the wild nomad Cossacks of the Don came to play a part in Russian literature. In 1834 Pushkin published a* History of the Pugachev Rebellion *(of the 1770s), a violent social revolt during which the Cossacks had set an example of hardy independence.*

Below *'The Cossacks write to the Sultan' by Ilya Repin (1888/91) who specialized in painting episodes from history. (Russian Museum, Leningrad)*

It was not the barrier of language alone that so long isolated Russia from the culture of the West. Until the present century, the Russian social system remained obstinately autocratic; and serfdom was abolished by the Emperor as late as 1861. Nor did Russians, being members of the Greek Orthodox Church, enjoy the cultural fellowship of the Roman Catholic religion. Though the Enlightenment had had the approval of the Empress Catherine the Great (who patronized Voltaire himself) its effects, even on the educated upper classes, were extremely limited; and only when the Romantic Movement swept through Europe did Russia begin to develop a literature that was essentially its own. Then it took shape under the influence of Byron.

Alexander Pushkin (1799–1837) was a peculiarly Byronic character, who was descended from a family of minor nobility, and as a young man associated with intellectual circles in St Petersburg, where his first important book came out – a long romantic poem *Ruslan and Ludmilla* (1820) – and immediately earned him fame. Meanwhile, he had been banished to Southern Russia as a dangerous young liberal by the Emperor Alexander I; and during his exile, which lasted five years, he travelled through some of the more distant parts of his gigantic fatherland – especially the Caucasus, a region whose wild mountainous landscapes provided the background of several of his poems and stories.

Pushkin's masterpiece, his great verse–novel *Evgeni Onegin* (1833) was also begun in exile. A drama of contemporary Russian life, as the poet had himself observed it, the poem has a Byronic hero, melancholy, rakish, attractive to women but deeply mistrustful of love. There is evidently a close connection between this brilliant narrative and Byron's *Don Juan*; but, according to many critics, Pushkin's is the better poem of the two, its blend of lyrical feeling and astringent social satire being even more accomplished. Pushkin was a many-sided genius; and, while his play *Boris Godunov* (1831) showed his gifts as an historical dramatist, his prose-works, for example his memorable short story *The Queen of Spades* (1834), are almost equally compelling. He died in 1837, when, provoked by malevolent gossip about his beautiful, frivolous wife, he challenged an unworthy adversary to a duel and received a mortal wound.

Russia's other great Romantic, **Mikhail Lermontov** (1814–1841) had also fallen under Byron's spell; but he lacked the English poet's strain of gaiety and humour. His was a melancholy, self-destructive spirit, as we see in his poem *The Demon* (1829/41), which describes a fallen spirit's conquest of a young and innocent girl, and in his loosely constructed novel *A Hero of our Times* (1840), where the chief character Pechorin, was meant, he said, to 'embody the vices of our whole generation' – its cynicism, disillusionment and frustrated quest for happiness. Lermontov shared Pushkin's fate. He had published *A Hero of our Times* when he was only twenty-five, and died a year later in an unnecessary duel.

Right *Lermontov, Guards officer, poet and novelist, addressed his* Death of a Poet, *describing the alleged 'murder' of Pushkin, to the Tsar – and was expelled from the Guards and banished to a line regiment in the Caucasus. Portrait by R. Sabolotsky. (Tretyakov Gallery, Moscow)*

Below *Pushkin, mortally wounded in the duel of honour said to have been forced on him by his enemies at the court of the new Tsar, Nicholas I.*

Right *A gallant officer leads his troop at the Battle of Antietam, 1862, in the American Civil War. The Civil War Years were to be notably evoked in 1895 when Stephen Crane wrote his classic story of a young man growing up during that time,* The Red Badge of Courage.

Below right *The romance of the New World had percolated through to such artists of the rococo style as the Italian painter Giambattista Tiepolo, who together with his sons painted the vast ceiling frescoes for the Grand Staircase in the Residenz Palace of Würzburg in Germany in 1752. Historical and allegorical scenes represent the four parts of the globe. This detail shows 'America' as a 'noble savage', plumed and jewelled.*

The nineteenth century was well under way before the New World made any important contribution to the literary culture of the West. During the second half of the eighteenth century, transatlantic men of letters, like the famous **Benjamin Franklin** (1706–1790) were nearly as much at home in England and France as they were on the other side of the Atlantic Ocean; and Franklin once went so far as to announce that Great Britain, though a very small island, 'enjoyed in almost every Neighbourhood more sensible, virtuous and elegant Minds than we can collect in ranging 100 Leagues of our vast Forests'. Thus, in the early nineteenth century, the development of American literature, as a completely original form, was both slow and tentative.

Washington Irving (1783–1859) was the first American writer to import and adapt the products of the European Romantic Movement; and his literary group in New York was called the 'Knickerbocker School', after his book *A History of New York ... by Diedrich Knickerbocker* (1809), a playful mixture of fantasy and fact. His short stories that make up *The Sketch Book* (first published serially in 1819/20 under the pseudonym 'Geoffrey Crayon, Gent.'), contained, among other items, the well-known story of 'Rip Van Winkle', and his *Tales of a Traveller* (1824) were inspired by the German 'Gothic novels' and the masterpieces of Sir Walter Scott.

James Fenimore Cooper (1789–1851) gained world-wide fame with his novels on the American Indians, *The Pioneers* (1823), *The Last of the Mohicans* (1826) and *The Deerslayer* (1841). Not only were they exciting tales, but they contained incomparable descriptions of the vast unexplored American wilder-

Above *'The Trapper's Last Shot' reflects the current American preoccupation with Man's battle against Nature and with the conquest of the wilderness. Coloured lithograph after a painting by W. Ramsay.*

Far left *James Fenimore Cooper, best-known for his stories of American Indians, was much admired by his contemporaries – Balzac, Victor Hugo (who set him above Sir Walter Scott) and later by Joseph Conrad. By contrast, Mark Twain was to accuse Cooper of breaking '18 out of 19 of the rules governing literature'. His Indian stories have always delighted the young; but beneath the surface lies a strain of genuine pathos and a feeling for the tragic conflicts of the age.*

Left *Book jacket for a Swedish edition of Cooper's 'Leatherstocking Tales' of 'Red Indian' life, a series of novels that started with his* The Pioneers *in 1823.*

Edgar Allan Poe in a daguerreotype of 1848 by S.W. Hartshorn. The Raven *(1845), written while he was literary critic on the* New York Mirror, *was the first of his poems to achieve great popularity.* **Below** *One of Gustave Doré's illustrations (1883).*

ness. Cooper also wrote historical novels and a seafaring narrative called *The Pilot* (1823).

Far more significant than either Irving or Cooper was **Edgar Allan Poe** (1809–1849), a citizen of the Southern States who lived and died in poverty, and, after the death of his pathetic young wife, declined into chronic alcoholism, which finally cut short a promising literary career.

As a critic, Poe defended the doctrine of 'art for art's sake'; and his poems at their best have a curious rhythmic fascination, which made a strong appeal to nineteenth-century French writers, including Baudelaire and Mallarmé. Death, loss and the passing of youth and beauty were the themes that haunted his imagination, and that recur in all his best-known verses, *To Helen, The Bells, The Raven, Ulalume* and *Annabel Lee.*

In his short stories, Poe both revived the tradition of the horrifying 'Gothic Novel' and helped to launch the modern detective tale, as the author, on the one hand, of *Ligeia* (1838) and *The Fall of the House of Usher* (1839), on the other of *The Gold Bug* (1843) and *The Mystery of Marie Roget* (1842). Simultaneously, in *The Narrative of Arthur Gordon Pym* (1838), he foreshadowed twentieth-century science fiction.

Irving, Cooper and Poe were all early Romantics; but, in the United States, between 1835 and 1850, the Movement took a more philosophic and less imaginative form. The so-called Transcendentalists, whose centre of operations was the north-eastern states, were influenced by German and Oriental thought, rebelled to some extent against puritan beliefs, and preached a generally idealistic approach to existence, seeking God in Nature and asserting the inborn goodness of the human soul. Besides issuing a magazine called *The Dial* (1840/44), they made bold attempts to engage in schemes for co-operative agriculture.

The leader of this group was **Ralph Waldo Emerson** (1803–1882), who expressed his views in collections of *Essays* (1841 and 1844) where, adopting a semi-lyrical style, he discussed such subjects as friendship, love and art. His opinions were a mixture of Jean-Jacques Rousseau's visionary creed and traditional American conservatism.

A fellow Transcendentalist, **Henry David Thoreau** (1817–1862), had so strong a passion for Nature that, for two years, he retired alone into the wilderness, and later described his experiences in *Walden* (1854), still one of the most widely read of all American prose-works.

From the late 1830s onwards a group of New England writers and intellectuals came together in occasional meetings, known as the 'Transcendental Club'. Among them were Ralph Waldo Emerson, Nathaniel Hawthorne and Henry Thoreau. Their concern was with the relation of the soul to Nature (Emerson's essay Nature *had appeared in 1836). In Nature they sought God; and they encouraged the sharing of manual labour as well as the exchange of thoughts. Transcendentalism had its roots in German philosophy and in the ideas of English writers, such as the poet Coleridge. Thoreau's protest against industrialism and his belief that Man must return to Nature is reflected in his painting of an American forest scene, 'View by Moonlight', by J. Shaw*

THE SECOND EMPIRE

In 1852 Napoleon III, nephew of the Great Napoleon, after a brief but bloody *coup d'état* became the Emperor of the French – a position he continued to hold for another eighteen years. During that period he transformed Paris, with the help of his architect Baron Haussman cutting broad modern thoroughfares through its ancient, still half-medieval quarters and creating a new metropolis that dazzled Europe. Yet, despite its superficial splendours and its bold parade of wealth and elegance the political framework of the Second Empire was built on insecure foundations. The Emperor's military exploits failed to equal those of his victorious uncle. Not only the working classes, whose conditions he failed to improve, though he had some vaguely liberal tendencies, but the educated middle class and the intelligentsia protested vigorously against his rule; Victor Hugo, now an exile in the Channel Islands, nicknamed him 'Napoleon the Little'. When the Franco-Prussian War broke out in 1870, the whole structure ignominiously collapsed; and the Second Empire was replaced by the Third Republic. Meanwhile, the Commune, which a conservative government savagely put down, had destroyed the Palace of the Tuileries and the Hôtel de Ville.

*The dazzling epoch of the Second Empire in France was to come to an abrupt end with the Franco–Prussian War of 1870–71. The French declaration of war in July 1870 was hailed ecstatically by Parisians (**right**). Barely six weeks later Emperor Napoleon III's army capitulated at Sedan, and William I of Prussia is depicted receiving the defeated Emperor (**above**). The result was a deep national sense of humiliation and of anger against the regime that had brought defeat. The Emperor was deposed. After the false confidence of the Empire, the atmosphere that pervaded the end of century – the* fin de siècle *– was one of doubt and spiritual malaise.*

BAUDELAIRE

Victor Hugo and **Charles Baudelaire** (1821–1867) were the two greatest French poets of the nineteenth century; but, except for the fact that both possessed genius, they could scarcely have been more unlike. Hugo had been famous since his youth, and remained extraordinarily successful. Baudelaire, during his comparatively short life, was regarded by many critics, including Sainte-Beuve, as a perverse eccentric; and the story of his personal existence is a long catalogue of failures and misadventures. When his elderly father died in 1827, Baudelaire enjoyed the happiest year he would ever experience; he and his young and attractive mother were a devoted, inseparable pair. Then Madame Baudelaire married again; she became the wife of a dashing soldier, General Aupick; and 'the green paradise of childish loves' was for ever laid waste. This blow seems to have been the ultimate origin of all Baudelaire's later aberrations. Having grown up, he rebelled against his family by developing such reckless habits that he was put under the control of a financial guardian, who doled out what was left of his father's fortune in miserably small sums. Until his death, he lived from hand to mouth, constantly struggling with his creditors.

Nor was his emotional life happy. For many years, his 'one pleasure', his 'only friend', was the half-caste actress Jeanne Duval; and she was neither faithful nor genuinely affectionate. Yet unhappiness was an element that suited his genius; and in 1857 he published *Les Fleurs du mal*, the only collection of poems that he issued in his lifetime; and, like Flaubert's *Madame Bovary*, which appeared at the same time, it was prosecuted by Napoleon III's police as immoral and obscene. The poet, his publisher and printer were fined and some of the poems banned.

The title, 'The Flowers of Evil', was not one that Baudelaire had himself chosen; and it is, to some extent, misleading, since it suggests that his preoccupation with evil may have limited and distorted the poet's view. This, of course, is altogether erroneous. 'The world of Baudelaire's thought, the country of his genius', wrote Marcel Proust in *Contre Sainte-Beuve*, is a landscape of which every poem is a separate fragment, that, 'while we read, joins up with other fragments'; and the huge landscape that gradually unfolds beneath our eyes includes a vast variety of attributes. It finds room for both evil and good, for vice and virtue, for misery and exaltation, for pagan despair and, now and then, religious faith. Though never an orthodox Christian, Baudelaire was by no means a determined sceptic. 'Even if God did not exist', he declared in a notebook-jotting, 'religion would still be sacred and divine.'

The poet spent most of his life in Paris; and Paris was the background of much of his most memorable verse and prose – the ancient city he remembered, and the new spacious, gaudy metropolis that the Emperor and his architect were busily creating. Baudelaire was fascinated by urban civilization. 'Paris', he said, 'is fecund in poetic and marvellous subjects'; and, elsewhere, *'il faut être de son temps'* – an

Above right *Baudelaire (c. 1862) by Étienne Carjat, a contemporary of the more famous French photographer, Nadar. They both portrayed many great men, including Balzac, Hugo and Zola.*

Right *Despite his allegedly 'decadent' and subversive tendencies, Baudelaire was one of the greatest and most influential poets in the history of French literature. Sketch (1862/68) by Édouard Manet.*

artist must belong to his own age; and he also delighted in minor aspects of the nineteenth-century scene, in contemporary fashions and feminine elegance. His finest critical essay, *Le Peintre de la vie moderne,* is devoted to the brilliant draughtsman Constantin Guys who depicted both the squalor and the fashionable splendour of the Second Empire.

The young Rimbaud, having styled Hugo 'a colossal vulgarian', decided that Baudelaire was a true *'voyant'*, or visionary poet; while the Symbolist Jules Laforgue said that he had brought a new voice, a 'plangent wail' – *'un nouveau miaulement'* – into French poetry. Sometimes, his verses are mediocre, even 'execrable', as Paul Valéry pointed out to André Gide; but Gide remarked that at least they show the poet's inclination to lessen the difference between himself and the ordinary reader. Despite these occasional weaknesses his poems have a haunting eloquence. Whereas Victor Hugo occupied an Olympian height, from which he now and then descended, Baudelaire is a poet who wanders through the streets and, though a poetic solitary by nature, mixes in imagination with the crowd.

Besides *Les Fleurs du mal,* he wrote *Petits Poèmes en prose* or *Le Spleen de Paris* (1857) – 'melodious, without rhythm or rhyme ... adapted to the lyric currents of the soul ... to the fitful leaps of the conscious mind' – and a series of excellent critical essays on literature, painting and music. His *Journaux intimes,* also published after his death, form a wonderfully acute record of the workings of his mind and heart.

Illustration from a French edition (1946) by Adolf Hallman of Baudelaire's Les Fleurs du mal. *One of the most influential collections of verse in French, it at first shocked and startled his contemporaries, but was supported by Théophile Gautier (to whom it was dedicated) and other gifted 19th-century critics. As a young man, Baudelaire became an aesthetic dandy, and boldly attacked the bourgeois social standards of his age. Sent away on a long sea-voyage by his anxious family, he left the ship en route and immediately returned to Paris.*

Spleen by Baudelaire

I'm like the king of a rain-country, rich
but sterile, young but with an old
wolf's itch,
one who escapes Fénelon's apologues,
and kills the day in boredom with his
dogs;
nothing cheers him, darts, tennis,
falconry,
his people dying by the balcony;
the bawdry of the pet hermaphrodite
no longer gets him through a single
night;
his bed of fleur-de-lys becomes a tomb;
even the ladies of the court, for whom
all kings are beautiful, cannot put on
shameful enough dresses for this
skeleton;
the scholar who makes his gold cannot
invent
washes to cleanse the poisoned
element;
even in baths of blood, Rome's legacy,
our tyrants' solace in senility,
he cannot warm up his shot corpse,
whose food
is syrup-green Lethean ooze, not
blood.

FLAUBERT

Among the nineteenth-century masters of French prose **Gustave Flaubert** (1821–1880) made a particularly strong impression – a realist, who in two great novels, *Madame Bovary* (1856/57) and *L'Education sentimentale* (1869), sought to draw a painstakingly accurate picture of contemporary social life; a stylist, who laboured day after day on the wording of a single sentence; yet a romantic, whose imagination often carried him back into the past. His first work, *La Tentation de saint Antoine* (The Temptation of Saint Anthony) he eventually decided to abandon; and his huge historical novel *Salammbô* (1862), a highly coloured evocation of ancient Carthage, is overloaded with elaborate archaeological detail that often makes it heavy reading. His masterpiece *Madame Bovary*, on the other hand, has an essentially prosaic subject – the story of a woman, the attractive wife of an obscure provincial doctor, who is betrayed by her romantic dreams, and her longing to escape from her tedious environment, into two illicit love-affairs that bring her only misery and ruin. Flaubert is said to have taken his story from a scandal that had occurred in a nearby Norman village, and treats it without sentimentality but with deep objective sympathy. 'I myself am Madame Bovary!' he once exclaimed. This was not surprising; Flaubert knew only too well the dangers of romantic dreaming. He was acquitted at his trial for immorality in this novel.

Left *Flaubert's remorseless analysis of his characters provoked this cartoon 'Flaubert dissecting Mme Bovary' by Lemot (1869). A resolutely professional writer, he devoted long hours to the pursuit of 'le mot juste' (exactly the right word) but was seldom altogether satisfied with his own efforts. Though a passionate and often pleasure-loving man, he lived a somewhat solitary, even at times ascetic, life. (Bibliothèque Nationale, Paris)*

Far left *The tombstone of Mme Delphine Delamare, whose life supposedly inspired Flaubert's novel* Madame Bovary. *Emma Bovary, like Mme Delamare the wife of a country doctor, yearns for romantic adventure, but her love affairs bring her nothing but unhappiness and at length she kills herself.*

DRAMA OF THE SALONS

Having flourished for a few years with Hugo and Musset, the Romantic Drama died out; and, meanwhile, a new kind of drama had begun to appear – 'melodrama' as it was first called, since it combined tragedy and comedy. The middle class was now asserting its tastes; and, while the dramatis personae of Hugo's *Hernani* include an emperor, a king and three dukes, the new audience, though it appreciated the picturesque, had tired of grandiose historic personages and high-flown rhetorical speeches. During the Second Empire, the 'drama of the salon' arose, plays that dealt with everyday social themes – skilfully constructed light-weight productions that soon captured the European stage. Successful dramas of this type were provided by **Eugène Scribe** (1791–1861) and the younger **Alexandre Dumas** (1824–1845) with his pathetic *La Dame aux camélias* (1852, the Lady of the Camellias), where the heroine is a golden-hearted courtesan. No significant social drama was evolved until in Norway, on the borders of the Western world, Ibsen and Bjørnson opened a new period of dramatic history.

'Salon des Artistes Français' (the 1911 Paris Salon) by J-A. Gruen (1922). In opposition to the influence of the earlier Salons ruled over by the Académie des Beaux-Arts (referred to by Ingres as 'literally no more than a picture shop') the Impressionists set up their rival shows, among them being the so-called Salon des Refusés. This revolutionary group was in close sympathy with the leading literary figures of the time. (Musée des Beaux-Arts, Rouen, France)

THE EXPERIMENTAL NOVEL

Three critical writers who helped to mould French thought during the second half of the nineteenth century were **Sainte-Beuve** (1804–1869) who, having passed through a Romantic phase, turned to literary criticism, applying a more scientific method to the art and attempting to determine the link between an author's achievement and the conditions of his age. His literary portraits and reviews appeared in his *Causeries du lundi* (1849/61), a collection of the essays he published every Monday, and in his famous *Histoire du Port-Royal* (1840/59), a study of the seventeenth-century religious sect that numbered Pascal among its most eloquent defenders.

Although **Ernest Renan** (1823–1892) wrote his *L'Avenir de la science* (The Future of Science) as early as 1848, this bold declaration of his faith in the scientific method was not published until 1890; and meanwhile his unorthodox views had cost him his professorship. His best-known work, *Vie de Jésus* (1863), an attempt to examine the origins of Christianity from a purely historical point of view, aroused a bitter controversy.

Hippolyte Taine (1828–1893) also attempted to apply a scientific approach to different fields of literature and art; he considered that the products of the human imagination obeyed the same laws, and might be judged by the same standards, as other natural phenomena. 'Our sins and virtues are products as natural as sugar and vitriol', he wrote. Among his works are *Philosophie de l'art* (1805) and *Histoire de la littérature anglaise* (1863).

During the Third Republic, French literary prose took a primarily realistic turn; but, on a more popular plane, it introduced Science Fiction, of which the earliest master was **Jules Verne** (1828–1905) whose heroes visit the Moon, explore the centre of the Earth or plunge 'Twenty-thousand Leagues beneath the Sea'. Verne was a genuinely imaginative story-teller, some of whose visions show a considerable degree of prophetic insight.

The most important novelists of the period, however, called themselves the Naturalists – a title coined in 1877 – since they believed that the modern novel should provide a naturalistic account of the contemporary social world, observed with pitiless exactitude. **Émile Zola** (1840–1902), for example, author of *Le Roman expérimental* (1880, The Experimental Novel) sought to become the literary historian of his age; and to each book he gave a separate subject.

Thus his series on the rise and fall

Below left *Toulouse-Lautrec's lithographed poster 'At the Printer's' (1893). Lithography opened new possibilities for the book trade.*

Below *Engraving by A. de Neuville of Captain Nemo taking bearings on the* Nautilus *for Jules Verne's* Twenty-thousand Leagues beneath the Sea *(1870).*

Cinq Centimes

ERNEST VAUGHAN

L'AURORE

Littéraire, Artistique, Sociale

J'Accuse...!

LETTRE AU PRÉSIDENT DE LA RÉPUBLIQUE

Par ÉMILE ZOLA

LETTRE

A M. FELIX FAURE

Président de la République

Above *'Zola awaits judgment' by L. Sabatier for* L'Illustration, *and* (**right**) *the front page of the Paris newspaper* L'Aurore *for 13 January 1898, carrying Zola's open letter to the President of the Republic, in which he attacked government institutions for conniving at injustice. Brought to trial and found guilty of 'defaming officers and authorities', he was fined and sentenced to a year's imprisonment, and spent some time as an exile in England. (Bibliothèque Nationale, Paris)*

of a family – *Les Rougon-Macquart,* (1871/93) includes the life of a Parisian market (*Le Ventre de Paris,* 1873), a coal-mine and its effect on its workers and owners (*Germinal,* 1885), even the growth of a great department store (*Au bonheur des dames,* 1883), that transforms and devours a whole district; and every theme he develops with an abundance of carefully collected and often savagely revealing details.

Zola's backgrounds are frequently more impressive than the characters who people them; but the panoramic impressions that he built up – of mankind in the mass struggling to survive, or wrestling for power and enjoyment – are often memorably vivid. Besides his literary gifts, he had a vigorous sense of justice, as he showed by his conduct during *'l'affaire Dreyfus'* when, in a courageous pamphlet entitled *J'Accuse* (1898), he pleaded most eloquently for the victim.

The brothers **Edmond de Goncourt** (1822–1896) and **Jules de Goncourt** (1830–1870) were both historians of art and exponents of Naturalism in the modern novel, and based their narratives on an elaborate documentation of facts and meticulous observation of the world beneath their eyes. Thus the subject of *Germinie Lacerteux* (1865) was their own devoted housekeeper, who, after her death, they found to have been a dissolute liar and persistent thief. Of much greater interest is the famous *Journal* they kept, and which Edmond continued to keep after his younger brother's tragic end. It provides a splendidly graphic, though often somewhat prejudiced record of the French cultural and social world between 1851 and 1896.

Guy de Maupassant (1850–1893) was the family-friend and literary protégé of Gustave Flaubert, whose concern with style he had inherited. Under Flaubert's tuition he became an exceptionally proficient story-teller; and, during his brief career – he suffered a complete mental breakdown in 1891 – he found time to produce six novels and almost three hundred short stories. His earliest and most effective story, *Boule de suif* (The Dumpling) came out in 1880 – an anecdote from the Franco–Prussian war, which describes the courage and patriotism

shown by a young prostitute as compared with the cowardice and hypocrisy revealed by her prudish middle-class companions. No less typical of Maupassant's approach to life is *La Maison Tellier* (1881), a study of a homely provincial brothel, its customers and denizens.

There is little sentimentality in his tales; but he did not lack sympathy; and his most moving work was the novel he called *Une vie* (1883, *A Life*) – the account of an ordinary woman's existence, her hopes and sorrows and decline towards old age, which concludes with the heroine's discovery that in life 'nothing is either as good or as bad as we think it's going to be!' Maupassant's personal character was a blend of dark melancholy and robust sensuality. His friends nicknamed him '*le taureau triste*', the gloomy bull.

Illustrations, to Maupassant's novel Pierre et Jean *by Geo-Dupuis in 1903* (**above**) *and to his short story* Bed Number 29 – *'The beautiful Irma shows herself to the officers'* (**right**) *by Jeanniot. Maupassant shared with Zola and the Naturalists a concern with the darker and more violent aspects of contemporary social life.*

THE VICTORIAN EPOCH

The word 'Victorian' was long a pejorative term, employed to signify the repressive moral standards that prevailed in Great Britain during Queen Victoria's long reign, from 1837 to 1901. The Victorian ethos, however, did not extend to standards of personal conduct alone. It sprang from economic causes; Karl Marx had based his theory of the inevitable progress of capitalism on his study of the nineteenth-century British scene. Since the Industrial Revolution, wealth had accumulated and poverty increased. Britain was now one of the richest countries in the world; but, as Benjamin Disraeli, later Prime Minister, pointed out in his novel *Sybil* (1845), the rich and the poor had become two separate nations; and, as Ruskin added, they might very soon conflict.

We must not forget, however, the tremendous progress, both spiritual and intellectual, made during the Victorian period, which was often ignored by the rebellious generation – among them, the Queen's biographer Lytton Strachey – who sprang up in the 1920s. English science achieved a revolution, almost as radical as that which Locke and Newton had led during the seventeenth century. Meanwhile, the economist, **John Stuart Mill** (1806–1873), made himself the spokesman of the Utilitarian Theory, or the philosophy of social usefulness, its aim being the greatest possible provision of happiness for the greatest possible number of people – an idea that was to inspire many nineteenth-century reformers. The scientific researches of **Charles Darwin** (1809–1882) into the origins of mankind and 'the survival of the fittest' helped to undermine the biblical story of the Creation still accepted by devout believers. Darwin also encouraged the belief in Progress, in the vision of a world continuously developing, that, at least until the Second World War, ran through European culture.

'Christmas at Windsor', a popular etching of the 1850s. After the scandals of the Georgian age, the virtuous domesticity of Queen Victoria and her consort seemed particularly appealing, and set an example that the middle-class public followed. Despite its moral prejudices, however, the English 19th century was an extraordinarily vigorous and creative epoch. (British Museum, London)

Historians and critics followed suit. They, too, whether revolutionary or reactionary, responded to the forward-looking spirit of their age. **Thomas Carlyle** (1795–1881), a dour Scotsman of hardy peasant stock, passionately opinionated and often wrong-headed, survives today neither as an historian, nor as an historical thinker, but as an imaginative writer who dramatized history. His greatest achievement, *The French Revolution* (1837), although his views about the origins of the Revolution (which he attributes in part to the frivolity and moral wickedness of the *ancien régime*) are absurdly simplified, is a wonderfully stirring narrative, enlightened with brilliant portrait-sketches of the main participants. Carlyle had a cult of the 'hero', set forth in a book he entitled *Heroes, Hero-Worship and the Hero in History* (1841), which expressed his conviction that such dominant figures must be the arbiters of human destiny – hence his admiration for Frederick the Great of Prussia. As he grew older, his point of view became increasingly conservative. He detested industrialism and the suffer-

ings it inflicted, yet opposed ideas of parliamentary reform.

His friend **John Ruskin** (1819–1900), also abominated industrial civilization. His first book, *Modern Painters* (1843) he devoted to the genius of a modern artist, J.M. Turner; but elsewhere, in *Seven Lamps of Architecture* (1849) and *The Stones of Venice* (1851/53), his subject was the art and architecture of the Middle Ages. Latterly, however, he adopted the role of prophet, and published a bold attack, *Unto This Last* (1862) on the modern economic system, that is said to have been 'the Bible of the British Labour Party' and Mahatma Gandhi's favourite reading. At the same time, he remained an influential art critic and the chief supporter of the new Pre-Raphaelite Movement. Ruskin was a master of English prose; and his unfinished autobiography *Praeterita* (1885/89), written in his old age, rivals Jean-Jacques Rousseau's *Confessions* as one of the most fascinating self-portraits in the history of European literature.

Above *Charles Darwin, whose* Origin of Species by Means of Natural Selection *(1859) provided the necessary body of observational data to support a scientific theory of evolution and a mechanism – selection by the survival of those individuals best fitted by adaptations to their environment – to explain it. It was an instant best-seller both for its controversial content and lucid literary style. With the publication of Darwin's* The Descent of Man *(1871), which proposed an evolutionary connection between Man and the apes, controversy reached fever pitch.*

Top *Evolutionary theories were seized on by cartoonists. An Austrian wit in* Der Floh *(The Flea) depicts the evolutionary development of a cellist as he gradually adapts himself to his functions. (Kunsthistorisches Museum, Vienna)*

Above *John Ruskin, an art critic for whom art was the crown of life; but he was also passionately interested in social reform and a fierce opponent of modern industrial society. By Hubert von Kerkhomer (1881). (National Portrait Gallery, London)*

DICKENS

Since the death of Shakespeare, few European writers have created more memorable and, even today, vividly recognizable characters than **Charles Dickens** (1812–1870), who adopted the traditions of the English eighteenth-century novel, on which he had been brought up, but enriched it and tremendously enlarged its scope. Much of his material he drew from his own youth. His good-natured, improvident father – the prototype of Mr Micawber – had spent some time in a debtors' gaol; while he himself, at the age of thirteen, was condemned to earn a pittance at a London blacking-factory. These experiences he never forgot. They inspired him with a horror of poverty and a fierce determination to succeed. In 1828 he set to work as a parliamentary reporter, and presently began to write fiction, and in 1833 he dropped a manuscript entitled *Sketches by Boz* 'into a dark letter-box in a dark office' that belonged to a popular monthly magazine. Having been accepted and published with engravings by the well-known caricaturist George Cruikshank, it was soon followed by the *Pickwick Papers* (1836/37), which after the fourth issue (where Sam Weller made his earliest appearance) proved extraordinarily successful.

Oliver Twist, a far more serious work and the first book he published under his own name, came out in 1838; and from that point triumph followed triumph. London, a city he loved and, because it had been the scene of his wretched childhood, also feared and hated, was usually the background of his greatest novels, *David Copperfield* (1850), *Bleak House* (1853), *Little Dorrit* (1857), *Our Mutual Friend* (1865); and he never tired of exploring and describing it. Dickens possessed prodigious

The versatile artist George Cruikshank (1792–1878) was to produce a memorable series of illustrations for Dickens's Oliver Twist.

Left *A page from Cruikshank's sketch-book showing versions for the figure of Oliver in the famous workhouse scene when the shameless boy asks for more, and* (**below**) *Oliver learns the trade of a pickpocket. (British Library, London)*

energy; whatever he did – writing, editing, organizing theatricals, entertaining his friends – he did with tireless zeal and gusto; and the wild enthusiasm he put into his public readings is said to have cut short his life. His imagination had often a sinister side; and his genius as a story-teller was sometimes qualified by a strain of moral humbug. His heroines, unlike his male characters, are apt to be paragons of stainless virtue; though his treatment of his own foolish wife was harsh, and he was by no means faithful to his marriage vows. Dickens had many of the fine qualities and some of the shortcomings of the age in which he lived.

Opposite, above *Charles Dickens signed his name with an extrovert flourish.*

Opposite *'Dickens's Dream'. This unfinished picture shows a whirling crowd of his imaginative creations surrounding the sleeping writer in his study. It was painted by R.W. Buss in 1873. When the* Pickwick Papers *were appearing in serial form in 1836, the original artist, Robert Seymour, committed suicide and a successor was urgently needed. Both Buss and W.M. Thackeray applied for the post, but it went to H.K. Browne, known as 'Phiz', who was to illustrate many more of Dickens's novels. (Dickens House Museum, London)*

THACKERAY

Above right *Portrait of William Thackeray (1864) by Samuel Laurence. (National Portrait Gallery, London)*

Above *One of the author's illustrations for his* Book of Snobs *(1848) which had first appeared the year before as a series of articles, 'The Snobs of England', in* Punch.

Right *The formidable Miss Crawley hears how Rebecca – Becky – has refused old Sir Pitt's offer of marriage, in Thackeray's* Vanity Fair. *Illustration by Robin Jacques for a 1963 Folio Society edition.*

Though he was almost as skilled a literary craftsman as Dickens, **William Makepeace Thackeray** (1811–1863) who regarded Dickens as his only serious rival, lacked the same demonic energy and imaginative fire. He, too, was a critic of society – he invented the useful word 'snob' – but on a somewhat more superficial plane. Nor did he succeed so rapidly; and his masterpiece *Vanity Fair*, after three workmanlike but less distinguished novels, did not appear until 1848, when he was applauded as 'the Fielding of the present age'. Thackeray studied drawing briefly in Paris in the early 1830s and was an accomplished illustrator.

Two emotional tragedies that overshadowed Thackeray's existence are reflected in his novels – his young wife developed acute melancholia and was pronounced incurably insane; and he conceived a romantic devotion for a friend's wife, who encouraged his friendship but did not return his passion. Such, in *Vanity Fair*, is Dobbin's hopeless devotion to Amelia, who, although virtuous and dutiful, has too little character ever to make him happy; and the central personage of the story is her exact antithesis – Becky Sharp, a woman born to exploit her attractions, as unscrupulous and strong-willed as Amelia is naturally gentle and submissive. She is her author's finest creation. Most Victorian novels present some kind of hero. Thackeray's aim, he said, was to produce 'A Novel without a Hero' – or, indeed, a satisfactory heroine – and 'to indicate, in cheerful terms, that we are for the most part abominably foolish and selfish ... I want to leave everybody dissatisfied and unhappy at the end of the story ...' Among the great Victorian novelists none is, in a quiet way, more cynical.

'BY A LADY'

Above left *The unassuming Jane Austen (c. 1810) by her sister Cassandra. (National Portrait Gallery, London)*

Above *The Brontë sisters (c. 1836) – Emily, Anne and Charlotte – by their brother Branwell. (National Portrait Gallery, London)*
The sisters' first publication was a joint collection: Poems by Currer, Ellis and Acton Bell *(1846), and they continued to use these pseudonyms for their individual publications.*

Left *The Yorkshire moors near Haworth, the Brontë home.*

Jane Austen (1775–1817) was one of the greatest, and certainly the most unassuming, of nineteenth-century English novelists; and when her first published novel, *Sense and Sensibility,* appeared in 1811, it was described on the title-page merely as 'By a Lady'. The daughter of a modest country clergyman, she always lived at home, and was seldom, if ever, seen writing. Although before her death she had achieved celebrity, and was admired by Sir Walter Scott and King George IV, she was not an author who sought attention, and wrote largely for her own amusement on the subjects that she knew best – the world of middle-class gentry and local squires and parsons, the quiet family lives they led, and the occasional balls that they attended. Her novels fall into two main groups – *Sense and Sensibility, Pride and Prejudice, Mansfield Park, Emma* between 1811 and 1816, and *Northanger Abbey* and *Persuasion,* which made a posthumous appearance. Each, particularly *Mansfield Park,* is a miniature work of art; she worked, she herself said, on a 'little bit (two inches wide) of ivory'; and each shows unerring wit and an acute insight into human nature. She possessed an extraordinary gift for enlarging and dramatizing the most apparently commonplace situations.

Very different, both in method and in subject-matter, were the women novelists who sprang into prominence during the mid-years of the nineteenth century – **Charlotte Brontë** (1816–1855) whose *Jane Eyre* (1847) startled and shocked some of her contemporaries as the portrait of a young woman whose passions, though she remains strictly virtuous, have an almost masculine intensity; and her still more talented sister **Emily Brontë** (1818–1848), whose wild rustic drama *Wuthering Heights* (1847) has a self-destructive hero, Heathcliff, that even Charlotte found alarming. Over the book hung a 'horror of great darkness'.

George Eliot (1819–1880), the pseudonym of Mary Ann Evans, was by comparison a literary realist, deeply concerned with the social conditions of her age and the plight of the Victorian labouring classes. But her grasp of personal character was also strongly developed; and her masterpiece *Middlemarch* (1871/72), subtitled *A Study of Provincial Life,* is both a study of her own period, against a background of industrial development and parliamentary reform, and a sympathetic analysis of conflicting human problems.

VICTORIAN POETS

All the early English Romantics, even Wordsworth during his revolutionary youth, had been to some extent rebels against the current social system; but **Alfred Tennyson** (1809–1892), who succeeded Wordsworth as Poet Laureate in 1850 and became a peer of the realm in 1884, developed with the passage of years into a pillar of conformity. His last poem to display a truly adventurous spirit, *Maud*, the poetic drama that he himself considered his finest work, appeared in 1855; but by that stage he was already the widely admired author of various official odes and patriotic pieces.

Yet Tennyson's youth had been restless and care-ridden. His third collection of verse (of which only 450 copies were printed) reveals an imagination that, a modern critic suggests, 'responded most deeply to the doubtful and the dismaying'. A strain of nostalgic melancholy, a sense of the futility of human effort, runs through all his earlier work. At that period, as we see from such memorable poems as *The Lotos-Eaters* (1833) and *Mariana in the South*, the future prophet of Victorian optimism was a visionary pessimist. The idea of death haunted him; and the loss in 1833 of Arthur Hallam, his dearest Cambridge friend, inspired his magnificent elegy *In Memoriam* (1833/50), a funereal tribute that, although the form it took was very different, and the feelings it records probably far more profound, deserves to rank with Milton's *Lycidas* and Shelley's *Adonais*. Tennyson was a poet who outlived his genius, yet never forfeited his mastery of words. He retained his gift of creating verbal harmonies; and his *Idylls of the King* (1859), a Romantic evocation of the Arthurian legends, would be admirable for its craftsmanship alone.

Above *Alfred Tennyson (c. 1840) by Samuel Laurence (National Portrait Gallery, London). While Tennyson was steeping himself in Arthurian legend with his* Idylls of the King, *other Victorians were turning to Celtic lore, and the mad artist, Richard Dadd, became obsessed with the world of fairies.*

Right *Dadd's unfinished painting (1855/64), 'The Fairy Feller's Master-Stroke', was produced while he was incarcerated in London's Bethlem Hospital. He wrote a long explanatory poem about it 'for the benefit of the common mind'. The fairy woodman is about to split a hazelnut in half to make a carriage for Queen Mab. It was eventually acquired by Sir Siegfried Sassoon, poet and author, who in 1963 gave it to the Tate Gallery, London.*

Of Tennyson's close contemporary **Robert Browning** (1812–1887) a modern Catholic writer, Graham Greene, has said that some of his lines 'have stayed in my memory for fifty years and have influenced my life more than any of the Beatitudes'; while, during his own lifetime, a distinguished fellow-poet, Walter Savage Landor, declared that, since Chaucer's day:

> No man hath walk'd along our roads
>   with step
> So active, so inquiring eye, or tongue
> So varied in discourse ...

Browning was a born inquirer, who liked to fasten on a problem, whether it were historical or psychological, and who, besides being at his best an admirable lyric poet, had some of the gifts of a novelist and dramatist. His first great success, *The Ring and the Book*, which appeared in 1863, tells the story of a murder and explores the secret motives of the crime. Elsewhere, in the series of shorter poems he entitled *Men and Women* (1855), he dramatizes personalities of the Italian Renaissance – a dying bishop, a priest more pagan than Christian, ordering his bastard sons to construct the sumptuous tomb that he deserves, and *Andrea del Sarto*, 'The Faultless Painter', apostrophizing his beautiful but faithless wife. Although, like Tennyson, he was a master of words, Browning tended to avoid poetic language and adopt a more colloquial idiom. Victorian critics, however, often accused him of being unnecessarily obscure, and of allowing his attempts to answer the questions he set himself to degenerate into 'mere grey argument'. From a modern point of view, a much more serious fault was his uninhibited verbosity. He was the wordiest of all Victorian poets; and his collected works run to well over a thousand crowded pages.

His wife, **Elizabeth Barrett Browning** (1806–1861), was for many years much the more famous of the two; and, until he published *The Ring and the Book*, the reading public continued to regard him as 'the man who married Elizabeth Barrett'. Compared with her husband, she was none the less a minor poet. Though the love-poems she addressed to Robert, *Sonnets from the Portuguese* (1850), contain some of her most effective and appealing work, she also wrote poems on public issues – in *Aurora Leigh* (1856), the education of women; and in *The Cry of the Children* (1844), the employment of children, condemned to Victorian factories and mines:

For oh, say the children, 'we are weary,
And we cannot run or leap –
If we cared for any meadows, it were merely
To drop down in them and sleep.
Our knees tremble sorely in the stooping –
We fall upon our faces, trying to go;
And, underneath our heavy eyelids drooping,
The reddest flower would look as pale as snow.
For, all day, we drag our burden tiring,
Through the coal-dark, underground –
Or, all day, we drive the wheels of iron
In the factories, round and round . . .'

Above right *Robert Browning and his wife Elizabeth, whom he married in 1846 after a dramatic elopement. Browning's abstruse allusions and touches of deliberate obscurity gave him a reputation as a 'difficult' poet. Here he anticipated later trends in English poetry, but his poetic innovations were often strikingly original, for example, his use of eloquent monologues in his* Men and Women *series. Portraits by M. Gordigiani (1858). (National Portrait Gallery, London)*
Right *Elizabeth Barret Browning campaigned against child labour; this sketch was appended to a parliamentary report on Lord Ashley's Mines Act of 1842 which forebade the employment of women and children beneath the age of 10 as workers underground. (British Library, London)*

THE TWO WAVES

*Before Hegel (**above**) earlier philosophies were seen as rivals to be assessed on equal terms. He saw them as stages in Man's spiritual development, which progressed by conflict between extremes, that yielded progressively more mature syntheses. Lithograph by L.J. Sebbers (1828).*

An historian has described the two huge waves that rolled over Western civilization during the nineteenth century, the one Socialist, the other Nationalist; and nowhere did they seem more likely to merge than in Germany, which, at the opening of the era, had begun to achieve national freedom accompanied by a measure of democratic reform. Yet nowhere else did these two movements prove more difficult to reconcile. After many reverses, national unification was at last achieved in 1871; but Prussian militarism developed simultaneously; and although Liberal aspirations persisted, they were hard pressed by powerful reactionary forces.

Meanwhile, industrialism and scientific progress brought to Germany new ways of thought that superseded the philosophic and artistic ideals of the Romantic period. **G.W.F. Hegel** (1770–1831), however, built a kind of bridge between the two epochs, with his conception of a 'universal spirit' that stood for universal Reason, and his 'dialectic' – his belief in a law of change that runs through human existence. Radical and purely materialistic thinkers, among them **Karl Marx** (1818–1883) and **Ludwig Feuerbach** (1804–1872), joined Hegel, although his own tendencies were more or less conservative. In 1848, Marx and Engels published their *Communist Manifesto* and, in 1867, the first part of *Das Kapital*. The political emergence of Socialism, which had alarmed the middle classes, tended to exasperate the social conflict; and the strife and anguish that resulted is expressed in increasingly realistic writing.

During the first half of the century, the philosopher **Arthur Schopenhauer** (1788–1860) delivered a vigorous attack on the intellectual idols of his day. His most important work, *Die Welt als Wille und Vorstellung* (*The World as Will and Idea*) appeared in 1819; but his philosophy did not come into vogue until the year 1851, when he published *Parerga und Paralipomena* (*Essays from the Parerga and Paralipomena*); and his pessimistic theory that human will-to-live is itself an evil was finally accepted as an alternative to the specious optimism of materialistic thinkers.

From **The Communist Manifesto**
by Karl Marx and Friedrich Engels

The working men have no country. We cannot take from them what they have not got. Since the proletariat must first acquire political supremacy, must rise to the leading class of the nation, it is, so far, itself national, though not in the bourgeois sense of the word.

National differences, and antagonisms between peoples are daily more and more vanishing, owing to the development of the bourgeoisie, to freedom of commerce, to the world market, to uniformity in the mode of production and in the conditions of life corresponding thereto.

The supremacy of the proletariat will cause them to vanish still faster. United action, of the leading civilized countries at least, is one of the first conditions of the emancipation of the proletariat.

In proportion as the exploitation of one individual by another is put an end to, the exploitation of one nation by another will also be put an end to. In proportion as the antagonism between classes within the nation vanishes, the hostility of one nation to another will come to an end.

The charges against Communism made from a religious, a philosophical, and generally from an ideological standpoint, are not deserving of serious examination.

Does it require deep intuition to comprehend that man's ideas, views and conceptions, in one word man's consciousness, changes with every change in the conditions of his material existence, in his social relations and in his social life?

What else does the history of ideas prove, than that intellectual production changes its character in proportion as material is changed? The ruling ideas of each age have ever been the ideas of its ruling class.

When people speak of ideas that revolutionize society, they do but express the fact, that within the old society, the elements of the new one have been created, and that the dissolution of the old ideas keeps even pace with the dissolution of the old conditions of existence.

When the ancient world was in its last throes, the ancient religions were overcome by Christianity. When Christian ideas succumbed in the eighteenth century to rationalist ideas, feudal ideas fought their death battle with the then revolutionary bourgeoisie. The ideas of religious liberty and freedom of conscience merely gave expression to the sway of free competition within the domain of knowledge ...

The Communist revolution is the most radical rupture with traditional property relations; no wonder that its development involves the most radical rupture with traditional ideas ...

The proletariat will use its political supremacy to wrest, by degrees, all capital from the bourgeoisie, to centralize all instruments of production in the hands of the State, i.e. of the proletariat organized as the ruling class; and to increase the total of productive forces as rapidly as possible ...

The Communists disdain to conceal their views and aims. They openly declare that their ends can be attained only by the forcible overthrow of all existing social conditions. Let the ruling class tremble at a Communistic revolution. The proletariat have nothing to lose but their chains.

They have a world to win.

WORKING MEN OF ALL
COUNTRIES, UNITE!

After 1849, Marx spent the rest of his life in England, but an English translation of Volume 1 of Das Kapital *did not appear until three years after his death. From the 1860s, Marx hardly aged at all, and apart from the sparkle in his eyes this 'coloured' photograph of the 1870s is very similar to those taken in 1882 while he was on a cure in Algiers and about which he wrote to his daughter, Laura: 'No art could make a man look worse.'*

'YOUNG GERMANY'

Below *Heine's* 'Krähwinkel', *a satire on small-town virtues, and* (**opposite**) *'Heine's sharp pen threatens authority and philistines'. Illustrations by Angelo Jank in* Jugend *(7:1906). Heine, who made his name with* Die Harzreise (1826, Tour in the Harz) *also inspired the Young German group of the 1830s with his attacks on German military conservatism.*

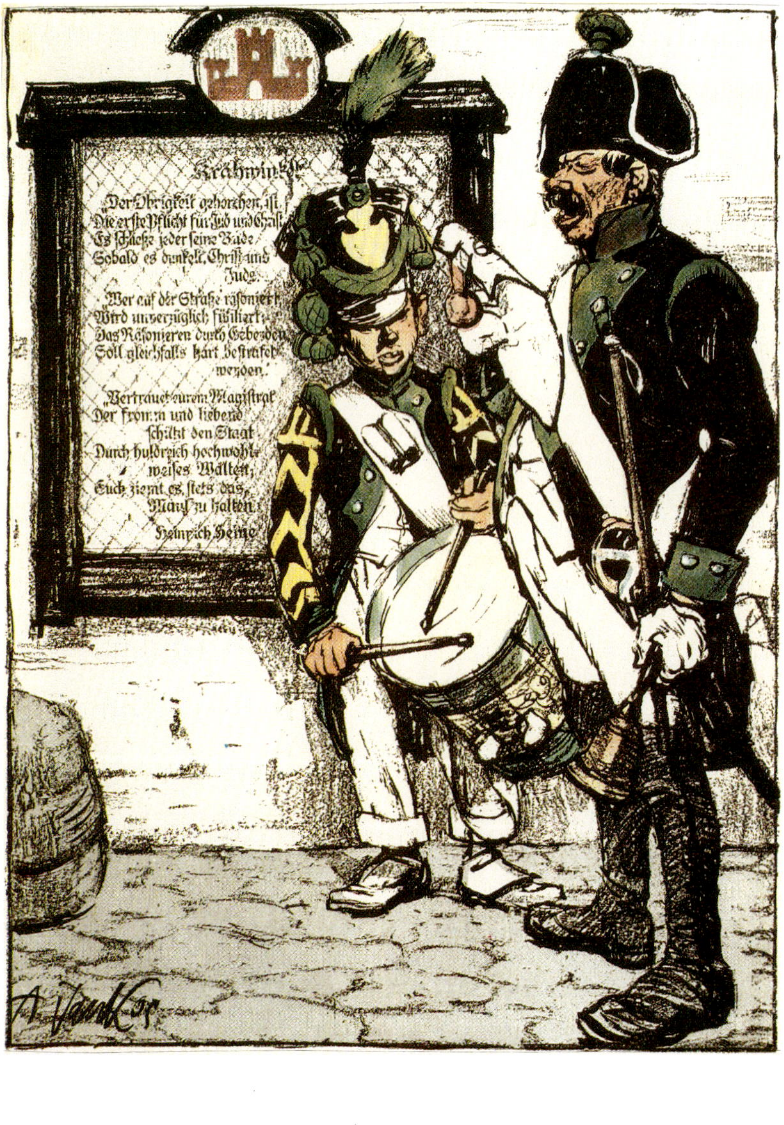

Most of the German Romantics had been politically conservative; but in their rebellion against the philistinism of ordinary life lay the seeds of a separate development, which came to fruition in the *Junges Deutschland* (Young Germany) movement in the 1920s when a phalanx of new writers entered the struggle for liberal reform.

Heinrich Heine (1797–1856), a leading poet of the group, was Jewish by birth, and, although he had abandoned his ancestral religion, never felt quite at home either in Germany or, later, in France, the country he loved and had adopted. His weapon was irony, which he employed to great effect. As a lyric poet, he delighted his own generation, especially the young; and his collection of poems, the *Buch der Lieder* (1827, *Book of Songs*) with its blend of simplicity and subtlety, melancholy and gaiety, as in *Lorelei*, *Die beiden Grenadiere* (*The Two Grenadiers*), and *Die Wallfahrt nach Kevlaar* (*Pilgrimage to Kevlaar*), became a classic of its kind:

The Virgin Mary at Kevlaar
Puts on her best array,
For she must be right busy
With the sick who come today.

And votive gifts are offered
By many sickly bands,
Limbs all from wax are modelled
And waxen feet and hands.

And he who a wax hand offers
His hand will be free from pain
And he who a wax foot offers,
His foot will be well again.

To Kevlaar went many on crutches
Who now on the tight-rope bound,
And many now play the viol
Who had never a finger sound.

Heine was also a brilliant prose-writer, the author of historical and critical works, *The Romantic School* and *Religion and Philosophy in Germany* (1835), and of imaginative discursions – *Reisebilder* (1826/29, Travel Pictures I–III) and *Florentinische Nächte* (Florentine Nights) published in *Salon III* (1837), where, among much else, he describes his single visit to London.

Having migrated to France, he enjoyed a freedom of expression from

Jugend
No 7 1906
M. 05

Despite his attacks on German life, Heine retained a romantic love of his homeland, symbolized by the scenery of the Harz mountains. **Theodor Storm** *(1817–1888), a native of Schleswig, was also an exile for some years during the conflict between Prussia and Denmark over Schleswig-Holstein (1853–64). It was the misty landscapes of the German coastlands* (**above**) *that inspired his nostalgic recollections. Among the finest German lyric poets of the 19th century, Storm was also a master of evocative prose.*

which he was debarred in Germany, and developed into a powerful controversialist. His epic *Atta Troll* (1841/46), the story of an old dancing bear who has returned to the forest, makes splendid fun of the German Socialist party and its vague idealism. Heine was also a political prophet who foretold the re-emergence of the ancient German gods, when Thor's hammer would demolish the Gothic cathedrals, and 'a drama will be enacted in Germany compared with which the French Revolution will appear a harmless idyll'.

Stricken by paralysis and condemned to a 'mattress-grave', Heine died in 1856 and his last volume of verse, *Romanzero* (1851), is a characteristic mixture of heroic ballads, satirical impieties and tragic references to his own approaching end.

In Germany as in England, some writers, poets for the most part, kept the Romantic tradition alive far into the Age of Realism. **August von Platen**, (1796–1835), was one of them – a despondent character who, through poetry, sought compensation for a sense of exclusion and alienation that arose from his homosexual tendencies. Yet this compensation was not easily achieved; and he regarded verse-writing as the sacrificial service he paid to a demanding god.

'The Romantic Agony', as a recent critic has called it, also destroyed the German-Hungarian poet **Nikolaus Lenau** (1802–1850), who finally lost his reason, and meanwhile expressed his gloom in a series of melancholy images – desolate landscapes through which it was his lot to wander. Lenau's gift of translating his own spiritual adventures into natural imagery made him a link between the earlier Romantics and the late nineteenth-century Symbolists.

Towards the middle of the century, Realism began to prevail among poets indifferent to political struggles and the growth of new ideas, of whom **Eduard Mörike** (1804–1875) was an important example. Timid by nature, shy of making human contacts and unsuited to his profession as a priest, he did his best to escape into mysticism and romantic personal relationships, but found refuge only in the world of simple and palpable things. That is the essence of his classically pure verses, collected in *Gedichte* (1838, Poems). He wrote, a literary historian tells us, 'about the first notes of the harp in the blue air of spring, the slumbering song of rushing rivulets at midnight, the dim green cool of the forest, the joyful eagerness of the river… the relief of summer rain, its brisk fall on the stones of the little street, the flight of clouds, the dreams of love and the light shifting of a young girl's mind'.

EVERYDAY PROSE

The leading prose-writers of the period were Swiss. Albert Bitzius (1797–1854), known by his pseudonym **Jeremias Gotthelf**, fought both as a priest and as a writer for his two ideals – Christianity and political freedom. Prepared to preach on morality, yet also a creative artist, he was a highly original writer, thanks not only to his narrative force but to his realistic grasp of his subject, based on a feeling for human grandeur and human miseries alike. Nearly all his novels and stories are set among Swiss peasants and villagers. In *Der Bauernspiegel* (1837, The Peasant Mirror) he tells of a parish child's spiritual development; in *Uli der Knecht* (1841, *Ulric the Farm-Servant*) and in *Uli der Pächter* (1848, Ulric the Factor) of a peasant boy's fall and redemption.

Gottfried Keller (1819–1890), in his *Der Grüne Heinrich* (1855, Green Henry), produced the nineteenth-century equivalent of Goethe's didactic tales. This powerful work describes a young painter, at last forced to admit that he lacks an artistic vocation, and that he can fulfil himself only by a prosaic adherence to the path of duty, who is finally converted to modern science and Feuerbach's philosophy in an anatomy lecture room. But the quality that makes *Der Grüne Heinrich* one of the great nineteenth-century German didactic novels is that this drama of ideas has living characters – Heinrich himself and the women round him. Keller's portrayal of people and of their rustic background has a glow of poetry and humour.

Keller strengthened his position as a realistic novelist by the admirable short stories published in *Die Leute von Seldwyla* (I, 1856; II, 1874, The People of Seldwyla) and *Züricher Novellen* (1878), of which the most absorbing is *Romeo und Julia auf dem Dorfe* (The Village Romeo and Juliet), a popular revival of the ancient tragedy.

Among the many realistic prose-writers active during the middle of the century, **Fritz Reuter** (1810–1874), is particularly notable. He wrote in his native dialect – low German (*platt-deutsch*), and raised it to the level of a literary language. Despite his own misfortunes – he was condemned to death for political agitation, reprieved and given a long prison sentence – he became his country's most popular humorist with his novel *Ut Mine Stromtid* (1863/64, Life in the Country) and its immortal personality Onkel Bräsig.

Above *Jeremias Gotthelf, devout Swiss pastor, always wrote with didactic intent. His realistic, unsentimental novels and stories, written primarily for his rural parishioners, are often in the local Bernese dialect. His* Die Schwarze Spinne *(1842,* The Black Spider*) evokes a medieval plague legend which he adapted to a modern setting. Woodcut by Hänny.*

Left *Gottfried Keller, the Swiss novelist, in 1887, sketched by K. Stauffer. His novel* Green Henry *is largely autobiographical;* The Village Romeo and Juliet *inspired Frederick Delius's opera of the same name.*

ALL IS TRAGIC

Franz Grillparzer was also a competent amateur musician, friend of Schubert and Beethoven (in the early 1820s they discussed plans for an opera), and his play Sappho *(1818) was originally intended to be an opera. Saddened by the decline of Austria as a European power, Grillparzer produced* Family Strife in Hapsburg. *Set in the early 17th century and a characteristically subtle piece of psychological analysis, it is a drama of religious and political conflict that clearly refers to the events of his own day. Portrait (1844) by F.G. Waldmüller. (Kunsthistorisches Museum, Vienna)*

As in other countries, drama was the stepchild of Realism, partly perhaps thanks to the actual possibilities of the art-form. So the Goethe–Schiller drama lived on, though it acquired a new realistic tone.

The Austrian **Franz Grillparzer** (1791–1872) associated himself with Greek Antiquity in his choice of subjects, as in the trilogy *Das goldene Vliess* (1821, The Golden Fleece), and also in his view of life, which regarded hubris, or arrogance, as the greatest of human sins. Above conflict and struggle he valued philosophical resignation, though, in his own existence, resignation often took the form of bitterness, as when, after a fiasco, he refused to allow his plays to be performed – *Ein Brüderzwist in Habsburg* (1848, *Family Strife in Hapsburg*), for instance, which is now accounted one of his best works. As he grew older, his scepticism increased and his plays, such as *Ein treuer Diener seines Herrn* (1828, A Faithful Servant of his Master), became more and more conservative.

Friedrich Hebbel was equally aware of the vanity of ambition, and his works have been characterized by the word 'pantragism', to signify that all is tragic. His plays usually depict the individual's attempts at self-assertion, which, though necessary, must still be punished. In *Maria Magdalena* (1844), he took a modern subject – the tragic life of a middle-class girl. Otherwise, his main personages are usually aristocratic, or derived from ancient literature. In *Judith* (1840), *Herodes und Mariamne* (1850), *Gyges und sein Ring* (1856, Gyges and His Ring) and *Die Nibelungen* (1862), a rebellious main character constantly appears, but is eventually routed and forced to admit his defeat.

Both Grillparzer and Hebbel looked back to the past in many of their plays, while the young **Georg Büchner** (1813–1837) tended to look forward, and during a short life, devoted to studies and revolutionary conspiracies, wrote plays that, until the present century did not receive the recognition they deserved – the comedy *Leonce und Lena* (1836), and the tragedies *Dantons Tod* (1835, *Danton's Death*) and *Woyzeck* (1836). The latter anticipates Expressionism, and inspired the opera by Alban Berg, 'Wozzeck' (1925).

German Naturalism long favoured the theatre; and the *Freie Bühne* (The Free Stage), founded in 1889, put on contemporary works by Strindberg, Ibsen and other forerunners of modern writing. Among German Naturalistic dramatists, however, most today are of historical interest alone. An exception is **Gerhart Hauptmann** (1862–1946), of whom Thomas Mann said, 'he did not speak in his own guise, but let life itself talk.' He made his name with *Die Weber* (1892, *The Weavers*), which portrays the revolt of the weavers in Schlesien during the 1840s, and, like Zola, subordinates the plight of the individual to the sufferings and struggles of the masses. In *Florian Geyer* (1896), the peasant revolt during the Reformation is similarly treated. Hauptmann's hilarious but savage comedy, *Der Biberpelz* (1893, The Beaver Fur Coat), is another comment upon social life, and shows Justice administering a different law for poor and rich. But, at length, Naturalism failed to satisfy this naturally poetic writer; and *Hanneles Himmelfahrt* (1893, Hannele's Journey to Heaven) forecasts a much more lyrical type of drama, while *Die versunkene Glocke* (1896, The Sunken Clock) is a fairy-tale play.

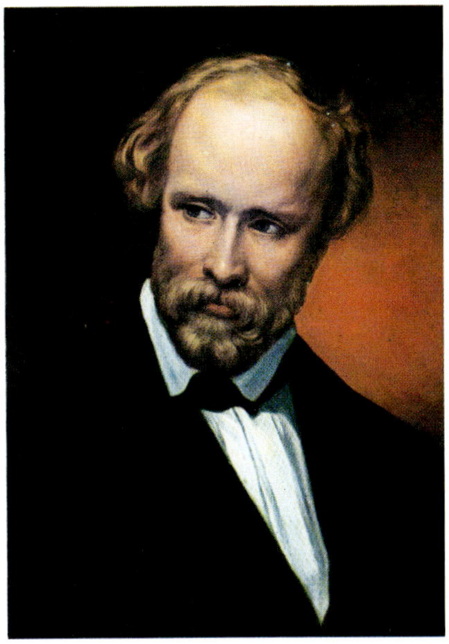

Far left *Friedrich Hebbel (1813–1863), whose themes were often mythological or biblical, but have an immediate bearing on the human condition as a whole. He was inspired by the Old Testament story of Judith* (**below left**). *Illustrated here is 'Judith showing the Head of Holofernes' by Gustave Doré, from the Doré Bible series (1865). Portrait by Karl Rahl. (City Museum, Vienna)*

Left *Berg's opera was inspired by Büchner's play* Woyzeck, *which had woven a powerful tragedy around the sordid tale of a distracted soldier who murders his faithless mistress. Poster by Jan Lenica for a 1964 Polish production.*

Above *One of a series, 'Weaver's Rising' (1893/97), based on Hauptmann's play* The Weavers *by the renowned German graphic artist, Kathe Kollwitz, whose work so often exposed the horrors of social evils. (Wallraf-Richartz-Museum, Cologne)*

Left *Gerhart Hauptmann, by the German realist artist Max Liebermann. (Kunsthalle, Hamburg)*

A STABLE SOCIETY

Scandinavian literature, in the middle of the nineteenth century, reflected both the virtues and the vices of a stable middle-class social system. Revolutionary writers were banned by the authorities; and controversial exchanges of ideas were on religious rather than on political issues. Almqvist, the most dangerous Swedish man of literature, had been rendered harmless and sent into exile. The great liberal writer **Viktor Rydberg** (1828–1895) shocked his contemporaries far more with his *Bible Teaching on Christ* (1862) than with the rebellious rumblings of his *Cave Song*.

The Danish thinker, **Søren Kierkegaard** (1813–1855) was also a rebel, but in the religious field alone. His ponderous works are not so much literature as romanticized theses. In *Either-Or, Stages on the Road of Life* (1843) he broke with the aestheticized Christianity of his day and demanded radical involvement, which he did not find in the established church. Christianity was to Kierkegaard a private question, and its inner essence was suffering, the last of the 'stages on the road of life'. But his importance grew. Strindberg recollects in *Son of a Servant* the pangs of conscience he experienced after reading the works of Kierkegaard, 'the pillar saint', and, far later, Kierkegaard was brought back into literary circulation by Sartre and the Existentialists.

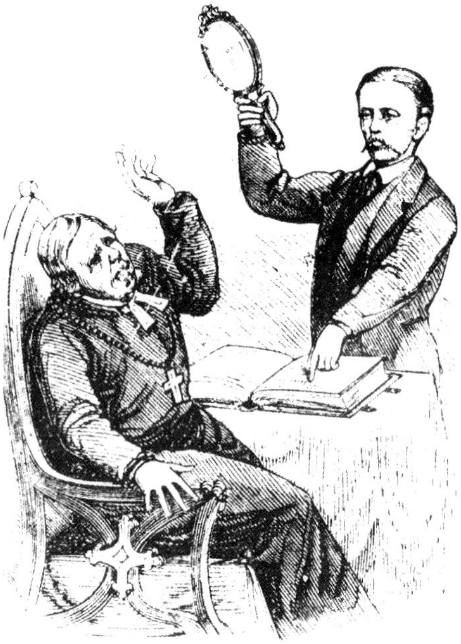

Above right *Swedish cartoon from* Söndagsnisse *(1868) of Viktor Rydberg, who shocked public opinion by his challenge to the doctrine of Christ's divinity; he confronts a churchman with the Mirror of Truth which he opposes to the Bible. (Royal Library, Stockholm)*

Right *Kierkegaard strolling in Copenhagen in the 1840s. (Royal Library, Copenhagen)*

Above *The doyen of Danish literature, Hans Christian Andersen, photographed at the age of 70. His first series of fairy-tales were published in 1835, and they were translated into English some ten years later. (Royal Library, Copenhagen)*

HANS CHRISTIAN ANDERSEN

Scandinavia's most famous writer, **Hans Christian Andersen** (1805–1875), was born in poverty and obscurity; and his fairy-tales – *The Ugly Duckling*, for example – are often symbolic representations of his early sufferings, which in his autobiography, *The Adventure of my Life* (1855) he described in a more prosaic style. His life for many years, as he himself said, had been a 'struggle against rough waves', while he worked and starved in Copenhagen, dreaming of getting into the theatre and trying out different literary forms. Of his early labours all that now remain are some novels – *The Improvvisatore* (1835), *The Two Baronesses* (1848) and *Only a Fiddler* (1837); and when his first volume of fairy-tales, *Tales Told to Children*, appeared in 1835, the only reviewer who noticed them suggested that it was improper that 'a sleeping princess should ride on a dog's back to meet a soldier, who then kisses her'.

Not until 1838, when he received a royal grant, which gave him the security he needed, could the duckling-turned-swan fully spread its splendid wings. Andersen was a highly neurotic man, obsessed by numerous quirks and phobias (as his host Charles Dickens soon observed); and, although his stories may be addressed to children, the underlying theme is often dark and sinister. His poetic imagination is apparent at its best in such stories as *The Snow Queen* and *The Marsh King's Daughter*, where hints of cruelty and adult wickedness lurk not far beneath the surface. Andersen was a prose-poet who translated the stuff of reality into memorable symbolic shapes.

The story quoted here, *The Teapot*, is one of his lesser-known works but is not without charm.

The Teapot
by Hans Christian Andersen

There was once a proud teapot, proud of its porcelain, proud of its long spout, proud of its broad handle. It had something in front, something behind – the spout in front and the handle behind – and that's what it liked to talk about. It never talked about its lid, for that was cracked, that was riveted, the lid had a defect and we don't care to talk about our defects – others will see to that. Cups, cream jug and sugar basin, the whole tea-set, would of course much more easily bear in mind the frailty of the lid and gossip about that rather than about the good handle and the excellent spout. The teapot was well aware of all this. 'I know them,' it said to itself, 'and I also know my own defects well enough to admit them. That's where my humility, my modesty, come in. We all have our failings, though we also have gifts, don't we? The cups have a handle, the sugar basin has a lid, but I have both, as well as one thing in front which they've never got. I have a spout, and that makes me Queen of the tea-table. The sugar basin and the cream jug are privileged to be the handmaids of taste, but I am the giver, the mistress. I pour out a blessing for thirsting humanity; in my inside the Chinese tea-leaves are brewed in boiling tasteless water.'

All this was said by the teapot in the confident days of its youth. It stood on the tea-table, it was lifted by the most delicate hand; but the most delicate hand was clumsy, and the teapot was dropped. The spout broke off, the handle broke off, and the lid – well the lid isn't worth mentioning; it's been talked about enough already. The teapot lay fainting on the floor with the boiling water running out of it. It was a hard blow that it got and yet the hardest blow was the way that they laughed; they laughed at the teapot and not at the clumsy hand.

'That's something I shall never forget', said the teapot, when it afterwards turned over in its mind the story of its own life. 'They said I was done for. I was put aside in a corner, and, the day after, given away to a woman who came begging for dripping. I was reduced to poverty; I couldn't say a word, whether outwardly or inwardly: yet as I stood there, a better life began for me. First you're a thing, and then you become something quite different. Earth was put into me. That means burial for a teapot, but in the earth was placed a bulb. Who put it there, who gave it, I have no idea; but given it was – a substitute for the Chinese tea-leaves and the boiling water, a substitute for the handle and the spout that broke off.

'The bulb lay in the earth, the bulb lay in me and became my living heart, such as I'd never had before. There was life in me, there was strength and energy. My pulse beat, the bulb sprouted till it almost burst with thought and energy; it broke into flower, I saw it, I carried it, I forgot myself in its loveliness – a wonderful thing it is to forget yourself in others. It never thanked me, never gave a thought to me. It was praised and admired. All this made me so glad; how glad it must have made the bulb. Then one day I heard someone say it deserved a better pot. They broke me across the middle, which hurt like anything. But the flower was moved into a better pot – while I was thrown out into the yard to lie there like an old potsherd ... But I have my memories; I can't be robbed of those.'

IBSEN AND BJØRNSON

No one has put forward Kierkegaard's demands for 'either-or' more powerfully than the Norwegian **Henrik Ibsen** (1828–1906), the most influential Scandinavian dramatist. Thus, in *Brand* (1866), the main character is a fanatical priest who allows his wife and children to rot in an unhealthy mountain village rather than capitulate to the 'spirit of compromise' and move away. Too late, he sees the divinity he should have served was not the merciless 'Will of Man', but the Christian God of Love.

In *Brand*, Ibsen judged himself and his people; and he performed the same task, though somewhat more joyfully, in his verse drama *Peer Gynt* (1867), which depicts a Norwegian northerner who finds it as easy to boast and dream as to 'get through' all his difficulties.

Like an Old Testament prophet, Ibsen rebukes middle-class society in a long series of realistic dramas. In *A Doll's House* (1879), he speaks for the independence of women; in *Ghosts* (1881), he exorcises the ghosts of the past who oppose free discussion of marriage, venereal disease and religious prejudice; in *An Enemy of the People* (1882), he dares to doubt if the opinions held by the majority are always well-founded.

Next comes another group of dramas in which he again descends into the dark depths of the individual character and tries to plumb 'the living-lie'. His masterpiece at this stage is *The Wild Duck* (1884), where he presents another 'Peer Gynt', Hjalmar Ekdahl, the failure with a thousand projects, and Gregers Werle, who thinks that he can strip his fellow men of their 'living-lies', but only causes misery and evil. Once more Ibsen is accusing and judging himself. His last dramas, *Rosmersholm* (1886), *Hedda Gabler* (1890) and others, suggest that Ibsen's knowledge of human character anticipated some of the discoveries of twentieth-century psychologists.

Although his international importance cannot be compared with Ibsen's, **Bjørnstjerne Bjørnson** (1832–1910) is the second Norwegian forerunner of the twentieth-century drama. As Ibsen had done, he began by producing historical plays in a light romantic spirit – such a play was *Sigurd Jorsalafar* (1872) – and then proceeded to criticize modern society. He attacks business morality in *The Bankrupt* (1875); and in *A Gauntlet* (1883) he shows a woman herself demanding the sexual standards a man demands of her – an idea that infuriated Strindberg and many others. *Beyond Our Power, Beyond Human Might* (1882/94), is a tragedy about religious miracles, of which the second part of the play is a political drama, as in some of Bjørnson's later works. He himself was a fanatical Norwegian patriot and politician, and a follower of Wergeland. His vigorous stories of folk-life, *Synnøve Solbakken* (1857) and *A Happy Boy* (1860), also won him international fame.

Above *Betty Henning as Nora in the dance scene in Ibsen's* A Doll's House *recorded at the opening performance of the world* première *at the Royal Theatre, Copenhagen, in 1879. Ten years later the London production led to controversial debates on Ibsenism.*

'SUBMIT PROBLEMS TO DEBATE'

Towards the end of the century, the established social system in Scandinavia first showed certain signs of breaking down. Denmark's defeat by Germany in 1864 put an end to Scandinavian chauvinism; while the increasingly stubborn resistance of the Norwegians to the Union with Sweden undermined the idealistic concept of a brotherhood of peoples. When industry developed, new ideas and modes of thought arose, as well as new political and economic factors. The Free Churches had long headed the opposition to the State Church; and the working men's movement and socialist politicians attacked the values of a privileged society. Literature, during the 1870s and 1880s, both reflected and inspired this revolution. Post-Romanticism was superseded by a critical Realism and, as in France, by Naturalism.

A brilliant herald of these new literary schools was the Danish **Georg Brandes** (1842–1927), who, in innumerable articles and literary essays, expressed his conviction that literature should 'submit problems to debate'. His biographies of Shakespeare, Tegnér, Caesar and others, show his radical theories clashing with his emotional sympathy for great men.

Otherwise, Danish writers of this period were less assertive than their Norwegian counterparts. **J.P. Jacobsen** (1847–1885) anticipates the 'tired' writing of the end of the century, with its descriptions of characters who are inhibited from action and doomed to defeat, as in *Fru Marie Grubbe* (1876) and *Niels Lyhne* (1880).

For Swedish literature, the new era opened in 1879, when **August Strindberg** (1849–1912) brought out *The Red Room*, the earliest Swedish novel.

Left *Georg Brandes was an influential critic and lecturer. He headed the literary avant-garde in Scandinavia, represented by the 'modern breakthrough' movement, and his critical writings earned him European fame. Portrait (1902) by P.S. Krøyer. (National History Museum, Frederiksborg, Denmark)*

Below *The Danish writer J.P. Jacobsen reads his work to the leading Copenhagen literary society in 1880. His early poems,* Gurresange, *based on medieval Danish legends, were set to music as* Gurrelieder *in 1913 by Schoenberg. Illustration (1910) by Erik Henningsen. (National History Museum, Frederiksborg)*

Elsewhere he achieved distinction through his Naturalistic tragedies, *The Father* (1887) and *Miss Julie* (1888), which were soon performed all over Europe. In both plays he uses the new psychology and an artistic form that relies for its effect on the unity of time and space. At this stage, his most remarkable work was his autobiography, *Son of a Servant* (1886/1909), a self-portrait almost as noteworthy as the confessions of St Augustine and Jean-Jacques Rousseau. His other important plays *Master Olof* (1874) and *The People of Hemsö* (1887), are aimed chiefly at a native audience. But in later dramas, *A Dream Play* (1901) and *The Road to Damascus* (1898/1901), and in his Expressionist *Chamber Plays* (1907), he again joined the international avant-garde. Eugene O'Neill is one of the modern dramatists who have admitted indebtedness to Strindberg.

On a different level, the Finnish writer **Aleksis Kivi** (1834–1872), wrote his festive peasant novel, *The Seven Brothers* (1870), the first masterpiece of Finnish prose – a realistic portrayal of the wilderness, with glimpses of folk-tales and touches of grotesque fancy. His comedy, *The Shoemaker of the Heath* (1864), remains the first product of the Finnish drama that is still performed today.

Above left *Strindberg, and a reconstruction of his study in the Nordiska Museet in Stockholm, and* (**above**) *in his Berlin days. An unhappy childhood and three failed marriages, combined with a neurotic disposition, convinced him that there was inevitably a struggle between the sexes. Portrait (1895) by the Norwegian artist Edvard Munch. (Nationalmuseum, Stockholm)*

THE LAST AUTOCRACY

Democratic movements in the rest of Europe had left the Russian Empire almost untouched for more than a hundred years. Though Western ideas of freedom now and then penetrated, they affected students and intellectuals rather than workers and peasants; the Decembrist Revolt of 1825, and the assassination of the Emperor Alexander II in 1881, had no immediate revolutionary sequel. Death-sentences and exile in Siberia constantly threatened any opponent of the Imperial regime.

At some time in his life, every important nineteenth-century Russian writer, though not necessarily a revolutionist himself, felt the need of social and political change. Writers made their contribution by criticizing society, not only the condition of the peasants but the life of the educated classes, who, as described by novelists, seem always slightly at a loss, unable to cope with their own problems, or find a purpose in existence, and tormented by a subconscious fear that the future is against them.

There may be little deliberate propaganda in the works of **Nikolai Gogol** (1809–1852). He was a natural Romantic; and his collection of stories *Evenings on a Farm near Dikanka* (1831/32) among which is the famous *Taras Bulba*, a brilliant picture of the Cossack race, shows his interest in traditional lore; but his most celebrated novel, *Dead Souls* (1842) ridicules both the anomalies of serfdom (by which a feudal landlord's estate consisted of the number of 'souls', or peasants, he had inherited) and the absurdities of officialdom in rural Russia. His books became powerful arguments for revolution, though he remained a conservative and an Orthodox believer.

Above *Gogol, who has been called the father of Russian realism in literature, lived for most of his adult life in Rome. With such stories as* The Nose *(1835) and* The Overcoat *(1842), and his novel* Dead Souls *– which he never finished – Gogol anticipated Kafka and the Symbolists. Portrait by F.A. Moller. (Tretyakov Gallery, Moscow)*

Above *Gramatté's grim illustration for* The Overcoat *reveals its Kafka-esque aspects.*

Top *An artist's impression of the assassination of the Tsar Alexander II on 13 March 1881. The Emperor's liberal views could not safeguard him against Terrorist attacks; and his death ushered in a new period of repression.*

Above *'The Volga Boatmen' (1873), a work by the Russian artist Ilya Repin, professor of historical painting at the St Petersburg Academy. Peasant life and the sufferings of the poor were among his favourite themes, as also for some contemporary writers. Repin's work provided a model for painters of the Soviet socialist realist movement. (Russian Museum, Leningrad)*

In the novels of **Ivan Turgenev** (1818–1883), however, the liberal tendency is always manifest, despite a strain of brooding pessimism. The book that made his name, his *Sportsman's Sketches* (1852), reveals his compassion for ordinary men and women, especially the serfs, whose sufferings he had watched in his mother's tyrannical household. Yet, as an aristocrat himself, he still belonged to the past and mistrusted the prophets of the future. Thus *Rudin* (1856) is a variety of self-portrait, in which, for the first time, a classic Russian literary type emerges – the 'superfluous man', the hopeless dreamer, who cherishes innumerable high-flown thoughts and ideals, but whose will to act is suffocated from the start. In *Fathers and Sons* (1862), on the other hand, a story based on the conflict between the old and the new, he draws the incisive portrait of a genuine revolutionary spirit – Basarov, who is determined to destroy the old world – a character Turgenev depicts with reluctant admiration. It was here that he first coined the term 'nihilism' for the views of certain revolutionary groups.

TOLSTOY

The fact that **Leo Tolstoy** (1828–1910), like Turgenev, was a member of the ruling class and a one-time officer, had a considerable effect upon his writing, although, in later life, he longed above all else to live and work among the peasants, and became what was sometimes called 'the repentant aristocrat'. In his autobiographical novels, *Childhood* (1852), *Boyhood* (1854), *Youth* (1857), he tells of Russian country-house life and of his own spiritual development; while in *Sketches from the Siege of Sebastopol* (1855/56) he records his memories of his military service in the Caucasus and the Crimea – a description of warfare without romantic glosses.

The success of these stories enabled him to launch out on a major theme and produce his first masterpiece, *War and Peace* (1869), an historical novel, in which he chronicled the reign of the Emperor Alexander I and Napoleon's disastrous Russian campaign. Here he glorifies not the great leaders but the Russian common people. Tolstoy is as critical of the French emperor, and of the Russian commanders who opposed him, as he is of aristocratic society in St Petersburg. He reserves his praises for the poor soldier Platon Karatayev and a host of humble characters.

The same critical view of the Russian ruling class appears in *Anna Karenina* (1877), which again exalts the values of simple, unambitious life. Levin, a hard-working landowner, who in some respects resembles Tolstoy, achieves faith and married happiness, whereas the lovely, fashionable Anna, wedded to a dull official, is ruined and broken by her passion for Vronski, a fascinating Guards officer.

Tolstoy's political radicalism, his hatred of war, his aversion from aristocratic social life and the pleasures of the flesh, steadily increased with time, and were strengthened by his desperate religious needs. He yearned for, but could not find, salvation. Even his ageing wife at length became a foe; and in his private life existence he made strenuous efforts to practise the original Christian ideals of monastic poverty and chastity. All forms of state organization and private property seemed evil to him, and art and literature mere sinful seductions. His moral crisis is narrated in *A Confession* (1879) and in *The Death of Ivan Ilyich* (1884/86); his fanatical struggle for purity, in a drama, *The Power of Darkness* (1886), and in his novels *The Kreutzer Sonata* (1890) and *Resurrection* (1899). At the age of eighty-two years he suddenly left home one night, and died in a lonely railway station, whither his unwanted wife pursued him. 'The peasants – how do peasants die?' were among his last words.

Left *Greta Garbo and Freddie Bartholomew in David O. Selznick's MGM film of Tolstoy's* Anna Karenina *(1935).*

Below *Besides his imaginative works, Tolstoy wrote numerous pamphlets and articles to promote his social and religious views. Portrait by J. Kramskol. (Tretyakov Gallery, Moscow)*

Tolstoy's novel Resurrection *of 1899 was successfully adapted as a play. Shown here:* (**right**) *the atmospheric prison scene from Act III of the Swedish world* première *in 1903 at the City Theatre, Gothenburg, and* (**below**) *the courtroom scene, with an uncompromisingly realistic setting, in the 1930 production at the Maxim Gorky Theatre in Moscow.*

DOSTOEVSKY

Feodor Dostoevsky (1821–1881) became acquainted with suffering and humiliation at a very early period of his life. His tyrannical father was murdered by the family's serfs; and he was himself an epileptic. Then, in 1849, when he had just begun to make a name as a writer, he was arrested, accused of involvement in a revolutionary conspiracy, and condemned to death. But his condemnation was a sadistic hoax, said to have been personally ordered by the Emperor; and he was reprieved at the last moment, when he had already climbed the scaffold. Instead, he received a long sentence of penal servitude and Siberian exile. Thenceforward the power of Evil and the martyrdom of mankind became the central theme of everything he wrote, tempered by a faith in human goodness, that, even in his gloomiest novels, he occasionally recognizes. From his own experiences he derived the raw material of his first outstanding book – *The House of the Dead* (1860/62), a deeply moving description of a Siberian prison-camp.

Politically, he was less 'engaged' than Tolstoy. He was concerned not so much with social change as with religious redemption. Evil, he believed, had a metaphysical origin; and the problems that haunted him were those of human responsibility and moral guilt. Here the dilemma he faced was that only freedom can ennoble mankind, but that only compulsion can remove our ills. For Dostoevsky, the solution lay in the paradox of Christianity; and he rejected both Western rationalism and the specious optimism of Socialist doctrinaires. In an early masterpiece, *Crime and Punishment* (1866), the rationalist point of view is represented by the student Raskol-

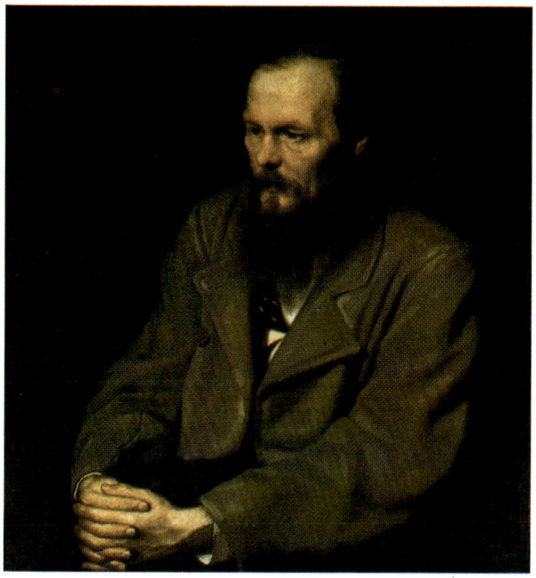

Left *Dostoevsky, who, because he had joined an association of enthusiastic young men who demanded social and political reform, was sentenced in 1849 to four years' hard labour in Siberia. Portrait by B. Perov. (Tretyakov Gallery, Moscow)*

Below *Forty years on, and prisoners are still being sent to work out their sentences in Siberia. From an illustration of 1891.*

Above *The 'rationalist' student Raskolnikov sits brooding at the dinner table in this illustration by P. Reisman for a 1944 edition of Dostoevsky's* Crime and Punishment.

Opposite *'Nihilist students arrested by the police, St Petersburg, 1880', a contemporary artist's impression. Turgenev had first used the term 'nihilism' in his novel* Fathers and Sons *(1862) to denote the views of numerous Russian revolutionary groups who held that the first step to any lasting reform was to destroy existing institutions, until nothing remained of the corrupt old order, no matter what the immediate consequences might be. Some ten years later Dostoevsky, now a staunch opponent of revolutionary ideas, also portrayed nihilism in his novel* The Possessed. *The assassination of Tsar Alexander II in 1881 was a classic act of nihilist terrorism. The Tsar had presided over the emancipation of the serfs and planned further reforms; but, in nihilist terms, such reforms must necessarily be tainted because sponsored by the old regime. Isolated groups, even individuals, carried out sabotage and assassinations inspired by the concept of nihilism throughout the later 19th century.*

nikov, who decides that he has the right to murder a 'worthless' old woman because he himself is her superior, while Sonja, the naive prostitute, stands for love and fellow feeling. She embodies Dostoevsky's human ideal, as in *The Idiot* (1868/69) does the epileptic Prince Myshkin, a pure-hearted fool of God. *The Devils* (1871/72) is an attack on revolutionary terrorists, who are portrayed as diabolic figures, straight from the inferno. Still more passionately, in his huge unfinished novel, *The Brothers Karamazov* (1880) he wrestles with the problems of suffering and freedom. Its action circles around the secret murder of the old rake, Karamazov, the trial of one of his sons and the unjust sentence that the law pronounces. But for Dostoevsky, the question is not primarily judicial. Everyone shares the assassin's guilt. The condemned Mitya accepts another mans' punishment that he may be able to atone; while Ivan, the talented rationalist, has a very different fate, and in his conversation with the Devil, which becomes the climax of the story, he hears the legend of Christ and the Grand Inquisitor, and learns that happiness and freedom can never be reconciled, and that the path for a true Christian is the road that leads to Calvary.

Dostoevsky lacked Tolstoy's magnificent descriptive gifts and literary sense of style. His realism was almost entirely subjective; his theme, the drama of the human soul. His genius consisted in his extraordinary ability to bring his ideas alive by translating them into terms of human character, and in his prophetic imagination, which foresaw many of the crises that afflict the world today.

From **The Idiot** by Dostoevsky
(On Capital Punishment)

'The criminal was a middle-aged man, intelligent, fearless, strong – Legros was his name. Well, believe it or not, I tell you he wept when he walked up the scaffold. White as a sheet, he was. Is such a thing possible? Isn't it horrible? Whoever heard of anyone crying for fear? I never thought that a grown-up man, not a child, could cry for fear, a man who has never cried before, a man of forty-five. What do you think is going on in such a man's soul at the time? Think of the mental anguish he suffers. It's an outrage on the soul, that's what it is! It is written. Thou shalt not kill. Does that mean that because he has killed we must kill him? No, that's wrong. It is a month since I saw it, and I can still see it as though it were happening before my eyes. I've dreamt of it half a dozen times.'

The prince grew animated as he spoke; a faint flush suffused his pale face,

although he spoke as quietly as ever. The servant watched him with sympathetic interest, as though he could not bring himself to take his eyes off him; he, too, was probably a man with imagination, with a capacity for reasoning.

'It's a good thing, sir,' he observed, 'that there is not much suffering when the head flies off.'

'Do you know,' cried the prince, 'you've just made that observation and lots of people are of the same opinion as you, and the engine, the guillotine, was invented for that very reason. But at the time the idea occurred to me – what if it is even worse? You may think such an idea absurd and ridiculous, but if you have some imagination you can't help getting such ideas. Just think: take, for instance, torture: you get suffering, wounds, bodily agony, all of which distracts the mind from mental suffering, for up to the very moment of your death you are only tormented by your wounds. Yet the chief and the worst pain is perhaps not inflicted by wounds, but by your certain knowledge that in an hour, in ten minutes, in half a minute, now, this moment your soul will fly out of your body, and that you will be a human being no longer, and that that's certain – the main thing is that it is *certain*. Just when you lay your head under the knife and you hear the swish of the knife as it slides down over your head – it is just that fraction of a second that is the most awful of all. Do you realize that it is not only my imagination, but that many people have said the same? I am so convinced of it, I will tell you frankly what I think. To kill for murder is an immeasurably greater evil than the crime itself. Murder by the legal process is immeasurably more dreadful than murder by a brigand. A man who is murdered by brigands is killed at night in a forest or somewhere else, and up to the last moment he still hopes he will be saved. There have been instances when a man whose throat has already been cut, was still hoping, or running away or begging for his life to be spared. But here all this last hope, which makes it ten times easier to die, is taken away *for certain*; here you have been sentenced to death, and the whole terrible agony lies in the fact that you will certainly not escape, and there is no agony greater than that. Take a soldier and put him in front of a cannon in battle and fire at him and he will still hope, but read the same soldier his death sentence *for certain*, and he will go mad or burst out crying. Who says that human nature is capable of bearing this without madness? Why this cruel, hideous, unnecessary, and useless mockery? Possibly there are men who have sentences of death read out to them and have been given time to go through this torture, and have then been told, You can go now, you've been reprieved. Such men could perhaps tell us. It was of agony like this and of such horror that Christ spoke. No, you can't treat a man like that!'

RUSSIAN REALISM

Left *Chekhov reading from his play* The Seagull *(a title changed from the original 'woodcock') to the Moscow Arts Theatre company in 1898.*

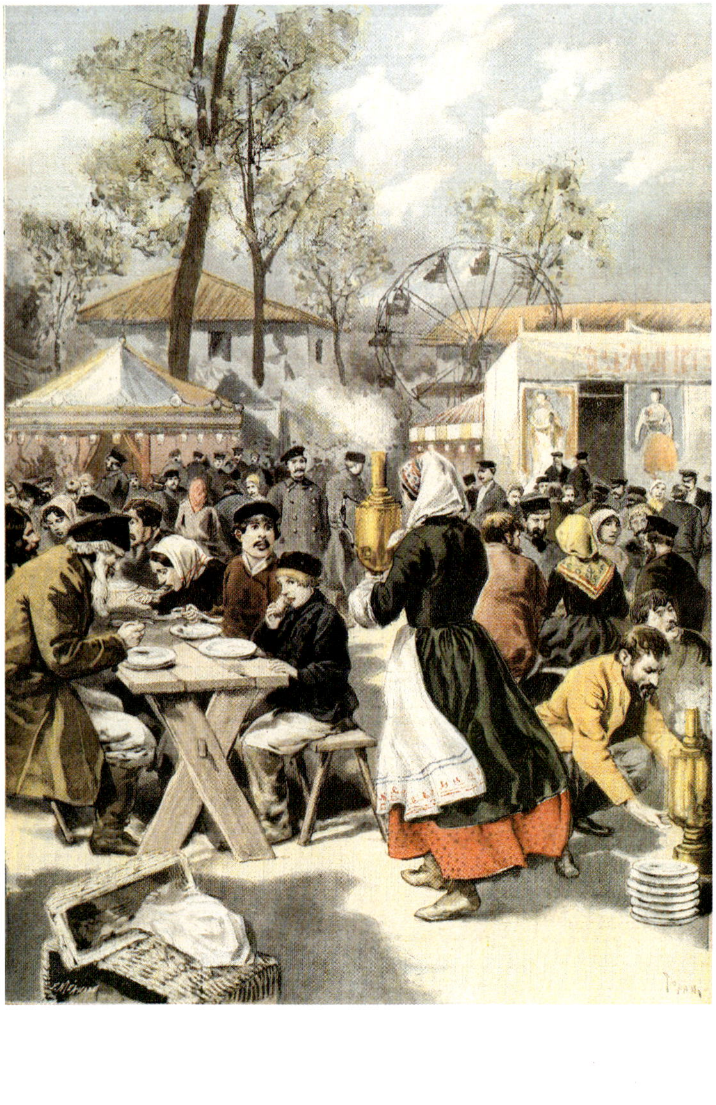

Right *Popular celebrations in Russia at the accession of Tsar Nicholas II (1894), an artist's impression for the French magazine* 'Le Petit Journal'. *Aged 26, Nicholas neither wished to be Tsar nor was prepared for his responsibilities. His one unswerving aim was to hand on to his heir the full powers of untrammelled autocracy, and he had earlier announced his view that popular aspirations to participate in government were 'senseless dreams.' His reign ended in February 1917, and he and his family were 'executed' within the year.*

For decades to come, the great Russian novelists had a powerful influence on modern writing. Dostoevsky had deepened our knowledge of character, and shown that the conflict of ideas was an immensely fruitful topic; while Tolstoy had developed the technique of the novel. His stories are constructed with masterly ease. In *War and Peace,* for example, he manipulates no fewer than 539 dramatis personae; and he made use of 'the interior monologue' long before James Joyce or Virginia Woolf. On the other hand, Naturalism of the kind that Zola practised is seldom found in Russian literature. A mechanistic view of the world, and of man as an amoral animal, could never have been combined with the religious and moral broodings of the Russian story-tellers.

Nikolai Leskov (1831–1895), unlike many of his contemporaries, had an idyllic turn of mind. A joyful observer, though he had a feeling for the macabre, in *Cathedral Folk* (1872) and *The Enchanted Wanderer* (1873), with their capricious and anecdotal style, he depicts many traditional aspects of the Old Russia, its enormous monasteries and ancient churches.

Anton Chekhov (1860–1904) began his literary life as the author of comic anecdotes for newspapers and magazines, but had become, before the age of thirty, a profoundly serious writer. His plays – *The Seagull* (1896), *Uncle Vanya* (1897), *The Three Sisters* (1901) and *The Cherry Orchard* (1904) – and his short stories (of which one of the finest and best-known is *The Lady with the Dog*) show the same subtlety of characterization and the same descriptive skill, which immediately fixes our appreciation of a character or landscape. It is a pensive, autumnal world he depicts. The people he introduces – students, professional men, actors and actresses, small land-owners – seem all more or less frustrated, and look despairingly towards the future. In *The Cherry Orchard*, the beautiful orchard itself has not yet been laid low; but the sound of the woodman's axe is rapidly approaching.

MORALISTS FALSE AND TRUE

The American Civil War of 1861–65 opened a new era, governed by the industrial development of the Northern States; but it was some time before the Machine Age found proper literary expression. Then Romanticism and Realism began to merge; and one of the more memorable Romantics was **Henry W. Longfellow** (1807–1882), the most popular poet of his day, whose chief service to literature were his evocations of the national past – in *The Song of Hiawatha* (1855) of native Indian life, and *Evangeline* (1847) and *The Courtship of Miles Standish* (1858), of Colonial times.

In his novels and short stories, **Nathaniel Hawthorne** (1804–1864) strove for psychological realism. He was a stern moralist. But in his best novel, *The Scarlet Letter* (1850) with its study of a wrecked marriage and an illicit love affair, he shows unusual human insight. Hawthorne's use of the 'American in Europe' theme is thought to have had some influence on Henry James.

Harriet Beecher Stowe (1811–1896) wrote in 1852 the world-famous novel *Uncle Tom's Cabin*, a sentimental romantic narrative aimed at the evils of slavery. So deep was the impression it made abroad, and so appealing was the character of the high-minded old negro Uncle Tom, that there was a run on the Bible in Parisian bookshops, and purchasers could be heard anxiously enquiring whether the volume offered them was indeed 'the real Bible', the book that Uncle Tom had read. The novel's political importance, however, has probably been overestimated; though Abraham Lincoln is said to have greeted the author as the woman whose book had helped to start the Civil War.

Above *America's three most popular writers in the mid-19th century: from the left, Nathaniel Hawthorne, Longfellow and Harriet Beecher Stowe. Melville and Whitman had not yet been discovered by the public.*

Left *A contemporary painting that records the conclusion of the American Civil War with the surrender of the Confederate General Robert E. Lee to the Federal (Northern) commander General Ulysses Grant at the Appomattox courthouse in April 1865. (Smithsonian Institution, Washington DC)*

Below left *President Lincoln rides through the streets of Richmond, Virginia, in April 1865 to celebrate the end of the Civil War. (Library of Congress, Washington DC)*

WHITMAN

Walt Whitman, who in his Bohemian youth loved to cultivate picturesque legends about himself. It is said that he was dismissed from his employment in 1855 for publishing 'an obscene collection of poems'. This was Leaves of Grass, *that was to make Whitman America's national poet. Popular opinion was at first shocked by the poems' glorification of universal love and perplexed by his free verse forms. The Transcendentalist Ralph Waldo Emerson, however, sent Whitman a letter of congratulation, calling the work 'the most extraordinary piece of wit and wisdom that America has yet contributed'.*

Walt Whitman (1819–1892), America's national poet, stands on the borderline between the two eras. He derived his tempestuous egotism, and his understanding of the writer's role as a prophet and a seer, from the Romantic movement, yet remained a Realist in his insatiable appetite for the contemporary American scene.

Whitman's great subjects are threefold – the poet's sense of his own identity and his almost ecstatic love of life, which finds its strongest expression in the tremendous *Song of Myself* (1855, rev. 1889); the United States, whose literary independence he proclaims in the poem, *Pioneers! Oh Pioneers!* (1865); and his visions of democracy and human brotherhood, voiced, for example, in *Song of the Open Road* (1856).

The first edition of his central work, *Leaves of Grass*, came out in 1855; and during the course of years he published nine editions, all with different texts, to which he was constantly adding new or rewritten poems; until the number of pages had risen from 55 to 550. The last edition came out in the year of his death; but meanwhile, despite his passionate self-absorption, he had never allowed his name to appear upon a title-page. His book was intended as an independent organism that spoke directly to the reader.

Whitman was a linguistic pioneer, with an immensely wide vocabulary, based on his intense observation of the sensuous world; and his verse, though free, was always carefully constructed. His method often anticipates that of twentieth-century Surrealists and Expressionists.

From **Song of Myself**
by Walt Whitman

Through me many long dumb voices,
Voices of the interminable generations
of prisoners and slaves,
Voices of the diseas'd and despairing
and of thieves and dwarfs,
Voices of cycles of preparation and
accretion,
And of the threads that connect the
stars, and of wombs and of the
father-stuff,
And of the rights of them the others
are down upon,
Of the deform'd trivial, flat, foolish,
despised,
Fog in the air, beetles rolling balls of
dung.
Through me forbidden voices,
Voices of sexes and lusts, voices veil'd
and I remove the veil,
Voices indecent by me clarified and
transfigur'd.

I do not press my fingers across my
mouth,
I keep as delicate around the bowels as
around the head and heart,
Copulation is no more rank to me than
death is.

MELVILLE

For five years, until he embarked on authorship, **Herman Melville** (1819–1891) had sailed the oceans as a seaman and whaler. His material was impressively realistic; but his style was strongly coloured by the influence of a turbulent, romantic nature. He tried many literary methods before he finally made his name in 1846 with his travel-book *Typee*, where he described his stay among the cannibal inhabitants of the Marquesa Islands. He also wrote poetry, psychological novels and short stories. His reputation as one of the great American prose-writers is based on his novel *Moby Dick* (1851) – a straightforward story of the whalers' hazardous life and a stirring prose–poem combined, in which both Captain Ahab, who hunts the great white whale, and the terrifying whale itself, are mysterious symbolic figures.

After the success of *Moby Dick*, Melville lost his popularity, and took up a post with the American Customs Service. But during that long period, he wrote several important works – a collection of short stories, *The Encantadas* (1854), material for which was taken from the Galapagos Islands, *Piazza Tales* (1856), and the sea-story *Billy Budd* (published posthumously in 1924), an exciting mixture of fact and fiction that again, like *Moby Dick*, had a strongly symbolic side, and inspired an opera by Benjamin Britten.

Gregory Peck as Captain Ahab battling with the whale in John Huston's film 'Moby Dick' (1956), with script by science-fiction writer Ray Bradbury.

AMERICA AND EUROPE IN LIFE AND LETTERS

Realism in America began modestly with short stories; and here the leading names are **Bret Harte** with his gold-mining tales, and **Mark Twain** (1835–1910), the pseudonym of Samuel Clemens. Twain created at least two memorable characters, and in his *The Adventures of Tom Sawyer* (1876), and *The Adventures of Huckleberry Finn* (1885), evoked the sleepy background of the Mississippi. Though he avoided direct social criticism, very often we can infer from his writing what perhaps he would have liked to say – for example, when he describes Huckleberry Finn's friendship with a fugitive negro slave. His travel-book *The Innocents Abroad* (1869) contains satirical impressions of Europe; and in his journalism he championed the cause of the oppressed, for example, Chinese insurgents during the Boxer Rebellion.

Henry James (1843–1916), American by birth, European, and latterly British, by adoption, was unquestionably among the most distinguished novelists of his epoch on either side of the Atlantic. His literary life can be divided into three periods. Of these the first began in 1876 with publication of *Roderick Hudson*, a comparatively direct and unambitious tale. To the second belong his finest short stories, including *Daisy Miller* (1879) and *The Aspern Papers* (1888), and his early masterpiece *The Portrait of A Lady*, which came out in 1881; while the third produced a trio of novels, *The Wings of the Dove* (1902), *The Ambassadors* (1903) and *The Golden Bowl* (1904), where, in seeking for greater clarity of expression, he employed a far more complex and allusive style.

A theme that always fascinated Henry James was the gulf between the Old and New Worlds, between American innocence and European sophistication; and his characters are usually leisured and privileged persons, who have the time and talent to cultivate their own separate ideas and dreams. He was an exceedingly shrewd psychologist and, at his best, a highly accomplished story-teller. Although no realist in the ordinary sense of the term, he never ceased to value what he called 'solidity of specification', and believed that only through art could human experience be raised to the plane of imaginative literature. He condemned mere reporting. Hence his sharp disagreement with his young friend H.G. Wells. The novelist's task, James declared, was to extract from his human raw material a 'tiny nugget of gold' which he could then 'hammer into a sacred hardness'.

Meanwhile, on the other side of the Ocean, two rising authors **Stephen Crane** (1871–1900) and **Frank Norris** (1870–1902) benefited from the example of the European Naturalists, and gave their works an aggressive slant, directed at the growing materialism of American society.

Above left *Mark Twain, photographed in old age.*
Opposite, above *Clemens's pseudonym came from 'mark twain', the river call for two fathoms of water. As a youth he had commanded a Mississippi river boat and his two most famous books –* The Adventures of Tom Sawyer *and* Huckleberry Finn *– immortalized his boyhood spent on the riverside. Both stories have been filmed (Museum of the City of New York). Fame as a humorist was assured with his* Jumping Frog *article in 1865, and he was to make lecture tours all over the world.*
Right *A teenage Jackie Coogan starred as Tom Sawyer in both of Norman Taurog's films. He is seen here in 'Huckleberry Finn' (1931).*
Far right *Henry James in 1913. The sitter wrote of Sargent's portrait: '... Sargent at his very best and poor old H.J. not at his worst ... a living breathing likeness ...' (National Portrait Gallery, London)*

FROM ROMANTICISM TO SYMBOLISM

Death waters the flowers in 'The Garden of Death' (1895), a painting by the Finnish artist Hugo Simberg who was inspired by the ideals of the Symbolist movement in literature. Like the Symbolist poets, the artist is using external objects – the monks' robes, the watering can, the simple towel, the ordered layout of a monastery garden – to convey or symbolize a deeper reality. Evocative though it is, the painting demonstrates the difficulties that confront an artist who attempts to transmit a visual image through the elusive medium of words. Whereas Simberg's pictorial metaphor may seem rather obvious, the poems of the Symbolists were often somewhat obscure because the symbols they chose were often recondite and not easily interpreted. (Atheneum Museum, Helsinki)

A word that concludes with the suffix 'ism' now and then inspires mistrust. It frequently performs a useful service, however, and helps us to understand the background and tendencies of any given literary period.

Just as Romanticism first emerged in the Age of the Enlightenment, during the nineteenth century two dominant isms, Realism and Naturalism, were followed by Symbolism, the gospel of a school of poets who sought to express themselves by suggestion, evocative imagery and the music of words, rather than by direct statement. Their founder, Charles Baudelaire, was saluted by the young Rimbaud as a modern 'king of poets' and the first of 'voyants' or 'visionary writers'; and, although the lifetime of genuine Symbolism was brief, its main principles had a profound effect on twentieth-century poetic literature.

Another agent of change was a growing interest in psychological research, stimulated by the fact that science had now entered the field. Dr Jean-Martin Charcot's experiments with hypnosis at the La Salpêtrière Hospital near Paris stimulated many European writers, among them August Strindberg.

Some literary groups, meanwhile, had not yet quite abandoned the Romantic tradition, and tired of 'shoemaker realism', as the Swedish writer Heidenstam called it, launched into exoticism or religious mysticism, even into reactionary nationalism. Then there were the aesthetes, devotees of beauty for its own sake, who preached the artist's moral freedom. At the same time, when the twentieth century dawned, a sense of melancholy and helplessness spread through the creative world, as if writers had vague premonitions of the coming World War. They no longer felt, like Victor Hugo or Tolstoy, that they had a prophetic role to play, but were resigned to becoming mere spectators.

SYMBOLISM

Paul Verlaine (1844–1896), was above all else a literary musician, whose art was 'the art that conceals itself', and who, during a disorderly life, produced a multitude of famous lyric poems, distinguished by their simplicity, verbal delicacy and deceptive air of spontaneity.

Like François Villon, he spent much of his existence, particularly his later years, 'between the brothel and the Holy Church'. When his astonishing *protégé* Arthur Rimbaud had lured him from his wife and home, he became a wandering bohemian (once imprisoned for murderously attacking Rimbaud) and a sometimes remorseful drunkard. But his poems would never lose the lightness and freshness that makes them almost impossible to translate. His *Il pleure dans mon coeur* (*There is Weeping in My Heart*) is quoted below:

> There is weeping in my heart as it rains on the town. What languor is this that pierces my heart?
>
> O gentle noise of the rain on the ground and the roofs! For a heart that is troubled, O the song of the rain!
>
> There is no cause for weeping in this sickened heart. What! No treason? This sorrow has no cause.
>
> Indeed, it is the worst grief not to know why, without love or hate, my heart has so much grief.

In the youthful **Arthur Rimbaud** (1854–1891) Verlaine, as soon as he had read *Le Bateau ivre* (*The Drunken Boat*), recognized a new poet of bewildering originality. Their relationship became passionate as well as poetic; and together they visited London and explored its slums and public houses. Rimbaud had concluded his literary career before he reached the age of twenty-one; *Le Bateau ivre* was written in 1870, when he was seventeen. Then, after publishing *Une Saison en enfer* (1873, A Season in Hell), an account of the spiritual inferno through which he had just passed, he abandoned literature and decided he would conquer the world as an adventurous man of action. We hear of him in many strange roles – Foreign Legionary, circus-performer, Abyssinian trader and arms-smuggler. He died in France, crippled by an accident on one of his African expeditions, towards the end of 1891.

Above *Paul Verlaine, an alcoholic and, though he was once married, latterly a homosexual. His passionate association with the young poet, Arthur Rimbaud, whose genius he immediately recognized, was another disturbing factor in his life. Verlaine became one of those writers at odds with society whom he himself described in a famous critical essay,* Les Poètes maudits *('accursed') of 1884. Etching (1895) by the Swedish portrait painter Anders Zorn. (Bibliothèque Nationale, Paris)*

Left *Cartoon by Charles Decaux in the 1890s of Rimbaud as an unruly child defacing language with his paint-box. It was prompted by his poem* Sonnet des voyelles *('vowels'), published in the Symbolist periodical* La Vague *(1886). Here Rimbaud evoked the delicate connection between words and colours.*

Above right *Detail of a group portrait by the French painter and writer Jacques-Émile Blanche (1861–1942), with the poet Mallarmé on the right. (Musée des Beaux-Arts, Rouen, France)*

Above *'The Afternoon of a Faun', woodcut by Édouard Manet for the special limited edition (1876) of Mallarmé's poem, published by the poet himself after the editors of* Parnasse contemporain *had rejected it the year before.*

Le Bateau ivre by Arthur Rimbaud

I've known the surf, the waterspout, the tide:
Lightning-split skies, the dusk; the dawn upheld
Like a swarm of doves; and I have spied
Sometimes, what Man believes he has beheld.

Lighting long wisps in violent panoramas
I have seen mystic horrors scrawl the sun:
For waves, like actors in the ancient dramas
Unroll their flickering shutters as they run.

I've dreamed the green night lit with dazzling frost
A kiss that to the sea's eyes slowly grew
The flow of saps, to human knowledge lost
And singing phosphorescence gold and blue.

Modernist poets of the 1900s probably owed more to Arthur Rimbaud than to any other nineteenth-century poet, both to his poems and to his theories. Victor Hugo he accounted a 'colossal vulgarian'. He was a poetic anarchist, determined to destroy as well as re-create. Writing verse was a magical operation; and, to achieve the vision it needed, the poet must seek a systematic 'derangement of all the senses', transforming himself into the universal Sick Man, universal Criminal, universal Damned Soul. The imagery of his poems is always vigorous and often violent. Of Rimbaud's *Le Bateau ivre,* Verlaine said, when he first received the manuscript, that it contained 'all the sea'.

Stéphane Mallarmé (1842–1898) was another poet who regarded his art as a magical manoeuvre; who reverenced words for their own sake, and often collected them and carefully put them aside, accompanied by significant images, before he used them in a poem. He cherished the idea of 'pure poetry', of 'the little flame' that illuminated the works of the greatest poets, and that he himself was constantly attempting to kindle. In his maturity, Mallarmé became the leader of a school, whose disciples gathered around him every Tuesday evening. The works collected in his slender volume, *Poésies complètes* (1887), include his famous *L'Après-midi d'un faune* (1876, *The Afternoon of a Faun*), which Debussy set to music as a 'symphonic poem' in 1894. It also inspired Nijinsky's first attempt at choreography for Diaghilev in 1912.

Verlaine is the most comprehensible of the three great French Symbolists; Rimbaud, the most revolutionary; Mallarmé, the most subtle and abstruse. Together, they immensely enlarged the horizon of nineteenth-century French poetic literature.

In 1886, the Greek-born poet **Jean Moréas** (1856–1910), pseudonym of Iannis Papadiamantopoulos, published a manifesto in the newspaper *Figaro*, where the word 'symbolism' was used for the first time to describe the whole movement; and the magazine *Le Symboliste* was launched the same year.

Symbolism also helped to renew the drama, a renewal foreshadowed in Ibsen's and Chekhov's later works. French Naturalistic drama had never fully developed; and its day had already passed when the Belgian **Maurice Maeterlinck** (1862–1949), wrote his poetic plays, *Les Aveugles* (1890, *The Sightless*) and *L'Oiseau bleu* (1909, *The Blue Bird*). They contain neither revealing action nor psychological analysis, but are lyrical, almost static works, of which the meaning is implied through symbols rather than openly declared.

'The Kingdom of the Future' – the Azure Palace 'where the children wait to be born' (Act V, scene iii). Illustration (1971) by Touchague for Maeterlinck's The Blue Bird *(1909), one of the most popular plays of its time. He was awarded the Nobel Prize for literature two years later. His* Pelléas et Mélisande *of 1892 provided Debussy with the book for his opera of the same name.*

'THE BANKRUPTCY OF SCIENCE'

Right *'Never lend books! My shelves are mostly filled with books lent by my friends', advised Anatole France, who was awarded the Nobel Prize for literature in 1921. Shortly after his death in 1924, a former secretary published an intimate account,* Anatole France en pantoufles *('in slippers') which revealed the secrets of the great writer's love life. Sketch of the writer in old age by Birger Lundquist.*

François Anatole Thibault, who wrote under the name of **Anatole France** (1844–1924), had the two qualities said to be typically French, irony and wit. Nicknamed 'the pocket Voltaire of his age', he was a skilful story-teller, seen at his most engaging in such light-hearted, amiably cynical novels as *Le Crime de Sylvestre Bonnard* (1881), *La Rôtisserie de la reine Pédauque* (1893, *At the Sign of the Reine Pédauque*) with its entertaining hero, the benevolent, pleasure-loving Abbé Coignard, and *La Révolte des anges* (1914, *The Revolt of the Angels*).Towards the end of the century, however, France became absorbed in a burning question that divided friends and broke up families – the Dreyfus Affair, caused by the unjust condemnation of a Jewish regular officer as a German secret agent. France, like Zola, became an ardent Dreyfusard and wrote a fantastic novel, *L'Île des pingouins* (1908, *Penguin Island*) in which the whole Affair is elaborately satirized.

Paul Bourget (1852–1935), a friend of Henry James, was a prolific novelist whom critics praised for his acute knowledge of feminine psychology and the technique of fashionable love-making. Latterly, nevertheless, he attempted more serious subjects; and in *Le Disciple* (1889) he warns his readers against taking a too scientific view of life.

Meanwhile, Renan's homage to science had been published in 1890; but, five years later, 'the bankruptcy of science' was already being discussed. Both are extremist points of view; and the tragedy of the new century was that it could not find a middle way.

From Anatole France's At the Sign of the Reine Pédauque, *by B.B. Hedlund for a 1945 edition.*

THE WILL TO POWER

There were many writers in Germany at this time who did not share the Naturalistic credo, among them being the Swiss **Conrad Ferdinand Meyer** (1825–1898). With psychological realism, but also with a Romantic's sense of the picturesque, he portrayed great historical figures in narrative verse and short stories, including *Huttens letzte Tage* (1871, The Last Days of Hutten) and *Die Versuchung des Pescara* (1887, The Temptation of Pescara). He was a neurotic; and in his verse he also expressed his private conflicts, but objectively, without emotional asides. He allows his subject-matter to speak for itself, thus anticipating both the Symbolists and such later poets as Rainer Maria Rilke.

Friedrich Nietzsche (1844–1900) who began his career as a disciple of Schopenhauer, soon shaped his own brilliant, desperate theories. Rejecting the democratic bias of the period, he put his faith in an élite, and evolved the concept of a 'Superman', who stands high above all laws and accepted moral standards. The starting-point of Nietzsche's philosophy was his hatred of the Christian religion. He wished to replace its 'slave-morality' with the 'master morality' he himself upheld; for his aim, pronounced with almost religious enthusiasm, was to achieve a 'revaluation of all values'.

Behind his wild theorizing lay perhaps some traces of the mental illness that first attacked him in the 1870s, when he was a Professor of Classical Philology at the University of Basle, and wrote his earliest critical works, including *Die Geburt der Tragödie* (1872, *The Birth of Tragedy*). In 1879, this illness, which would persist until his death, obliged him to leave his academic post, though it did not prevent him from writing and publishing his most influential books.

What heightened his influence was the fulminating style in which he framed his new gospel, particularly in *Also sprach Zarathustra* (1883/92, *Thus Spoke Zarathustra*), where his mouthpiece was the ancient Persian religious leader, Zarathustra, whose recorded precepts, however, bear little resemblance to his own. The titles he often employed show the direction of his thought: *Jenseits von Gut und Böse* (1886, *Beyond Good and Evil*), *Zur Genealogie der Moral* (1887, *The Genealogy of Morals*) and *Der Wille zur Macht* (which was revised and adapted posthumously in 1906 as *The Will to Power*).

Nietzsche not only protested against the intellectual trends of his day, but to some extent reflected them. It is a fairly short step from Darwin's 'survival of the fittest' to Nietzsche's 'will to power'; and his teaching was a brew in which the best and worst tendencies of the period were combined. A German historian has described him as a 'demonic' creature, divided both in his mind and in the effect that he produced. During the twentieth century, Nietzsche's ruthless 'Superman' would come to play a sinister part in the history of the German people.

A somewhat uncharacteristic portrait of Friedrich Nietzsche by the Norwegian artist Edvard Munch. He called this an 'idea' portrait as it was done posthumously in 1905/06 from other portraits and photographs. (Thielska Gallery, Stockholm)

From **Thus Spoke Zarathustra**
by Friedrich Nietzsche

Behold, I teach you the Superman.

The Superman is the meaning of the earth. Let your will say: The Superman *shall be* the meaning of the earth!...

It is not your sin, but your moderation that cries to heaven, your very meanness in sinning cries to heaven!

Where is the lightning to lick you with its tongue? Where is the madness, with which you should be cleansed?

Behold, I teach you the Superman: he is this lightning, he is this madness!

THE GOETHE HERITAGE AND THE EMPIRE

Emperor William II of Germany, on horseback, greeted by the once all-powerful Chancellor Otto von Bismarck in 1895. The Young Emperor had dismissed Bismarck in 1890 but they became reconciled a few years later. The Emperor's condescension and the submission of the old statesman sum up the situation in William's new Germany. Many outside Germany believed that the destinies of that great country were in the hands of the ambitious and unstable sovereign, and German literature itself became increasingly critical in the years that preceded the First World War. Drawing by C.W. Albers (1895).

The new German state, Bismarck's creation, soon demonstrated its explosive strength. German industry captured world markets; and the Imperial regime showed itself the equal of other European governments in the acquisition of fresh colonies. But, as Germany grew stronger and more aggressive during the years that preceded the outbreak of the First World War, an atmosphere of resignation and pessimistic apathy crept through its spiritual and intellectual life. Writers and thinkers seem to have suspected that beneath the surface all was not well; that the bad seed of the nineteenth century was ripening, and that its good seed – the heritage of Goethe, the regard for civilization and the sense of moral responsibility – was being trampled underfoot.

Though German literature during those years was more than ever critical, it appeared, at the same time, to have lost its nineteenth-century ambition to redress the injustices of modern life, and concentrated on far more general themes – the tragedy of human existence, the hopelessness of the individual's position in a universe without God, and the artist's solitude in a world without poetry.

Heading the group of poets who contributed to the magazine *Blätter für die Kunst* (1892/1909, Journal of the Arts) was **Stefan George** (1868–1933), who had adopted some of his ideas – his contempt for mass-thinking and material values – from the works of Nietzsche. In his verse, which was deliberately formal and obscure, he spoke to a few initiates alone. A prophet of beauty, he considered that the writer had as important a task to perform as any other social being. The following is from *Der Sterne des Bundes* (1913, The Star of the Covenant):

When the lightning-flash of the
  tempest shatters the sky,
When storm-winds blow ill, and topple
  battlemented towers,
Is it unhallowed work to stalk the
  ringing rhymes?

'The solemn harp-string and the lilting
  lyre
They utter, ever, my will, as ages wax
  and wane,
Give voice to the unchanging pattern
  of the stars.'

Yet George was aware of the vocation of the people; those who accuse him of too narrow a nationalism forget what high and stern ideals he set himself. Among his other works, he published three collections of poems, *Das Jahr der Seele* (1897, The Year of the Souls), *Der siebente Ring* (1907, The Seventh Ring) and *Das neue Reich* (1928, The New Kingdom). Despite its title, the latter should not be considered an advertisement for Hitler's 'Kingdom of a Thousand Years'. Indeed, as early as 1930 he was to go into voluntary exile.

Nor can the Austrian poet **Hugo von Hofmannsthal** (1874–1929) be ranked among irresponsible aesthetes, despite his semi-religious cult of beauty. His most significant productions were his verse dramas – *Der Tod des Tizian* (1901, Death of Tizian), *Der Tor und der Tod* (1893, The Fool and Death), and the medieval morality play that has been performed in many different countries, *Jedermann* (1911, *Everyman*). Here he blends the ideals of Romanticism and Classicism, but gives them an eloquent contemporary form. In the spiritual values of poetry he sees the only escape from death and chaos.

Far left *Stefan George, friend of Mallarmé and Verlaine, who greatly influenced Hofmannsthal and Rilke. Portrait 'The Last Swan' by Hermann Frobenius.*

Left *Hugo von Hofmannsthal, who until 1905, although he associated himself with the aestheticism of Stefan George, was well aware of its dangers. There followed his long and famous collaboration as librettist with the composer Richard Strauss, notably in 'Der Rosenkavalier'. Portrait by A. Faistauer (Austrian Gallery, The Belvedere, Vienna)*

Below *Illustration for* Everyman, *Hofmannsthal's 'festival drama'. In 1920 Max Reinhardt staged it in the square before the Cathedral at the first Salzburg Festival, which he and Hofmannsthal had founded, and it was frequently repeated there. Woodcut by Erwin Lang for a 1961 edition.*

RILKE

Rainer Maria Rilke (1875–1926), whom many critics claim as the greatest German poet after Hölderlin, was for a while in Stefan George's enchanted circle, but soon broke away; and his many-faceted temperament makes him difficult to describe. After a troubled childhood, weakly and tied to his mother, he found that he could only solve the problems of adult life by relying on the support of generous and sympathetic women; and in his thinly disguised autobiography, *Die Aufzeichnungen des Malte Laurids Brigge* (1910, *The Notebooks of Malte Laurids Brigge*), he portrays himself as a neurotic personality, who, since his early youth had been a homeless outsider. That sense of personal alienation is apparent in the poem *Kindheit* (*Childhood*) quoted here:

The school's long stream of time and
 tediousness
winds slowly on through torpor,
 through dismay.
O loneliness, O time that creeps
 away ...
Then out at last: the big streets ring
 loud and gay,
and in the big white squares the
 fountains play,
and in the parks the world seems
 measureless. –
And to pass through it all in children's
 dress,
with others, but quite otherwise than
 they: –
O wondrous time, O time that fleets
 away,
O loneliness!

Despite his agonized compassion for every kind of human suffering, Rilke was too egocentric to take an interest in public life. What concerned him were the crises of the individual soul. In *Stundenbuch* (1905, *Book of Hours*), he struggles with the idea of religious faith; but Rilke's spiritual road would never lead to Christianity. He was a mystic who exercised his calling through art. Yet the impression his poems make is marvellously concrete; and *Neue Gedichte* (1907, New Poems), are said to have been inspired by Rodin's monumental sculptures.

During the war years, Rilke's inner crisis worsened. His *Duineser Elegien* (1923, *Duino Elegies*) where he pours out his anguish, faced with the cruelty of death and life, is one of the most important collections of modern European poetry, and has often been likened to T.S. Eliot's *The Waste Land*. Their basic tone is tragic and resigned. He compares (in the Eighth Elegy) the unsettled life of man with the placid world of animals and angels:

... We only see death; the free animal
has its decease perpetually behind it
and God in front, and when it moves,
 it moves
into eternity, like running springs.
We've never, no, not for a single day,
pure space before us, such as that
 which flowers
endlessly open into ...

Yet *Die Sonette an Orpheus* (1923, *Sonnets to Orpheus*), which appeared shortly afterwards, is an ecstatic tribute to the joys of living. At this stage Rilke appears to have achieved the vision of a spiritual reality that both accepts and overcomes extinction.

Top *Rilke, by his friend the expressionist painter Paula Modersohn-Becker (1906). (Ludwig-Roselius Coll., Bremen)*
Above left *Rilke's* Sonnets to Orpheus *appeared three years before Cocteau's* Orphée, *which Rilke had begun to translate before he died. 'Orpheus' (1896) by Melchior Lechter. (Westphalian Landesmuseum, Münster)*

ESCAPISTS AND OBSERVERS

German prose before the First World War showed little enthusiasm for the German Empire's rapid material progress. Some writers, it is true, foresaw the approaching catastrophe; but others merely rebelled against the evils of city-life and international culture, and sought a refuge in the country. This escapism took a variety of shapes, ranging from artistic realism to the mystical and anti-Semitic expressions of the Primitive Teutonic spirit.

In the early work of Thomas Mann (who is described more fully in the next chapter) we find no patriotic illusions about the benefits of national progress. His elder brother, **Heinrich Mann** (1871–1950), whose most important work belongs to the pre-war period, was equally free of illusions. At first he was attracted to the kind of worldly fiction fashionable at the end of the nineteenth century, stories with rich, often somewhat decadent backgrounds. But his approach to his subjects quickly sharpened; and his novel, *Professor Unrat* (1905), achieved worldwide fame when it reached the film-screen as 'The Blue Angel', with Emil Jannings as the professor and Marlene Dietrich as the singer. He was even more caustic in *Der Untertan* (1918, *Man of Straw*), the description of a little parvenu's climb up the social ladder, and a savage and far-sighted criticism of the Prussian way of life.

Top *Heinrich Mann (left), and his younger brother, Thomas (described in the following chapter). Heinrich was more 'left' politically than Thomas, and his early novels satirized pre-war life in Germany. Although in exile from the Nazis since 1933, he was interned by the French authorities in 1940 but managed to escape to the US.*
Right *Marlene Dietrich in 'The Blue Angel' (1930), Josef von Sternberg's classic film based on Mann's novel* Professor Unrat.

THE REVOLT AGAINST VICTORIANISM

Queen Victoria's visit to France in the Diamond Jubilee year, 1897, from Le Petit Journal, *and* (**below**) *a typical family portrait, 'Swinburne and his Sisters' by G. Richmond – images of respectability behind which stirred a turbulent, creative life. (National Portrait Gallery, London)*

During the last decades of the nineteenth century, economic progress in England was combined with cautious liberal reforms. The British Empire maintained its power and prestige, though, both at home and abroad, the Boer War of 1899–1902 aroused much hostile criticism. In domestic life, the Victorian moral code had not yet been seriously challenged.

There were rebels, however – for example, **Algernon Charles Swinburne** (1837–1909), the Etonian son of a retired admiral who, like Shelley, broke with the beliefs and dictates of his own class, and became an enthusiastic atheist. His verse–drama, *Atalanta in Calydon* (1865), first delighted his young readers, among them the Pre-Raphaelite Brotherhood, and shocked the older generation. Swinburne had a prodigious flow of words and a feverish poetic fancy, of which, later, he made full use in his collection of *Poems and Ballads* (first series, 1878), where he defied Victorian 'good taste' by his bold introduction of erotic and sadistic themes. Swinburne was also a fervent republican and in *Songs before Sunrise* (1871) he had attacked monarchical tyrants all over Europe and championed the democratic cause.

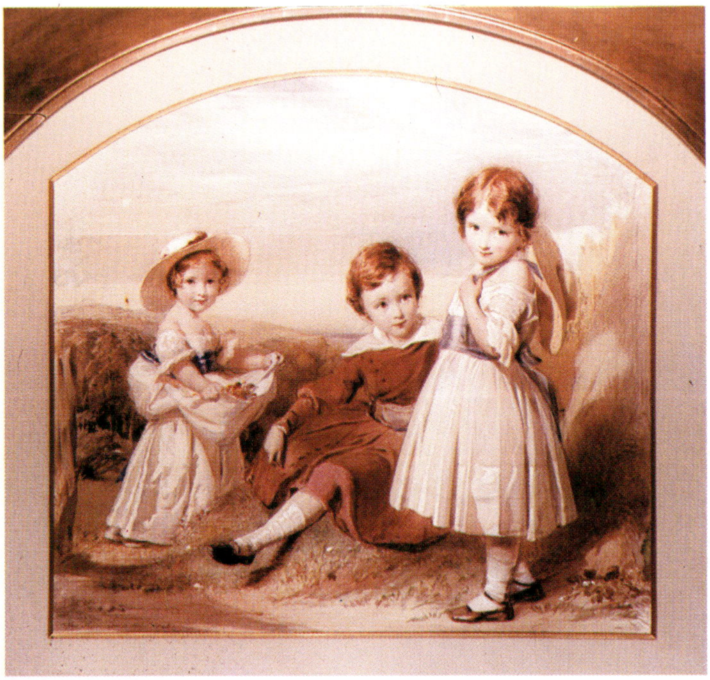

Oscar Wilde (1854–1900) was a rebel of a different kind, a wit, an aesthete and a dilettante, who, while he was still at Oxford, had already announced that he wished to eat 'the fruit of all the trees in the garden of the world'. Some of the fruit he later consumed was dangerous; and, having been convicted of homosexual offences, he was thrown into gaol, from which he emerged a broken man.

Of his dramatic works – 'modern drawing-room plays with pink lampshades', as he himself described them – only *The Importance of Being Earnest* (1895), an enchanting comedy, 'written', he said, 'by a butterfly for butterflies', is frequently performed upon the twentieth-century stage. Otherwise, his productions were often derivative. His novel, *The Picture of Dorian Gray* (1891) – the tale of an unscrupulous hedonist, who remains permanently young and handsome, while his hidden portrait grows more and more deformed – is partly borrowed from a French original; and his verses, even *The Ballad of Reading Gaol* (1898), in which he revived his horrible memories of prison-life, very seldom ring quite true. It was his wit that counted, his aphorisms and paradoxical *bon mots*. In them he showed a touch of genius, as an intellectual dandy and a hammer of the philistines.

A series of gifted novelists attacked the Victorian social system in the second half of the nineteenth century.

One was **George Meredith** (1828–1909), whose most important work, *The Ordeal of Richard Feverel* (1859), criticizes the sacred institution of the family; while, in *Diana of the Crossways* (1885), he took his stand among the earliest male champions of women's rights. Another social critic, the clergyman's son **Samuel Butler** (1835–1902) also attacked Victorian humbug. *Erewhon* (1872) – 'Nowhere' reversed – is a satirical fantasia about an imaginary country that reflects his idiosyncratic views on how a good society might be organized; and in his autobiographical novel, *The Way of all Flesh* (1903), he drew a cruelly vivid picture of his own middle-class upbringing and his pious, stupid parents.

A leading prose writer of the time, **Thomas Hardy** (1840–1928) does not blame society for human happiness, but 'the gods' who rule our fate. Like the ancient Greek dramatists, he saw his characters as the victims of an inexorable destiny, whether they have really incurred guilt as in *The Mayor of Casterbridge* (1886), or are innocent victims, as is *Tess of the d'Urbervilles* (1891). The book's summing-up, as his heroine pays the last penalty – she has murdered her seducer – is a paraphrase of Aeschylus: '"Justice" was done, and the President of the Immortals, in Aeschylean phrase, had ended his sport with Tess.'

Not all his fellow novelists admired Hardy. Henry James, for instance, having just read *Tess*, remarked in a letter to Stevenson, that 'the pretence of sexuality is only equalled by the ab-

Left *'Enter Herodias', one of Aubrey Beardsley's censored illustrations (it lacked the obligatory fig-leaf) for the first English edition (1894) of Wilde's French verse-play,* Salomé. *Sarah Bernhardt was to play the part in London, but* Salomé *was banned from the public stage in England until 1931.* The Times *of London reviewed it as '. . . an arrangement in blood and ferocity, morbid, bizarre, repulsive, and very offensive in its adaptation of scriptural phraseology to situations the reverse of sacred . . .'*

Below *Charles Laughton and Elsa Lanchester as Dr Chasuble and Miss Prism in the London Old Vic's production of* The Importance of Being Earnest *in 1934.*

Oscar Wilde in 1882, self-proclaimed aesthete and brilliant playwright, photographed by Napoleon Sarony, top theatrical photographer of New York, for his first American lecture tour.

Conan Doyle, chained to Sherlock Holmes but wreathed in clouds of spiritualism – his last belief, by Bernard Partridge (1926).
Below *Basil Rathbone and Nigel Bruce, cinema's most acclaimed 'Holmes and Watson' pair (1939).*

sence of it, and the abomination of the language by the author's reputation for style'. Certainly Hardy's style was apt to be rugged, and his characterization often rather clumsy. Where he excelled was in the evocation of the English landscape – the south-western country he called 'Wessex' – that he had known and loved since childhood, with its inhabitants and local customs.

In his later life, Hardy turned from the novel to poetry and drama. His historical epic *The Dynasts* is a ponderous but impressive piece of work, and his *Wessex Poems*, published in 1898, contains some deeply moving lyrics.

As a portrayer of landscape, Hardy has no equal among the English prose writers of the day. The tragedy of human lives is somehow softened by its absorbing natural background.

A popular literary form that now developed was Detective Fiction, of which **Wilkie Collins** (1824–1889) is usually held to have been the inventor. T.S. Eliot described his novel, *The Moonstone* (1868), as 'the first and greatest of English detective stories'. It includes mysterious details; but the centre of this admirably constructed tale is the search for a priceless Indian gem and the misfortunes that it causes.

The fame of **Arthur Conan Doyle** (1859–1930) in this new field rests upon a single character, Sherlock Holmes, the master-sleuth, with his violin, his addiction to drugs, his bachelor's den above Baker Street, and his admiring disciple, Dr Watson. Sherlock Holmes was so beloved by his millions of readers that, when the author attempted to kill him off, he was presently forced to resurrect his hero. No other writer of detective stories has managed to weave them around so dominant a personality.

RULE BRITANNIA!

Towards the end of the century, English readers acquired a romantic interest in strange lands, encouraged, no doubt, by the expansion of the British Empire.

A much-travelled novelist was the Scottish **Robert Louis Stevenson** (1850–1894), who died in the South Sea Islands, whither he had gone hoping to find a cure for the pulmonary tuberculosis that eventually killed him. He made his name in 1883 with *Treasure Island*, a splendid adventure story intended for young readers. But his masterpieces, *Kidnapped* (1886), *Catriona* (US: *David Balfour*, 1893) and *The Master of Ballantrae* (1889) are all set in eighteenth-century Scotland. *Dr Jekyll and Mr Hyde* (1886), on the other hand, has a comparatively modern setting; the hero–villain is the symbolic recreation of a paranoiac personality, split between two opposing selves, virtuous and insanely wicked.

A master of narrative prose, Stevenson was also an engaging minor poet; and, shortly before his death, he wrote his own epitaph:

Under the wide and starry sky,
Dig the grave and let me lie.
Glad did I live and gladly die,
And I laid me down with a will.

This be the verse you grave for me:
Here he lies where he longed to be;
Home is the sailor, home from sea,
And the hunter home from the hill.

Like the twentieth-century Russian, Vladimir Nabokov, the Polish **Joseph Conrad** (1857–1924) became a successful English novelist; but, whereas Nabokov had learned the language as a child, Conrad did not acquire it until he had reached adult life. Meanwhile, he had spent many years at sea, very often sailing through the tropics. In 1884 he became a British citizen, and decided he would take up writing, married an Englishwoman in 1896, and, a year earlier, published his first novel *Almayer's Folly*. Here, as in his subsequent works, he portrays not only the beauty and violence of Nature, but the effect of some dramatic crisis upon the individual human soul, and describes how the hero's sense of honour and his commitment to duty help him overcome the dangers he is facing. Conrad had chivalric ideals; he remained all his life an old-fashioned Polish gentleman. His life was always hard; and, although his books were praised, he was disappointed by his failure to achieve immediate popularity, and spoke of his 'great isolation

In its heyday the British Empire extended round the globe, a fact that aroused keen interest in tales of foreign lands.

Below left *R.L. Stevenson (1887), master of stories set in faraway places, by Sir W.B. Richmond (National Portrait Gallery, London)*

Below *A French print shows the armed forces of the British Empire from India, Australia, Canada, Africa, Borneo and British Guiana.*

Right *'The Council Rock' where the Pack Meeting of wolves was held to decide whether to adopt the man's cub – Mowgli, and where he was to learn the law and life of the jungle. Scene from Walt Disney's animated film (1967) of Kipling's* The Jungle Book.

Far right *Kipling in 1899, the year before he found himself in South Africa when 'there happened to be a bit of a war on' (the Boer War), became a war correspondent and 'had the time of my life.' Portrait by his first cousin, Sir Philip Burne-Jones, son of the famous Pre-Raphaelite painter. (National Portrait Gallery, London)*

Right *Joseph Conrad, the Polish-born writer who had never heard English spoken until he was 21, yet became a famous English novelist and original prose stylist.*

from the world'. His two most effective books, *The Nigger of the Narcissus* and *Lord Jim*, appeared in 1898 and 1900; but it was *Chance* that in 1914 finally brought him the popular acclaim and financial security he had so long needed and demanded.

Rudyard Kipling (1865–1936) became the literary prophet of the British Empire. Born in India, he became deeply attached to the country when he returned there as a young journalist. His first collection of stories, *Plain Tales from the Hills* and *Soldiers Three* (both came out in 1888) present a wonderfully life-like picture of the old Anglo–Indian world, of its soldiers and civil-servants at work and play, and of their dealings with the alien races they governed.

Less realistic were *The Jungle Books* (1894/95), the story of the young boy Mowgli, brought up by friendly, human-minded wolves, who protect him against the perils of the forest. Kipling's animals have often a strong resemblance to the products of an English public school, whether they be benevolent wolves, bears and panthers, or wicked, cruel, ungentlemanly tigers; and the stories Kipling relates are always fascinating, though frequently incredible. *Kim* (1901), however, his tale of an Anglo–Indian waif, and of his footloose wanderings across the Indian sub-continent, accompanied by a saintly Buddhist sage, is based on first-hand observation, and still praised, even in India, as a brilliant record of Indian life and landscapes during the last years of the nineteenth century. Kipling ranks high among European story-tellers; and, during his middle period, he published two volumes of short historical tales that summon up the ghosts of England's past, *Puck of Pook's Hill* (1906) and *Rewards and Fairies* (1910). Kipling had tremendous gifts, but a strangely limited outlook. He understood friendship; but sexual love was a subject that he very seldom dealt with. He preserved his boyish tastes – a passion for machinery, a schoolboy's code of honour and a respect for brute strength. Only in his last stories does he reveal an insight into the darker and more complex side of adult life. He wrote verse and prose with equal facility; and his achievements as a poet were warmly praised by T.S. Eliot.

THE WONDERFUL JOURNEY

The 1890s was one of the great decades of Swedish literature. Nationalism, exoticism, mysticism, almost all the traits of Romantic art, were present in its composition.

A typical figure, **Verner von Heidenstam** (1859–1940), made his entrance as early as 1888 with his collected poems, *Pilgrimages and Wandering Years,* a blend of eastern myths, enthusiasm for his native landscape and a cheerful lack of faith, complicated by a Nietzschean contempt for the 'slave religion', Christianity. His historical stories, *Soldiers of Charles XII* (1847/48), celebrate the myth of that unlucky sovereign's reign.

Poetry was then still the strength of Swedish writing. In 1891, **Gustaf Fröding** (1860–1911), published *Guitar and Concertina*; and charmed his readers with his Värmland humour and his ironic love-poems. Fröding's religious broodings, which appeared in his later collections of verse, showed the effects of his approaching mental breakdown; but *New Poems* (1894) helped to establish his genius; and *Splashes and Shreds* (1896) was the modest title he gave to the volume of poems now accepted as probably the most poignant and accomplished work yet written in the Swedish language.

Like all Swedish poets, both Fröding and Heidenstam were hampered by linguistic barriers and this is particularly true of **Erik Axel Karlfeldt** (1864–1931), the third great poet of the period. His first work, *Songs of Love and the Wilderness* (1895) and, later, his *Fridolin* poems with their Nordic appreciation of Nature, are nearly impossible to translate.

Yet the prose-writer **Selma Lagerlöf** (1858–1940), has kept a firm place in European literature. Her first book, *Gösta Berlings saga* (1891) was distinguished by its exotic charm, and it was filmed, starring Greta Garbo, in 1924. With *Jerusalem* (1901/02) she shows her imaginative characterization and her passionate moral involvement and her children's book *The Wonderful Journey of Nils* (1906/07) has been translated into many languages.

Norwegian literature, too, sounded a fresh note at the end of the nineteenth century. **Knut Hamsun** (1859–1952) made his name in the 1890s with his short lyrical novels, *Hunger* (1890), *Pan* (1894) and *Victoria* (1898), in which lonely dreamers confer with Nature, and pay not the smallest attention to the social problems of the day. Hamsun's ideas, his conception of the 'superman' and his rampant individualism, occasionally confuse the issue; but in his great novel, *Growth of the Soil* (1917), he produced an important message for the war-torn world – his belief in Man as a power for good and in the healing influence of natural scenes. His later novels are concerned

Left *Gustaf Fröding, in 1909, after his mental breakdown. Portrait by Richard Bergh.*

Centre *'Charles XII on the Field of Narva'. Although outnumbered by the forces of Tsar Peter the Great, the Swedish king won a famous victory over the Russians at Narva in the first year of the Great Northern War (1700–21). Verner von Heidenstam celebrated the Swedish soldier king in his stories. Painting (1905) by Gustav Cederström. (Nationalmuseum, Stockholm)*

Below *The Norwegian novelist and critic Knut Hamsun as a young man. He was to win international recognition and received the 1920 Nobel Prize for literature.*

Above *From S. Hansen's book jacket design for a 1956 Danish edition of Johannes V. Jensen's early* Himmerland *stories, first published in 1898. His Nobel Prize award came much later, in 1944.*

Right *Book jacket for a 1949 Swedish edition of the internationally famous* Kristin Lavransdatter, *an epic trilogy set in the 14th century, by the Norwegian writer Sigrid Undset. On receiving the Nobel Prize for literature in 1928, she had no time for interviews, '... I am studying scholastic philosophy', was how she excused herself to reporters.*

with a variety of themes, and reveal his mastery of the language.

During the Second World War and the German occupation of Norway, the ageing writer paid for the gallant line he took by being temporarily committed to a lunatic asylum; and in his autobiographical *On Overgrown Paths* (1949) he gives a vivid account of his experiences in that traumatic period.

Weightier and more prosaic was **Sigrid Undset** (1882–1949), who, like Hamsun, won the Nobel Prize. In her first novels – for example in *Jenny* (1911) – she appeared as a portraitist of women and a critic of her age, although her ethical preoccupations sometimes impeded her artistic gifts. But in *Kristin Lavransdatter* (1920/22), she managed to give her material an independent literary shape. The main theme of this huge medieval epic is the transformation of one of those strong, domineering women who may, in the novelist's words, 'be brought to maturity before being harvested'. Sigrid Undset revives the past, and shows extraordinary descriptive skill, as when she writes of sexual love, of the death of a child and of death itself; while, in her novels, *The Wild Orchid* (1929), and *The Burning Bush* (1930), she is inspired by the renewal of her early Catholic faith.

The Danish **Johannes V. Jensen** (1873–1950), was also a Romantic, who, both in his critical writings and in his novels, made somewhat hazardous speculations on the importance of work and environment, on the superiority of the Nordic races, and on the possible advance of science and technology. His lasting works include realistic stories of Jutland, his unique *Himmerland* 'myths' (1898), and his great series of novels *The Long Journey* (1908/22) attempts to describe, in a Darwinian spirit, the development of the human race from the Ice Age to Columbus.

The tradition of social debate was carried on by the proletarian Danish author, **Martin Andersen Nexø** (1869–1954), who displayed his creative ability in his important novels, *Pelle the Conqueror* (1906/10) and *Ditte: Girl Alive* (1917/21); but political sympathies sometimes tempted him into misleading simplifications.

SMOKE AND STEEL

Few notable literary results were achieved by the socially-conscious American Naturalists; but their work provided a starting-point for twentieth-century transatlantic prose, which at first, was divided into two main streams, one primarily propagandist. **Upton Sinclair** (1878–1968) is among the writers who belonged to this faction. His novel *The Jungle* (1906) describes the filthy conditions of the meat-packers of Chicago. This led to a federal investigation and the passing of the US Pure Food and Drug Act the same year. Sinclair and his school were nicknamed 'The Muckrakers' by conservative journalists and book-critics.

For a time, the immensely popular story-teller, **Jack London** (1876–1916) wrote books that revealed his socialist leanings – such as, in 1907, *The Iron Heel*, a prophetic vision of an authoritarian state. His later works, besides recording his own experiences, incorporate many current literary trends – in *The Sea Wolf* (1904) and *Martin Eden* (1909) the cult of 'superman'; in *The Call of the Wild* (1903) and other exciting tales, gathered from the Klondike during the period of the Gold Rush, the attraction of primitive life.

The second stream of American prose-writing was less overtly propagandist. The novels of **Theodore Dreiser** (1871–1945) are often documentary in form and portray not only the failings of American civilization, but the cruelty of life itself. *Sister Carrie* (1900), a novel based on his memories of his sister's sufferings when she migrated to Chicago to seek her fortune, was the book that made his name; and in two successive novels, *The Financier* (1912) and *The Titan* (1914), he chronicled against carefully observed backgrounds, the progress of a modern American financier who triumphantly builds up a fortune; while Clyde, the hero of *An American Tragedy* (1925), although equally greedy and ambitious, comes to a disastrous end. The story of Clyde's rise and fall, though he remains a reprehensible character, is told with understanding and compassion. Because Dreiser never passed judgment on his amoral, and

Top *American novelist and journalist Jack London. As a youth he lived rough on the California waterfront, went to sea, spent time as a tramp and joined the Klondike Gold Rush. He drew on his experience in Alaska for* The Call of The Wild, *which centres on the dog Buck, sold as a Klondike sledge-dog, befriended by the gold-prospector Thornton who is killed by Indians, whereupon Buck breaks away to the wilds. The story has often appealed to film-makers. In early Biograph days the first version was made (1908), then Darryl F. Zanuck at 20th Century-Fox produced his much-romanticized version in 1935.*

Left *The degrading conditions of work in a Chicago meat-packing factory of the 1880s, the setting for Upton Sinclair's* The Jungle, *one of several novels with socially committed themes.*

Left *Scene from Ken Annakin's film (1972) of* The Call of the Wild *starring Charlton Heston.*

Top *Courtroom scene from Josef von Sternberg's film (1931) of Theodore Dreiser's* An American Tragedy. *An early example of the use of factual case-history material (the Chester Gillette–Grace Brown case) in fiction, it provoked official and popular indignation by its subject matter and by its indictment of industrial society.*

Right *Emily Dickinson, from the frontispiece of a 1924 edition of her* Complete Poems. *Only a few of her more than a thousand poems were published in her lifetime.*

Far right *The Dickinson family on a visit to the 18-year-old Emily at the Mount Holyoke Female Seminary in Massachusetts. This silhouette was cut by a family friend in 1848.*

even criminal personages, a number of his books incurred the censor's wrath.

Before the First World War, however, poetry out-distanced prose; and it was the influence of American poets that, in the post-war age, helped to liberate the art of prose-writing.

After Whitman, nineteenth-century verse had produced only one distinguished figure – **Emily Dickinson** (1830–1886), an over-sensitive solitary who published nothing in her lifetime, and whose earliest collection of *Poems* did not appear until 1890. She wrote short, apparently spontaneous lyrics. Their fragile substance hides intense feeling, expressed in profound reflection on death and on her own emotional solitude.

A poetic revolution occurred in 1912, when a magazine entitled *Poetry* was founded in Chicago; and the poems that there emerged had something of Whitman's tempestuous strength. The original leader of this movement was **Carl Sandburg** (1878–1967), whose collected poems, *Chicago Poems* (1916) were prefaced by some famous lines:

Hog butcher for the World,
Tool maker, Stacker of Wheat
Player with Railroads and the Nation's
  Freight Handler;
Strong, husky, brawling,
City of the Big Shoulders:

Sandburg was then accused of being coarsely unpoetic; but, perhaps for that reason alone, he was a poet suited to the twentieth century. Sandburg attacks his subject like a stone-breaker; but he is capable, at the same time, of distilling an atmospheric beauty from his observations of the natural world. The victims of modern industrialism were always close to his heart; and the titles of his later books suggest the material he chose – *Smoke and Steel* (1920), *Good Morning America* (1928), *The People, Yes* (1936).

Vachel Lindsay (1879–1931) was another American poet who did his best to keep pace with contemporary existence, and who dreamed of winning over the masses to poetry. A master of rhyme, in *General Booth Enters Into Heaven* (1913) and *The Congo* (1914), he often adapted current idioms from Salvation Army slogans and the vocabulary of Negro jazz.

A third Chicago poet, **Edgar Lee Masters** (1869–1950) entered the literary world with a single book of verse, the original *Spoon River Anthology* (1915), which consists of a series of free-verse epitaphs on the citizens of the town thus named (of which *Knowlt Hoheimer* is quoted below). His pattern was the classic Greek epigram, revived to serve a modern purpose; and his poetic vignettes are a terrible commentary on the limitations of American provincial life:

I was the first fruits of the battle of
Missionary Ridge.
When I felt the bullet enter my heart
I wished I had stayed at home and
gone to jail
For stealing the hogs of Curl Trenary,
Instead of running away and joining
the army.
Rather a thousand times the county jail
Than to lie under this marble figure
with wings,
And this granite pedestal
Bearing the words, 'Pro Patria.'
What do they mean, anyway?

Top *Study of Carl Sandburg by his brother-in-law, the famous painter and photographer Edward Steichen. Sandburg won his second Pulitzer Prize (1940) for 'The War Years', part of his great 6-volume biography of Abraham Lincoln (1926, 1939).*

Above *One of the New Orleans brass bands who turned marches into jazz, around the 1890s. Vachel Lindsay was inspired by the scenes and sounds of American life, from brass bands and revivalist hymns to the words of Negro jazz.*

GERMAN BANKRUPTCY

In Germany, all the ominous forebodings of the years between 1914 and 1945 were destined to come sadly true, during a period that proved even more calamitous than the gloomiest prophets had foreseen. Economically, the country's resources had been drained by war. Politically and morally, as elsewhere in Western Europe, life went through a long-drawn crisis; and the counter-measures adopted were particularly desperate. Adolf Hitler's brand of National Socialism exploited both middle-class fears of Socialism and proletarian demands for change, thus doubly out-manoeuvring resistance.

The most important attempt to remedy the sickness of the age was made through twentieth-century psychology, which questioned the unity of the individual character, emphasized the role of the subconscious, and shook traditional notions of responsibility and guilt. On literature, the technique of psychoanalysis, launched at the beginning of the century by the Austrian alienist, **Sigmund Freud** (1856–1939), had a considerable effect; while analytic psychologist **C.G. Jung** (1875–1961), who was less preoccupied with sexual impulses than Freud, and spoke of 'archetypes' and mankind's common stock of symbols, attracted many literary followers.

Right *Hitler gives the Nazi salute in Berlin at a march-past on 30 January 1937 to celebrate the 4th anniversary of his accession to power.*

Above *'Where books are burnt, people will also finally be burnt' wrote Heinrich Heine, the German-Jewish poet, whose 'un-German' books were among the 20,000 incinerated by the Nazis on the night of 10 May 1933 outside Berlin's Opera House.*
Right *Sigmund Freud in his Vienna home in 1938, the year he chose to become an exile in England.*

THOMAS MANN AND HERMANN HESSE

In 1901, **Thomas Mann** (1875–1955) published *Buddenbrooks,* a novel subtitled 'The Decay of a Family', which debated the problems that had preoccupied Mann throughout the previous stages of his literary career – the conflict between the artist's demand for individual freedom and the standards of orthodox morality. For Mann, the descendant of a rich merchant family in Lübeck, both had necessary virtues. After this first success, Mann wrote many long short stories including *Tristan* (1903), *Tonio Kröger* (1903) and *Der Tod in Venedig* (1911, *Death in Venice*); and here again his main theme was the individual's need of integrity and solitude, as opposed to his equally justifiable desire to participate in ordinary human life. That Mann was dubious of all political and democratic programmes is evident from his *Betrachtungen eines Unpolitischen* (1918, Observations of an Unpolitical Man).

At the end of the First World War, however, it became clear to Mann that this position was untenable; and he sought to discover a new path that both Europe and mankind at large could take. In his novel, *Der Zauberberg* (1924, *The Magic Mountain*), set in a Swiss sanatorium, the whole post-war struggle of ideas is gathered into a single stormy narrative. The hero of the book, Hans Castorp, 'an ordinary young man', sets out to find the proper escape route; which he does by exchanging a narrow German nationalism for humanism and the creed of individual love.

The National-Socialist revolution obliged Mann to become a voluntary exile, first in Switzerland and then in the United States where the one-time non-political writer 'did his war service with the weapons of the mind'. Over a ten-year period – 1933–43 – he also wrote his series of Biblical novels, collected under the title *Joseph und seine Brüder* (*Joseph and his Brothers*). Despite its convoluted, heavily symbolic style, it is a fascinating attempt to probe the depths of family relationships and investigate the origins of culture. At the same time, profiting from the opportunities of objective examination that an exile's life now offered him, he scrutinized his own country's national temperament and educational ideals. *Lotte in Weimar* (1939) is an amusing novel about the ageing Goethe, whose 'representative on earth' Mann himself had once been called; and in the masterpiece of his old age, the novel *Doktor Faustus* (1947), he attributes to his chief character, the brilliant composer Adrian Leverkühn, features both of Nietzsche and his own personality. The Faustian pact that Leverkühn makes with the Devil symbolizes not only the penalty an artist has to pay for genius, but also the co-operation of the luckless German race with the insidious powers of Evil.

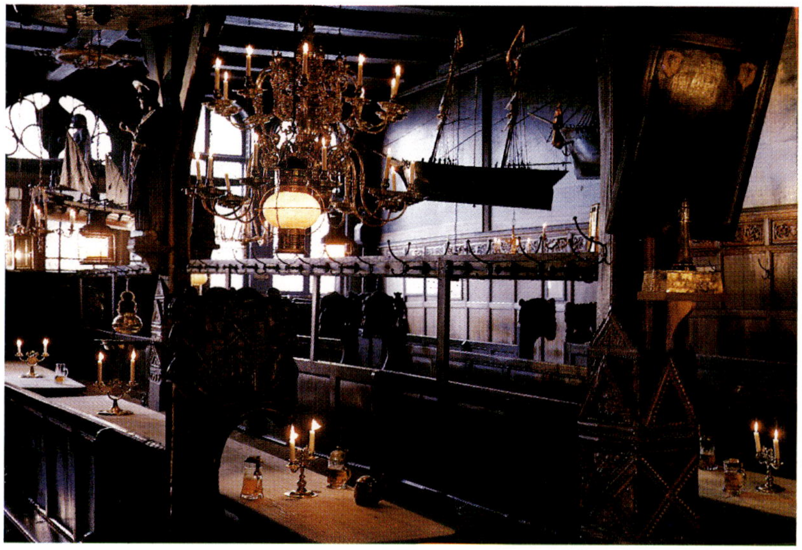

Above *Thomas Mann. He began life as an insurance official and always distrusted false artistic attitudes. 'If anything can make a literary man into a writer', he wrote, 'it is bourgeois love of the human, the living, the ordinary.'*

Top *'The Club' in Lübeck where the black sheep of the Buddenbrook family, Christian, did his virtuoso act, in Mann's* Buddenbrooks.

Hermann Hesse (1877–1962) began his literary life as a Romantic. His first poems, called *Romantische Lieder* (Romantic Songs) came out in 1899; and his prose work, *Peter Camenzind* (1904), is an idyllic autobiographical picture of his native background. But these subjects soon proved insufficient; and his experience of the First World War gave his mind a darker turn. At the same time, he suffered personal misfortunes and passed through a grievous inward crisis.

After a breakdown, Hesse was analysed by one of Jung's disciples; and, during a visit to India, he came under the spell of Buddhism and other Eastern schools of thought; with the result that his novels *Demian* (1919) and *Siddharta* (1922) are strongly critical of our ailing Western culture.

After a second crisis in the mid-1920s, Hesse published his most celebrated novel, *Der Steppenwolf* (1927), a study of psychic illness, where both the importance and the dangers of giving human cravings free play are vigorously described.

Towards the end of his life, Hesse managed to bring the struggling forces he recognized within himself under some kind of harmonious control. The novels he then wrote, *Narziss und Goldmund* (1930) and *Die Morgenlandfahrt* (1932, *The Journey to the East*), combine elements of mysticism, Indian philosophy and an undenominational religious faith – a blend that has helped to revive his popularity among the soul-starved modern young. Hesse's best-written book, his Nobel Prize-winning novel, *Das Glasperlenspiel* (1943, *Magister Ludi/The Glass Bead Game*), is an account of Kastalia, an imaginary country where no one exercises power, and an apparently useless game with glass beads is mankind's noblest occupation. It is a tale that seems to hark back to the days of Hesse's romantic youth; but its romanticism has been much tempered by a long life of suffering and thought.

Top *In 1972, the young American producer/director Conrad Rooks made a film of Hermann Hesse's novel,* Siddharta. *It was filmed in India with Indian actors, starring Shashi Kapoor.*

Left *The author Hermann Hesse. His father and grandfather were missionaries in India and he visited the sub-continent in 1911. Thereafter he lived in Switzerland, working for the Red Cross in the First World War, taking Swiss nationality in 1923 and being much influenced by the Swiss psychiatrist, Carl Jung.*

EXPRESSIONISM

The revolt against the past and all that it signified first found literary utterance through the movement called Expressionism, which demanded a break-down of outward forms in the search for inner meaning. On the plane of visual art, a similar movement was led by such painters as Klee and Kandinsky.

Poetry and drama were the vehicles that Expressionist writers chose; and they had begun work before the First World War in a German magazine called *Die Aktion*. The most prominent Expressionist poet, **Georg Trakl** (1887–1914), published his single volume of poems in 1913; but Expressionism did not find the conditions it needed until the difficult between-wars period, when it was often linked with activities of the radical Left Wing.

In his play *Die Bürger von Calais* (1914, The Burghers of Calais), **Georg Kaiser** (1878–1945) launched an attack on traditional patriotism and military ideals. But in *Gas* (1918/20) he wrote a purely expressionistic drama with a chorus and rapid changes of scene.

Ernst Toller (1893–1939) employed drama for a revolutionary purpose in *Masse Mensch* (1921, *Masses and Man*), *Die Maschinenstürmer* (1922, *The Machine Wreckers*), and *Hoppla, wir leben!* (1927, *Hoppla, Such is Life!*). The last play reflects the mad Witches' Sabbath of political and sexual passions that, after 1918, bedevilled German life. Here, for the first time in the history of drama, a film was used on the stage to illuminate the background.

Georg Trakl, the Austrian 'visionary poet', drawn by Oskar Kokoschka (1888–1980) in his Expressionist style. Trained as a pharmacist, Trakl was called up as a Medical Corps lieutenant in the First World War but within a few months he attempted suicide and then took an overdose. He was appalled by the wounds and fearful sufferings of the soldiers he had to treat. His fellow-poet, Franz Werfel, selected the poems to be included in his first volume.

Left *Gas attacks and the horrors of the war were to transform many writers. Ernst Toller volunteered in 1914 but emerged an embittered pacifist. Erwin Piscator, the controversial stage director, produced Toller's post-war play* Hoppla, Such is Life! *with film sequences, moving scenery and other new effects. The cartoon* (**below**) *shows an actor being helped to gain the right effect!*

Die Aktion

WOCHENSCHRIFT FÜR POLITIK, LITERATUR, KUNST

III. JAHR HERAUSGEGEBEN VON FRANZ PFEMFERT NR.29

INHALT: Richter-Berlin: Haus zwischen Hochbahn und Kanal (Titelzeichnung) / Franz Pfemfert: Die Revolutions G. m. b. H. / André Gide: Die Rückkehr / Ernst Stadler: Ueber ein Essaybuch / Hellmuth Wetzel: Nomaden / Ignotus: Paris von Gütersloh / Franz Vallentin: Wenn ich mein Hemd fallen lasse / Oskar Kanehl: Breslauer Vergnügungspark / Benno Weis: „Weder - weder" / Friedrich Eisenlohr: Seine Brücke / Stöffel: Buschbeck. Eine Tragikomödie / Alfred Lichtenstein: Die Welt / Gustav Specht: An Heinrich Mann

VERLAG / DIE AKTION / BERLIN-WILMERSDORF

HEFT 30 PFG.

During the early days of the Expressionist literary movement (c. 1910–25), two magazines were founded to cater for its followers – Die Aktion *(a 1913 issue shown here) and* Die Sturm.

Right *Robert Musil in 1930 by his wife Marta. 'Discovered' in the late 1940s, Musil was little known during his lifetime. Despite a distinguished World War record and promising career prospects, he devoted himself to writing and died in Geneva in the middle of the Second World War, an impoverished exile from Nazi Vienna. (Gaetano Marcovaldi Collection, Rome).*

Below *Book jacket for a Swedish edition (1960) of* The Death of Virgil *by Hermann Broch, translated, and book jacket designed, by Harry Järv. Like Musil, Broch abandoned good prospects (he was manager of his father's textile works) for writing. In 1938 he was able to emigrate to the US on the intervention of foreign friends, among them James Joyce.*

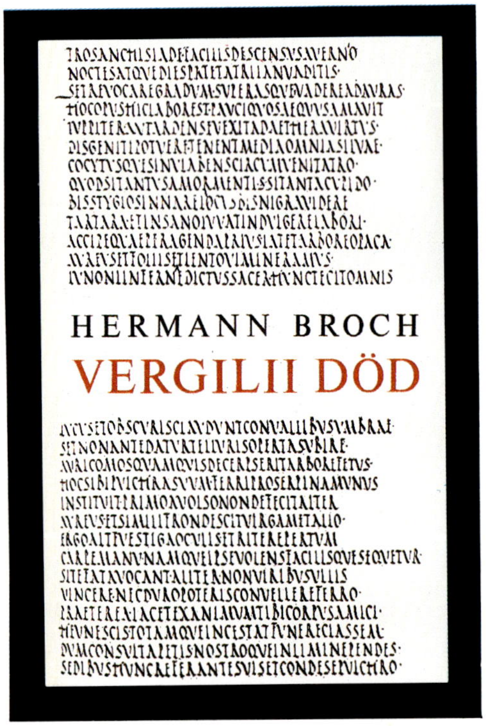

A powerful sense of social justice inspired the works of **Franz Werfel** (1890–1945); but, for him, the only escape from chaos was through religious experience. In his poems he sees the image of a creature whose face is shrouded in mist, but of whose presence he is still aware behind the confusion and squalor of the external universe. The following is taken from his *Gottes Name in Menschen* (1935, God's Name in Man):

He, the hidden maker, marked no
  message
Upon this image of himself,
Save a sign that will not fade
Yet scarcely can be seen,
Set deep in the corner where the paint
  lies thick.
There only, his signature shows.

The revolt of Werfel's contemporaries against the previous generation appears in his novel, *Nicht der Mörder, der Ermordete ist schuldig* (1920, Not the Murderer, but the Murdered is Guilty). At the same time, he wrote verse and produced expressionistic plays and, later, he wrote realistic novels.

In his earlier works, the Austrian **Robert Musil** (1880–1942), was an Expressionist; but he attracted little notice, and his reputation rests entirely on his great unfinished novel *Der Mann ohne Eigenschaften* (1930/43, 1952/57, *The Man Without Qualities*), only published ten years after his death – a blend of psychological analysis and topical satire, where the plot is slight, but serves as a pretext for long searching conversations. It concerns a Ruritanian state called Kakania, which vaguely resembles Austria, whose rulers, despite the inexorable approach of the First World War are making preparations for an idiotic jubilee. Besides being a somewhat heavy-handed satire on unawakened pre-war Europe, it is a symbolic representation of the general vanity of human efforts.

It was again with a single work, his novel *Der Tod des Virgil* (1946, The Death of Virgil), that another Austrian, **Hermann Broch** (1886–1951), joined the ranks of noteworthy modern authors. Begun in 1938, while he was imprisoned for a few weeks by the Nazis, in method and style it is as complicated a narrative as James Joyce's *Ulysses*, and has a semi-lyrical flow of words, that sometimes runs into sentences covering four or five pages. The story is slight; the dying writer returns to his homeland and meets the Emperor Augustus and his own immediate predecessors. But the description of events is unimportant. What holds us are the writer's emotions and thoughts, his subjective experience of life and love, of evil and beauty, of power versus art, and, most of all, the idea of death.

KAFKA

Above *Franz Kafka. The author's work and personality seem to demand the kind of psychological speculation that he himself indulged in. His relationship with his domineering father may have lain behind his anguish over the power of the social system. Many of his stories and aphorisms were published in his lifetime but his three best-known novels* (The Trial, The Castle, *and* America) *were published posthumously, and against his wishes.*

Above left *Illustration by Herbert Fronius for* The Castle, *which catches the mood of this novel, and the hero 'K' (who is not unlike the author) has a Kafka-esque face.*

Though **Franz Kafka** (1883–1924) also represented a kind of Expressionism, he is extremely difficult to classify. He belonged to the German–Jewish minority in Prague; and, apart from some spells in hospital with tuberculosis, he spent his short life in his native city, cut off from German literary groups. While he lived, he published only a few minor works, *Betrachtung* (1913, Reflections) and the collection of short stories, *Der Hungerkünstler* (1923, The Hunger Artist). After his death, however, and then against his stated wishes, his most important work was published by his friend Max Brod.

The basic experience behind his writing is solitude. His characters are always helplessly isolated in an impersonal and feelingless society; and their plight symbolizes Man's imprisonment in a universe that allows him no appeal. Thus in *Der Prozess* (1925, *The Trial)* the main character, Josef K., is imprisoned, accused, condemned and executed without ever discovering precisely what his crime has been. Similarly, in his unfinished novel, *Das Schloss* (1926, *The Castle),* human existence is regulated by the secret powers who occupy the castle, and whom no one is permitted to meet. The castle is Kafka's symbol of the normal existence that for him proved unattainable, but also of the inescapable paternal authority that he has always fought against. *Amerika* (1927) contains elements of farce and burlesque; and its capricious swiftness of action reflects the lack of a coherent meaning that for a pessimist distinguishes the whole universe. Apart from publishing Kafka's three unfinished novels, Max Brod also dramatized both *The Castle* and *Amerika.*

These three books form a 'trilogy of solitude'. Despite his use of symbolism, Kafka wrote in a sharply realistic style and with touches of astringent humour. He has become important today because his nightmares about the helplessness of the individual have proved to be grimly true.

THE NEW OBJECTIVITY

Right *Lew Ayres (in foreground) in a scene from Lewis Milestone's film (1930) of Remarque's classic war novel,* All Quiet on the Western Front.

Below *Bert(olt) Brecht. Much influenced by the pioneer stage director Erwin Piscator, Brecht was noted both for the experimental nature of his staging and for his political didacticism. His self-proclaimed 'anti-dramatic' theatre made use of* Verfremdung *('estrangement' or 'alienation') to distance the audience from what was being enacted and thus to draw their attention to it more objectively. The Berliner Ensemble, directed by Brecht and his wife Helene Weigel in East Berlin (at the Deutsches Theater from 1949 to 1954 and then at the Theater am Schiffbauerdamm) was renowned for its productions of his plays which employed numerous devices such as on-stage commentaries, masks, placards, film projections and so on.*

Expressionism found its proper place during the uneasy years that followed the First World War; but the writers who appeared at the end of the 1920s paid more and more attention to social problems, which they attacked by means of a realistic technique called *'Neue Sachlichkeit'* (The New Objectivity). Some time passed before the actual experiences of the First World War received adequate literary expression. Then **Erich Maria Remarque** (1898–1970) published *Im Westen Nichts Neues* (1929, *All Quiet on the Western Front*), where the brutality and boredom of trench warfare was graphically portrayed. In his next book, *Der Weg zurück* (1931, *The Road Back*), Remarque went on to describe the plight of homecoming soldiers as they struggled to adapt themselves to a civilian way of life; and in his later novel, *Strandgut* (1941, Flotsam), he became one of many émigré writers to bear witness against the Nazi regime.

No less objective in his approach to his subject, even when he appeared to be the boldest of Expressionists, was **Bertolt Brecht** (1898–1956). A Communist since the 1920s, he gave his dramas a political and propagandist turn; and in *Trommeln in der Nacht* (1919, *Drums in the Night*), he showed how the revolutionary ideals of the front-line soldier were destroyed both by his economic needs and by his dreams of commonplace domestic happiness.

Brecht's first masterpiece – *Die Dreigroschenoper* (*The Threepenny Opera*), which Kurt Weill set to music – appeared in 1928. It is a kind of modern *Beggar's Opera*, with thieves and rogues as the dramatis personae; and behind his acrid cynicism lie powerful political feelings. The same blend of cynicism and political passion, with a few strong drops of sentimentality, distinguishes both the two collections of poems produced at the time, and his play, the prophetic *Aufstieg und Fall der Stadt Mahagonny* (1930, *The Rise and Fall of the City of Mahagonny*).

In 1933, Brecht was driven into an exile that lasted fifteen years; it was then that he developed his 'epic theatre', which, with the help of a narrator, achieved epic size and strength. To this group of plays belong *Leben des Galilei* (*The Life of Galileo*) and *Mutter Courage and ihre Kinder* (*Mother Courage*), both written in 1939; while *Der gute Mensch von Sezuan* (1943, *The Good Woman of Setzuan*) and *Der kaukasische Kreidekreis* (1948/49, *The Caucasian Chalk Circle*) preach Marxist doctrine in an oriental disguise.

With two novels and the young people's classic, *Emil und die Detektive* (1929, *Emil and the Detectives*), **Erich Kästner** (1899–1974) himself practised the New Objectivity; while, on a grander scale, his collections *Herz auf Taille* (1927, The Tailored Heart) and *Lyrische Hausapotheke* (1935, Lyrical Medicine Chest) revealed his true poetic gifts. Kästner often expresses his generation's sense of failure.

After the advent of National Socialism in 1933, almost all the writers listed above were exiled, or in some other way silenced; and thenceforward German writing was divided between émigré literature and work tolerated or patronized by the Nazi regime.

Above *Ulla Sjöblom in Brecht's* Mother Courage *at the Skåne Theater, Malmö, Sweden in 1978.*

Right *The Berliner Ensemble's 1968 production of* Die heilige Johanna der Schlachthöfe *(1932,* St Joan of the Stockyards*), Brecht's satire on American capitalism, set in Chicago.*

CRISIS IN PHILOSOPHY

French society was spared none of the twentieth century's trials and problems. Two world wars, fought on French soil, and a period of German occupation, were followed by economic crises, themselves aggravated by corruption and financial scandals.

France's spiritual crisis was equally disturbing. Science had destroyed the old conception of existence, and swept away traditional values without producing new standards. Although the spirit flourished, and modern technology advanced beyond all expectations, the failure of contemporary ideas in the fields of morality, ethics and human relationships had become rapidly more and more apparent; and, once the Second World War had exploded the nineteenth century's belief in continuous human progress, there was little that could take its place.

Already, before the end of the nineteenth century, Naturalism as a philosophy had met increasingly powerful counter-currents. The philosopher **Henri Bergson** (1859–1941), maintained that man's psyche follows laws quite different from those of material reality, and that intuition is above reason.

Despite the official division between Church and State that occurred in 1905 – or, perhaps, because of it – the Catholic Church showed signs of reinforcing its position, which had been weakened by its attitude during the Dreyfus Affair, when it had tended to support the anti-Dreyfusard cause.

Meanwhile, on the political battlefield, both Right and Left took a fiercely propagandist line, and sometimes advocated the use of violence. The worker's movement was splintered; and the Left did not achieve political power until the formation, in the 1930s, of Léon Blum's Popular Front. On the extreme Right, contributors to the daily newspaper *L'Action française* (1908/44), preached an almost totalitarian doctrine.

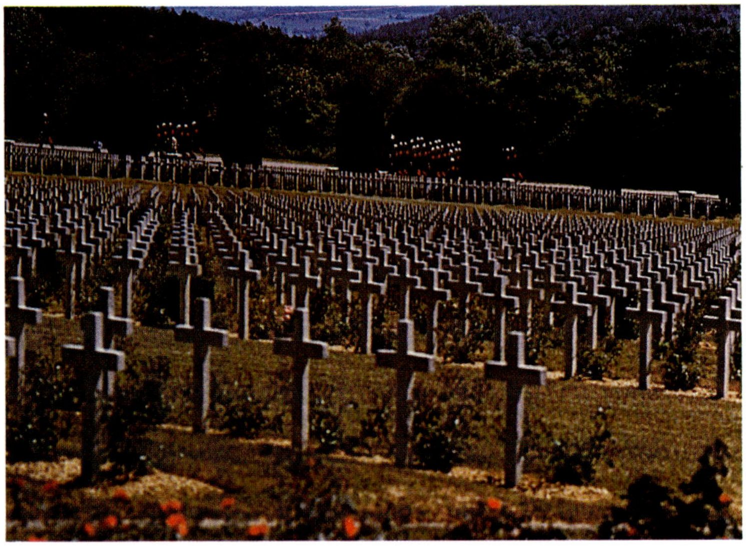

Above *The war graves on the battlefield of Verdun. The battle, which was to be hailed as a French 'victory', raged from February to November 1916, during which time some 600,000 French and German soldiers were killed.*

Right *French philosopher Henri-Louis Bergson, drawn by Michael Cauvet. His book,* L'Evolution créatrice *(1907,* Creative Evolution*) expounded his belief in a life-drive (*élan vital*) at work in the evolutionary process. It influenced many thinkers, notably the playwright George Bernard Shaw. To less sanguine spirits the carnage of the Great War suggested that human affairs might be governed by a death wish. (Bibliothèque Nationale, Paris)*

GIDE

A writer who, for many years, played a conspicuous part in French intellectual life, both as an artist and as an exponent of new ideas (which many of his critics considered highly subversive) was **André Gide** (1869–1951). His was a divided personality – the product of a puritanical background, yet a man devoted to the adventures of the flesh. His inherited puritanism was constantly at war with his rebellious hedonism; and he suffered all his life from what a Swedish psychologist has called 'morality sickness'. His inclinations, which he made no attempt to disguise, were strongly homosexual; and his marriage to a pious, dutiful cousin, seems to have remained platonic. This unhappy relationship caused him a life-long sense of guilt. On an ideological plane, he embodied a moral dilemma of his period. He had renounced religion, but was unable to rid himself of Christian values.

It was during a visit to North Africa that, assisted by a new English acquaintance, Oscar Wilde, he first broke through the barrier of his sexual inhibitions; and the literary result of this experience were the prose–hymns that appeared in *Les Nourritures terrestres (Fruits of the Earth)*, published in 1897, which became the gospel of romantic hedonists and 'life-worshippers' during the decades between the two wars. But in his next works, *L'Immoraliste* (1902, *The Immoralist)* and *La Porte étroite* (1909, *Strait Is the Gate*), Gide already recognizes the personal problems involved and admits to moral doubts.

Another attribute that troubled this painfully self-centred writer was his lack of strong impulsive feeling; and he dreamed of *l'acte gratuit* – the spontaneous, entirely gratuitous action, as when, in *Les Caves du Vatican* (1914, *The Vatican Cellars*), his young hero suddenly decides to push a harmless stranger off a speeding train. Yet in his short masterpiece, *La Symphonie pastorale* (1919, *Two Symphonies*) he suggests that no human being should imagine that he or she is a completely free agent.

Among Gide's most absorbing books is his autobiography, *Si le grain ne meurt* (1920/26, *If It Die*), where he tells of his emotional education and of his life before his marriage. Its merciless candour offended many critics who overlooked its underlying moral tendency. That same year, 1926, his great novel *Les Faux-Monnayeurs* (*The Coiners*), was also published; and there once again Gide broke with his earlier ideas. The title he chose refers to the counterfeiting of values in modern society; and his basic subject, as always, is the writer's own predicament – that of a Christian youth who first accepts his antipathy to women as a virtue, but then discovers it is merely a manifestation of his secret homosexual leanings. *The Coiners* has contributed much to the technical development of the twentieth-century novel.

Later, in his diary, *Journal 1889–1949*, which began to appear in the 1930s, Gide explained the change both of his political and of his literary views. For a while he was a member of the Communist Party; but, after a journey to Soviet Russia he dissociated himself in *Retour de l'URSS* (1937, Return from USSR) from his difficult allegiance.

Below *The young André Gide. 'Our actions possess us as the light possesses phosphorus', he wrote. 'They devour us, it is true, but they give us our power of light. And if our soul has any worth, then it is because it has burnt more brightly than others.' He was awarded the Nobel Prize for literature in 1947.*

Right *Book jacket of a 1933 Swedish edition of* The Coiners *(sometimes known as* The Counterfeiters*). The intensity of Gide's expression suggests both his passionately self-centred character and the strong effect he had on the intellectual world of his time.*

THE INDIVIDUAL AND THE COLLECTIVE

Above *Marcel Proust by J-E. Blanche. His admiration for John Ruskin, whose work he translated, may have helped him realize his own genius. (Collection Mme Proust, Paris)*

Below *A fashionable pastry-cook's establishment in Paris. It was from Parisian social life that Proust drew his subjects for his panoramic masterpiece,* Remembrance of Things Past.

Although **Marcel Proust** (1871–1922) being half-Jewish himself was deeply concerned with the Dreyfus Affair, otherwise he took little interest in social or political questions. His immense novel, *À la recherche du temps perdu* (1913/17, *Remembrance of Things Past*), deals exclusively with the life of the individual, with the nature of love, with the narrator's complex and often-changing relationship to the people whom he loves or hates, and with his observations of the somewhat limited world that he enters and explores as an inquisitive outsider. Apart from some sketches and essays, he published little else.

The son of a brilliant physician and the sympathetic and well-read daughter of a prosperous Jewish family, Proust suffered from severe asthma and regarded himself as a chronic invalid, obliged to spend much of his life in bed.

One of the hall-marks of a great novelist is his ability to create characters, and, however slightly, to change our view of life. This Proust certainly did in his novels. Such personages as the baron de Charlus, Madame Verdurin, Swan, Odette, Saint-Loup, the duchesse de Guermantes, have now become a part of our imaginative existence; while his studies of love and jealousy, and of the interaction of past and present, have helped to transform our vision of the world in which we live.

Throughout the novels of **François Mauriac** (1885–1970), the sense of sin is omnipresent. They are nearly always set in one of the households which owns an estate or vineyard near Bordeaux. *Le Noeud de vipères* (1932, *The Vipers' Tangle*) describes the unending conflict between man's lust for sensual satisfaction and his longing for spiritual salvation – a theme constantly repeated in his books, *Thérèse Desqueyroux* (1927), *Le Fleuve de feu* (1923, *River of Fire*) and in the play *Les Mal-Aimés* (1945, The Ill-loved).

Even more challenging to the Western civilization were the novels of **Georges Bernanos** (1888–1948), whose combination of somewhat anti-social personality with a brand of radical Catholicism resulted in the point of view – alarming to Christians and pagans alike – that produced *Sous le soleil de Satan* (1926, *Star of Satan*) and *Journal d'un curé de campagne* (1936, Diary of a Country Priest).

The first French novel that sprang directly from the author's experiences of the First World War was *Le Feu* (1916, *Under Fire*) by **Henri Barbusse** (1873–1935); and in *Clarté* (1918, *Light*) he preached the gospel of Peace and Socialism, which was to launch the international *'Clarté'* movement. **Romain Rolland** (1868–1944) was Barbusse's fellow-campaigner for Peace and Internationalism. His great ten-part novel, *Jean-Christophe* (1903/12), had as its hero a German composer not unlike Beethoven. Rolland's pacifism, however, aroused considerable hostility and he was obliged to take refuge in Switzerland, where, during the year 1915, he published *Au-dessus de la melée* (1915, *Above the Battlefield*), a vigorous protest against the insanity of modern warfare.

Georges Duhamel (1884-1966) who had served as a medical officer on the Western Front, recorded his impressions of the conflict in *Vie des martyrs* (1917, *The New Book of Martyrs*) and *Civilization* (1918). Later, he became increasingly conscious of the problems of the individual; and, in *Vie et aventures de Salavin* (1930/32, Life and Adventures of Salavin) he told the story of a little clerk struggling to overcome his limitations. Anxious to join the saints, Salavin ventures into politics, and finally sacrifices himself through his altruistic efforts. Duhamel's series of novels, *Chronique des Pasquier* (1933/44, *The Pasquier Chronicles*) are a moralist's review of contemporary society as a whole.

Society, rather than the individual, is the subject of the first of a sequence of narratives, which eventually ran to 27 volumes, under the general title *Les Hommes de bonne volonté* (1932/47, *Men of Goodwill*) by **Jules Romains**, the pseudonym of Louis Farigoule (1885–1972). The dramatic focus of the work is the First World War; and *Verdun* is devoted to a powerful description of the conflict, where we catch only glimpses of the individual soldier amid the general horror of the scene. Romain formulated his belief in the soul and in the unity of the collective human consciousness through the theory that he called 'unanimism'.

In his succession of novels entitled

Above left *Henri Barbusse (centre) with friends, 1923. In* Under Fire, *one of the most widely read of First World War books, he describes the lives of front-line soldiers as men made to fight for a cause they scarcely understood. In the early 1920s his views became militantly Communist, and he later wrote lives of Lenin and Stalin.*

Above right *Romain Rolland as an exile in Switzerland during the war. An ardent pacifist, he received the Nobel Prize for literature in 1916, the year his* Above the Battlefield, *which official circles considered grossly defeatist, was first given to the public. Rolland is also remembered for his life of Beethoven (1903).*

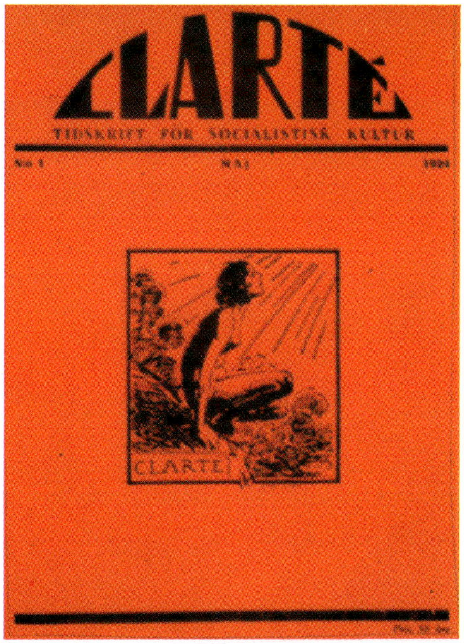

First issue cover (May 1924) of the Swedish-language edition of Clarté *(Light), organ of Barbusse's movement for Peace and Socialism.*

Les Thibault (1922/40, *The World of the Thibaults*), **Roger Martin du Gard** (1881–1958) provides a panorama of French life up to the end of the First World War. Here two brothers represent two different aspects of the national character – revolutionary enthusiasm and reasoned objectivity. The Thibaults' authoritarian father commits one son to a reformatory which he himself has founded, and embodies the unconscious hypocrisy that sometimes characterizes members of a class whose dissolution and defeat the author chronicles. The epilogue of *Les Thibault*, written in 1940, is a plea for total pacifism.

André Malraux (1901–1976) was always known for his fierce political involvement. An active Communist, he worked in China with Chou En-lai during the 1920s, and fought on the government side in the Spanish Civil War. *Les Conquérants* (1928, *The Conquerors*), and *La Condition humaine* (1933, *Man's Estate*), take their raw material from the Chinese struggle; and *Le Temps du mépris* (1935, *Days of Contempt*) was one of the first books by a French author to attack the Nazi regime. *L'Espoir* (1937, *Days of Hope*), describes Malraux's own experience in the Spanish Civil War, and both its style and content have won it a high place in modern Western literature.

Antoine de Saint-Exupéry (1900–1944), a professional airman, killed on a reconnaissance flight over Occupied France, was also passionately concerned with the future of mankind. The comradeship of Air Force life had given him a passionate faith in human solidarity, irrespective of all political issues; and, in his own lyrical style, he did more than any other novelist to make a literary conquest of the sky. *Vol de nuit* (1931, *Night Flight*), *Terre des hommes* (1939, *Wind, Sand and Stars*), *Pilote de guerre* (1942, *Flight to Arras*) are full of the writer's personal musings; but his melancholy fairy-tale, *Le Petit Prince*, (1945, *The Little Prince*), the story of the little boy who descends from a mysterious star, and then returns, leaving behind his body as an empty shell on earth, is still one of his most often read and best-loved books.

Above *Antoine de Saint-Exupéry's own drawing of his character, 'The Little Prince'. 'I've recently tried', he wrote, 'to draw him and this was the best I could do . . . of course, it is not as delightful as he was himself.'*

Centre *Saint-Exupéry, an aristocrat by birth, was a pioneer aviator and, during the Second World War, a leading figure in the Free French movement.*

Bottom *André Malraux (at left), in 1938, back from the Spanish Civil War, in which he led a fighter squadron on the government side. Man of action and dedicated writer, Malraux soon became a legend. He saw the Great War as the suicide of the liberal European tradition and modern life as a laughable conflict between the dead tradition of progressive human reason and Man as he really existed – a 'monster of wish-fulfilment' imprisoned in solitude and suffering. His political views changed from pro-Communist to Gaullist and in the 1960s he was appointed French Minister for Culture.*

THE NEW DRAMA

Actors and actresses and brave theatrical directors – Jacques Copeau, Louis Jouvet, Jean Vilar, Jean-Louis Barrault – were mainly responsible for bringing the French theatre to life again in the period between the two wars. Some remarkably original plays had already been written, among them the fantastic *Ubu Roi* (1896) of **Alfred Jarry** (1873–1907); but no one had yet dared to put them on the stage.

Paul Claudel (1868–1955), although the most gifted poetic dramatist of his age, cared little for the orthodox technique of play-writing. He was primarily a poet, who, as a professional diplomatist, had spent a great deal of his life abroad; and his reconversion to Catholicism and a tragic love affair were the disturbing emotional experiences to which he constantly reverts. *Partage de midi* (Noontide) deals so frankly with his own conflict that he would not allow it to be performed; written as early as 1906, it was not produced until 1948. In his huge uneven drama, *Le Soulier de satin* (1928/29, *The Satin Slipper*), the slipper that his heroine dedicates to the Virgin appears to symbolize mankind's limping progress, torn between love of God and the claim of earthly passion:

> I give myself over to you! Virgin mother, I give you my shoe, Virgin mother, keep in your hand my luckless little foot!
>
> I warn you that presently I shall see you no longer and that I am about to set everything going against you!
>
> But when I try to rush on evil let it be with limping foot! The barrier that you have set up,
>
> When I want to cross it, be it with crippled wing.

Like *Partage de midi*, *Le Soulier de satin* was held back for many years. Claudel's drama *Le Livre de Christophe Colomb* (1927), with music by Darius Milhaud, is on an even grander scale – a Christian mystery-play, almost as hard to perform as the second part of Goethe's *Faust*, but distinguished by the same eagle-flights of fantasy.

Otherwise, the introduction of religious themes was not typical, at this period, of the French drama, which devoted itself instead to social problems and attacks on war-time chauvinism. In *Siegfried et le limousin* (1922, *My Friend from Limousin*), called simply *Siegfried* when staged, the witty, paradoxical **Jean Giraudoux** (1882–1944) gave a well-observed interpretation of the contrasted aspects of the German national character – its Goethe-esque humanity and the Prussian military spirit; while, in *La Guerre de Troie n'aura pas lieu* (1935, *The Tiger at the Gates*), he showed how powerless against the warmongers was enlightened goodwill.

The cleverest playwright of the younger group was **Jean Anouilh** (*b.*1910), who revived the elegant traditions of Marivaux and Musset. He divides his plays into 'red' and 'black', among the red being his remarkable production *Le Bal des voleurs* (1938, *Thieves' Carnival*), that he himself has called a comedy–ballet; among the black, those in which he exhibits the conflict between youthful innocence and the vulgarity and squalor of the ordinary world – for example, in his variations on classic Greek themes, *Eurydice* (1942) and *Antigone* (1944). Now and then, as in *Colombe* (1951), he makes fun of his own idealistic pathos. Anouilh is so skilful a writer that critics are inclined to neglect his underlying seriousness.

Top *Jarry's* Ubu Roi, *which anticipated the Theatre of the Absurd. Malmö City Theatre 1978 production.* **Centre** *Claudel's* L'Annonce faite à Marie *(1912,* The Tidings Brought to Mary*), was more successful abroad than at home. Scene from Stockholm's Royal Dramatic Theatre (1974).* **Bottom** *Anouilh, who said, 'If there is a message in my plays, it is by mistake . . .'*

THE EXISTENTIALISTS

Above *Jean-Paul Sartre, writer and Existentialist philosopher, and his life-partner Simone de Beauvoir (1908–86). In 1941 they founded the periodical* Les Temps modernes. *Like Sartre, she used fiction to propagate her views on the importance of freedom and individual decision in the personal day-by-day creation of one's own life.* Le Sang des autres *(1944,* The Blood of Others*) is set in the France of the 1930s and during the wartime Resistance while* Les Mandarins *(1954) vividly evokes the Parisian intellectual world.* Le Deuxième sexe *(1949,* The Second Sex*) is a foundation text in the canon of the feminist movement.*

Above right *Gertrud Fridh and Max Von Sydow in Sartre's play* Loser Wins, *where he uses the theme of (German) war guilt on which to build his theme of personal responsibility. Scene from Stockholm's Royal Dramatic Theatre in 1960.*

Right *Albert Camus studied philosophy at university and gained his experience of life as a journalist, teacher, and stage actor/writer/director. He was awarded the Nobel Prize for literature in 1957, a few years before his fatal car accident.*

Jean-Paul Sartre (1905–80), particularly in his philosophical work *L'Être et le néant* (1943, *Being and Nothingness*), helped to found the doctrine of Existentialism, which remained the background of almost everything he wrote. For him and his disciples, radical pessimism and a recognition of the absurdity of life provided the only honest and reasonable starting-point for human action. Paradoxically enough, this gloomy view of existence led him to fierce political involvement. Sartre was long a Communist. He described himself as having 'no illusions, but full of faith in the greatness of mankind'.

His novel *La Nausée* (1938, *Nausea*) and his collection of short stories, *Le Mur* (1939, *Intimacy*), both illustrate his attitude. But his chief contribution has been in his dramas. *Les Mouches* (*The Flies*) came out in 1949, and in a legendary disguise portrays the moral dilemma that confronted Frenchmen during the German occupation. Later plays, *Huis-clos* (1959, *In Camera*), *Les Mains sales* (1949, *Crime Passionel*), *Les Séquestrés d'Altona* (1959, *Loser Wins*), carry on his Existentialist gospel; but here he shifts from the description of individuals to a consideration of society and politics.

For the French-Algerian **Albert Camus** (1913–1960) the absurdity of human existence is again a dominant theme; and in his novel, *L'Étranger* (1942, *The Outsider*) and his philosophical work *Le Mythe de Sisyphe* (1942, *The Myth of Sisyphus*), he expressed a view of life very similar to that of the Existentialists. Camus' great novel *La Peste* (1947, *The Plague*) symbolizes Fascism as a destructive epidemic. Always aware of present-day problems and conscious of the role he ought to play, Camus found it increasingly difficult to take a definite political position. *L'Homme révolté* (1951, *The Rebel*) is a brave attempt to establish his view of Stalinism and the revolutionary principle; while, in his last novel, *La Chute* (1957, *The Fall*) he does his best to settle accounts with self-confident party-liners.

SURREALIST JUNGLE

During the twentieth century, the novel was the literary form that attracted most notice; but poets contributed far more to the world of the imagination; and the efforts they made to find new methods of expression are usually labelled Modernist.

In France, the earliest, **Guillaume Apollinaire** (1880–1918), worked in close conjunction with the young contemporary painters, including Picasso, Braque and Modigliani, whose prophet and spokesman he became. 'We should love our own times', he wrote. '... We are living in a marvellous age full of burning imagination and fascinating progress'; and he and his friends looked forward to 'a profound renewal ... of societies, myths, the arts, philosophy'. Apollinaire was an industrious writer who among much else, produced an elaborate pornographic novel; but it was in his lyric poems, witty, allusive, haunting, that he showed his real genius.

Meanwhile, in 1916, the birth of Dadaism had been announced by its chief exponent the Romanian **Tristan Tzara** (1896–1963), who declared that it was no literary phenomenon but a protest against the whole existing social system, particularly against middle-class culture, then being shaken by the horrors of the First World War.

More important and lasting than Dadaism (which had a somewhat childish side) was Surrealism, an offspring of Symbolism, that set out to overturn all the earlier means of artistic and literary expression, and show us the world, through fresh, unclouded eyes, as a stranger and wilder place than we imagined, where a phantom lurks round every corner. The Surrealists had abandoned Reason, and derived their material from the unconscious and

Above *'Apollinaire and his Friends' (1909) by Marie Laurencin, his mistress at that time. Shown in this detail are: Gertrude Stein and Alice B. Toklas (far left), Apollinaire (centre), with on his left Picasso and his mistress Fernande Olivier, possibly Ezra Pound (with the beard), and the artist herself. (Collection Apollinaire, Paris)*

Left *'Gigantic Days' (1928) by the surrealist painter René Magritte. Apollinaire coined the word 'surrealism' when he described the Cocteau/Massine ballet 'Parade' (1917), designed by Picasso, as 'a sort of sur-realism in which I see a point of departure for a series of manifestations of that New Spirit which . . . promises to transform arts and manners from top to bottom with universal joy. 'Parade' was meant to bring Cubist theory to the lyric stage. Apollinaire also called his burlesque play produced the same year,* Les Mamelles de Tirésias, *a surrealist drama. (Musée des Beaux-Arts, Bruxelles)*

'At the Rendezvous of Friends' (1922) – the originators of Surrealism – by German-born painter and sculptor Max Ernst. In front (left to right) are: René Crevel (at the 'piano'), Ernst sitting on the knee of Dostoevsky's ghost and Jean Paulhan on his other knee, with Théodore Fraenkel's face behind, Benjamin Peret, Johannes Baargeld and Robert Desnos. Second row (left to right): Philippe Soupault, Hans Arp with his arm raised, Max Morise, the ghost of Raphael, Éluard, Aragon, framed by Breton's arm, Giorgio de Chirico and Gala Éluard. At the time many of these artists had also been involved with Dadaism. The Surrealist interest in the irrational unconscious and automatism in writing, had obvious affinities with Dada, as with Symbolism and the theories of Freud. (Private Collection, Hamburg)

Left *Paul Valéry by J-E. Blanche. He started out as a Symbolist under the influence of Mallarmé, then gave up writing poetry for a time but continued working on his* Cahiers (Notebooks) *which were published posthumously in 29 volumes (1957/61) and proved to be an important addition to his prose work. T.S. Eliot believed that Valéry would be considered 'the representative poet' of the first half of the 20th century. The 'Cemetery' of his famous poem is at his birthplace, Sète, in southern France. (Musée des Beaux-Arts, Rouen, France)*

from the imagery of dreams. The First Surrealist Manifesto was drawn up in 1924 by **André Breton** (1896–1966), one of the leading poets of the movement, whose best-known collection of verse is provocatively entitled *Le Revolver à cheveux blancs* (1948, The White-Haired Revolver). This includes *The Man and Woman Absolutely White* from which the following is taken:

> I see their breasts that place a point of
> sunlight in the night's darkness,
> And the time these take to fall and rise
> is the only exact measure of life.
> I see their breasts which are stars on waves
> Their breasts in which weeps for ever
> the invisible blue milk.

For writers, surrealism represented a true break with all forms of literary convention.

Other poets who arose from the Surrealist jungle were **Paul Éluard** (1895–1952), author of moving love–poems, and the Communist **Louis Aragon** (1897–1983), who went on to publish a series of well-written novels that show his strong political sympathies.

Two French poets more or less independent of contemporary trends were **Jules Supervielle** (1884–1961) and **Saint-John Perse** (1887–1975), the pseudonym of Alexis Saint-Léger Léger. Supervielle's poems, in *Gravitations* (1925) and *L'Escalier* (1975, The Staircase), despite their modern imagery, are carefully and rationally constructed; while Perse's main achievement *Anabase* (1922, *Anabasis*) is the epic account of an ancient conquering people, with associations that run through world-history. In *Vents* (1946, Winds) and *Amers* (1957, *Seamarks*) he celebrates the splendours of the natural universe, and the beauty of the wind and sea and love:

> And on the shore of my body man born of the sea lies stretched out. May he refresh his face even at the spring beneath the sands; and rejoice on my soil, like the god tattooed with male fern . . . My love, are you thirsty? I am woman at your lips keener than thirst. And my face in your hands as in hands fresh from shipwreck, ah! may there be for you in the warm night freshness of almond and flavour of dawn, and first awareness of fruit on the foreign shore!

Paul Valéry (1871–1945) stands alone, and belongs not to any modern movement, but to the great tradition of poetic French literature. For Valéry, pure thought is the only ally that a poet needs. His masterpiece, *Le Cimetière marin* (1920, *The Graveyard Beside the Sea/The Cemetery by the Sea*) is a long, harmonious, and beautifully disciplined meditation on the theme of love and death and past happiness. Elsewhere, for example in his philosophical poem *Le Serpent*, his method is somewhat more indirect, and, now and then, recalls Mallarmé's devious approach.

Valéry also wrote distinguished prose – an essay on the method of Leonardo da Vinci and *La Soirée avec Monsieur Teste* (1895, *Monsieur Teste*), in which he recommends a kind of intellectual quietism.

PRE-WAR PROSE

At the beginning of the twentieth century, an Englishman could sleep more soundly than his Continental brethren. The English social system was comparatively stable; which did not mean, of course, that it showed no signs of strife. During the 1900s, opposition to Victorian moral standards sharpened, particularly after the First World War, when so many attractive ideas and ideals had been proved meaningless. It would be wrong, however, to regard English post-war literature as largely argumentative and controversial. What it frequently expresses, on the other hand, are Man's attempts to adapt himself to a world that, with the progress of science and technology and the growth of industry, has suffered more radical changes in a shorter time than at almost any other period.

Herbert George Wells (1866–1946) was always much preoccupied with his visions of the future. By training a scientist, who had studied under T.H. Huxley, he first made his name as an author of science fiction in a series of admirably told stories, of which *The Time Machine* (1895) and *The War of the Worlds* (1898) are particularly good examples.

During his next stage, he published realistic novels, *Love and Mr Lewisham* (1900), *Kipps* (1905), *Tono-Bungay* (1909) and others, which usually depict the kind of life he knew best – that of the English lower middle-class. Between the wars, he became both a propagandist and an ardent educationalist, producing, for example, a survey of civilization from a self-taught historian's point of view.

Except perhaps in *Love and Mr Lewisham*, Wells was not a very good novelist. His characters are apt to be wooden; his aim was to arouse and instruct his readers rather than to satisfy their sense of style. Henry James (whose exquisite craftsmanship he ridiculed) once explained how much they differed. Wells, he said, did not love his fellow men, but believed he could reform them, while he himself loved humanity, but did not suppose that it could ever change. Latterly, Wells despised art; the qualities that make his books readable are his natural energy and humour. Though his optimism was often disappointed, he retained his staunch belief in progress.

Arnold Bennett (1867–1931) belonged, like Wells, to the lower middle-class, but came from the industrial north of England, the pottery-making 'Five Towns', which he described with lingering affection, though with little admiration, in *Anna of the Five Towns* (1902); and of his many novels, *The Old Wives' Tale* (1908), the story of a woman's lengthy, unsatisfying life (inspired by the works of the Goncourts and the other French Naturalists) has the greatest literary

Left *Wells in 1923. His genial optimism was steadily undermined by the threatening world situation. Cartoon by Boardman Robinson, one of the contributors to the New York socialist periodical* The Masses *(1911/17).*

Above *Illustration for the Swedish edition (1969) of Wells's* The First Men in the Moon *(1901), by Ann Margaret Dahlquist-Ljungberg.*

Galsworthy's Forsyte Saga *was one of the first of such modern novels to be adapted to the small screen, which brought the novelist a surge of new readers. BBC Television launched their remarkable series in 1968. 'A Forsyte never dies; it is against their principles' wrote the author, but when the inadmissible happened they all 'rallied' to old Roger Forsyte's funeral, with its traditional end-of-the-century trappings* (**above**).

Right *Galsworthy and his wife in 1926. The first Forsyte trilogy)*The Man of Property, In Chancery *and* To Let*) was completed in 1922 and Galsworthy received the Nobel Prize for literature ten years later.*

value. Otherwise, he often sacrificed his art to commerce, and threw off a succession of 'best-sellers' that kept his well-filled pot boiling.

John Galsworthy (1867–1933) was another highly successful writer who owed something to the French Naturalists, and had a first-hand knowledge of his subjects. His famous series of novels, *The Forsyte Saga*, of which the first part, *The Man of Property*, came out in 1906, bears some resemblance to Thomas Mann's *Buddenbrooks*, and follows the progress of a rich middle-class family, self-satisfied and self-centred, but already showing signs of dissolution. Property is sacred to the Forsytes. Galsworthy's main character, Soames Forsyte, always appears to behave with unimpeachable correctitude, but has an inhuman strain that drives away his wife; for he cannot help regarding her as merely a part of his domestic apparatus. In *The Dark Flower* (1913) Galsworthy took up a different theme, though his background was the same milieu – the destructive effect of sexual passion on a quiet, well-ordered world. His plays, *The Silver Box* (1909) and *Justice* (1910), show his attitude towards society in general, and illustrate the cruel errors of the Law.

Edward Morgan Forster (1879–1970) wrote his first novels and short stories in traditionally realistic style. He lived a sheltered life, and grew up protected by his mother and his aunt, from whose household he found it difficult to escape, though he presently rebelled against their moral influence. By nature he was a life-long homosexual; and in his books he often described the conflict between inhibited Englishmen and the warm-blooded Southern races, between puritanical ethics and the romantic paganism that his chief English characters wistfully admire. *Passage to India*, published in 1924, is without doubt his finest novel, an extraordinarily vivid picture of Anglo–Indian society and of the Indians themselves. For the latter most of his sympathy is reserved; and the hero's championship of an engaging Indian friend, accused of a crime that he had not committed, involves him in disgrace and social exile. The story ends on a vaguely mystical note. So far as the English traveller is concerned, India has won the day.

William Somerset Maugham (1874–1965), an able story-teller and an accomplished popular dramatist, was a man with few illusions, embittered by the misfortunes he had encountered in early life – his harsh unbringing, the loss, while he was still young, of a mother he adored, and the humiliating stutter he could never wholly overcome. Many of his characters suffer some defect. In *Of Human Bondage* (1915), the bonds he describes are both physical and mental, while in *The Moon and Sixpence* (1919), based on the biography of the painter Gauguin, we read of an artist's painful struggle against his philistine environment. Maugham's view of the world was keen yet limited; he could not see far beyond his own experiences.

Gilbert Keith Chesterton (1874–1936), on the other hand, was a determined lover of life, who, in novels and short stories, *The Man who was Thursday* (1908), *Manalive* (1911) and *The Flying Inn* (1914), explored the realms of fun and fantasy, which he did with realistic skill. He was also a devout Catholic; and his faith remained unshaken. Chesterton appreciated the good things of life, particularly good wine. He was a prolific writer; and besides his stories and ballads, he produced a host of lively critical essays. But his most memorable creation was the great detective Father Brown, a Catholic priest, apparently as innocent as a dove, yet as cunning as a fox.

Above *G.K. Chesterton. His style is so larded with puns and paradoxes that his works are now difficult to read at any length. He loved surprising antitheses: 'The worst and most dangerous hypocrite is not he who plays the unpopular role of the virtuous, but he who plays the popular role of sinner'.*

Left *The notable portrait of Somerset Maugham (1949), by Graham Sutherland. Maugham was Maupassant's pupil in the art of writing realistic short stories that end with a forceful point. Many of them concern Europeans in the tropics, one of the most famous being* Rain *(1932). His novel* Cakes and Ale *(1930), perhaps based on the life of Thomas Hardy, traces a writer's career, with some acidulous comments on the literary scene. (Tate Gallery, London)*

IRISH DRAMATISTS

The Irish 'literary renaissance' had started with the antipathy to politics felt by many writers after the Parnell scandal of 1890. The later Irish 'Troubles' both inspired and repelled the leading literary figures of the early 20th century.

Above *Dublin's famous Sackville Street which saw fierce fighting during the Republic's unsuccessful Easter Rising of 1916, the subject of W.B. Yeats's famous poem,* Easter 1916.

Right *Sinn Fein suspects searched by British soldiers in the north during the Troubles that led up to the establishment of the Irish Free State in 1921.*

Many well-known English novelists tried their hands at writing plays. But the English-speaking theatre owed its renaissance to a group of Irish dramatists, who, although they succeeded on the London stage, remained extremely Irish in their sympathies and points of view.

George Bernard Shaw (1856–1950), who was born and brought up in the Dublin back-streets, came to London at the age of twenty; and, while his mother supported them both by giving singing lessons, he attempted to write novels and, between 1876 and 1885, produced no less than five, none of which a publisher accepted. He then became a literary and, in 1888, a musical critic, and, under a pseudonym, 'Corno di Bassetto', first attracted appreciative notice. Wagner and Ibsen were his twin heroes; and his earliest play, *Widowers' Houses*, which discussed the problem of slums and slum-landlords, was staged in 1892. Equally controversial was its immediate successor, *Mrs Warren's Profession* (1893, but not performed until 1902). Here his subject was organized prostitution. Controversy was the breath of Shaw's life, even when he dealt with legendary or historical themes; and he professed to despise Shakespeare because the Elizabethan poet, he said, had lacked 'ideas'.

Shaw's own ideas, his dramatic stock-in-trade, were always brilliantly expressed, aggressively put forward and sometimes wildly paradoxical. A Fabian Socialist, he criticized nearly every part of modern English society – in *Arms and the Man* (1894), the patriotic spirit; in *Pygmalion* (1913), the absurdities of the modern class-system. His greatest popular success, the historical drama *Saint Joan*, appeared in 1923.

William Butler Yeats (1865–1939) was, in many ways, Shaw's exact antithesis – in his youth, a passionately Romantic poet, haunted by the Celtic past; in later life, a meditative philosopher and master of the English language, who exerted a deep and lasting influence on the development of modern poetry. Among his great concerns was the Abbey Theatre in Dublin, founded (1904) as a rival to London playhouses, for which he wrote essentially Irish dramas, including *The Land of Heart's Desire* (1894) and *Cathleen ni Houlihan* (1902). At the beginning of the twentieth century, Yeats discarded much of his youthful Romanticism, and simplified and sharpened his poetic style. A collection of poems, *The Tower*, published in 1928, contains some of his most memorable works.

As a dramatist, **John Millington Synge** (1871–1909) was more prosaic and direct than Yeats. Such plays as *Riders to the Sea* (1904) and *The Playboy of the Western World* (1907), besides a strong poetic strain, include close observations of ordinary life and pleasant strokes of Irish humour. **Sean O'Casey** (1884–1964), on the other hand, had vigorous political sympathies, and his fine plays, *Juno and the Paycock* (1924) and *The Plough and the Stars* (1926), take their dramatis personae from Dublin's ancient, decaying slums.

Above left *'GBS' (1945) by Erik Hermansson. Shaw made his career in London from the age of 20 but his first play was not staged for another 15 years. This Fabian Socialist harried the public with barbs of puckish commonsense and, in the* Prefaces *to his plays, expounded his views in powerful, lucid prose.*

Above *W.B. Yeats (c. 1910) by Augustus John. Like Shaw, Yeats had begun his career in London, but he returned to Ireland in 1896 to become a leader of the Irish 'literary renaissance'. The Irish theatre enjoyed a golden age when the famous Abbey Theatre of Dublin was founded in 1904, with Yeats and Lady Gregory as its first directors. Yeats had fallen in love with the Irish revolutionary Maud Gonne, but she refused him, and in 1917 he married and settled down in 'The Tower', after which he called a memorable book of verse that marks the highest point of his achievement. (National Portrait Gallery, London)*

BRAVE NEW WORLD

The First World War provoked no political crisis in England such as had occurred in Germany. The war-years, nevertheless, marked a borderline between two literary periods. No one, after the collective insanity of the war struggle, could accept the omnipotence of human Reason. The teachings of Freud and other psychiatrists on the subconscious origins of human behaviour seemed especially applicable. At the same time, religion reasserted its claims; standards of sexual morality changed, women made further bids for equality and freedom.

Both in prose and in poetry this was an experimental period; and among the boldest of the experimentalists was **David Herbert Lawrence** (1885–1930), who has been called the modern Rousseau. In his first novels he himself appears, the consumptive son of a northern miner, tied to his mother, but tormented by his longings for a larger, better life. His first novel, *The White Peacock*, which came out in 1911, was followed in 1913 by *Sons and Lovers*, and, in 1915, by *The Rainbow*. All these stories have an autobiographical colouring; and all of them foreshadow the gospel that he would afterwards preach with such prophetic energy – that the Age of the Machine and the worship of intellect had destroyed Man's deepest roots; and that our only salvation was to obey the Dark Gods, listen to the call of the blood and release the life-giving forces of sexual attraction.

Above *D.H. Lawrence late in life, and* (**right**) *his own sketch for the jacket of his novel* The Rainbow. *This book was banned as obscene when first published in 1915. (An expurgated edition appeared in the US a year later.) In 1929 the police closed an exhibition of his paintings in London – on the grounds that they were indecent.*

In pursuit of these aims Lawrence travelled around the world, and described his experiences against the background of the places that he visited. For example, *Aaron's Rod* (1922) is set in Italy; *Kangaroo* (1923) in Australia; *The Plumed Serpent* (1926) in Mexico. He wrote vividly and beautifully of landscapes and of *Birds, Beasts and Flowers* (1923, 1930, the title of a delightful book of poems), but often less convincingly of human characters. His views on the supreme value of perfect sexual satisfaction became an important feature of his works; and *Lady Chatterley's Lover* expressed them so clearly and frankly that the novel was prosecuted and, for a time at least, banned. (An expurgated edition was published in 1928, an unabridged version in Paris in 1929, and a full edition in England in 1960.)

While Lawrence aspired to salvation through the flesh, **Aldous Huxley** (1894–1963) sought it first through the mind, then through the soul. He was an intellectual unbeliever, who ultimately became a mystic. His first novel, *Crome Yellow* (1921), an enchanting social satire in the style of Shelley's old friend Thomas Love Peacock (1785–1866), is his best-written and undoubtedly his most amusing book. Its successors, *Those Barren Leaves* (1925) and *Point Counter Point* (1928), are more ambitious but a good deal less shapely. *Brave New World*

(1932) is a prophetic glance into a dreadful totalitarian future; and in his last novels his mystical tendencies predominate. He had become increasingly preoccupied with mankind's spiritual redemption, and believed that illumination might sometimes be achieved through an adventurous use of drugs.

Whereas Huxley adopted to some extent the technique of the nineteenth-century novel, the Irishman, **James Joyce** (1882–1941), after publishing a volume of short stories, *Dubliners* (1914), and an autobiographical novel, *A Portrait of the Artist as a Young Man* (1916), in 1922 gave the world his revolutionary narrative *Ulysses.* His intention was to produce a modern variant of the *Odyssey;* and its 800 pages relate the adventures of a single day in the life of a small Jewish businessman, Leopold Bloom, as he wanders round Dublin. Bloom's exploits parody those of Odysseus, but are often both scandalous and squalid. Yet Bloom himself is a sympathetic character; and his background – the crowded Dublin streets – is drawn by Joyce with a telling blend of retrospective love and hatred. His use of words is masterly; and he may be said almost to have invented a new literary language. Particularly effective is his employment of the 'interior monologue' to record the mazy flow of Bloom's thoughts, his recollections of past and his hopes of future happiness. Joyce wrote each chapter in a different style, adopting the professional jargon of schoolmen, lawyers, soldiers, milliners, butchers and bawds. Joyce made good use of his literary learning, and, besides imitating the structure of the *Odyssey,* sometimes parodied the English classics. His last book, *Finnegans Wake* (1939), however, though it contains many splendidly evocative passages, does not quite achieve its aim. His experiments with language are so bold that he is apt to mystify his readers.

Another novelist who employed the interior monologue was **Virginia Woolf** (1882–1941). Her first novel, *The Voyage Out* (1915), tells a comparatively straightforward story; but by the time she produced *Mrs Dalloway* (1925) and *To the Lighthouse* (1927), which is probably her best book, she had begun to employ an entirely new technique, linking together a series of vivid though disconnected impressions, with a record of the thoughts and feelings that pass across her personages' minds. The beauty of her novels consists not in the tale she unfolds but in the texture of her writing, in the delicate pattern of characters and scenes, of ideas and visual

Top *Aldous Huxley photographed by Cartier-Bresson and Leonard Rosoman's illustration (1971) for the Folio Society's* Brave New World, *where the drug* soma *controls the population.* **Above** *Marc Allégret's film (1955) of* Lady Chatterley's Lover *starring Danielle Darrieux. New York attempted to ban it for showing adultery as 'a proper pattern of behaviour', but this 'thematic' type of obscenity was not considered grounds for censorship.*

Virginia Woolf at the age of 20, one of a famous series of photographs by G.C. Beresford in 1902. This was the time when her father, Sir Leslie Stephen, was editing the Dictionary of National Biography *and Virginia was attending the Academy Schools – with a certain success – but failing dismally in 'high society', especially when it came to acquitting herself gracefully on the dance floor. (National Portrait Gallery, London)*

imagery. Her last books – *The Waves* (1931), for example – show a certain falling off. The effect they make is a little too elusive, and her prose-style too poetic.

The prose writers who appeared shortly before, or during, the Second World War have partly continued the traditions of the psychological novel, and depicted a world that, in their own experience, seemed to be growing more and more chaotic. A brilliant newcomer was **Graham Greene** (*b.*1904). His earliest stories, highly accomplished 'thrillers', he has described as 'entertainments'; but the themes he attacked, between 1940 and 1961, in novels that range from *The Power and the Glory* to *A Burnt-Out Case*, grew more and more serious. Greene is a Catholic; and, like his French admirer François Mauriac, an equally troubled Catholic, he shows a haunting sense of sin.

Arthur Koestler (1905–1983), Hungarian by birth, was one of the politically involved writers, and he produced observant and grim analyses of an existence increasingly dominated by mechanical and human robots, *Darkness at Noon* in 1940 and *Arrival and Departure* (1943), the former being a vivid account of a Soviet spy-trial, the latter being the first literary account of Nazi extermination camps.

Left *Arthur Koestler in 1967 and illustration by Jaroslav Bradáč (1970) for* Darkness at Noon *that shows Rubashov, the Bolshevik leader who fell victim to Stalin's purges in the 1930s, being dragged to execution. Koestler later become absorbed in the study of parapsychology.*

Opposite *Caricature (1967) of James Joyce by David Levine, and detail of portrait (1935) by J-E. Blanche. Joyce's* Ulysses *was published in 1922. (National Portrait Gallery, London)*

From **Ulysses** by James Joyce (the end of Molly Bloom's 50-page monologue)

I love flowers Id love to have the whole place swimming in roses God of heaven theres nothing like nature the wild mountains then the sea and the waves rushing then the beautiful country with fields of oats and wheat and all kinds of things and all the fine cattle going about that would do your heart good to see rivers and lakes and flowers all sorts of shapes and smells and colours springing up even out of the ditches primroses and violets nature it is as for them saying theres no God I wouldnt give a snap of my two fingers for all their learning why dont they go and create something I often asked him atheists or whatever they call themselves go and wash the cobbles off themselves first then they go howling for the priest and they dying and why why because theyre afraid of hell on account of their bad conscience ah yes I know them well who was the first person in the universe before there was anybody that made it all who ah that they dont know neither do I so there you are they might as well try to stop the sun from rising tomorrow the sun shines for you he said the day we were lying among the rhododendrons on Howth head in the grey tweed suit and his straw hat the day I got him to propose to me yes first I gave him the bit of seedcake out of my mouth and it was leapyear like now yes 16 years ago my God after that long kiss I near lost my breath yes he said I was a flower of the mountain yes so we are flowers all a womans body yes that was one true thing he said in his life and the sun shines for you today yes that was why I liked him because I saw he understood or felt what a woman is and I knew I could always get round him and I gave him all the pleasure I could leading him on till he asked me to say yes and I wouldnt answer first only looked out over the sea and the sky I was thinking of so many things he didn't know of Mulvey and Mr Stanhope and Hester and father and old captain Groves and the sailors playing all birds fly and I say stoop and washing up dishes they called it on the pier and the sentry in front of the governors house with the thing round his white helmet poor devil half roasted and the Spanish girls laughing in their shawls and their tall combs and the auctions in the morning the Greeks and the jews and the Arabs and the devil knows who else from all the ends of Europe and Duke street and the fowl market all clucking outside Larby Sharons and the poor donkeys slipping half asleep and the vague fellows in the cloaks asleep in the shade on the steps and the big wheels of the carts of the bulls and the old castle thousands of years old yes and those handsome Moors all in white and turbans like kings asking you to sit down in their little bit of a shop and Ronda with the old windows of the posadas glancing eyes a lattice hid for her lover to kiss the iron and the wineshops half open at night and the castanets and the night we missed the boat at Algeciras the watchman going about serene with his lamp and O that awful deep down torrent O and the sea the sea crimson sometimes like fire and the glorious sunsets and the figtrees in the Alameda gardens yes and all the queer little streets and pink and blue and yellow houses and the rosegardens and the jessamine and geraniums and cactuses and Gibraltar as a girl where I was a Flower of the mountain yes when I put the rose in my hair like the Andalusian girls used or shall I wear a red yes and how he kissed me under the Moorish wall and I thought well as well him as another and then I asked him with my eyes to ask again yes and then he asked me would I yes to say yes my mountain flower and first I put my arms around him yes and drew him down to me so he could feel my breasts all perfume yes and his heart was going like mad and yes I said yes I will Yes.

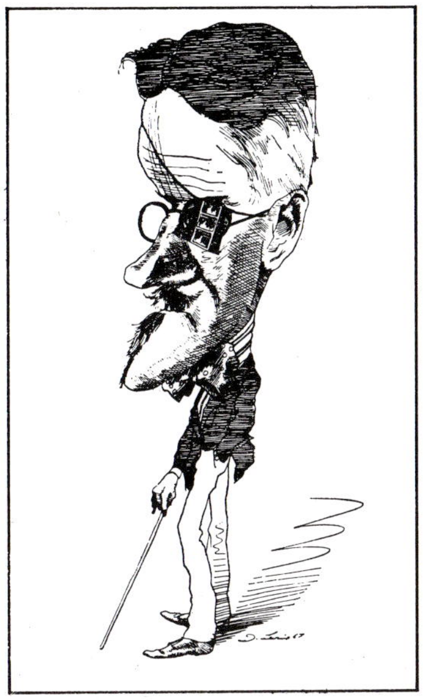

THE NEW LANGUAGE OF POETRY

A prophet of the new poetic literature was Ezra Pound (see page 280), an American who had made Europe his home; and, although the importance of his gigantic poem, *The Cantos*, on which he worked for 50 years, has occasionally been questioned, there is no doubt of his value as a leader and a teacher.

In September 1914, Pound met **Thomas Stearns Eliot** (1888–1965), who was also born in America, but became a British citizen. Encouraged and inspired by Pound, who thoroughly revised *The Waste Land*, he presently took his place as the foremost English poet and critic of his generation.

Above *The martyrdom of St Thomas à Becket in Canterbury Cathedral in the year 1170, from a manual on ecclesiastical lore,* The Golden Legend *(1484/85). T.S. Eliot hoped to revive poetic drama with his account,* Murder in the Cathedral. *After his conversion in 1928, Eliot proclaimed he was 'Anglo-Catholic in religion . . . classicist in literature, and royalist in politics.'*

Right *Eliot (1949) by the British painter, Patrick Heron. (National Portrait Gallery, London)*

In his first collection of poems, *Prufrock and Other Observations* (1917), he followed the French Symbolist poet Jules Laforgue, to whose blend of ironic wit and lyrical pathos he gave a fascinating new turn. Eliot was an authoritative critic; and in 1919 he formulated a famous theory – that the writer should always seek 'the objective correlation'; that is to say, he should not directly display his personal experiences, but should do his best to find an 'objective' equivalent.

In his famous cycle of poems, *The Waste Land* (1922), where his indebtedness to Laforgue largely disappeared, he no longer designs sharp poetical vignettes, but produces a boldly imaginative vision of the tragic modern world, and portrays its barrenness with something of the same cold passion Dante reveals in his *Inferno*:

The river's tent is broken: the last fingers of leaf
Clutch and sink into the wet bank. The wind
Crosses the brown land, unheard. The nymphs are departed.
Sweet Thames, run softly, till I end my song.
The river bears no empty bottles, sandwich papers,
Silk handkerchiefs, cardboard boxes, cigarette ends
Or other testimony of summer nights. The nymphs are departed.
And their friends, the loitering heirs of city directors,
Departed, have left no addresses.
By the waters of Leman I sat down and wept . . .
Sweet Thames, run softly till I end my song,
Sweet Thames, run softly, for I speak not loud or long.
But at my back in a cold blast I hear
The rattle of the bones, and chuckle spread from ear to ear.

In *The Hollow Men* (1925) and *Ash Wednesday* (1930) Eliot enlarges his picture of the twentieth-century world; but now it is seen from a conservative and Christian point of view. That attitude is also reflected in his successful poetic dramas – *The Rock* (1934), of which the subject is a church being built despite all opposition; *Murder in the Cathedral* (1935), which recalls the murder of St Thomas à Becket, and implies that true martyrdom is not to sacrifice one's own life, but to relinquish one's egocentric will. *The Family Reunion* (1939) and *The Cocktail Party* (1950) again have a strongly Christian message; they resemble medieval mystery plays in modern dress. *The Four Quartets* poems (1935/1942), are melodious and, at times, mysterious. Here he speculates on the link between past and present, experience and belief, memory and imagination.

Among the young poets who succeeded Eliot, the most original was **Wystan Auden** (1907–1973). His efforts to find a secure foothold in the modern Waste Land involved many dramatic changes, as he moved from Freudianism and Marxism to the kind of mysticism that Aldous Huxley eventually embraced. During these vicissitudes – a more important step – he developed an extraordinary sense of words and became a genuinely original writer.

THE POETRY OF REVOLUTION

After the Bolshevik revolution in 1917, the position of Russian writers long remained doubtful. As, for a while, they had neither readers nor publishers, they frequented taverns and cafés, where they found an outlet for their pent-up energies in endless literary discussions. This was the 'café period' of Soviet literature. When publishing at last began again, their work was dominated by revolutionary activities which extended to the art of writing. A conspicuous figure was **Alexander Blok** (1880–1921), a prominent Symbolist before the War, whose political beliefs were combined with the ancient conviction that Russia's destiny was to save the world. In his poem, *The Scythians* (1918), he proudly adopts the tribal name that Western critics had since bestowed upon the Russian people; for he was persuaded that their primitive strength might enable them to launch a new period of world-history. In his group of poems, *The Twelve* (1918), he imagines Christ himself marching ahead of twelve shouting and marauding soldiers through a perilous winter night.

Another vigorous champion of new literary forms was **Vladimir Mayakovsky** (1893–1930), most vocal and decisive of the so-called Futurists. His first collection, which came out in 1915, was called *The Cloud in Trousers*. After the Revolution, he offered 'all his high-sounding strength' to Communism, and wrote short lyrical causeries, and held readings of them both inside and outside the Soviet Union. The following is from his *My Soviet Passport* (1929):

    . . . hammered fast
sickle clasped
    my red Soviet Passport
I'd tear
    like a wolf
    at bureaucracy
For mandates
    my respect's but the slightest
To the devil himself
    I'd chuck by the way without mercy
every red-taped paper
    But this . . .
I pull out
    of my wide trouser-pockets
duplicate
    of a priceless cargo
        You now;
read this
    and envy
        I'm a citizen
of the Soviet Socialist Union.

Top right *The annual May Day parade in Red Square, Moscow, celebrates the triumph of the Bolshevik Revolution of 1917.*

Above *The attack on the Winter Palace, Petrograd, in October 1917 when the Bolsheviks seized power from Kerensky's Provisional government. Lenin and his party, who had no hand in the February Revolution, which overthrew the Tsar, took some years to fasten their hold on Russian life. Up to the mid 1920s the arts and literature, seen as allies of the Revolution, were exciting and adventurous. Public readings by poets like Mayakovsky* (**right**) *were eagerly received and are still part of the officially approved literary scene.*

Top *Esenin and Isadora Duncan. Passion soon died in their brief marriage (1922) marked with riotous escapades, while he sank into alcoholism. Esenin had innocently hailed the Bolshevik Revolution as the resurgence of Peasant Russia: later he came to see it as a betrayal. In 1919 he sought spiritual refuge with the 'Imaginist' poets, whose wild Bohemianism is depicted in his* Moscow of the Taverns *(1924). A second marriage – to a granddaughter of Tolstoy – did nothing to relieve his despair.*

Above *Boris Pasternak, by his father Leonid. His* Dr Zhivago *is a vivid, though disillusioned account of life in early Communist Russia behind the myths of the Revolution.*

Unfortunately, no doubt, for Mayakovsky, he was not a simple propagandist, and, towards the end of the 1920s, his poetry acquired a suspect inner note. In 1930 he committed suicide, probably as the result of an unhappy love affair. But, despite this escape into what the authorities regarded as bourgeois individualism, thanks to Stalin's support, even after his death, he remained a national poet.

Sergei Esenin (1895–1925) was yet more unlucky. For all his goodwill, he could not commit himself to revolutionary violence with as much enthusiasm as Mayakovsky; he was far too attached to the old Russian countryside, where he had grown up, and to which he dedicated some of his most beautiful poems. Esenin was akin to a medieval wandering poet, and never at home in an industrial society. His brief, unhappy marriage to the American dancer Isadora Duncan symbolized his desire to break free; and, a few years later, as Mayakovsky would do, he committed suicide.

Boris Pasternak (1890–1960) was the third great poet of the Revolution. For many years he avoided becoming too closely involved in politics; and the subjects of his bold experimental poems were such universal themes as nature, love and death. He first made his name in 1922 with a collection entitled *Life, my Sister*. But, when, in his novel *Dr Zhivago* (1957), which ends with a series of poems, he appeared to turn not only against the Soviet regime, but against a materialistic view of life, the book was banned in the Soviet Union, and first issued by an Italian publisher. When, in 1958, he was forbidden to accept the Nobel Prize, Pasternak became a representative of the poetic spirit that does not submit to temporal powers.

Long before this episode, Russian literature – and most of all poetry – had begun to freeze. By a number of Party decrees, towards the end of the 1920s, it had been harnessed to the task of building a Communist society. The time for experimental writing had passed. Lenin himself considered that a poem that was to speak to the masses should not break with old traditional forms. Literature was to be a method of propaganda in the service of the Party, which indeed it became – with catastrophic consequences.

Hamlet in Russia, a Soliloquy
by Pasternak

I love the mulishness of Providence,
I am content to play the one part I was
  born for ...
quite another play is running now ...
take me off the hooks tonight!

The sequence of scenes was well
  thought out;
the last bow is in the cards, or the
  stars –
but I am alone and there is none ...
All's drowned in the sperm and the
  spittle of the Pharisee –

To live a life is not to cross a field.

SOCIALIST REALISM

In the field of prose, too, writers were divided after 1917 by their differing attitudes towards the Communist regime. Among these who continued to flourish after this date was **Ivan Bunin** (1870–1953), a winner of the Nobel Prize, whose novels and short stories are written in the spirit of Chekhov, and often, as in *The Village* (1910) and other of his works, describe the twilight world of old-fashioned Russian country-houses.

Writers who shared his sympathies formed a rapidly dwindling group, largely made up of older men who could not entirely cast off the influence of pre-revolutionary culture. For a while, they formed a small literary society and issued a manifesto based on their belief that art was its own justification – a doctrine that, in the climate of the period, was unlikely to survive.

Maxim Gorky (1868–1936) on the other hand, who had been a revolutionary writer since the beginning of the century, was a staunch supporter of the government, and is regarded as the founder of Socialist Realism. At first, he portrayed rogues, beggars and failures without any direct political bias – for example, in his plays *The Lower Depths* (1902) and *The Night Lodgings* (1905). But, at the same time, encouraged no doubt by Nietzsche, he attempted to raise his lost souls almost to the rank of supermen. Later, his revolutionary sympathies became still more evident; and he was imprisoned by the Tsarist authorities and lived for many years in exile. His greatest literary contribution was his trilogy of linked autobiographical novels, *Childhood* (1913/14), *In the World* (1915/16) and *My Universities* (1923), while his portrait of the aged Tolstoy – a master he knew and loved well – is an admirably revealing little book. On his return to the Soviet Union, he became Chairman of the Writers' Union, and won Stalin's warm approval.

The first generation of orthodox Communist writers frequently chose their subjects from the Civil War – **Alexander Serafimovitch Popov** (1863–1949) in *The Iron Stream* (1924); **Isaak Babel** (1894–1941) in *Budyonny's Red Cavalry Army* (1926), and **Mikhail Sholokhov** (1905–1984) in his fine novel, *And Quiet Flows the Don* (1928/33). The last describes the part that had been played in the Revolution by the Cossacks, and was the earliest Soviet novel to reach the same heights as some of the best products of Western–European fiction. More deliberately propagandist, however, is Sholokhov's *Virgin Soil Upturned* (1935), a rather naive story of the struggle caused by the collectivization of land, which had cost so many lives and caused so much misery.

Konstantin Fedin (1892–1977) in his novel *Cities and Years* (1924), also dealt with the history of the revolution; and, in *The Brothers* (1928), he portrayed the difficult life of the intelligentsia, when faced with the problem of adjusting themselves to a new system. The masterly journalist, **Ilya Ehrenburg** (1891–1967), on the other hand, visited the West and frequented literary circles there. In *The Life of Automobiles* (1930) and *Thirteen Pipes* he accused the capitalist system of impoverishing and mechanizing human life. *The Fall of Paris* (1941), where he gives his views on the defeat of France during the Second World War, is a mixture of direct reportage and descriptive literary prose. Towards the end of his life, Ehrenburg, as a Jew, was often in a dangerous position, and

Below *'Babushka' (granny), the eternal symbol of Russian peasant motherhood.* **Bottom** *Maxim Gorky, who guarded his independence against the Bolshevik government, lived in voluntary exile for most of the 1920s. Although officially approved by Stalin and now considered the father of Soviet literature, he came to a mysterious end.*

occasionally obliged to renounce his deviations from the Party line.

In the Soviet Union, 1928 saw the beginnings of the industrial Five Year Plan; and, for men of letters, conditions then hardened. From the first years of the 1930s, literature was officially dedicated to the advancement of the Plan; and writer after writer became, as Stalin directed, 'an engineer of the human soul', and wrote on cement factories, electricity-generating stations, canal-construction and collective farming. The results had all the weaknesses that such propagandist writing invariably shows.

It was the ageing Gorky who finally protested against books being turned out to suit a prescribed pattern; and from the middle of the 1930s onwards, writers were once again permitted to describe the individual. Now that Russian nationalism was growing more and more pronounced, they were also allowed to choose their subjects from the pre-revolutionary past. In *Peter the Great* (1929/45) by **Alexis Tolstoy** (1882–1945), that far-seeing tyrant is praised as a nation-builder and reformer, who broke down ancient prejudices; while in two plays about Ivan IV (Ivan the Terrible, who was crowned as Tsar in 1547) he portrays that sadistic despot as essentially a Man of the People.

Both in his writing and attitudes, Mikhail Sholokhov (**above**) *increasingly became the spokesman for the Soviet literary establishment against Solzhenitsyn, among others.*

Above right *'Peter the Great Inspecting a New Harbour' by Valentin Serov (1907) and* (**right**) *'Ivan the Terrible with his Murdered Son' by Ilya Repin (1885). Such works found official favour as examples of Socialist Realism applied to history, and 'correct' interpretations of the Tsarist past. (Tretyakov Gallery, Moscow)*

Opposite *Gorky visits Leo Tolstoy at his home in Yasnaya Polyana in 1901. Tolstoy's towering genius was necessarily accepted by the Communists, though his mystical advocacy of peasant virtues might not suit the dictatorship of the industrial proletariat. Gorky was also to present a problem. Of Tolstoy he once wrote: 'I am not fatherless on this earth while this man lives.' A father-figure in his turn to many young writers, despite his position as Chairman of the Writers' Union, he was to protest in vain during the purges.*

MAMMON WITH FEET OF CLAY

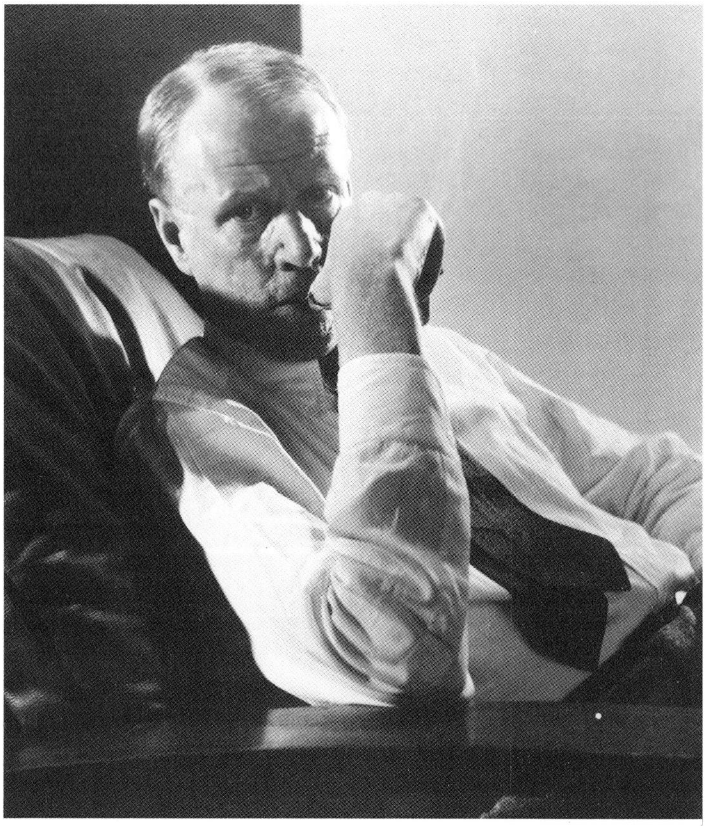

Right *Crowds outside a New York bank during the Wall Street Crash of 1929. The collapse of the New York stock market put a sudden end to the heady optimism and social frivolity of the 1920s. Banks all over the country failed, and millions of families in small towns as well as in financial centres lost their life savings. During the next decade disaster struck the agricultural communities of the Middle West when a long drought reduced the once-prosperous prairie lands to dust bowls. This gave John Steinbeck the theme for his novel* The Grapes of Wrath *(see page 278). In the space of two decades America's traditional small-town life came near to collapsing. Sinclair Lewis* (**right**), *creator of 'Babbitt', the type of small-town businessman and his world that Lewis attacked for their limitations. But today nostalgia sometimes prompts a reassessment. In 1930 Lewis was the first American to be awarded the Nobel Prize for literature.*

America's post-war boom collapsed suddenly and disastrously with the Stock Exchange Crash of 1929; but during the 1920s, even among intellectuals, some illusions still remained; and what writers criticized were the spiritual shortcomings of an increasingly prosperous society.

Like the Chicago poet Edgar Lee Masters (referred to in the previous chapter), **Sinclair Lewis** (1885–1951) in *Main Street* (1920) and *Babbitt* (1922) ridiculed the stultifying limitations of American small-town life; and *Babbitt* explodes the pretensions of the 'average citizen', the 'little man in the street', then a transatlantic hero. This he usually does with a saving touch of humour; and *Martin Arrowsmith* (1925) suggests that he can still see light ahead. On the other hand *Elmer Gantry* (1927) is a savage caricature of a loud-mouthed barn-storming evangelist.

This protest against the American way of life was reiterated by **Sherwood Anderson** (1876–1941), who attacks the deadly mechanization of a world where healthy sexual impulses are cruelly repressed. In *Winesburg, Ohio* (1919) and *Dark Laughter* (1925), there are reminiscences of Freud and D.H. Lawrence. The hero of the latter novel abruptly leaves his suffocating office and dull middle-class background for an unknown but freer mode of existence, as only a few years earlier Anderson himself had done.

Lewis and Anderson had not played an active part in the First World War. Younger men, who witnessed trench-warfare, had a less optimistic point of view, and employed a somewhat different literary technique. **Gertrude Stein** (1874–1946) labelled them 'The Lost Generation'. She was a powerful Jewish–American prophetess, whose more ambitious works were written in a style that Wyndham Lewis called 'a gargantuan mental stutter'; she also produced a rewarding book of memoirs, *The Autobiography of Alice B. Toklas* (1933), and gathered around her most of the clever young expatriates living in Paris at the time.

One of her protégés was **Ernest Hemingway** (1899–1961). The First World War he had seen in the hospital service; later, he observed the Spanish Civil War as a roving journalist; and all his life he was fascinated by strenuous masculine pursuits, in which a man could prove his strength and powers of endurance – shooting, boxing, deep-sea fishing. Of his first books, *The Sun Also Rises* (1926, UK: *Fiesta*) and *A Farewell to Arms* (1929), one describes the adventures of a group of Americans visiting a Spanish bull-ring; the second, war on the Italian front in 1917 and a hazardous love-affair behind the lines. Hemingway's narrative style, vivid, sparse and clear-cut, was certainly his greatest asset; his chief weakness, however, is that his cult of masculine fortitude occasionally strikes a false note. He was both a more neurotic, and a more sensitive and sympathetic character than he would have had his readers think.

During his youth, Hemingway's father had committed suicide; and he himself, though he had become prosperous and famous, was to follow his parent's sad example. The malady from which many of his heroes suffer is their inability to admit their own fears. Perhaps his grimmest short story is *The Short Happy Life of Francis Macomber* (1938), which introduces a lion-hunter, who at first succumbs to a fit of cowardice, and is therefore betrayed by his wife, but then shows unexpected courage, only to be rewarded with a bullet through his head. In his long novels, *To Have and to Have Not* (1937), the story of an ill-fated Cuban smuggler, and *For Whom the Bell Tolls* (1940), a picture of the Spanish Civil War, he takes a broader view of human problems. Latterly, his gift of telling a story weakened; but, meanwhile, he had revolutionized the technique of the modern American novel. An extract from his *Death in the Afternoon* (1932) is given on page 277.

Above left *Gertrude Stein with 'Basket', for whom she bought an Hermès coat (and had it fitted by a specialist in race-horse coats) with the money earned from* The Autobiography of Alice B. Toklas. *Her daring experiments with language and her dominating character made her house in Paris a favourite resort of many itinerant intellectuals. Painted in 1935 by Breton artist Pierre Jacob Tal Coat. (Collection H. Benezit, Paris)*
Above right *Ernest Hemingway, whose 'iceberg' technique aimed at short phrases, resonant with hidden meaning; and* (**right**) *Bogart and Bacall in Howard Hawks's film (1944) of Hemingway's tale,* To Have and Have Not.

Right *Gospel singers in New Orleans. Even after the Civil War the blacks remained an exploited class who could only express themselves fully in their own music, traditionally brought by Negro slaves from West Africa to the New World. Hymns turned into spirituals; work songs, brass bands, march music, the Blues (with its characteristic lyrics handed on from singer to singer, allowing for improvisation) turned into jazz.*

Below *William Faulkner, to whom the South is a Promised Land cursed by the memories of its past.*

The myth of the 'Happy Twenties', the intoxicating 'Jazz Age', evaporated soon after the American stock-market collapsed in 1929. But, while it lasted, **Francis Scott Fitzgerald** (1896–1940) and his somewhat unbalanced wife enjoyed its bohemian pleasures to the full. Besides dashing off a host of lucrative short stories, Fitzgerald became its literary historian with his masterpiece, *The Great Gatsby* (1925). Money fascinated him, as Hemingway once pointed out; he believed that 'the rich were different'; and this is the story of a very rich man, a romantic parvenu, whose riches and whose romantic dreams are both founded on self-delusion and deception. Gatsby gives magnificent parties to dazzle the woman he loves, and who, he imagines, must love him, and is then murdered, more or less by accident.

William Faulkner (1897–1962), invalided by a plane crash, was another member of the same 'Lost Generation'. He was preoccupied with the idea of life being perpetually confronted with defeat and death; and most of his books are set in a narrow corner of the Deep South, and overclouded by its heavy atmosphere. His characters return in book after book. Often they are sickly or grotesque, sometimes war-casualties, who cannot adapt themselves to the ordinary civilian world, as in *Soldier's Pay* (1926), sometimes degenerates or imbeciles, as in his experimental novel *The Sound and the Fury* (1929), or ruined wastrels, as in *As I Lay Dying* (1930). A basic belief that runs through his work is that strong and energetic people frequently bring evil, but, since they are destroyed by their own passions, cannot be held totally responsible for the havoc they have caused. This we see in what is perhaps his most important novel, *Light in August* (1932), of which the chief character is the half-caste Christmas. Though never a propagandist, Faulkner has always spoken up for the Negroes of the Southern States, and in *Requiem for a Nun* (1951), a blend of novel and play, he exposes white hypocrisy.

As pronounced as Faulkner's obsession with death was the ravenous hunger for life we find in **Thomas Wolfe** (1900–1938), which was no doubt the result of the war-experiences through which he and his generation passed. Wolfe's whole output was autobiographical. He hoarded up feelings and impressions, to form huge mountains of notes, from which his chaotic novels were then hewn. He survives largely thanks to his lyrical declamatory style and his gift of vividly recreating scenes. *Look Homeward, Angel* (1929) and *Of Time and the River* (1935) were published during his short career; but, after his death, two gigantic and shapeless, but memorable books were also added to his record.

From **Death in the Afternoon**
by Ernest Hemingway

Until the dead are buried they change somewhat in appearance each day. The colour change in Caucasian races is from white to yellow, to yellow-green, to black. If left long enough in the heat the flesh comes to resemble coal-tar, especially when it has become broken or torn, and it has quite visible tarlike iridescence. The dead grow larger each day until sometimes they become quite too big for their uniforms, filling these until they seem tight enough to burst. The individual members may increase in girth to an unbelievable extent and faces fill as taut and globular as balloons. The surprising thing, next to their progressive corpulence, is the amount of paper that is scattered round the dead. Their ultimate position, before there is any question of burial, depends on the location of the pockets in the uniform. In the Austrian army these pockets were in the back of the breeches, and the dead, after a short time, all consequently lay on their faces, the two hip pockets pulled out and, scattered around them in the grass, all those papers their pockets had contained. The heat, the flies, the indicative positions of the bodies in the grass and the amount of paper scattered are the impressions one retains.

The first thing that you found about the dead was that, hit badly enough, they died like animals. Some quickly from a little wound you would not think would kill a rabbit. They died from little wounds as rabbits sometimes die from three or four small grains of shot that hardly seem to break the skin. Others would die like cats, a skull broken in and iron in the brain, they lie alive two days like cats that crawl into the coal bin with a bullet in the brain and will not die until you cut their heads off. Maybe cats do not die then, they say they have nine lives, I do not know, but most men die like animals, not men. I have never seen a natural death so called, and so I blamed it on the war . . .

Above *Defeated government troops heading for the French frontier in the last stages of the Spanish Civil War in the winter of 1938–39. The savage conflict between Franco's rebel forces and the Republic divided opinion throughout the Western world. Volunteers, many writers among them, joined the International Brigade to fight against Franco's Falangists in what they saw as a crusade against Fascism. George Orwell and André Malraux were two who volunteered, and Pablo Neruda, the Chilean diplomat and poet, said his life-view was transformed by his tour of duty in Spain. Hemingway acted as a newspaper correspondent there, basing* For Whom the Bell Tolls *on his experiences.*

In his Death in the Afternoon *(1932), Hemingway not only explains the spectacle of Spanish bullfighting both 'emotionally and practically' but within the text he uses the device of a continuing dialogue with an 'Old Lady'. He discourses on his consuming passion – the bullfight; she interrogates; he informs her on such esoteric facts as the sexual habits of Raymond Radiguet, the origins and consequences of venereal disease, and in chapter 12 provides 'A Natural History of the Dead' (from which the extract here is taken). It is based on his knowledge of the Italian front during the Austrian offensives in 1917–18.*

'WE' REPLACES 'I'

Below *John Steinbeck, and* (**right**) *a scene from John Ford's film (1940) of* The Grapes of Wrath, *starring Henry Fonda as Tom Joad.*

Bottom *Richard Wright, whose autobiography* Black Boy *(1945) aroused Gertrude Stein's admiration, which persuaded him to settle in Paris. Ellen Glasgow (1874–1945) was among the white writers, such as Caldwell, who showed an understanding of black problems in the South. According to one critic, she 'almost single-handedly rescued Southern fiction from the glamorous sentimentality of the Lost Cause.'*

The economic catastrophe of 1929 and the crisis that followed, together with the threat of a Second World War, encouraged a renaissance of the social novel. The novel of the 1920s had often concentrated on the first person singular; but, during the 1930s, in the work of some novelists at least, 'I' tended to become 'we'. As a literary subject, the agony of the individual seemed less engrossing than the general anguish of society.

This approach was introduced by **John Dos Passos** (1896–1970), whose *Three Soldiers* (1921) is one of the most powerful of the many pacifist novels. Although his experience of warfare had a decisive effect on his work, as his technique developed, he became more and more politically involved. His best novels, *Manhattan Transfer* (1925) and the trilogy *USA* (1930/36), have no single hero; but he follows the individual destinies of the men and women he portrays, often inserting extracts from contemporary newspapers and films – a plan that other authors of such 'documentary' novels were very soon to take up.

John Steinbeck (1902–1968), too, with his broad humour and sharp realism, usually did his best to avoid, though he was not always successful, producing straightforward propaganda. He began by experimenting with different forms, including the comic novel, *Tortilla Flat* (1935), and his description of a strike, *In Dubious Battle* (1936). It was with his short novel, *Of Mice and Men* (1937) (which he later dramatized) and *The Long Valley* (1938), a collection of short stories, that he achieved maturity. Then came his major work, *The Grapes of Wrath* in 1939, a narrative that depicts the migration of white day-labourers to California, and certainly merits a place among the major realistic novels of our age.

This critical line dominated American prose until the Second World War, and works of this type often maintained a very high artistic level. One of its most consistent followers was **James T. Farrell** (1903–1979), who portrayed semi-working-class Chicago youth in his trilogy, *Studs Lonigan* (1932/35); and another was **Erskine Caldwell** (*b.*1903), who described the terrible poverty of the white working-class in his novels *Tobacco Road* (1932) and *God's Little Acre* (1933), and, later, the plight of many of America's black citizens in such novels as *Trouble in July* (1940).

Black writers who dealt with America's treatment of their race belonged to the same literary group – notably **Richard Wright** (1908–1960), the first to make his name by recording in *Native Son* (1940) the contemporary tragedy of his own people.

NATIVE AMERICAN DRAMA

The United States at last achieved a drama that was essentially American; and its earliest exponent was **Eugene O'Neill** (1888–1953) a writer who employed several different styles without becoming enslaved by any of them. He usually built up his plays on a basis of brutal fact; but his dramatis personae have always a second dimension in their baffled spirituality and longing for religious faith. The material of his earliest one-act play was derived from his experiences as a seaman; and here his technique is purely realistic, as in his country tragedy, *Desire under the Elms* (1924). But in others he uses an Expressionist method, as in the monologue play, *The Emperor Jones* (1920), or in *The Great God Brown* (1926), where masks amid naked faces symbolize Man's conventional, everyday self and the deepest aspect of the ego. Similarly, in *Strange Interlude* (1928), he breaks up the dialogue with lengthy inner monologues, and in *Lazarus Laughed* (1927), presents a variation of the Greek chorus. O'Neill's dramatic trilogy, *Mourning Becomes Electra* (1931), translates the stories of Electra and Orestes into twentieth-century terms, but explains the action with the help of Freudian psychology.

After writing his masked-play, *Days without End* (1934), in which he was feeling his way towards a spiritual faith, O'Neill was silent for twelve years, and after this period in his plays he seems to have overcome his memories of personal suffering – he was an alcoholic and suffered from Parkinson's Disease. Thenceforward his works voice a humbler philosophy and contain less metaphysical speculation. *The Iceman Cometh* (1946), though superficially a record of drunken talk in a bar, is also a multi-voiced fugue that illustrates the human condition as a whole. O'Neill's most important posthumous drama, *Long Day's Journey into Night* (1956), portrays the breakdown of a family through disease and drug addiction. All are to blame; but no one is judged – 'a novel by Dostoevsky, in which Strindberg has written the dialogue', a contemporary critic announced.

America's other distinguished dramatist, **Maxwell Anderson** (1888–1959), had not quite the same stature. He favoured an anti-realistic, almost classical line, and declared that, as a play could never be more than a stylization of reality, he wished to experiment with verse–drama. First he tried the poetic form on historical subjects – *Elizabeth the Queen* (1930) and *Mary of Scotland* (1933), and then returned to the present day in *Winterset* (1935) and in *Key Largo* (1939), both versified attempts to create a lofty drama of ideas against a background of criminal activity.

During these years, several other American dramatists gained an international renown that subsequently faded. The most original was the Armenian **William Saroyan** (1908–1978). In his short stories and novels, he showed some of the gifts of an oriental story-teller; and his plays, for example, *My Heart is in the Highlands* (1939), are romantically undisciplined. But his optimistic belief in the perfectibility of mankind after the Second World War now seems a little out of date.

An extremely skilled dramatic craftsman was **Tennessee Williams** (1914–1983) whose *The Glass Menagerie*, produced in 1944, and followed in 1947 by *A Streetcar Named Desire* – the pathetic picture of a frail pretentious woman living in a vulgar dream-world – are not only psychologically acute but enormously effective on the stage. His contemporary, **Arthur Miller** (*b.*1915), on the other hand, has never quite repeated the success in 1949 of *Death of a Salesman*, which presents a 'little man' whose life is distorted by the false values of modern industrial society.

Below *Eugene O'Neill's autobiographical play,* Long Day's Journey into Night, *at Stockholm's Royal Dramatic Theatre in 1956. In 1914 O'Neill worked with George Baker's influential '47 Workshop' at Harvard, and was a founder of the Theatre Guild.*

Bottom *Eugene O'Neill, who had the capacity to invest sordid lives with poetry and tragic dignity.*

'I, TOO, AM AMERICA'

The most influential poet of this period was **Ezra Pound** (1885–1972), who began his creative life as an Imagist – a poetic school that owed something to the nineteenth-century French Symbolists – and believed that emotion should be expressed in short precise poems with a concrete image at the centre. Pound maintained that poems should be 'equations of human emotions'. His own poetry is often difficult, despite its carefully disciplined structure; and one of his rules was that, in a poetic image, the abstract and the concrete must never be combined.

His earlier poems, gathered in *Personae* (1908/10), were filled with classical references, the more ancient and abstruse the better. He even quoted from the Chinese, and inserted Chinese characters. Pound's loathing of American capitalism at length threw him into the arms of Fascism; and, after the Second World War, he was accused of collaboration with the enemy, and first relegated to a military prison-camp, then to a lunatic asylum. His *Cantos*, however, which began appearing in 1925, and on which he was still at work just before he died, show that his creative force was undiminished. Determined to rival Dante, he tried to produce in his *Cantos*, a contemporary epic poem.

Before Pound was cast out of society, he had been the indefatigable spokesman of his fellow modern poets, and (as already noted) had revised and much improved T.S. Eliot's *The Waste Land*. Many new poets first made their bow in *Poetry*, the magazine he edited, at a time when bookshops were crowded with 'best-sellers', including such flimsy novels as Margaret

Ezra Pound in 1938 by Wyndham Lewis, painter and writer. They were both contributors to the Vorticist magazine Blast *(1914), and Lewis, too, flirted dangerously with Fascism. Lewis's* Apes of God *(1930) was a brilliant satire on the* literati *of the 1920s, to which the Sitwells took great exception. (Tate Gallery, London)*

Mitchell's *Gone with the Wind* (1936).

Other highly original poets, though their value was only recognized by the cognoscenti, were published in very small editions. **E.E. Cummings** (1894–1962) experimented boldly with words, verse forms, and typographical oddities in his *Tulips and Chimneys* (1923) and *Is 5* (1926), the latter title being meant to signify the poet's gift of making two-plus-two come to five. Meanwhile, **Archibald Macleish** (1892–1982) wrote an epic poem, *Conquistador* (1932), on the Conquest of Mexico and poetic commentaries like *Frescoes for Mr Rockefeller's City* (1933); and the short-lived **Hart Crane** (1899–1932) wrote *The Bridge* (1930), where Brooklyn Bridge symbolizes the apogee of the Machine Age. Negro poets also contributed to modern American literature, of whom probably the best was **Langston Hughes** (1902–1967).

I, too from **The Dream Keeper**
by Langston Hughes

I, too, sing America.

I am the darker brother,
They send me to eat in the kitchen,
when company comes,
but I laugh,
and eat well,
And grow strong.

Tomorrow
I'll sit at the table
when company comes,
Nobody'll dare
Say to me,
'Eat in the kitchen,'
Then.

Besides,
They'll see how beautiful I am
And be ashamed –
I, too, am America.

Left *Brooklyn Bridge, for the poet Hart Crane a splendid symbol of man's inspiration and achievement.*

Below left *Vivien Leigh as Scarlett O'Hara in Selznick's film (1939) of* Gone With the Wind. *Leigh and Clark Gable gave electric performances and the film has become a landmark in film history, though the book itself had no great literary value.*

Below *Racial prejudice found its most extreme expression in the activities of the Ku Klux Klan, a member of which is seen here under their blasphemous sign, the Fiery Cross.*

ENTER THE PROLETARIAT

Top *Scene from Jan Troell's film (1966) 'Here Is Your Life' from Eyvind Johnson's* The Novel of Olof. *Troell was also the film's cameraman.* **Above** *Danish writer Vilhelm Moberg takes part in a demonstration.*

During the 1900s, the Scandinavian working-class played a more important literary part than would have been possible in other European countries. This they did thanks to the growth of democracy, and to the development of popular education. **Dan Andersson** (1888–1920), a writer from the wilds, attended one of the new High Schools, as did the epic poet, **Vilhelm Moberg** (1898–1973), who also learnt to think boldly and independently, to judge by his *Soldier with Broken Rifle* (tr. *When I Was a Child*, 1957).

Proletarian writing very often was just as much a social as a literary achievement. When **Eyvind Johnson** (1900–1976) and **Harry Martinson** (1904–1978) received the Nobel Prize, the welcome they received was particularly significant, since both came from an impoverished background and had fought their way to fame against all the odds.

Johnson had acquired an international reputation with his story *The Novel of Olof* (1934/37). The poet Martinson showed in prose and verse alike, from *Cape Farewell* (1933) to *The Road* (1948), great imaginative distinction. But, as a poet, he faced the restrictive language barrier; and not even his best work, the space epic, *Aniara* (1956), can be translated without some clumsiness or crudity.

An early leading figure in Danish proletarian writing mentioned in the previous chapter, was Martin Andersen Nexø; and an interesting psychological variation of the working-class novel came from the Norwegian **Axel Sandemose** (1899–1965), most of whose early books, such as *A Fugitive Crosses his Tracks* (1933), are based on his own experience of seafaring.

The Icelandic writer and Nobel Prize winner, **Halldór Kiljan Laxness** (*b.*1902), himself writes about the life of the poor in his novel *Salka Valka* (1931/32); but he observes it from a safe and comfortable distance, like the Finn, **Eemil Sillanpää** (1888–1964), also awarded the Nobel Prize for his story about the peasant girl, *The Maid Silja* (1931).

After the death of Strindberg, the great days of Scandinavian drama had passed. The Expressionist one-act plays by Swedish **Pär Lagerkvist** (1891–1974), were interesting and stimulating, but never reached an international audience. This he was to achieve through his novels, *The Dwarf* (1944), *Now Barabbas* (1950) and *The Sibyl* (1956).

The Danish **Kaj Munk** (1897–1944), the most often performed among Scandinavian playwrights in the 1900s, had little real originality; and what gave his dramas so much life was his involvement in contemporary questions and his ability to create splendid theatrical roles. In *An Idealist* (1928), he portrays the tragedy of a ruler; and in *He Sits at the Melting Pot* (1938), he turns to Fascist racial persecution. His own death, at the hands of a Nazi murderer, which aroused horror and amazement – and yet seemed at the same time to provide an Aristotelian catharsis – was the writer's last tragedy.

Nordahl Grieg (1902–1943), a Norwegian, started out on a promising career with *Our Honour and Power* (1935); but the war cut short his life as an essayist and poet. In Scandinavian countries, more than any living writer, he came to represent one of 'the dead youth'.

Top *Harry Martinson, whose early wanderings are recounted in the poem* Nomad *(1931). His innovative use of Swedish matched Strindberg's.*
Above *Lagerkvist's* The Man Who Relived his Life, *at Stockholm's Royal Dramatic Theatre (1961).*

FREEDOM OR DEATH

To do justice to all the musicians in the vast orchestra of world-literature is impossible in so limited a space, and only a few other internationally famous authors can be mentioned here.

In this century, probably the best-known Italian writer was **Luigi Pirandello** (1867–1936). In his plays, *Right You Are (If You Think So)* (1917), *Six Characters in Search of an Author* (1921) and *Henry IV* (1922), he experiments with time and space, and stresses the human need of illusion. His starting-point is that he denies the unity of personal character. He insists that the parts we perform are indistinguishable from our real selves, and that our separate identity is an optical illusion. Also a skilful writer of short stories, Pirandello was awarded the Nobel Prize in 1934.

Top *Lorca's travelling theatre company ran from 1931–35. 'I am a poet, they do not kill poets', he said, but he was murdered as war broke out.*

Above *Picasso's great monochromatic mural 'Guernica' (1936), which expresses his horror of violence. (Prado, Madrid)*

The Spanish poet and dramatist, **Federico García Lorca** (1898–1936), was murdered, probably by Fascists, during the Spanish Civil War. His rustic plays combine bold and bloodthirsty realism with lyrical poetry, as in a Shakespearian drama. Despite his social empathy, he deals with the timeless conflicts created by primitive urges and concepts of honour. *Blood Wedding* (1933) concerns a bride-snatching and the revenge that it provokes; the subject of *Yerma* (1934) is an infertile woman who strangles her husband. Lorca used to sing his lyrics (including poems published in his collection of *Gypsy Ballads* of 1928), to the accompaniment of his own guitar. They are a remarkable blend of extreme modernism and echoes of ancient Spanish folk songs. The following is from his *Somnambule Ballad*:

Green, how much I want you green.
Green wind. Green branches.
The ship upon the sea
and the horse in the mountain.
With the shadow on her waist
she dreams on her verandah,
green flesh, hair of green,
and eyes of cold silver.
Green, how much I want you green.
Beneath the gipsy moon,
all things look at her
but she cannot see them.

The Greek writer, **Nikos Kazantzakis** (1885–1957) was born in Crete while it was still under Turkish rule, a fact that is said to explain his rebellious disposition. Having received a philosophic training, he drew his material both from world history and from the present day. His enormous output includes nearly every type of literary work – plays on the demi-god Heracles, and on Prometheus and Jesus

Christ, as well as a gigantic revolutionary epic, *I Odysseia* (1938), a free continuation of the *Odyssey*. Outside Greece, he became known for the novels that he wrote in later life – *Zorba the Greek* (1949), *Freedom or Death* (tr. 1957) and the remarkable story of Christ entitled *The Last Temptation of Christ* (1953), which portrays Jesus as a forbidding malefactor, and yet unmistakably divine.

Some of Latin America's leading poets come from Chile. Though childless herself, Lucila Godoy Alcayaga, writing under the pseudonym of **Gabriela Mistral** (1889–1957), has been styled the poet of maternal love, largely on the strength of her moving poem *Poema del hijo* (Song for a Son) from *Dolor* (Pain) in her collection *Desolación*, 1922. Her poetry is fairly conservative in form; but it is carried along by its intense feeling for the abused and the rejected. She was the first woman poet and the first Latin–American to be awarded (in 1945) the Nobel Prize.

Her countryman **Pablo Neruda** (1904–1973), another Nobel Prize winner, became, on his death, the collective symbol of the Chilean people, a position he had hoped to assume in his lifetime and had done much to establish through his works. Neruda's solemn funeral was a gesture of resistance against the reigning military junta. For all his modernism, he did not always succeed in striking a popular note. His name was made by a volume of love-poems; but he then moved closer to politically committed verse, as in *Canto a Stalingrado* (1943, Song to Stalingrad). His central work, *Canto general* (1950, Great Song) was intended to be the mighty epic of the South–American continent – a huge uneven group of poems, which, besides revealing his self-absorption, reflect his love of Chile and its citizens, and his hatred of political antagonists, whom he very often names. The following extract is from *Canto general*:

Love, America (1400) by Pablo Neruda

Before wig and frockcoat
were the rivers, the arterial rivers,
the cordilleras, on those scraped
escarpments
the condor or the snow seemed immobile
humidity and density, the thunderclap
not-yet-named, the planetary pampas.

Man was earth, a vessel, the eyelid
of the quivering clay, a shape of
potter's earth,
Carib spout, Chibcha stone,
Imperial cup or Araucanian silica:
he was gentle and bloody, but on the
hilt
of his wetted glass weapon
the earth's initials were written.

No one
could later recall them: the wind
forgot, the water's idiom
was buried, the code was lost
or inundated by silence or blood . . .

. . . . . .

An Inca out of the slime, I
touched the stone and said:
Who
is waiting there? And closed my hand
around a fistful of empty glass.
And I walked among Zapotec flowers
and the light was tender as a deer
and the shade was like a green eyelid.

My land without name, without
America,
equinoctial stamen, lance-like purple,
your aroma rose through my roots
into the cup I drained, into the most
tenuous
word not yet born on my mouth.

Top *King Gustav VI Adolf of Sweden greets Neruda at the Nobel Prize celebrations in 1971.*
Above *Illustration by José Venturelli for the German edition (1953) of Neruda's* Canto general. *Born Neftali Ricardo Reyes Basualto, son of a railwayman, Neruda published his* Twenty Poems of Love and One Desperate Song *in 1924 and soon after worked in the consular service abroad. During the 1930s in Barcelona he published a Surrealist magazine, and he became a Communist after the Civil War. Thereafter he saw poetry as a mark of human solidarity with 'simple people'. He was Ambassador to Mexico (1940/42) and to Paris (1970/72), and 'died' in Chile within days of Pinochet's political coup.*

'HIGH TIME TO SHARE THE SOIL AND THE FIELDS'

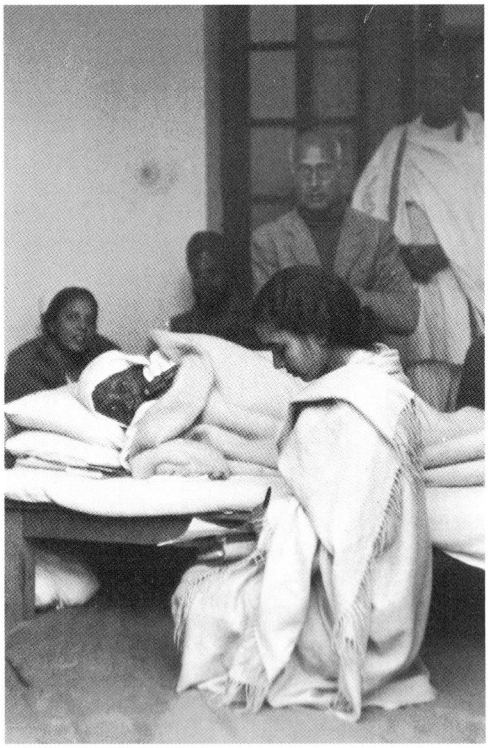

Above right *Rabindranath Tagore, one of the famous figures in the history of Bengali literature. Born in Calcutta of wealthy parents, he was influenced by the family belief that Western practical genius could be harmonized with the spiritual insight and aestheticism of traditional India. He translated much of his work into English, and accepted a knighthood, only to resign it in 1919 in protest againt the Amritsar massacre. The school he founded became the Visva-Bharati University in 1922.*

Above *Mohandas Karamchand Gandhi, the 'Mahatma' ('Great Soul'), during his last fast. His hunger-strikes were a weapon against the British authorities, but in 1947 he began a fast in a resolute attempt to stop the Hindu–Mohammedan sectarian slaughter that followed partition and independence. In January 1948 he was killed by a Hindu fanatic.*

In 1913 the Bengali poet, **Rabindranath Tagore** (1861–1941) was awarded the Nobel Prize – an historic occasion since this was the first time that a modern non-Westerner had received an international award; and it caused a considerable stir both among Indians and throughout many other Asian countries. Tagore had studied for a while in London, and his philosophy and poetry are a synthesis of ancient Indian thinking and Western humanism. If the Western reader cannot always sufficiently appreciate the lofty romantic poems collected in *Gitanjali* (1913) and *The Herb Gardener* (1912), that is partly due to our ignorance of their strict linguistic form. Tagore also wrote novels, for example, *The Shipwreck*, and such plays as *The Sacrifice* and *The Post Office* (1912).

The great Irish poet, William Butler Yeats, who was much influenced by Tagore's works, paid him an eloquent tribute. There, he wrote, 'An immense simplicity that one does not find elsewhere in literature makes the birds and the leaves seem as near to him as they are to children, and the changes of the seasons, great events, as before our thoughts had arisen between them and us.'

Tagore wrote in Bengali; **Mahatma Gandhi** (1869–1948) composed his remarkable autobiography, *My Experiments with Truth* (1927/29), in Gujarati; while Pakistan's national poet, **Mohammad Iqbal** (1873–1938) employed partly Persian, partly the great literary language, Urdu, for his poetry and his political essays. It is not only the language barrier that often prevents us from translating and enjoying Eastern verse, but also the fact that it was usually meant to be recited by the poet himself. Urdu poets frequently meet at a *mushaira*, or poetry symposium; and anyone who has heard them will know that their verses are almost impossible to reproduce either in translation or in print.

Its ideological background has made modern Chinese literature particularly interesting from a Western point of view. After the revolution in 1911, when the Imperial regime was brought down, and the linguistic reforms of 1917, Chinese authors abandoned the old Mandarin language and began to employ that of the people, *pai-hua* (*pinyin*). The first to weld it into a literary medium was the prose-writer, **Lu Hsun** (**Luxun**, 1881–1936), who has been hailed as the 'Gorky of China'. For many years, Chinese prose-writers were much influenced by Soviet Social Realism. Thus **Tien Chun** (**Tian Shun**, *b.*1908) in 1935 published a novel entitled *Village in August*, that describes the struggle of the Chinese against the Japanese invasion of Manchuria, and was the first modern Chinese novel to be translated into a Western language. Among the prose-writers of the 1930s, **Mao tun** (**Mao dun**, 1899–1980), **Pa chin** (**Ba Jin**, *b.*1904) and **Lao she**

Far left *A scene from the Kabuki theatre by the 17th-century Japanese artist Hishikawa Moronobu. Kabuki was a popular lyric adaptation of the austere classical tradition of Noh drama, which in turn had developed from ancient ritual temple dance. Richly costumed but without scenery, and with only two principal characters, it was court drama at its most refined. Kabuki had its own conventions but allowed somewhat freer scope – for instance the actors might approach the stage along 'flower ways' through the audience. Both forms survive and companies often tour Europe.*

Left *Mao Tse-tung during the Long March. Mao wrote poems as well as his 'Thoughts' and was reckoned a fine calligrapher. The art, an essential aspect of Chinese painting and literature, was once a necessary accomplishment of China's emperors.*

(1898–1967) have also reached the West, Lao she with his novel *Rickshaw Boy*. His realism, however, was so merciless that the English translator felt obliged to invent a happy ending.

Poets who appeared before the Communist Revolution of 1948–49 were **Kuo mo-jo** (**Guo Moro**, 1892–1978), **Wen yi-to** (**Wen Yido**, 1899–1946), **Tsang ko-chia** (**Cang Gojia**, *b.*1910), **Ai ching** (*b.*1910) and the party-chairman, **Mao Tse-tung** (**Mao Zedong**, 1893–1976), whose revolutionary poems are written in the classical literary language, with eleventh-century stylistic patterns.

Japanese literature has also interested contemporary Western critics. Seventeen-syllable *haiku* have been translated, and *Noh* plays performed on Western stages; and prose, too, has attracted foreign notice. Partly as a winner of the Nobel Prize, **Yasunari Kawabata** (1899–1972) saw a number of his novels, including *Snow Country* (1935/37) and *Thousand Cranes* (1947), rendered into Western languages; and **Yukio Mishima** (1925–1970) achieved fame as a novelist – *The Sound of Waves* (1950) is a good example of his work – and, at the same time, as a dramatist. His ritual suicide, before a large audience, was in the self-destructive Japanese tradition.

The Warlords Clash (1929)
by Mao Tse-tung

Wind and clouds suddenly rip the sky
and warlords clash. War again.
Rancour rains down on men who
dream of a Pillow of Yellow Barley.
Yet our red banners leap over the calm
Ting River on our way
to Shanghang and to Lungyen the
dragon cliff.
The golden vase of China is shattered.
We mend it,
happy as we give away its meadows.

THE WORLD WOULD NOT BE THE SAME

Right *'The atom bomb has radically changed the nature of the world we know, and as a result, the human race now finds itself in a new situation to which it has to adapt its thinking.' – Albert Einstein in 1946.*

Below *J. Robert Oppenheimer the American physicist who, as director of the Manhattan Project, ensured the successful development of the atom bomb – which was to put an end to the war in the Pacific. The first bomb was dropped on Hiroshima on 6 August 1945, the second on Nagasaki three days later and the Japanese surrendered within a week, although the formal terms were not signed until 2 September.*

In 1945, after the gates of Auschwitz had been opened, the German writer **Adorno** (1903–1969) said that nothing could ever be written again; by which he meant that the world of Man had become so terrible and so incomprehensible that writing and painting could neither truly reflect nor have any real pretensions to reshape it.

Although Adorno was clearly proved wrong by the vast body of novels, plays and poems that have since appeared, writers and artists have been obliged to study the human condition, and the potentialities of human nature, from a very different and deeply disturbing point of view. They have generally ceased to regard themselves as leaders or reformers, and are often content merely to describe and lament the chaotic pattern of twentieth-century life.

Among our age's positive achievements, however, have been at home the rapid emancipation of women and, abroad, the liberation of most former colonies. But, at the same time, technological development has widened the gulf between industrial and underdeveloped countries; while industry and the population explosion together have done incalculable harm to man's environment. We can no longer, like H.G. Wells, see scientific advance as necessarily a benefit. In the words of J. Robert Oppenheimer, the father of the atomic bomb, 'the physicists have known sin; and this is a knowledge which they cannot lose'. Oppenheimer added that the world would never be the same; and a succession of writers have echoed his opinion. From two American novelists we have had particularly vivid accounts of humanity's collective madness during the Second World War.

Joseph Heller (*b.*1923) wrote a novel, *Catch 22* (1961), based on his own wartime experiences. It is a 'black comedy', a macabre farce parodying the nightmare logic of war. Yossarian, a bomber pilot, tries to prove he is mad since this would mean he need not fly any further missions. But the fact that Yossarian wishes to abandon flying proves that he is sane; and therefore there is no escape. That is the 'catch' of the title. In Heller's next book, *Something Happened* (1974), with its quiet American background, he still manages

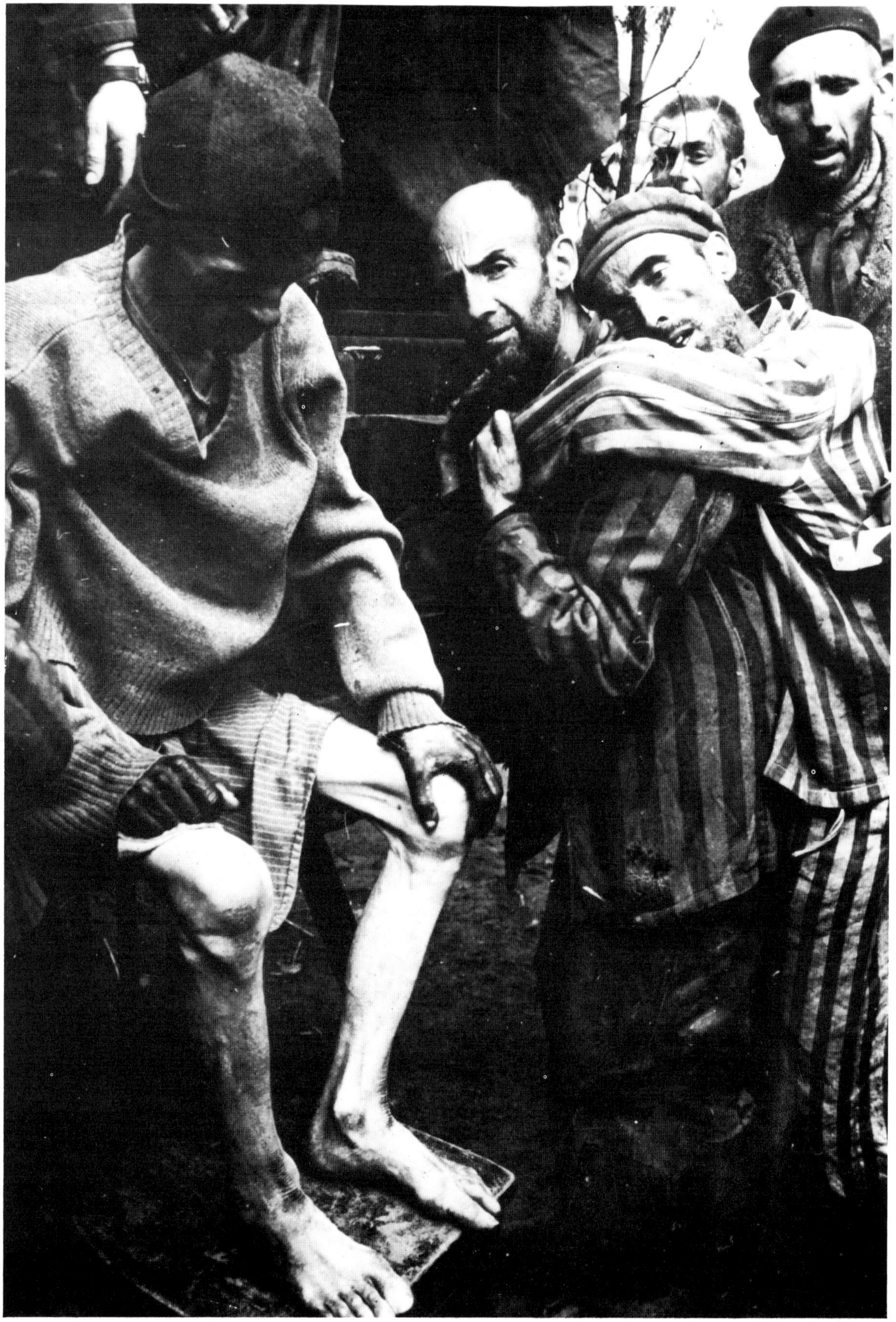

Survivors of the Nazi death camps of the Second World War. The urge to destroy life, whether on the pretext of military necessity or in pursuit of some conviction or ideology, seems to have been part of civilization since its beginnings. Yet in our age, the Nazi plan to exterminate the whole Jewish population under its control must appear the most purely Satanic manifestation of this urge; and it is not surprising that some writers should have rejected the whole concept of progress. The age-old paradox that, while as private citizens people may yearn for peace, their political organizations often produce brutality and war, led Kurt Vonnegut (while brooding over why people write books when presidents and generals and senators don't read them) to suggest that: 'one must catch people before *they become generals and senators and presidents and* poison their minds with humanity.'

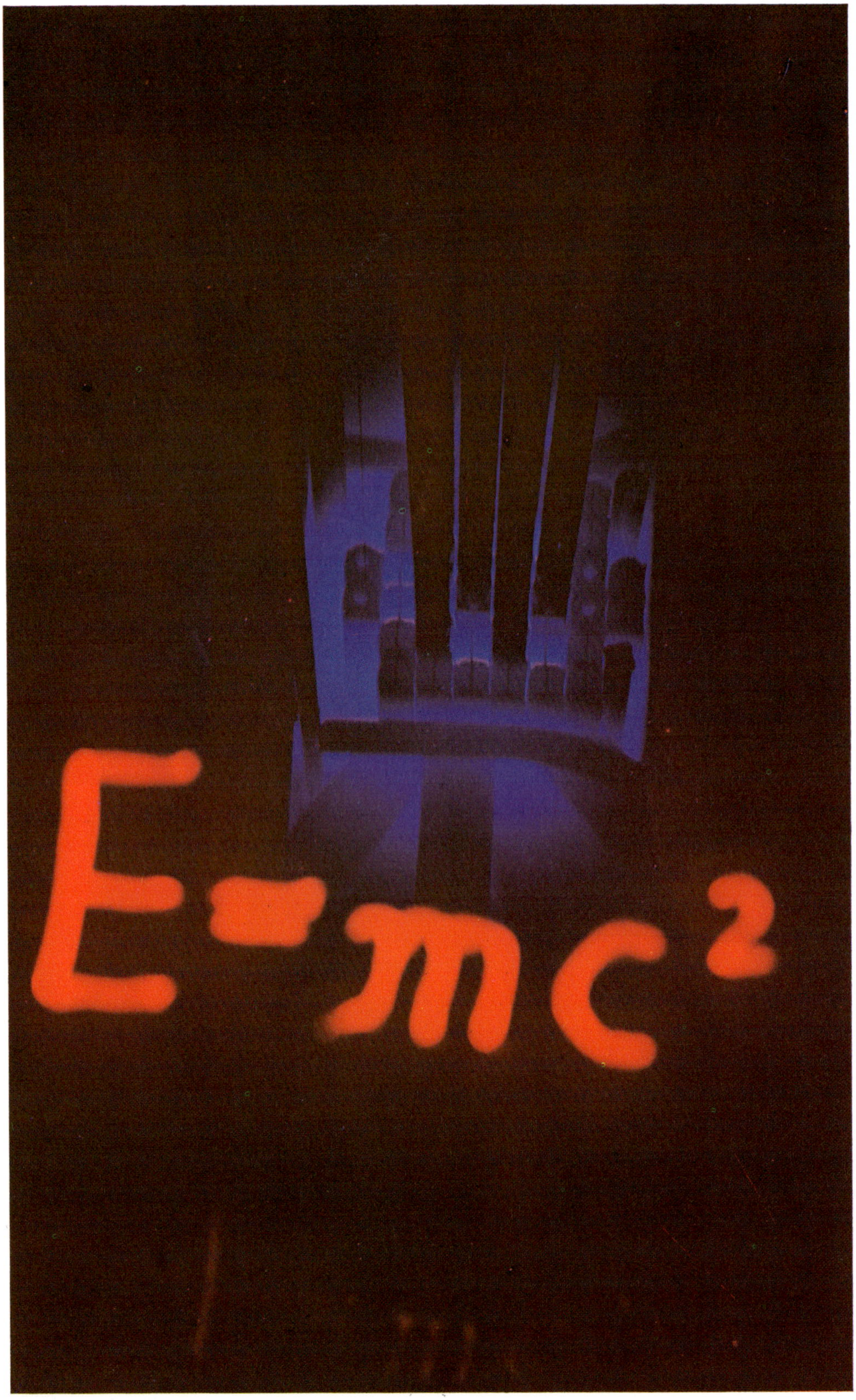

to conjure up a sense of panic terror.

Kurt Vonnegut (*b.*1922), another 'black humourist', made his name with *Slaughterhouse 5* (1969), a mixture of parodied science-fiction and the author's own terrible memories of the bombing of Dresden, which he observed as a prisoner-of-war. Behind the lunatic eccentricities of books like his *Slapstick* (1976), lies a profoundly serious criticism of modern society.

For German writers of the same age as Vonnegut or Heller, the problem of coming to terms with the post-war world had the added dimension that they had grown up in a now discredited society.

Günter Grass (*b.*1927) wrote an experimental novel *Die Blechtrommel* (*The Tin Drum*) in 1959 that soon attracted international notice. It consists of an immensely protracted monologue; but the speaker, who has somehow never grown up, remains a physical and intellectual dwarf. His picture of Germany is reflected in this comic distorting mirror and has a slightly gruesome verisimilitude. After his first success, Grass was more and more drawn towards the Left Wing.

Though Sweden was neutral during the Second World War, her writers reveal the same preoccupations as those of other European countries. Indeed, Swedish poetry reached a high point during the 1940s with the poets **Erik Lindegren** (1910–1968) and **Gunnar Ekelöf** (1907–1968). Their constantly expressed anxiety involved not so much the poet himself as the fears of the entire Nuclear Age. Ekelöf, who has the greater international reputation, was an early advocate of simple socially-conscious writing.

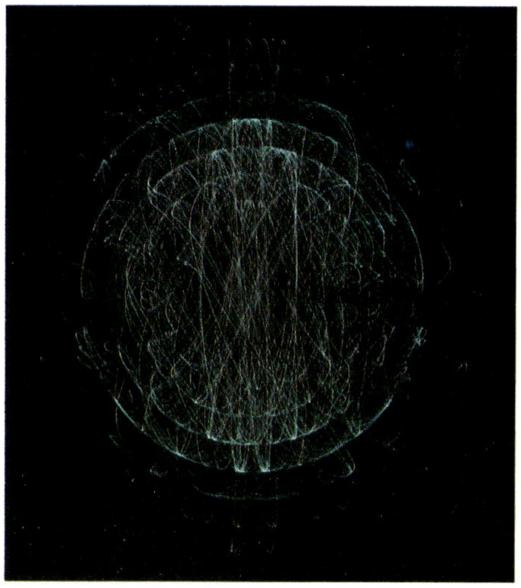

Opposite, far left *Fundamentals of atomic physics – an atomic pile with, superimposed, the Einsteinian formula expressing the equivalence of mass and energy – the energy release is equal to the mass times the square of the speed of light, and* (**left**) *Plexiglass model of a uranium (U235) atom, the element used for the Hiroshima bomb.*

Below right *Kurt Vonnegut, and* (**right**) *Swedish jacket for his novel* Slapstick. *The Allies' terror-bombing of Dresden in 1945 (where he was a P.o.W.) killed some 80,000 people. Cynics consider the A-bomb as a more efficient tool for a policy of destruction that was already being carried out. Whereas the Dresden holocaust used hundreds of bomber planes, that of Hiroshima required only one. Vonnegut's ruthless indictments of civilized man are savage, precise and extravagantly comic.*

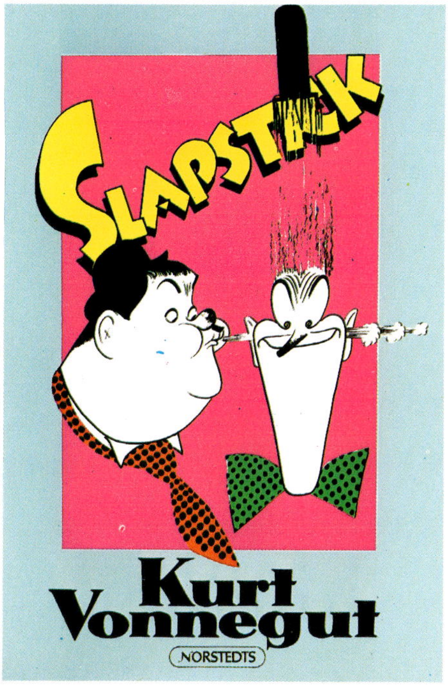

Above *Günter Grass. The German film of his novel* The Tin Drum *won an Oscar in 1979. He himself designed the jacket* (**right**) *for the original edition. In his novels,* Hundejahre *(1963,* Dog Years*) and* Der Butt *(1977,* The Flounder*), he experimented with new techniques.*

THE FLIGHT FROM REASON

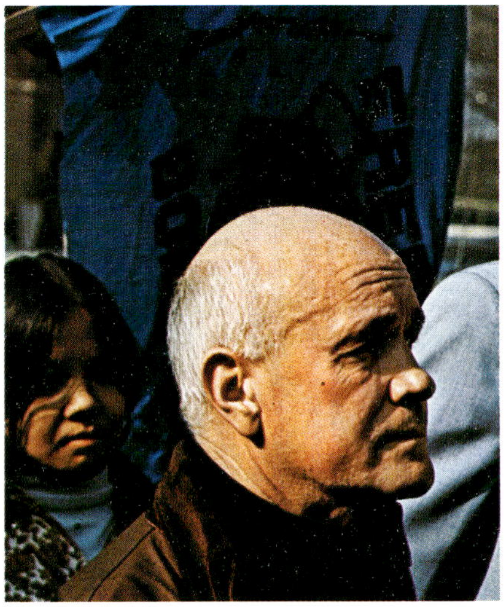

Above right *Jean Genêt in 1973, bastard son of parents he never knew, pederast and self-confessed delinquent. When he describes the crimes for which he was imprisoned, he attempts to dignify his own inverted universe with the help of a fine literary style. Sartre's* Saint-Genêt *(1952) is an Existentialist analysis of the man.*

Above *Scene from Stockholm City Theatre's production (1964) of Genêt's* The Screens.

The grimly comic distortions of Günter Grass or Kurt Vonnegut are direct reflections of war-time experience, their general thesis being that Man's existence is absurd, and that life is a cruel farce. This conviction, one of the main themes of European post-war literature in the 1950s, was frequently expressed upon the stage; though the chief prophet of Absurdism, the French dramatist Artaud, had already died before his influence was widely felt. **Antonin Artaud** (1896–1948), writer, actor, director and artist, spent some ten years in different psychiatric hospitals. His most famous work, *Le Théâtre et son double* (*The Theatre and its Double*), was published in 1938. Artaud believed that his view of life as desperate and brutal could only be expressed in what he termed 'The Theatre of Cruelty'.

Jean Genêt (1910–86), another French writer, without necessarily borrowing from Artaud, seemed to follow much the same line. In his novels and plays, which have a criminal and homosexual background, he welded his own experiences of human degrada-

:ion into a dark nihilistic philosophy, expressed through a remarkably powerful use of language. His prose works, *Journal du voleur* (1948, *Thief's Journal*) and *Miracle de la rose* (1946, *Miracle of the Rose*), contain passages where religious speculations are interspersed with scraps of pimps' and robbers' slang. His plays, *Les Bonnes* (1947, *The Maids*) and *Les Paravents* (1961, *The Screens*), glorify crime and treachery by means of paradoxical arguments and great dramatic skill.

Samuel Beckett (*b.*1906) is an Irishman who lives in France and writes in French as an intellectual discipline. He was a member of James Joyce's circle in Paris; and, like Joyce, he has a fastidious and wide-ranging concern with language for its own sake. This preoccupation which involves a love of complex, often scatalogical, puns, is a reminder that Beckett, like Joyce, despite all their apparent innovations belongs to an Irish literary tradition that embraces Swift, Yeats and Synge; a tradition of helplessness, passionate despair and pointless passion. Beckett translates all his own work; and his best-known play *En attendant Godot* (*Waiting for Godot*) was first performed in English in 1955. The central characters, two tramps, wait for the mysterious Godot, who never materializes; many critics have fallen into the trap of trying to explain its meaning. *Happy Days* (1961) portrays a married woman slowly sinking into a heap of sand while her husband fusses idiotically around her. The novels *Murphy*, *Watt* (both 1953) and the trilogy: *Molloy* (1951), *Malone meurt* (1951, *Malone Dies*) and *L'Innommable* (1953, *The Unnameable*), present equally ludicrous yet tragic heroes. Beckett received the Nobel Prize for literature in 1969.

From **Waiting for Godot** by Samuel Beckett

ESTRAGON: Why don't we hang ourselves?
VLADIMIR: With what?
ESTRAGON: You haven't got a bit of rope?
VLADIMIR: No.
ESTRAGON: Then we can't.
Silence.
VLADIMIR: Let's go.
ESTRAGON: Wait, there's my belt.
VLADIMIR: It's too short.
ESTRAGON: You could hang on to my legs.
VLADIMIR: And who'd hang on to mine?
ESTRAGON: True.
VLADIMIR: Show all the same. (*Estragon loosens the cord that holds up his trousers which, much too big for him, fall about his ankles. They look at the cord.*) It might do at a pinch. But is it strong enough?
ESTRAGON: We'll soon see. Here.
They each take an end of the cord and pull. It breaks. They almost fall.
VLADIMIR: Not worth a curse.
Silence.
ESTRAGON: You say we have to come back tomorrow?
VLADIMIR: Yes.
ESTRAGON: Then we can bring a good bit of rope.
VLADIMIR: Yes.
Silence.
ESTRAGON: Didi.
VLADIMIR: Yes.
ESTRAGON: I can't go on like this.
VLADIMIR: That's what you think.
ESTRAGON: If we parted? That might be better for us.
VLADIMIR: We'll hang ourselves tomorrow. (*Pause.*) Unless Godot comes.
ESTRAGON: And if he comes?
VLADIMIR: We'll be saved.

Top *Samuel Beckett, Irish playwright and novelist, whose* Waiting for Godot *was much analysed and discussed by the critics when it was first performed. It may well have more to do with 'Charlot' (Charlie Chaplin) than God(ot).*

Above *The universally famous characters – tramps Estragon and Vladimir – of* Waiting for Godot*, seen here in Stockholm's Royal Dramatic Theatre production in 1978.*

Above *Ionesco, the playwright, and Laurence Olivier (at left) with Duncan Macrae in the 1960 production of his* Rhinoceros *at London's Royal Court Theatre. The play is an allegorical picture of a man in a small town who changes, ever-so-gradually into a rhinoceros. When more and more people are similarly affected, the transformation becomes first fashionable and then obligatory.*

Opposite *Edward Albee at a rehearsal of his play* Who's Afraid of Virginia Wolf?, *notable for its searing assault on marriage as an institution.*

Eugène Ionesco (*b.*1912), though Romanian, has become a French dramatist. His plays exhibit the element of absurdity in human life by displaying farcical actions, or, indeed, by lack of action. This he does in *La Cantatrice chauve* (1950, *The Bald Prima-Donna*), where the characters merely exchange phrases that they have learned from an antiquated traveller's guide. *Le Leçon* (1951, *The Lesson*) is a variation on a similar theme – the general incomprehensibility and cruelty of the world. During a lesson the heroine has been instructed to learn, she cannot understand anything; and she is finally murdered by her teacher. In *Les Chaises* (1952, *The Chairs*), however, and *Le Rhinocéros* (1960), Ionesco also shows a touch of social concern, though the author has expressly stated that he detests any kind of political and propagandist writing.

Max Frisch (*b.*1911) is Swiss. His novels, such as *Stiller* (1954, *I'm Not*

Far left *Swiss dramatist Friedrich Dürrenmatt, who made his first success with the tragi-comedy* Der Besuch der alten Dame *(1956,* The Visit*), the story of a rich woman's revenge on the money-worshipping hypocrites of her native town.*
Left *Dürrenmatt's* The Physicists, *where the world falls into the clutches of a madman. Three 'madmen' (who are sane) impersonate Einstein, Newton, and an emissary of King Solomon (in fact the brilliant physicist Möbius). Christopher Wilkinson (Möbius), John Pickles (Inspector Voss) and Barrie Smith (Newton) at a Sheffield Playhouse production in 1968.*

Stiller), and his plays, *Andorra* (1961) and *Biedermann und die Brandstifter* (1958, *The Fire-Raisers*), not only insist on the absurdity of the roles society obliges human beings to adopt, but demonstrate how often we are the prisoners of artificial concepts and 'received ideas'. Sometimes we cannot see evil, even when it emerges undisguised; and the simple-minded Herr Biedermann himself provides the wicked arsonists with matches, just as the Germans accepted Hitler, despite the fact that he had openly declared his aims in *Mein Kampf*.

For Frisch's fellow-countryman, **Friedrich Dürrenmatt** (*b.*1921), the world resembles one of Kafka's nightmares. The action of his plays is frequently bizarre, but the problems that concern him grow more and more topical – for example, the question of Science's responsibilities to mankind, debated in *Die Physiker* (1962, *The Physicists*).

A sympathetic interest in their fellow men is not unusual among writers said to be Absurdists. Both Beckett and Albert Camus, for example, who largely invented the philosophical concept of Absurdist writing, were passionately anti-Nazi and, during the War, members of the French Resistance. But it would be wrong to regard such novelists and dramatists as forming a 'movement' or having a direct political aim.

In the United States **Edward Albee** (*b.*1928) has been associated with the Absurd view of life. *The Zoo Story* (1958) depicts a young homosexual who persuades an innocent man to kill him; while *Who's Afraid of Virginia Woolf?* (1962) is a piece of brilliant black humour with biting dialogue that reveals the sinister beneath the trivial. *Tiny Alice* (1964) tells of the evil influence of the 'richest woman in the world' and has a complex symbolism, but *A Delicate Balance* (1966) is more realistic on the horrors of family life.

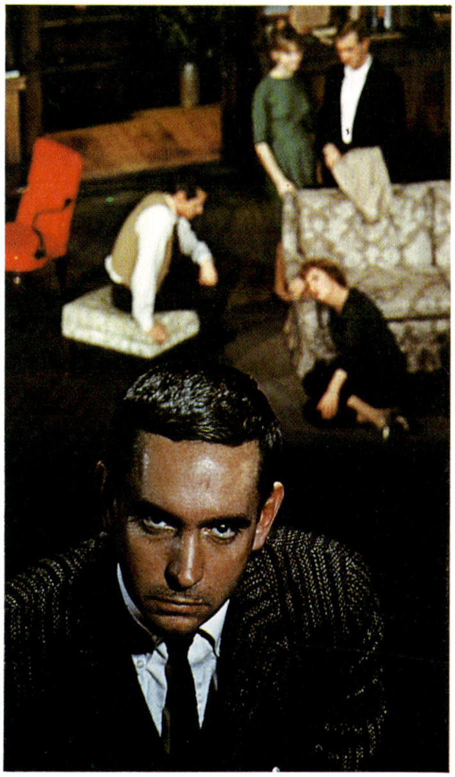

NEW SUBJECTS, NEW FORMS

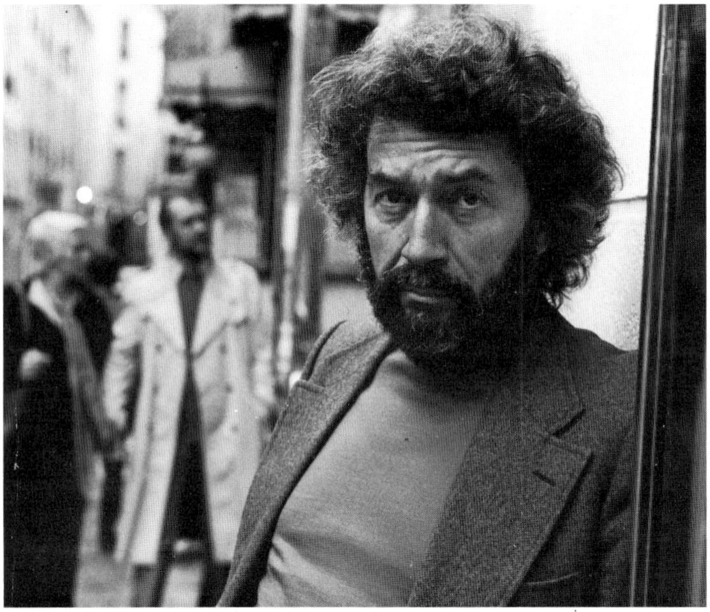

Right *Alain Robbe-Grillet, novelist, film-maker, critic and a leader of the 1950s French 'new novel'. His juggling with past and present in his screenplay for* Last Year in Marienbad *(1961) baffled viewers of Alain Resnais's much-praised film.*

Below *William Golding, whose work teems with mystical undercurrents. In* The Inheritors *(1955), which he considers his best book, he depicts the world's primeval innocence through the plight of the last group of Neanderthal Men, fleeing from a hunting tribe of* Homo sapiens *– the 'inheritors'.*

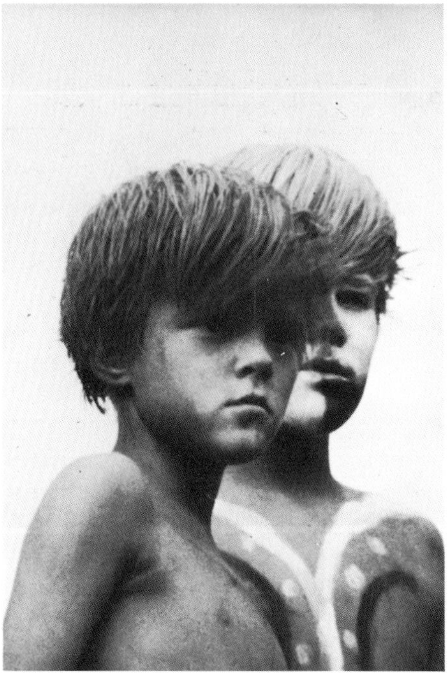

Above *Two of the castaways who bully and terrorize the other boys stranded on the desert island in Peter Brook's film (1963) of Golding's* Lord of the Flies, *where delightful children are shown turning into savage little tyrants.*

In the novels of **Alain Robbe-Grillet** (*b.*1922) – *Le Voyeur* (1955, *The Voyeur*), *La Jalousie* (1957, *Jealousy*) and *Dans le labyrinthe* (1959, *In the Labyrinth*) – there is neither plot nor psychological development. His books are built up of a series of vivid, yet often inconsequential images; and his characters are less men and women than 'holes with human contours surrounding them'. Robbe-Grillet also clears the decks of morals, 'messages' or symbolic pretensions. His text has as few, or as many, undertones or overtones and secret messages as the reality we all confront. We shall gain nothing if we look for a meaning in life, Robbe-Grillet declares; 'the world is neither meaningful nor absurd: it *is*.'

Michel Butor (*b.*1926) and **Claude Simon** (*b.*1913) employ a similar technique. In their works there is little external action; all time-schemes are mixed; characters are constantly dispersing or merging into others. The novels they have published are not so crisply constructed as those of Robbe-Grillet, perhaps because the authors – Simon most of all – are not dedicated novelists but primarily poets. Simon's *La Route de Flandres* (1960, *The Flanders Road*) consists of a lengthy monologue that describes several riders on a night retreat. Though monotonous and difficult to read, it possesses a suggestive lyrical beauty.

In the same literary movement, which has been named *le nouveau roman*, are the novels of **Nathalie Sarraute** (*b.*1902): *Le Planétarium* (1959, *The Planetarium*) and *Les Fruits d'or* (1963, *The Golden Fruits*).

Apart from Beckett, post-war English prose cannot be said to have followed James Joyce's lead. But the 1983 Nobel Prize winner, **William**

Golding (*b.*1911), is certainly an exception. When he was 43, he published *The Lord of the Flies* (1954), where his subject is the plight of a planeload of schoolboys, evacuated because a nuclear war threatens, whose plane crashes on a desert island. Their adult companions are killed, and the boys create their own society, which takes a brutally primitive form. Golding's later works are more experimental. *The Spire* (1964), for instance, concerns the building of a medieval spire on insecure foundations. Then, after many years of silence, in 1979 he wrote *Darkness Visible* and, in 1980, *Rites of Passage*, the supposed journal of one Edmund Talbot, who, some time during the nineteenth century, makes a hazardous voyage from England to Australia.

Anthony Burgess (*b.*1917) has made numerous experiments with style and even written books in a musical tempo. His best-known work, *A Clockwork Orange* (1962), is a hideous picture of Britain's future moral breakdown, seen through the eyes of a sadistic young gangleader. Among more conventional novels that appeared in the 1950s and 1960s was *Lucky Jim* (1954) by **Kingsley Amis** (*b.*1922). The hero, or anti-hero, Jim Dixon, is angry, sly, boorish, accident-prone, but essentially honest and, as a character, wonderfully amusing.

At this time, three distinguished women novelists also began to emerge – **Muriel Spark** (*b.*1918), whose cruel insight was first shown in *The Prime of Miss Jean Brodie* (1961) and *The Mandelbaum Gate* (1965); **Iris Murdoch** (*b.*1919), who has studied mankind from the point of view of a highly imaginative Professor of Moral Philosophy in *The Bell* (1958) and *A Severed Head* (1961); and **Olivia Manning** (1915–1980), author of penetrating semi-autobiographical novels, of which *The Balkan Trilogy* (1960/65) is probably the most successful.

Left *Alex and the Droogs all set for violence in Stanley Kubrick's film (1971) of* A Clockwork Orange. *Malcolm McDowell as the 'hero' who enjoyed Beethoven and brutality alike.*
Below *Maggie Smith won an Oscar for her performance as the eccentric Scottish teacher in Ronald Neame's film (1969) of Muriel Spark's masterly tale* The Prime of Miss Jean Brodie.
Bottom *Jennie Linden and Lee Remick in Dick Clement's film (1970) of Iris Murdoch's* A Severed Head, *a story that deals with both incest and adultery. Frederick Raphael wrote the script.*

French poetry, since the First World War, has produced no man of genius, though **Henri Michaux** (*b.*1899) won critical acclaim as a poet and travel-writer with *Un Barbare en Asie* (1932, *A Barbarian in Asia*). The romantic Catholic **Pierre Jean Louve** (1887–1976), the 'poet of loneliness', also deserves a mention.

One of the most remarkable poets of the twentieth century was the Portuguese, **Fernando Pessoa** (1888–1935), most of whose work appeared some time after his death. He wrote under four different names – his own and those of the modernist **Alvaro de Campos**, the classical traditionalist **Ricardo Reis**, and **Alberto Caeiro**, a headstrong but intellectual rustic. As such, Pessoa alone represents the four greatest Portuguese poets since Camoẽs.

Among English poets of the post-war period, especially noteworthy are **Ted Hughes** (*b.*1930), who published his first collection, *Hawk in the Rain*, in 1957; the urbane yet embittered romantic, **Philip Larkin** (*b.*1922), who first made his name with *The Less Deceived* (1955); and the dionysiac young Welsh word-master, **Dylan Thomas** (1914–1953), who loved language and handled it with a bold exuberance. His collection of poems, *Deaths and Entrances* (1946), reveals both his fascinated preoccupation with his own childhood and his Celtic cult of Nature.

During the same decade, the 1950s, new dramatists appeared. **John Osborne** (*b.*1929) in *Look Back in Anger* (1956) fixed the type of 'angry young man', the furious opponent of established values; and **Harold Pinter** (*b.*1930) set *The Birthday Party* (1957) and *The Caretaker* (1960) in ordinary surroundings, inhabited by commonplace people, where nothing romantic or extraordinary ever happens, but the protagonists' dialogue, which is notably clipped and colloquial, evokes an atmosphere of anxiety, terror and suspense.

More recent arrivals are **Alan Ayckbourn** (*b.*1939) and **Tom Stoppard** (*b.*1937). Ayckbourn situated *How the Other Half Loves* (1970) simultaneously in two different rooms; and Stoppard's *Rosencrantz and Guildenstern are Dead* (1966) focuses the audience's attention on a pair of minor characters from *Hamlet*, courtly nonentities quite oblivious to the great events that happen all around them.

Above *Dylan and Caitlin Thomas with their daughter, Aeronwy, in 1945. He had already started work on 'a play for voices' –* Under Milk Wood *(1953), which he first read at a US lecture.* **Right** *Warren Mitchell in the revival of Pinter's first major success,* The Caretaker, *at London's National Theatre in 1980.* **Far right** Rosencrantz and Guildenstern are Dead *with Christopher Timothy and Richard O'Callaghan as 'R' and 'G', Philip Locke as Player, in London's Young Vic revival (1975) of Tom Stoppard's remarkable play. In* Jumpers *(1972), a philosophic* tour de force, *he combines wit with virtuosity of language, and in his television film* Professional Foul *(1978) exhibits the hazards of free thought in a closed society.*

THE WIND OF CHANGE

On 3 February 1960 the British Prime Minister, Harold Macmillan, spoke in Capetown of the 'Wind of Change' blowing through the African continent; and since 1960 most former colonies throughout the world have achieved their independence, which has produced a remarkable literary flowering, as writers have employed the language of their one-time masters to discuss the peoples, history and landscapes of their own countries, and sometimes to condemn what they observe.

Most books in the former African colonies are published in French, English or Portuguese, as tribal languages are too numerous and various to provide a satisfactory common tongue. The two pioneers of 'Black' poetry, the Senegalese **Léopold Sédar Senghor** (*b.*1906), who became the president of his country, and the West Indian, **Aimé Césaire** (*b.*1913), have both preferred to write in French.

Today the centre of African prose-writing is in the Bay of Guinea where the Nigerians, **Amos Tutuola** (*b.*1920), **Chinua Achebe** (*b.*1930) and **Mongo Beti** (*b.*1932), a native of the Cameroons, are all at work. Nigeria has by far the greatest number of talented black poets who write in English, among the best known being **John Pepper Clark** (*b.*1935), **Christopher Okigbo** (*b.*1932) and **Gabriel Okara** (*b.*1921), who publishes prose–narratives as well as verse.

South Africa's leading black writer, **Peter Abrahams** (*b.*1919), has for many years been obliged to live in exile. The most notable of his many novels, *A Wreath for Udomo* (1956), takes Kwame N'Krumah (then President of Ghana) as the central character.

The Dead by Léopold Sédar Senghor

They are lying out there beside the captured roads, all along the roads of disaster
Elegant poplars, statues of sombre gods draped in their long cloaks of gold,
Senegalese prisoners darkly stretched on the soil of France.

In vain they have cut off your laughter, in vain the darker flower of your flesh,
You are the flower in its first beauty amid a naked absence of flowers
Black flower with its grave smile, diamond of immemorial ages.
You are the slime and plasma of the green spring of the world
Of the first couple you are the flesh, the ripe belly the milkiness
You are the sacred increase of the bright gardens of paradise

And the invincible forest, victorious over fire and thunderbolt.
The great song of your blood will vanquish machines and cannons
Your throbbing speech evasions and lies.
No hate in your soul void of hatred, no cunning in your soul void of cunning.
O Black Martyrs immortal race, let me speak the words of pardon.

Above right *Léopold Senghor, since the 1930s a passionate believer in Negritude and the value of African culture: 'We are the leaven that the white flour needs', to counteract the failings of Western civilization – 'no mother's breast but only nylon legs . . .'. This poet was elected the first president of the West African Republic of Senegal in 1960.*

Above *Mexican novelist and critic Carlos Fuentes, who at one time worked in the cinema with Buñuel. His panoramic novel* La Région más transparente *(1958,* Where the Air is Clear*), influenced by Joyce and others, traces social changes effected by the Mexican revolution. The technically ambitious 'open novel'* Cambio de piel *(1967,* Change of Skin*), explores the changing relationships of four main characters.*

Above right *Original jacket for* The Green Pope*, central volume of a trilogy by Miguel Asturias, Nobel Prize winner in 1967. That year an English translation had appeared of his* Mulata de tal *(1963,* Mullatta and Mr Fly*) which carries his technique of 'magical realism' to its extreme.*

Much of Latin America has long been independent; but its nineteenth-century writers, with the exception of the Brazilian novelist **Machado de Assís** (1839–1908), showed comparatively little original talent. During the twentieth century, however, especially since the Second World War, it has taken its place in world literature; and, apart from Neruda, the best-known author of the new school is the Argentinian novelist, **Jorge Luis Borges** (*b.*1899), a sceptical and labyrinthine writer, whose novels, poems and stories, for instance *Informe sobre Brodie* (1970, *Dr Brodie's Report*), have a speculative and philosophical basis. Meanwhile, the Cuban writer, **Alejo Carpentier** (1904–1980), has exhibited a characteristically Latin American distrust of political change, just as, in the works of **Carlos Fuentes** (*b.*1929) – notably in *La Muerte de Artemio Cruz* (1962, *The Death of Artemio Cruz*) – where the young Mexicans he describes begin to imitate the corrupt elder generation whom they once scorned. *La Ciudad y los perros* (1962, *The Time of the Heroes*) by the Peruvian, **Mario Vargas Llosa** (*b.*1936), portrays South American militarism with the help of a technique borrowed from the French modern novel, while the immensely popular *Cien años de soledad* (1967, *A Hundred Years of Solitude*) by the Colombian, **Gabriel García Márquez** (*b.*1928), tells – in parody – the story of a solitary little Latin American town.

After Borges, the late **Miguel Ángel Asturias** (1899–1974) is considered to be the most distinguished of Latin American novelists. He came from Guatemala; and his *El Señor presidente* (1946, *The President*), *Hombres de Maíz* (1949, Men of Maize), *El Papa verde* (1954, *The Green Pope*) and *Los Ojos de los enterrados* (1960, *The Eyes of the Interred*), are often fierce attacks on North American capitalism – huge pictures of the plight of American Indians and poor banana workers. Although Asturias's plots resemble those of adventure stories, his villains are always 'the lords of cheques and knives' and 'merchants in men's sweat'.

Other important post-war literary figures are the Mexican poet **Octavio Paz** (*b.*1914) and Brazilian Communist novelist, **Jorge Amado** (*b.*1912). Paz remained in Europe for many years, being influenced primarily by Surrealism. His later, more mature poetry took solitude as its point of departure: poetry itself being the reconciling principle for the lone spirit of Man. Immensely prolific, Amado was first preoccupied with social concerns, as in his realist novel *Terras do sem fim* (1942, *The Violent Land*), but in later works politics give way to humanism.

Left *'A Bush Road', an 1863 engraving of life in the pioneer days of the Australian 'outback'. Nineteenth-century novels and thrillers of bushranger life prepared the way for an Australian literature based on the Australian, rather than the European, experience. The tradition has come to maturity in the post-Second World War writings of such authors as Patrick White* (**below**) *who was awarded the Nobel Prize in 1973. In* The Aunt's Story, *White is considered to have taken on the Nietzschean concept of 'the lonely atheist's agonized capacity for insight into the nature of existence.'*

A distinctive Australian literature has emerged very slowly; and, apart from the poetry of **Kenneth Slessor** (1901–1971) and his contemporary **R.D. Fitzgerald** (*b.*1902), little of note appeared before the Second World War. Both these poets loved their own country, its history and pre-history. **A.D. Hope** (*b.*1907), on the other hand, whose first collection did not appear until 1955, has a wider scope and sometimes refers bitterly to modern social conditions. **Judith Wright** (*b.*1915) writes clear, intelligent verses on Australian subjects and domestic life. **Peter Porter** (*b.*1929), despite many years spent in England, produces sensitive poems that often reflect his antipodean background.

When the drama *The Summer of the Seventeenth Doll* (1956) by **Ray Lawler** (*b.*1921) was staged, Australian audiences heard, for the first time, Australian characters speaking the racy Australian idiom of the streets.

Since **Patrick White** (*b.*1912) published his first major novel, *The Aunt's Story*, in 1948, he has written a series of powerful books with an Australian setting, especially *The Tree of Man* (1955) and *Voss* (1957), the last a penetrating attempt to come to terms with himself, and which also describes the relationship between Man and Nature during a disastrous nineteenth-century expedition into the outback. Among younger novelists, **Thomas Keneally** (*b.*1935) has earned a rising reputation with books such as *A Dutiful Daughter* (1971), *The Chant of Jimmie Blacksmith* (1972) and *Schindler's Ark* (1982).

New Zealand's best-known poets are **Allen Curnow** (*b.*1911), **James K. Baxter** (1926-1972) and **Fleur Adcock** (*b.*1934). Of her prose writers probably the most important has been **Frank Sargeson** (1903–1982), whose talent first fully appeared in *That Summer* (1946).

Right *Salman Rushdie. In his highly acclaimed* Shame *(1983) – a veiled allegory apparently inspired by recent events in Pakistan – Rushdie depicts the corruption of individual life by a corrupt regime.*
Below *V.S. Naipaul, one of the most sensitive stylists of his generation. His preoccupation with, and reassessment of, his own origins has inspired* An Area of Darkness *(1964) on India, and* The Loss of El Dorado *(1969) on the history of Trinidad.*

Derek Walcott (*b.*1930), a Caribbean poet who writes in English, has published several collections of verse, among them *In a Green Night* (1962) and *The Castaway* (1965). He has an acute eye for detail, a fine ear and a masterly control of language. Walcott has also produced a number of successful plays. Meanwhile, Caribbean fiction has prospered. In the words of **George Lamming** (*b.*1927), 'The West Indian novel, by which I mean the novel written by the West Indian about West Indian reality, is hardly twenty years old' and is still developing. Barbados-born Lamming's own work, which includes a strong autobiographical element, shows an unusual literary gift.

V.S. Naipaul (b.1932) comes from an Indian Brahmin family settled in Trinidad, where Indians make up a third of the population; and some of his best books, including *A House for Mr Biswas* (1961) and *The Mimic Men* (1967) describe the setting of his youth. Educated at Oxford and now resident mainly in Britain, he shows a sense of personal rootlessness, well-described in a volume of short stories, *In a Free State* (1971), and in his novel *Guerrillas* (1975).

Similarly uncertain as to just where they belong are several other Indian authors who write in English. The delicate melancholy stories of **R.K. Narayan** (*b.*1907) have been called 'comedies of sadness'; and in *The Painter of Signs* (1976) Narayan has largely invented his own language to express an Indian's bewilderment confronted with modern Western values. A far younger novelist, **Salman Rushdie** (*b.*1947), also brilliantly sums up the dilemma of his generation, no longer dominated by an alien political authority, yet still torn between Western and Eastern standards. The hero of *Midnight's Children* (1981) is born at midnight on 14 August 1947, exactly the hour when India gained her independence.

Irish writers have always made an extremely important contribution to English literature; but during this century, stimulated by political independence in the South and the Civil War of the 1920s, the citizens of the Free State, particularly since the Second World War, have developed a strongly self-critical strain as we see in the plays of **Brendan Behan** (1923–1964) and in the vigorous semi-autobiographical novels of **John McGahern** (*b.*1935): *The Barracks* (1936) and *The Dark* (1965).

In Northern Ireland a notable school of writers, who have recently come to the fore, dig deep into the fabric of society, exploring its political, cultural and religious problems. Both poets and novelists relate the people they portray to their native landscape. Although **Brian Moore** (*b.*1921) left Belfast for North America in 1948, he has written a number of harrowing studies of men and women entrapped by the society he left behind, such as *The Lonely Passion of Judith Hearne* (1955), *The Feast of Lupercal* (1958) and *I am Mary Dunne* (1968). Graham Greene called him his 'favourite living novelist'. Moore's *Black Robe* (1985) is an extraordinarily powerful story of Jesuits and Indian tribal chiefs in 17th-century Canada.

During the 1960s and 1970s a series of gifted Northern Irish poets made their appearance. Most distinguished are **Derek Mahon** (*b.*1941), **Paul Muldoon** (*b.*1951), and **Seamus Heaney** (*b.* 1939), and though they seldom refer directly to the bloody civil strife of the last fifteen years and more, it often casts its depressing shadow across their prose and verse. Here and there, for example, in Heaney's *Field Work* (1979) he refers to the British Army's unwelcome presence.

Seamus Heaney, 'the best Irish poet since Yeats' according to the late Robert Lowell. His recent collection, Station Island, *was successfully publicized by a series of live readings around the country in 1984, a field in which Heaney is the leader. He has also recorded some of his poems on cassette (1983).*

The Toome Road from **Field Work**
by Seamus Heaney

One morning early I met armoured cars
In convoy, warbling along on powerful tyres,
All camouflaged with broken alder branches,
And headphoned soldiers standing up in turrets.
How long were they approaching down my roads
As if they owned them? The whole country was sleeping.
I had rights-of-way, fields, cattle in my keeping,
Tractors hitched to buckrakes in open sheds,
Silos, chill gates, wet slates, the greens and reds
Of outhouse roofs. Whom should I run to tell
Among all of those with their back doors on the latch
For the bringer of bad news, that small-hours visitant
Who, by being expected, might be kept distant?
Sowers of seed, erectors of headstones ...
O charioteers, above your dormant guns,
It stands here still, stands vibrant as you pass,
The invisible, untoppled omphalos.

THE NEW MEDIA

Above *The charismatic Bob Dylan, about whom a cult film was made in 1967, 'Don't Look Back', by D.A. Pennebaker (with Joan Baez, Beat poet Ginsberg and Alan Price). It was the letters to, from and about Byron in the years at Pisa with the Shelleys (edited by Peter Quennell) that inspired Pennebaker. '. . . I had a sense I was watching them create the legend that dominated literature for the next 200 years. It seemed like a film worth doing. All it needed was to find the right person. A film for – or instead of history.'*

The worldwide spread of television, radio and recorded music during the post-war period has affected many aspects of literary production, as has the huge development of the paperback book industry. Radio and television have naturally influenced dramatic writing, most noticeably in the work of Harold Pinter; while the cultural services of the European broadcasting system have done something to introduce poetry to a wider public. Dylan Thomas, for example, owed much of his popular fame to his delightful radio play, *Under Milkwood* (1953). Such was the Welsh poet's success that one American singer adopted his name.

Bob Dylan (Robert Zimmerman, born in 1941) is a controversial figure whom many critics dismiss, but others, including a Cambridge Professor of Literature, regard as an original and significant poet. Because his songs often criticize contemporary society they have been entitled 'protest songs'. On long-playing discs Bob Dylan's songs were distributed throughout the world in the 1960s; and his fame was only exceeded by that of the English pop group, The Beatles. The words of the Beatles' songs, largely written by **John Lennon** (1940–1980), had often a genuinely lyrical quality; and their message, like that of most of Bob Dylan's work, had usually an optimistic ring. Written and sung by youthful enthusiasts for a generation that had hardly known the war, they suggested that, in the words of one song, 'It's getting better all the time.'

Left *The 'Beatles', Liverpool's Famous Four – Paul McCartney, John Lennon, George Harrison and Ringo Starr – burst on the world in the early 1960s. They rode the youth culture wave with some fine music and lyrics and went on to succeed with their own individual interests.*

FANTASY, SCIENCE FICTION, AND CHILDREN'S BOOKS

The cheapness and wide distribution of paperbacks, despite the alternative charm of television, has immensely enlarged the reading public. Many classics and technical works have been reprinted in this form; but it has also encouraged the development of escapist science fiction. Here the most popular writers are those who invent a whole fantasy world, even an entire universe, with its own governments, moral systems and life-forms. Authors tend to write several books in the same story-cycle; for instance, the *Foundation Trilogy* (1963) of **Isaac Asimov** (*b.*1920) or the *Dune* stories of another American, **Frank Herbert** (*b.*1920). The plots and atmosphere of these huge sagas have something in common with the legendary framework of early medieval epics. A particularly ingenious creator of new worlds was the Oxford Professor of Medieval Literature, **J.R.R. Tolkien** (1892–1973), who used his specialized knowledge of the past to build up an immense fantastic landscape, called 'Middle Earth' for his children's benefit. His collection of stories in *The Lord of the Rings* trilogy (1954/55) became an international best-seller.

Not all science fiction is purely escapist, however. **Ray Bradbury** (*b.*1920), the American author of *Fahrenheit 451* (1953) and *Golden Apples of the Sun* (1953), snipes from behind a barrier of fantastic fiction at contemporary society; while **Arthur C. Clarke** (*b.*1917), employs the form to prophesy actual scientific advances.

A curious adult taste for children's books has popularized the characters of that very English tale *Winnie-the-Pooh* by **A.A. Milne** (1882–1956), and, elsewhere, *Moomins Family* by Finnish writer, **Tove Jansson** (*b.*1914) and *Pippi Longstocking* by Swedish authoress, **Astrid Lindgren** (*b.*1907). In the United States, the *Charlie Brown* strip-cartoon by **Charles Schultz** (*b.*1924), now syndicated throughout the world, and clearly written with an eye to amusing adults, depicts the family life of small-town America. More erudite are the Belgian authors **Goscinny** (1926–1977) and **Uderzo** (b.1927), who created their comic-strip hero *Astérix* to suit youthful tastes, but include learned linguistic puns and ingenious adult jokes.

Ray Bradbury's chilling story (named after the temperature at which paper burns), Fahrenheit 451, *is set in a future society where all books – the source of ideas and hence of subversion – have to be destroyed by fire. François Truffaut filmed it in 1966, with Cyril Cusack, glimpsed behind a curtain of fire* (**left**) *as captain of the savage firemen. One of his men, who begins to read the books he has been ordered to burn, is betrayed by his own wife and lured by a girl (both played by Julie Christie in the film) into joining her alternative community, who have resolved to memorize and thus preserve the greatest masterpieces of literature.*

TOWARDS THE MID 1980s

Right *George Orwell. During the war he worked (1941–43) for the BBC, having been refused for the army on medical grounds as he was already a consumptive. Despite his deep social and political commitment, Orwell jealously guarded his independence as a writer. 'When an author goes into politics,' he wrote, 'he must do it as a citizen, as a human being, but* not *as* an author.*'*

Below *Saul Bellow, whose books are as stimulating, and occasionally as tiring, as a witty, brilliant, endless monologue.*

German post-war poets, who distrusted the values of the previous age, asserted that the obscurity of much poetic language might suggest that the writer regarded himself as superior to the rest of mankind. They sought what they called 'the new simplicity'. One of the earliest of these literary democrats was **Hans Magnus Enzensberger** (*b.*1929). His new simplicity also expressed a spirit of resignation that the Second World War engendered. 'Those who live in the shadow', he wrote, 'are difficult to kill.'

The Englishman, **George Orwell** (the pseudonym of Eric Blair, 1903–1950), was deeply concerned with current political problems. His own experiences – he was a comparatively poor scholar at a very rich conservative school, a policeman in a British colony and a volunteer in the Spanish Civil War – helped to determine his beliefs; and his undogmatic left-wing views are set forth in his novels, in his records of the Spanish struggle – *Homage to Catalonia* came out in 1938 – and in his pugnacious controversial essays. But Orwell was a kindly, gentle character; and, revolted by tyranny under any guise, he produced *Animal Farm* (1945) – a splendid Swiftian satire, a picture of a Communist farmyard, where 'all animals are equal, but some are more equal than others' – and *1984* (1949), a nightmare vision of a future totalitarian state. *1984* introduces a little citizen, Winston Smith, who defies a mighty dictator and not only has his meagre existence crushed, but his inner life reshaped by the nefarious 'Thought Police', until finally he betrays everything that he has hitherto held dear.

In the United States, Jewish writers flourished during the post-war period. Nobel Prize winner **Isaac Bashevis Singer** (*b.*1904) first writes all his books in Yiddish and then usually translates them himself into English. A subject that shows him at his most able is the Jewish past of his native Poland. **Saul Bellow** (*b.*1915), another Nobel Prize winner, has made racial differences the starting-point of a discussion about the loneliness of Man in modern society. The heroes of his novels, Augie March of *The Adventures of Augie March* (1953), *Henderson the Rain King* (1959) and *Herzog* (1964), all make determined attempts to establish contact with their fellows and find some meaning in their own existence – Herzog by writing innumerable, but never-posted, letters to people alive and dead, both the known and the entirely unknown. The most distinguished American poet since the War was no doubt **Robert Lowell**

(1917–1977), much of whose best work appears in *Life Studies* (1959), though his *Imitations* (1961) – versions rather than translations of European poets – and *For the Union Dead* (1964), have also received an enthusiastic welcome.

At the same time, the vigorous but nihilistic poems of **Allen Ginsberg** (*b.*1926) brought him both fame and notoriety. His poem, *Howl* (1955) was prosecuted as obscene; and he and his associates were nicknamed 'the Beats', after the phrase 'Beat Generation', originally coined by his prose equivalent, the self-absorbed vagabond, **Jack Kerouac** (1922–1969).

Henry Miller (1891–1980) was no less typical of his age. The freedom he allowed himself in his erotic reminiscences was a deliberate attack on American puritanism. In his great series, *Tropic of Cancer* (1934), *Tropic of Capricorn* (1939) and *The Rosy Crucifixion* (1945/60), he records his personal experiences when he lived close to destitution, philandering and drinking and writing, in Parisian Bohemia between the wars.

Right *Henry Miller, with a copy of the first volume of his autobiographical trilogy,* The Rosy Crucifixion – Sexus, Plexus *and* Nexus. *His impressions of Greece in* The Colossus of Maroussi *(1941) were much admired, and from his retreat at Big Sur, in California, he has recorded his rejection of the American way of life in* The Air-Conditioned Nightmare *(1945). His rampaging prose shows his human warmth and anarchic passion for experience.*

Below *Allen Ginsberg at a 'flower power' gathering of hippies in London's Hyde Park in 1967. 'We love you' said the hippies as they handed out flowers to police and 'straights' alike. 'We may not be able to turn on with the pot (marijuana), but at least we can turn on with a chant', said Ginsberg.*

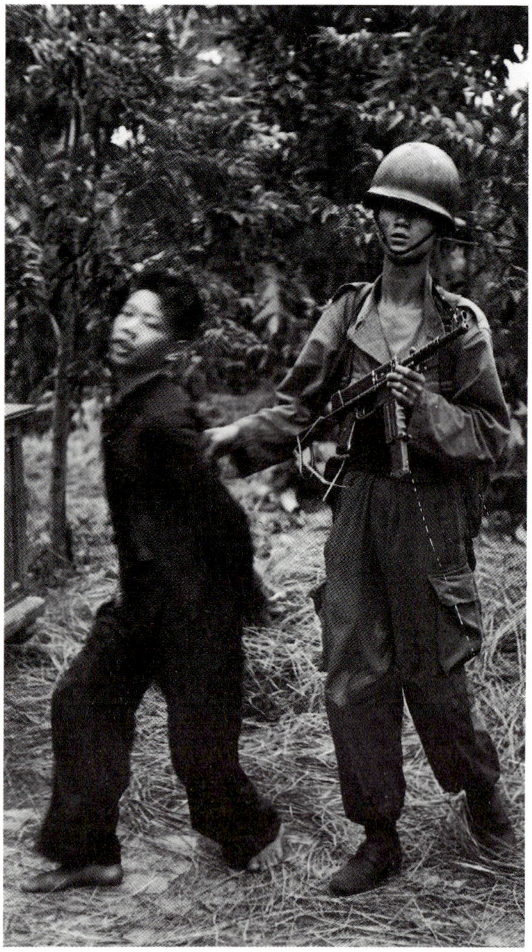

Above *An American soldier with Viet Cong prisoner during the Vietnamese War, which seriously damaged America's reputation as a champion of human rights.*

Above right *A member of Black Power, the aggressive American organization, demonstrates in Washington. The increase in black protest was predicted in James Baldwin's* The Fire Next Time *(1963). This great polemic against racialism is but one aspect of Baldwin's wide-ranging talents.* Giovanni's Room *(1956), with its theme of sexual conflict, derives from his period in Paris, where he came to terms with his own Americanism. In his later work, especially the essays, he continues to deepen his analysis of the American racialist malaise.*

Many writers in the United States have naturally studied the condition of American Negroes. For the black writer, **James Baldwin** (*b.*1924), antagonism between the races is merely a symptom of underlying anxiety and guilt; and the solution he recommends in his novels, *Go Tell It On the Mountain* (1953) and *Another Country* (1961), is the kind of sexual liberation D.H. Lawrence once preached.

The late 1960s saw the end of British and American optimism, with the worsening of the Irish conflict and the growing American commitment to the struggle in Vietnam.

Norman Mailer (*b.*1923), always a destructive critic of some of the fondest American myths, in 1948 published *The Naked and the Dead*, a novel that shocked those Americans, who, under the influence of official propaganda, had simplified the war against Japan into a conflict between decent whites and savage yellow sadists. During the Vietnamese War, he lived up to his reputation with *Why Are We in Vietnam?* (1967) and *The Armies of the Night* (1968). Several young Americans, who had actually served in that war, also recorded their impressions; and *Dispatches* (1977) by **Michael Herr** (*b.*1940) gives us a particularly vivid and convincing picture of modern warfare at its worst. In America itself, as the struggle dragged on, curious 'sub-cultures' developed among restless young inhabitants of big American cities, and **Tom Wolfe** (*b.*1931) in *The Pump House Gang* (1968) gives a memorable account of such a desperate little group.

It is not surprising that post-war German writers should have hesitated to become involved in political or racial issues; but they could not permanently stand aside, and **Heinrich Böll** (1917–85) soon became the literary conscience of the West German Republic. In his earliest books – *Haus ohne Hüter* (1954, *The Unguarded House*) and *Billard um halbzehn* (1959, *Billiards at Half-past Nine*) – he refuses to accept an aesthetic escape. His monologue–novel, *Ansichten eines Clowns* (1963, *The Clown*), is a settlement of accounts with those who betrayed their compatriots during the Nazi years, not least with his fellow Christians.

The position of the writer in countries under an authoritarian government is necessarily difficult; and South Africa is not an easy place for its black inhabitants. **Athol Fugard** (*b.*1932) is a white man; but in plays such as *Sizwe Bansi Is Dead* (1974), he examines the blacks' predicament and the relationship between the black and white citizens of a country where the theory of apartheid is still so firmly rooted. Although the novels of **Alan Paton** (*b.*1903), especially *Cry the Beloved*

Country (1948), plead for equality and peaceful conciliation, he opposed the idea of revolutionary violence. **Nadine Gordimer** (*b.*1923), today perhaps the most outstanding white South African writer, has done her best work in novellas and short stories; and, in her most recent collection, *Something Out There* (1984), she speaks for whites and blacks alike.

The Turkish epic writer, **Yasar Kemal** (*b.*1922) cherishes the traditions and myths of his homeland. Yet the central character of his novels *Undying Grass* (tr. 1963) and *The Wind from the Plain* (1961) is almost invariably that poorest and most wretched of Turkish citizens, the simple peasant; and his borrowings from folklore are deliberately intended to serve a revolutionary purpose.

Above left *West Berliners wave to friends on the other side of the Berlin Wall, a prime symbol of today's divided world.*

Above *Jacket for Swedish edition of Heinrich Böll's* The Clown *in which this radical Catholic writer addresses 'the authentic human condition' in a time-span of a few hours, increased by flashbacks.*

Left *John Kani and Winston Ntshona in Athol Fugard's* Sizwe Bansi is Dead, *at London's Royal Court Theatre (1974). This white actor and playwright has ignored the racial divisions enforced by apartheid, to work with black colleagues in multi-racial theatre projects in his homeland. Any assertion of a common humanity must contend against the opposition of the existing South African government.*

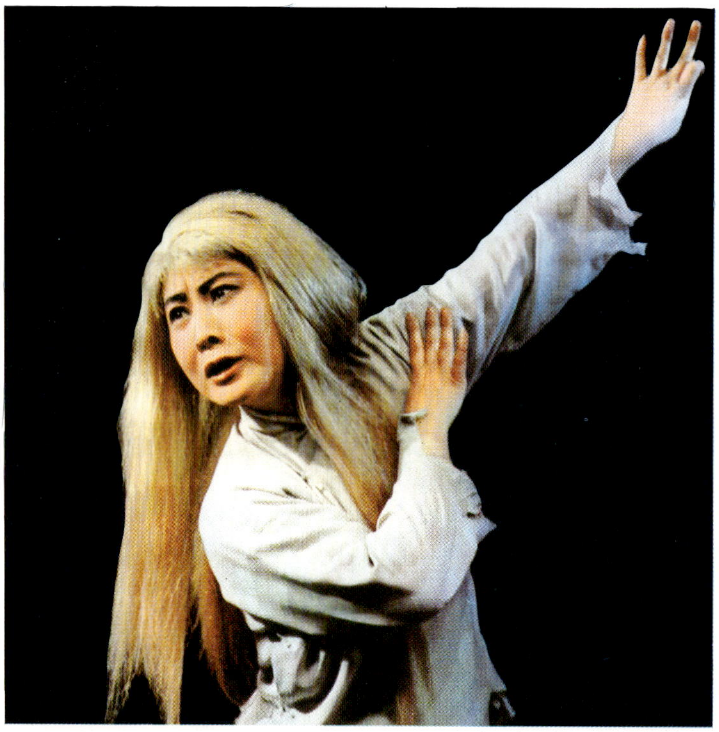

Xieri, 'The White-haired Girl', in the Chinese music–drama of that name. During the 'Cultural Revolution' the Peking Opera, perhaps the world's most venerable theatre company, was obliged to mount such propagandist pieces. But Chinese, the world's oldest, continuous, living literary tradition, has long been familiar with such official pressures and often successfully resisted them. Confucius taught 'the Way' (Tao) in which upright men could be critical of a government and yet remain loyal to it. A path, however difficult, could always be found through a minefield.

Tom Courtenay in the lead part in Caspar Wrede's film (1971) of Solzhenitsyn's One Day in the Life of Ivan Denisovich, *a classic account of the fate of the dissident in an authoritarian society and, in particular, the terrible fate of Russian dissidents.*

Opposite, top *Solzhenitsyn at a press conference in Washington in May 1975. In exile he continued to attack the Soviet regime in speeches and books, his views becoming more and more conservative and his declarations increasingly vehement on the moral decline in western society.*

Even before the disastrous Cultural Revolution (1965–69), Chinese writers were strictly enjoined to produce literature that 'served the people'; and today, despite the overthrow of the 'Gang of Four', it is uncertain whether new movements will at length result in the production of what the West calls imaginative writing. Yet, both before and during the Revolution, poets and dramatists attempted to combine the graceful old forms with a revolutionary content. Thus, in the so-called 'Peking Opera', they drew their subject-matter from the War of Liberation and the Revolution, as, for example, in *The Red Lantern* and *The White-haired Girl*, yet still preserved something of the sophisticated artistry of their ancient prototypes. These modernized operas are no longer performed today; and the Chinese workers and peasants can once again enjoy the old stories about the generals and sovereigns of the T'ang Dynasty. As to the spoken drama, some attempts have been made to introduce modern Western forms, rather than the dull, Ibsen-influenced drama preaching Sunday School morals that has dominated the Chinese stage since 1949.

In Russia several writers took advantage of the brief thaw that followed Stalin's death. **Yevgeny Yevtushenko** (*b.*1933) attracted huge audiences at his readings of his poems, notably *Stalin's Inheritors* and *Babiy Yar* (1961). The latter, though ostensibly a description of how the Nazis had massacred 30,000 Jews in a ravine outside Kiev, has at the same time a message to anti-Semitic zealots among his own countrymen.

It was during this same period that the Russian novelist **Alexander Solzhenitsyn** (*b.*1918) was at last, in 1962, able to publish *One Day in the Life of Ivan Denisovich*, which seemed to confirm George Orwell's vision of a future totalitarian regime. Simply and dispassionately it chronicles the events of an ordinary winter's day at one of Stalin's slave-labour camps, where any trace of human dignity vanishes during the struggle for a bowl of soup or a single cigarette; but Solzhenitsyn also describes how the brow-beaten and degraded prisoners manage, nevertheless, to endure and survive. The novel, based on real experience, was welcomed as a masterpiece by the Soviet and foreign press alike. Solzhenitsyn had himself spent eight years in prison camps and three years of exile in the wastes of Kazakhstan as a village schoolmaster.

By 1970, he had fallen from favour with the Russian authorities and did not travel to Sweden to receive his Nobel Prize for literature for fear of not being allowed to return to his homeland. During the intervening eight years he had written two major novels, *The First Circle* (tr. 1968) and *Cancer Ward* (tr. 1968), and many stories, and had written a series of open letters to the Union of Soviet Writers. Simultaneously he had been working on the *Gulag Archipelago*, a vast factual compilation, 1800 pages long, based on his own research and on hundreds of letters, in which he attempted to follow the whole history of Soviet persecution and repression from 1918 onwards. In 1973 he allowed a French edition to appear. In February 1974 he was deprived of his Soviet citizenship, and after spending some time in Switzerland he decided to settle in the US, where he is said to be writing a history of the Bolshevik Revolution.

From **Babiy Yar**
by Yevgeny Yevtushenko

Over Babiy Yar
rustle of the wild grass.
The trees look threatening, look like
judges.
And everything is one silent cry.
Taking my hat off
I feel myself slowly going grey.
And I am one silent cry
over the many thousands of the
buried;
am every old man killed here,
every child killed here.
O my Russian people, I know you.
Your nature is international.
Foul hands rattle your clean name.
I know the goodness of my country.
How horrible it is that pompous title
the anti-semites calmly call themselves,
Society of the Russian Race.
No part of me can ever forget it.
When the last anti-semite on the earth
is buried for ever
let the International ring out.
No Jewish blood runs among my
blood,
but I am as bitterly and hardly hated
by every anti-semite
as if I were a Jew. By this
I am a Russian.

From **An open letter to the Congress of the Union of Soviet Writers, 1967**
by Alexander Solzhenitsyn

Literature cannot develop in between the categories of 'permitted' and 'not permitted', 'about this you may write' and 'about this you may not'.

Literature that is not the breath of contemporary society, that dares not transmit the pains and fears of that society, that does not warn in time against threatening moral and social dangers – such literature does not deserve the name of literature . . . and its published works are used as waste-paper instead of being read.

Left *Yevgeny Yevtushenko, garlanded, during one of his world-wide poetry-reading tours. On his first English tour in 1962 he immediately became a popular celebrity. He has said that he chose 'the tribune' as his battleground – factories and research institutes, schools and villages '. . . so that by speaking of what was wrong in our society, I was strengthening, not destroying, their (the Russian people's) faith in our way of life.' The Society of the Russian Race referred to in the* Babiy Yar *extract was a pre-Revolutionary Russian group who directed anti-Jewish pogroms.*

NOBEL PRIZE WINNERS – LITERATURE

The Nobel Prize for Literature is one of the five prizes founded by Alfred Bernhard Nobel (1833–1896), the Swedish manufacturer, inventor and philanthropist, the other four being awarded for Physics, Chemistry, Medicine and Peace. This prize for literature is given to the person 'who shall have produced in the field of literature the most distinguished work of an idealistic tendency.' The award consists of a gold medal with an inscription suitable to the recipient and a sum of money (originally amounting to $40,000) that fluctuates through the years. The Swedish Academy in Stockholm administers the award and the official presentation is made annually on the anniversary of Nobel's death – 10 December. This prize is awarded to an author for his or her total literary output and not for any single work. It is not for competition and no one may apply for it.

1901 **Sully Prudhomme**, French poet
1902 **Theodor Mommsen**, German historian
1903 **Bjørnstjerne Bjørnson**, Norwegian dramatist, poet, and novelist
1904 **Frédéric Mistral**, Provençal poet and philologist, and **José Echegaray y Eizaguirre**, Spanish dramatist
1905 **Henryk Sienkiewicz**, Polish novelist
1906 **Giosuè Carducci**, Italian poet
1907 **Rudyard Kipling**, English novelist and poet
1908 **Rudolf Eucken**, German philosopher
1909 **Selma Lagerlöf**, Swedish novelist and poet
1910 **Paul von Heyse**, German novelist, playwright, and poet
1911 **Maurice Maeterlinck**, Belgian dramatist, poet, and essayist
1912 **Gerhart Hauptmann**, German dramatist, poet, and novelist
1913 **Rabindranath Tagore**, Hindu essayist and poet
1914 **No award**
1915 **Romain Rolland**, French novelist and dramatist
1916 **Verner von Heidenstam**, Poet Laureate of Sweden
1917 **Karl Gjellerup**, Danish novelist and poet, and **Henrik Pontoppidan**, Danish novelist
1918 **No award**
1919 **Carl Spitteler**, Swiss novelist and poet
1920 **Knut Hamsun**, Norwegian novelist
1921 **Anatole France**, French novelist, poet, and playwright
1922 **Jacinto Benavente y Martínez**, Spanish dramatist
1923 **William Butler Yeats**, Irish poet and dramatist
1924 **Wladyslaw Stanislaw Reymont**, Polish novelist
1925 **George Bernard Shaw**, Irish dramatist and novelist
1926 **Grazia Deledda**, Italian novelist
1927 **Henri Louis Bergson**, French philosopher
1928 **Sigrid Undset**, Norwegian novelist
1929 **Thomas Mann**, German novelist
1930 **Sinclair Lewis**, American novelist
1931 **Erik Axel Karlfeldt**, Swedish lyric poet. Posthumous award. Karlfeldt had refused the award ten years before on the grounds that he was an official of the Academy
1932 **John Galsworthy**, English novelist and dramatist
1933 **Ivan Bunin**, Russian novelist and poet
1934 **Luigi Pirandello**, Italian novelist and dramatist
1935 **No award**
1936 **Eugene O'Neill**, American dramatist
1937 **Roger Martin du Gard**, French novelist
1938 **Pearl S. Buck**, American novelist
1939 **Frans Eemil Sillanpää**, Finnish novelist
1940–43 **No awards**
1944 **Johannes V. Jensen**, Danish novelist and poet
1945 **Gabriela Mistral**, Chilean poet
1946 **Hermann Hesse**, Swiss (born in Germany) novelist, poet, and essayist
1947 **André Gide**, French novelist, essayist, philosopher, and poet
1948 **T.S. Eliot**, English (born in the United States) poet and critic
1949 **No award**
1950 **William Faulkner**, American novelist (award held over from 1949), and **Bertrand Russell**, English philosopher and mathematician
1951 **Pär Lagerkvist**, Swedish novelist, poet, essayist, and philosopher
1952 **François Mauriac**, French novelist, journalist, and poet
1953 **Winston Churchill**, English historian and statesman
1954 **Ernest Hemingway**, American novelist
1955 **Halldór Kiljan Laxness**, Icelandic novelist
1956 **Juan Ramón Jiménez**, Spanish poet
1957 **Albert Camus**, French novelist and playwright
1958 **Boris Pasternak**, Russian poet and novelist (prize declined)
1959 **Salvatore Quasimodo**, Italian poet and critic
1960 **Saint-John Perse**, French poet
1961 **Ivo Andrić**, Yugoslavian novelist
1962 **John Steinbeck**, American novelist
1963 **George Seferis**, Greek poet
1964 **Jean-Paul Sartre**, French philosopher, novelist, and playwright (prize declined)
1965 **Mikhail Sholokhov**, Russian novelist
1966 **S.Y. Agnon**, Israeli novelist, and **Nelly Sachs**, German poet
1967 **Miguel Ángel Asturias**, Guatemalan novelist
1968 **Yasunari Kawabata**, Japanese novelist
1969 **Samuel Beckett**, Irish novelist and playwright
1970 **Alexander I. Solzhenitsyn**, Russian novelist
1971 **Pablo Neruda**, Chilean poet
1972 **Heinrich Böll**, German novelist
1973 **Patrick White**, Australian novelist
1974 **Harry Martinson** and **Eyvind Johnson**, Swedish authors
1975 **Eugenio Montale**, Italian poet
1976 **Saul Bellow**, American novelist
1977 **Vicente Aleixandre**, Spanish poet
1978 **Isaac Bashevis Singer**, Yiddish author
1979 **Odysseus Elytis (Alepoudellis)**, Greek poet
1980 **Czeslaw Milosz**, Polish poet, essayist and translator
1981 **Elias Canetti**, Bulgarian novelist, dramatist and essayist
1982 **Gabriel García Márquez**, Colombian novelist
1983 **William Golding**, English novelist
1984 **Jaroslav Seifert**, Czech poet
1985 **Claude Simon**, French novelist

ACKNOWLEDGMENTS

Quotations

The author and publishers would like to thank all copyright-holders for permission to quote copyright material in illustration of the text. Every effort has been made to trace holders of copyright and secure their permission; if any material is unattributed or wrongly attributed we apologise to those concerned. The publishers would also like to thank John Scotney for his research concerning the following literary quotations and on new writers for Chapter 12.

CHAPTER ONE

8–9 **Gilgamesh** tr. N.K. Sanders from the *Epic of Gilgamesh* (Penguin Classics, rev. edn, 1972). (Copyright © N.K. Sandars, 1960, 1964, 1972.) Reprinted by permission of Penguin Books Ltd. 10 **'Dispute Between a Man and His Ba'** tr. Miriam Lichteim, from *Ancient Egyptian Literature – A Book of Readings*, 2 vols. (Copyright © 1973 by University of California Press.) Reprinted by permission of the Publishers. 10 **Akhenaten** 'Hymn to the Sun' tr. Sir Alan Gardiner, from *Egypt of the Pharaohs* (The Clarendon Press, 1961). Reprinted by permission of the Oxford University Press. 12–16 **The Bible** extracts from the *Authorized King James Version* (Crown Copyright in the United Kingdom) are reproduced by permission of Eyre and Spottiswoode, Her Majesty's Printers London. 18 **Confucius** tr. Joan Tate from *Lun Yu*. 18 **Lao Tzu** prose poem tr. Paul Garus, from *The Canon of Reason and Virtue*. (The Open Court Publishing Co., 1913). 18 **Chuang Tzu** from 'The Dream of the Butterfly' tr. Herbert Giles, from *Chuang Tzu* (Bernard Quaritch, 1882).

CHAPTER TWO

22 **The Iliad** from Book VI tr. E.V. Rieu from *Homer: The Iliad* (Penguin Classics 1950). (Copyright © Estate of E.V. Rieu, 1950.) Reprinted by permission of Penguin Books Ltd. 25 **Archilocus** elegy tr. Maurice Bowra, from *The Oxford Book of Greek Verse in Translation* (The Clarendon Press, 1938). Reprinted by permission of the Oxford University Press. 26 **Theognis** elegy tr. F.L. Lucas, from *Greek Poetry* (Everyman's Library 1951) Reprinted by permission of J.M. Dent and Sons Ltd. 26 **Sappho** poem tr. J.M. Edmonds, from *Lyra Graeca* (Loeb Classical Library 1922). Reprinted by permission of William Heinemann Ltd. 27 **Simonides** epitaph tr. John Scotney. 31 **Aeschylus** from 'Agamemnon' tr. Robert Lowell, from *The Orestia of Aeschylus* (Farrar, Straus & Giroux, Inc.; Faber and Faber, 1978). (Copyright © 1978 by Robert Silver and State Street Bank and Trust Company, Executors of the **Estate of Robert Lowell**.) Reprinted by permission of the Publishers. 32 **Sophocles** from 'Oedipus at Colonus' chorus tr. Walter Headlam, from *A Book of Greek Verse* (Cambridge University Press, 1907). 33 **Euripides** from 'The Bacchae' chorus tr. Gilbert Murray, from *The Collected Plays of Euripides* (George Allen & Unwin, 1954). Reprinted by permission of the Publisher.

CHAPTER THREE

42 **Catullus** love-poem tr. James Mitchie, from *The Poems of Catullus* (Hart–Davis McGibbon, 1969). Reprinted by permission of Granada Publishing Ltd. 46 **Horace** Ode XVI, Book II tr. James Mitchie, from *The Odes of Horace* (Hart–Davis, McGibbon, 1964) Reprinted by permission of Granada Publishing Ltd. 50 **St Augustine** from 'Confessions' tr. Peter Quennell.

CHAPTER FOUR

54 **'The Song of Roland'** tr. Dorothy L. Sayers, from *The Song of Roland* (Penguin Classics 1957). Reprinted by permission of Penguin Books Ltd. 60–61 **Dante** from 'Inferno' Canto V and 'Purgatorio' Canto XXX tr. Dorothy L. Sayers, from *Dante: The Divine Comedy* (Penguin Classics 1955 and 1962) Reprinted by permission of Penguin Books Ltd. 63 **Villon** 'Villon's Epitaph' version by Robert Lowell, from *Imitations* (Farrar, Straus & Giroux, Inc. and Faber and Faber, 1962). (Copyright © 1958, 1959, 1960, 1961 by Robert Lowell.) Reprinted by permission of the Publishers. 65 **Havamal** tr. D.C. Martin Clarke, from *The Havamal Edda* (Cambridge University Press, 1923). Reprinted by permission of the Publisher. 70 **The Koran** Sura LXXXI tr. Arthur J. Arberry, from *The Koran Interpreted* (George Allen & Unwin, and Macmillan Publishing Company, 1955). Reprinted by permission of the Publishers. 72 **Lady Kasa** poem tr. Geoffrey Bownas and Anthony Thwaite, from The Penguin Book of Japanese Verse (The Penguin Classics, 1964). (Copyright © Geoffrey Bownas and Anthony Thwaite, 1964.) Reprinted by permission of Penguin Books Ltd. 72 **Li Po** 'Drinking Alone by Moonlight' tr. Arthur Waley, from *More Translations from the Chinese* (George Allen & Unwin, 1919). Reprinted by permission of the Publisher. 72 **Li Po** (caption) 'Tsing ye si' transliteration by Göran Malmqvist. 72 **Po Chu-I** 'The Cranes' tr. Arthur Waley, from *One Hundred and Seventy-Five Chinese Poems* (George Allen & Unwin, 1946). Reprinted by permission of the Publisher.

CHAPTER FIVE

85 **Ronsard** Sonnet XLII tr. Geoffrey Brereton, from *The Penguin Book of French Verse 2*, ed. Geoffrey Brereton (The Penguin Poets 1958). Copyright © Geoffrey Brereton, 1958.) Reprinted by permission of Penguin Books Ltd. 88 **Cervantes** tr. J.M. Cohen, from *Don Quixote* (Penguin Classics 1950). (Copyright © J.M. Cohen, 1950.) Reprinted by permission of Penguin Books Ltd. 90 **Lope de Vega** 'Cradle Song for the Madonna' tr. George Ticknor, from *A History of Spanish Literature* (New York, 1849). 91 **Calderón** from *Life's a Dream* (Act II) tr. Frank Birch and J.B. Trend, (W. Heffer and Sons, 1925). Reprinted by permission of the Publisher. 94 **Marlowe** from *Tamburlaine the Great* (Act V, scene i). 98–99 **Shakespeare** Sonnet LXXIII; First Folio extracts from *The Merchant of Venice* (Act V, scene i), *Hamlet* (Act IV, scene vii), *Measure for Measure* (Act III, scene i) and *The Tempest* (Act IV, scene i). 100 **Donne** from *Devotions* XVII. 102 **Milton** Sonnet: 'On his Blindness' and from *Paradise Lost*, Book I.

CHAPTER SIX

110 **La Fontaine** 'The Grasshopper and the Ant' tr. Edward Marsh, from *More Fables of La Fontaine* (William Heinemann, 1925). Reprinted by permission of the Publisher. 111 **La Bruyère** from 'De l'homme' tr. Henri van Laun, from *La Bruyère: Characters* (Oxford University Press, 1963). Reprinted by permission of the Publisher.

CHAPTER SEVEN

114 **Swift** from 'The Voyage to Brobdingnag', *Gulliver's Travels*. 117 **Dryden** from *The Secular Masque*. 118 **Gray** stanza XXII from 'Elegy Written in a Country Churchyard'. 120 **Blake** from the preface to *Milton*. 127 **Rousseau** from 'Discourse on the Origin of Inequality', part II tr. G.D.H. Cole, from *The Social Contract and Discourses* (Everyman's Library 1913): extract tr. Barbara Foxley from *Émile* (Everyman's Library 1911). Reprinted by permission of J.M. Dent and Sons Ltd. 133 **Goethe** 'The Blessed Yearning' tr. 'The Book of the Singer' tr. Edward Dowden, from *The West–East Divan* (J.M. Dent and Sons, 1914). 138–39 **Carlyle** from *The Life of Schiller* (Chapman and Hall, 1845).

CHAPTER EIGHT

146 **Eichendorff** tr. Charles G. Leland, from *Memoirs of a Good-for-Nothing* (Leypoldt & Holt, 1866). 150 **Hölderlin** from 'Hyperion's Song of Fate' and 'To the Fates' tr. Michael Hamburger from *Hölderlin: Poems and Fragments* (Cambridge University Press, 1980). Reprinted by permission of the Publisher. 151 **Wordsworth** extracts from 'Lines Written above Tintern Abbey' in *The Lyrical Ballads* and from *The Prelude*, 156 **Shelley** from 'Lines written in Dejection near Naples'. 158 **Keats** from 'Ode to Melancholy' and 'Hyperion'. 163 **Hugo** from 'The Legend of the Centuries' tr. John Scotney. 164 **Musset** from 'La Nuit de mai' in 'Les Nuits' tr. Walter Herries Pollock, from *Musset: Poems* (Richard Bentley and Sons, 1880). 165 **Gautier** from 'L'Art' tr. Alan Conder, from *Cassell's Anthology of French Poetry* (Cassell and Co., 1950). (Copyright © Alan Conder, 1958.) Reprinted by permission of Macmillan Publishing Company. 172 **Leopardi** from 'The Infinite' version by Robert Lowell, from *Imitations* (Farrar, Straus & Giroux, Inc. and Faber and Faber, 1962). (Copyright © 1958, 1959, 1960, 1961 by Robert Lowell.) Reprinted by permission of the Publishers. 173 **Wergeland** from 'Jan van Huysums Blomsterstykke' tr. John Scotney.

CHAPTER NINE

182 **Baudelaire** 'Spleen' version by Robert Lowell, from *Imitations* (Farrar, Straus & Giroux, Inc. and Faber and Faber, 1962). Copyright © 1958, 1959, 1960, 1961 by Robert Lowell.) Reprinted by permission of the Publishers. 194 **Walter Savage Landor** from *The Morning Chronicle*, 1845. 195 **Elizabeth Barrett Browning** from 'The Cry of the Children'. 196 **Marx** extracts tr. Samuel Moore, from *The Manifesto of the Communist Party*, 1888 (Foreign Languages Publishing House, Moscow). 198 **Heine** 'Pilgrimage to Kevlaar' tr. Charles G. Leland, from *Heine's Book of Songs* (Leypoldt and Holt, 1868). 205 **Hans Christian Andersen** 'The Teapot' tr. P. Keigwin, from *Hans Christian Andersen's Fairy Tales*, ed. Svend Larsen (Flensted Forlag, Odense, Denmark, 1960). Reprinted by persmission of Skandinavisk Bogforlag. 214 **Dostoevsky** from *The Idiot* tr. David Magarshack (Penguin Classics 1955). (Copyright © David Magarshack, 1955.) Reprinted by permission of Penguin Books Ltd. 218 **Walt Whitman** from 'Song of Myself', *Leaves of Grass* (1889 edn).

CHAPTER TEN

223 **Verlaine** 'There is Weeping in My Heart', tr. Anthony Hartley, from *The Penguin Book of French Poetry 3*, ed. Anthony Hartley (The Penguin Poets 1957). This selection and introduction © Anthony Hartley, 1957.) Reprinted by permission of Penguin Books Ltd. 224 **Rimbaud** from 'The Drunken Boat' tr. Roy Campbell, from *Collected Poems – Roy Campbell*, vol. 3 (The Bodley Head, 1960). Reprinted by permission of Francisco Campbell Custodio and Ad. Donker (Pty) Ltd. 227 **Nietzsche** from *Thus Spoke Zarathustra* tr. R.J. Hollingdale, (Penguin Classics rev. edn, 1969). Copyright © R.J. Hollingdale, 1961, 1969.) Reprinted by permission of Penguin Books Ltd. 228 **Stefan George** from 'The Star of the Covenant' tr. John Scotney. 230 **Rilke** from 'Childhood' tr. J.B. Leishman, from *Selected Works* – Rilke, vol 2 (Hogarth Press, 1960); extract from *The Duino Elegies* tr. (and introduced by) J.B. Leishman and Stephen Spender (Hogarth Press, 1939). Reprinted by permission of the Publisher. 235 **Robert Louis Stevenson** epitaph from 'Requiem', *Underwoods*. 240 **Carl Sandburg** extract from *Chicago Poems* (Henry Holt and Co. 1916). Reprinted by permission of Harcourt Brace Jovanovich, Inc. 241 **Edgar Lee Masters** 'Knowlt Hoheimer' from *The Spoon River Anthology* (The Macmillan Company, 1915) Reprinted by permission of Mrs Ellen C. Masters.

Acknowledgments

CHAPTER ELEVEN
246 **Franz Werfel** from 'Gottes Name in Menschen' tr. John Scotney, from *Schlaf und Erwachen* (1935). 255 **Claudel** tr. Fr John O'Connor from *The Satin Slipper* (Sheed and Ward, 1931). Reprinted by permission of Editions Gallimard and the Publisher. 258 **André Breton** from 'A Man and Woman Absolutely White' tr. Kenneth White, from *Selected Poems – André Breton* (Jonathan Cape, 1969). Reprinted by permission of Editions Gallimard and the Publisher. 258 **Saint-John Perse** from 'Narrow are the Vessels' tr. Wallace Fowlie, from *Seamarks* (Bollingen, series 67, Princeton University Press). (Copyright by Wallace Fowlie, 1958.) Reprinted by permission of Madame Alexis Léger and the Publisher. 267 **James Joyce** from *Ulysses* (Random House Inc., 1934; The Bodley Head, 1936). (Copyright © 1914, 1918 by Margaret Caroline Anderson and renewed 1942, 1946 by Nora Joseph Joyce.) Reprinted by permission of the Publishers. 268 **T.S. Eliot** from 'The Fire Sermon' in 'The Waste Land', *Collected Poems 1909–1962* (Faber and Faber and Harcourt Brace Jovanovich Inc., 1963). Reprinted by permission of the Publishers. 269 **Mayakovsky** from 'My Soviet Passport' tr. Herbert Marshall from *Mayakovsky*, tr. and ed. Herbert Marshall (Dennis Dobson and Hill and Wang, 1965). Reprinted by permission of the translator. 270 **Pasternak** 'Hamlet in Russia. A Soliloquy.' version by Robert Lowell, from *Imitations* (Farrar, Straus & Giroux, Inc. and Faber and Faber, 1962. (Copyright © 1958, 1959, 1960, 1961 by Robert Lowell.) Reprinted by permission of the Publishers. 277 **Hemingway** from *Death in the Afternoon* (Jonathan Cape, 1932; Charles Scribner's Sons, 1948). (Copyright © 1932, copyright renewed 1960 by Ernest Hemingway.) 281 **Langston Hughes** 'I, Too' in 'The Dream Keeper' from *Selected Poems of Langston Hughes* (Alfred A. Knopf, 1932). (Copyright © 1926 by Alfred A. Knopf, Inc.) (Copyright renewed 1954 by Langston Hughes.) Reprinted by permission of the Publisher. 284 **Lorca** from 'Somnambule Ballad' tr. J.L. Gili and Stephen Spender, from *Selected Poems of Federico García Lorca* (The New Hogarth Library vol. XI, The Hogarth Press, 1943; New Directions, 1955). (Copyright © 1955 by New Directions Publishing Corporation.) Reprinted by permission of the Publishers. 285 **Neruda** from 'Love, America (1400)' tr. Anthony Kerrigan, from *Selected Poems of Pablo Neruda* tr. Alastair Reid, ed. Nathaniel Tarn (Jonathan Cape, 1970). (Copyright © 1970 by Anthony Kerrigan, W.S. Merwin, Alastair Reid and Nathaniel Tarn.) (Copyright © 1972 by Dell Publishing Co. Inc.) Reprinted by permission of the Estate of Pablo Neruda, Delacorte Press/Seymour Lawrence and the Publishers. 287 **Mao Tse-Tung** The Warlords Clash' tr. Willis Barnstone, from *The Poems of Mao Tse-Tung* (Bantam Books, 1972). (Copyright © 1972 by Willis Barnstone.) Reprinted by permission of the translator.

CHAPTER TWELVE
293 **Beckett** from *Waiting for Godot* (Copyright © 1955 by Grove Press, Inc. and Faber and Faber, 1956.) (Copyright © by Samuel Beckett, 1955, 1965.) Reprinted by permission of the Publishers. 299 **Léopold Senghor** 'The Dead' in 'Shadowsong' tr. Gerald Moore and Ulli Beier, from *The Penguin Book of Modern Poetry from Africa* (Penguin Poets 1963). Reprinted by permission of Editions du Seuil. 303 **Seamus Heaney** from 'The Toome Road' in *Field Work* (Faber and Faber and Farrar, Straus & Giroux, Inc., 1979). (Copyright © 1976, 1979 by Seamus Heaney.) Reprinted by permission of the Publishers. 311 **Yevtushenko** from 'Babiy Yar' tr. Robin Milner-Gulland and Peter Levi from *Yevtushenko: Selected Poems* (Penguin Modern European Poets 1962). (Copyright © Robin Milner-Gulland and Peter Levi, 1962.) Reprinted by permission of Penguin Books Ltd and the Pergamon Press. 311 **Solzhenitsyn** from 'Solzhenitsyn's Open Letter to the Fourth Soviet Writers Congress, 1967' tr. Leopold Labedz, from *Solzhenitsyn: A Documentary Record* ed. Leopold Labedz (Copyright © 1971 by Harper and Row, Publishers, Inc. and Penguin Books, 2nd edn. 1974). (Copyright © 1970 by Leopold Labedz). Reprinted by permission of the Publishers.

Illustrations

APN, Sovjetunionens pressbyrå, Stockholm. Det Arnamagneanske Institut, Köpenhamn. Fotograf Beata Bergström, Stockholm. Bildhuset, Stockholm. Etablissements J.E. Bulloz, Paris. Cinema International, Stockholm. Stud. Mats Dahlström, Höganäs. Löjtnant Ulf Dahlström, Linköping. Walt Disney Productions Sweden AB, Stockholm. Filmhuset, Stockholm. Gustaf Frödingsällskapet, Karlstad. Ny Carlsberg Glyptotek, Köpenhamn. Fotograf K.W. Gullers, Stockholm. IBL AB, Ljungbyhed. Fil.dr. Harry Järv, Stockholm. Fotograf Günes Karabuda, Stockholm. Lunds Universitetsbibliotek, Lund. Kungliga Biblioteket, Stockholm. Fotograf Anders Mattson, Malmö stadsteater. Medelhavsmuseet, Stockholm. Nationalmuseum, Stockholm. Oslo Kommunes Kunstsamlinger, Munkmuseet. Reportagebild, Stockholm. Fotograf Enar Merkel-Rydberg, Kungl. Teatern, Stockholm. Sanderew Film & Teater AB, Stockholm. Schiller-Nationalmuseum, Västtyskland. Fotograf Eva Siao, Peking. Roto Smeets Illustrated Projects, Holland. Svenska Filminstitutet, Stockholm. Svenskt Pressfoto, Stockholm. Sveriges Radio, Stockholm. Konstnär Stig Södersten. Tate Gallery, London. Thielska Galleriet, Stockholm. Östasiatiska museet, Stockholm.

Additional illustrations for the English language edition were supplied by the following sources:
BBC Hulton Picture Library Frontispiece 117L, 120R, 153, 266T, 288. John Calder Publishers/Jerry Bauer 296T. Camera Press 294R, 295L. Jonathan Cape Publishers 301B. Donald Cooper 295R, 298BL & BR, 309B. Faber and Faber Publishers 303. Mark Gerson 302L & R. Robert Hunt Library 289. Kobal Collection 149B, 296BL & BR, 297T, C & B, 305. Mansell Collection 24, 301T. Popperfoto 298T, 307B. Secker & Warburg Publishers/Jerry Bauer 300L. John Timbers 294L.

INDEX

NOTE Main page references for names with more than one entry are in **heavy** type. All titles are listed under the author in *italics* and given mainly in English (whether published in translation or not). Specific titles that are illustrated, or from which extracts are quoted in the text, are also listed alphabetically. Page references for illustrations are in *italics*, and artists' names are followed by the title or subject of their work in brackets.

Index

Index

Index